Preparing to Teach Writing
Research, Theory, and Practice

Second Edition

Preparing to Teach Writing
Research, Theory, and Practice

Second Edition

James D. Williams
Governors State University

LAWRENCE ERLBAUM ASSOCIATES, PUBLISHERS

1998   Mahwah, New Jersey   London

Lawrence Erlbaum Associates, Inc., Publishers
10 Industrial Avenue
Mahwah, New Jersey 07430

Cover design by Kathryn Houghtaling Lacey

Library of Congress Cataloging-in-Publication Data

Williams, James D. (James Dale).
Preparing to teach writing : research, theory, and practice /
James D. Williams. — 2nd ed.
p. cm.
Includes bibliographical references and index.
ISBN 0-8058-2266-6
1. English language—Rhetoric—Study and teaching—The-
ory, etc. 2. English language—Rhetoric—Study and teaching
—Research. 3. English language—Composition and exer-
cises—Research. 4. Report writing—Study and teaching —
Theory, etc. 5. Report writing—Study and teaching—Research.
6. English teachers—Training of. I. Title.
PE1404.W54 1998
808'.042'07—dc21   97-28118
                                                          CIP

Books published by Lawrence Erlbaum Associates are
printed on acid-free paper, and their bindings are chosen for
strength and durability.

Printed in the United States of America
10   9   8   7   6   5   4   3   2   1

*This book is dedicated to the memory
of my mother and father,
Jessie and Elmer Williams.*

Contents

Preface

When I began teaching high school many, many years ago, it never occurred to me that one day I might be helping prepare future teachers. I was too busy to think that far ahead. I juggled six different classes and monitored the restrooms during lunch hours while trying to understand why my students could not write and why they did not love literature as much as I did. In spite of my English degree and credential, I really had not been prepared to teach writing. It just was not part of the education curriculum in those days. So when I entered my own classroom for the first time, I was overwhelmed by how much I did not know. I began reading everything I could about the subject, but it never seemed to be enough, and I hope that the students I had during those years did not suffer too much from my ignorance.

A decade later, Ph. D. in hand, I began training people who wanted to teach, and like many others before me, I was certain that I had answers to most of the questions I had asked when I began my own career at a high school in California. The first edition of this book emerged out of those early years as a professor at UCLA when I discovered that there were no available books that tried to bring together all the disparate theories and research that influence writing instruction. This first edition provided many answers but posed few questions. Positioned firmly in the cognitive approach that dominated composition studies during those years, the first edition explored writing as a psychosocial action and advocated a pragmatic approach to instruction before the ideas of social constructivism had fully jelled in the profession.

Another decade has passed and I'm still training people who want to teach, but I discovered that I only knew a fraction of what I thought I knew, and most of that is not germane to the issue of how we help young people become better writers. The world is a different place. Education has changed. Students have changed. The challenges we face in turning children into literate human beings are greater now. Therefore, it is appropriate that this second edition of *Preparing to Teach Writing* offers fewer answers but asks more questions.

Like the first edition, it offers a fairly comprehensive examination of the research and theories that influence what teaching writing is about and it strives to separate the wheat from the chaff. Readers who want a quick overview of the history of rhetoric from classical times to the present will appreciate chapter 1, which is far more detailed than anything the first edition offered. I thoroughly revised and updated all the chapters, but those dealing with reading and writing, psychology and language, and ESL and nonmainstream students are almost completely new because so much has changed in these areas over the years. More important, perhaps, is that I tried to make this second edition more open-ended, allowing more room for readers to strike out on their own after seeing what the various experts have to say.

This open-ended approach puts the second edition even more at odds with those who are looking for a cookbook that will guide them through the frightful first year or two in the classroom. However, as I noted in the past, such cookbook does not exist. Even so, students in my classes and those who have read the first edition frequently ask me to tell them what they should consider to be the most important factor in becoming a good teacher. Over the last several years, the answer has become clearer to me, although I am not sure I communicate it convincingly to those who ask: They need to love children and know that teaching is a caring profession.

ACKNOWLEDGMENTS

I owe much to my students who, over the years, have taught me new things, and I thank them. Thanks go to Naomi Silverman at Lawrence Erlbaum Associates, the best editor I have had on any project. I also thank the many colleagues around the country who used the first edition and who were kind enough to send me notes detailing their successes and failures with the book. This information has been invaluable. I would like to thank the many great teachers I had in school, especially Lou Waters, Hans Guth, and the late Phil Cook, all of San Jose State University, and Ross Winterowd, Jack Hawkins, and Steve Krashen of the University of Southern California. A special thanks goes to Erika Lindemann for being my colleague, mentor, and friend at the University of North Carolina at Chapel Hill. Finally, thanks to my wife, Ako, for everything: *Anata-wa boku-no taiyo desu.*

—*James D. Williams*

1

Rhetoric and Writing

OVERVIEW

Many people use the terms *rhetoric* and *composition* interchangeably, but they aren't quite the same. During the classical period of Greece and Rome, rhetoric dealt primarily with oral language. Teachers in Athens, for example, helped their students become better speakers for the law courts and the governing assembly.

Rhetoric was initially tied to democracy, but as social circumstances changed and democracy gave way to empire, rhetoric also changed. For example, Athens was a democracy, whereas Rome was not, and the nature of rhetoric was quite different in the two cities. In Athens, rhetoric was used in the courts as well as in the governing assembly, which was characterized by free debate. In Rome, rhetoric was limited largely to the law courts, but eventually, it assumed a modest role there.

Christianity brought another change to rhetoric as the new religion sought to establish its doctrine as well as its popularity. Three to four hundred years after Christ's Crucifixion, Christianity was criticized for its lack of literary tradition that characterized the pagan sects. It was also torn by internal disputes over what was or was not official doctrine. St. Augustine (A.D. 354–430), who was trained in rhetoric, applied rhetorical analysis to the Bible to show that it was equal if not superior to pagan writing. In addition, his own compelling writing served as a bridge to link the rhetorical traditions of classical pagan culture to Christianity, providing a model that later writers attempted to emulate. An important result of St. Augustine's efforts was that the primary focus of rhetoric shifted from speech to writing.

This shift did not end the oral tradition immediately. It remained strong through the Middle Ages, the Renaissance, and into the 19th century because Western education continued to follow the model developed in ancient Greece and Rome, a model that valued oral composition. Nevertheless, the shift in focus from speaking to writing already had occurred. During the late 18th and early 19th centuries, several factors— such as the belles-lettres movement and an emphasis on specialization advocated by the German educational system—pushed the shift across the threshold, and oral rhetoric was replaced by writing. In the late 19th century, influential educators such as Alexander Bain argued that rhetoric was writing and that those who taught rhetoric were generalists who lacked the specialization necessary to teach content, which meant that all they could teach was style. By the turn of the century, American educators largely accepted Bain's views. Writing predominated, and composition instruction focused on style.

The seeds for these changes always existed in rhetoric. Even in the classical period, rhetoric meant somewhat different things to different people—the Sophists, Plato, and Aristotle, for example. The Sophists taught a pragmatic rhetoric, one that was useful in the courts. Plato argued against rhetoric in favor of dialectic but in the process, he developed a rhetoric that saw truth as its goal, not winning points of law. Aristotle criticized both Sophists and Plato, defining rhetoric as the "art of persuasion." In ancient Rome, Cicero had little use for philosophical inquiry but saw legal rhetoric as a means of influencing government policy.

In many ways, the tensions underlying these views continue to influence rhetoric, although ideas about its nature have multiplied in ways that neither the Greeks nor the Romans could have visualized. For example, rhetoric has become concerned almost exclusively with classroom writing, although courses in public speaking make attempts at keeping alive some vestige of traditional rhetoric. In fact, Aristotle remains the most influential figure in this field, even though his work on rhetoric had little to say about writing. Some scholars mark the birth of modern rhetoric with the publication of Kinneavy's *A Theory of Discourse* (1971), a work that explicitly linked Aristotle to college composition. Berlin (1990), however, argued convincingly for an earlier date, around 1960. As we see later in this chapter, a flurry of activity in rhetoric and composition characterizes the early 1960s, which suggests that Berlin's date is fairly accurate.

Rhetoric changed again in 1985, when several presenters at the Conference on College Composition and Communication urged teachers and researchers to abandon rhetorical models in favor of literary ones. In the ensuing years, rhetoric drifted into today's postmodern phase, in which questions of application have been largely supplanted by questions of social consciousness.

WHAT IS RHETORIC?

Rhetoric is a term that people use all the time, but not everyone knows what it means, partially because *rhetoric* has several different meanings. One sense of the word means speech that does not convey anything of substance. Politicians who do one thing and say another, for example, are said to use "empty rhetoric." There are also books that teach people how to write; these represent another meaning of rhetoric.

In this text, *rhetoric* is defined in two ways—first, as a field of study that examines the means by which speakers and writers influence states of mind and actions in other people, and second, the application of those means. Thus, the discussions that follow explore rhetoric as something people study and something they apply to influence others. This definition is different from traditional ones because it treats rhetoric as an intellectual discipline as well as an art, skill, or ability that people may possess and use. Consider that the Greek philosopher Aristotle defined rhetoric as "an ability, in each [particular] case, to see the available means of persuasion" (Kennedy, 1991, p. 36). Developing this ability, however, typically involved studying the structure of effective arguments, psychology, proof, and so forth, as well as practicing how to deliver a speech.

Modern rhetoric is characterized by several specialties, such as the history of rhetoric and public speaking, but composition is, by far, the largest of these. In addition, the specialty of composition is made complex by the fact that it is interdisciplinary, linked to such fields as education, linguistics, and psychology.

The multifaceted nature of rhetoric causes many people to be suspicious of broad definitions like the one above. They argue that the question "What is rhetoric?" is meaningful only in relation to the cultural characteristics of a given society in a specified period. There is much truth in this argument, especially insofar as rhetoric can be applied pragmatically to garner support for a given position. In classical Greece, rhetoric was, by and large, viewed as the use of language for purposes of persuasion. But almost from the very beginning there existed different emphases and purposes, and thus slightly different notions not only of what rhetoric did but also of what it was. These notions certainly changed over time, but through all the changes there was at least one constant—the focus on examining how people use language to attain certain ends.

History and Theory

Teachers who are concerned about helping students become better writers tend to be pragmatic. They want ideas and suggestions that they can use immediately to improve student performance. This admirable trait can make discussions of the history and theory of rhetoric seem like obstacles that delay grappling with practical issues. However, teaching writing has become a complex endeavor, informed by a huge body of research and competing aims that have a significant influence on methodologies. Focusing on methods without considering their historical and theoretical foundation would be shortsighted, if for no other reason than that students and classes differ to such an extent that no one method works for everyone or in all situations. Writing teachers must understand this foundation so they can make adjustments to classroom activities to meet the needs of students. They must understand not only what to do as effective teachers but also why these methods work. Because a large part of current theory and practice is based on ideas developed in ancient Greece, it seems appropriate to start our voyage of discovery there.

CLASSICAL GREEK RHETORIC

Tradition holds that Corax, a teacher from Sicily, and his student Tisias "invented" rhetoric in the Greek colony at Syracuse. This tradition cannot be entirely accurate because language is inherently rhetorical, making its "invention" impossible. More likely is Kennedy's (1980) and Enos' (1993) suggestion that Corax and Tisias were the first whose teachings about rhetoric were transferred into writing as handbooks on public speaking.

According to the tradition, Corax and Tisias responded to public need. Around 467 B.C., the tyrant Thrasybulus abused the citizens of Syracuse in many ways, including confiscating much of their property. The citizens responded by rebelling within a year of his assumption of power, and they established a democracy that lasted about 50 years. Those whose property had been confiscated sought to get it back and took their claims to court. There were no attorneys in those days, so each litigant had to plead his own case before a large jury. Observers noted that litigants with rhetorical training were more skillful speakers than those without and that they tended to win their cases. Apparently, the resulting demand was high for the services of teachers like Corax and Tisias.

Perhaps Corax and Tisias had more students than they could handle and decided to write handbooks detailing the principles of persuasive speaking. Perhaps their students developed class notes into handbooks. We do not know. We also do not know whether these handbooks were circulated among friends and copied or whether they were sold in the marketplace. We do know, however, that these books proved to be popular, and they opened up a new arena for teaching and rhetoric.

Democracy was never strong in Sicily, but the 50 years of democratic rule in Syracuse led to a flowering of rhetoric that had an important influence on Athens, where democracy and a less systematized form of rhetoric were well established. Democracy and rhetoric were greatly stimulated in Athens in the middle of the 7th century B.C., when the ruler Draco codified Athenian law, thereby setting limits on aristocratic power and laying the foundation for democracy. Vernant (1982) argued that Draco's laws were revolutionary because they articulated a new way of governing: The sword ceased being the sole—or even the primary—means of governing the populace. Vernant also argued that after the 7th century B.C., speech gained increasing importance as a means of exercising political power, largely because of the explosion of literacy that occurred in Athens during this time.

These changes in Athenian government, education, and social structure were significant, and scholars have proposed many explanations for them. Patterson (1991), for example, argued that a shifting economic base was responsible. Agriculture in Greece shifted from grain to olives, figs, and wine, which were far more profitable, owing to scarcity and higher prices. These crops, however, also required large sums of capital because it took years for the trees and vines to bear fruit. Small farmers and sharecroppers were displaced by the changing economy, and they flocked to Athens in search of work. The social and economic consequences were complex. Patterson proposed that the displaced small farmers created a farm labor shortage, and the landowners responded by relying increasingly on slave labor to tend and harvest their crops. Meanwhile, the large number of free but destitute displaced farmers in Athens gained political power by using the threat of revolution as leverage. They sought to blunt abuses of power by the elite and to assert their status as freemen.

In Patterson's view, as the number of slaves rose ever higher, the value of freedom grew until it was more important to the majority of Athenian citizens than material wealth. In fact, wealth became desirable only insofar as it allowed freemen to enjoy the luxury of their status, which apparently never involved the debased hedonism that characterized the behavior of wealthy Roman citizens during some periods of the empire. Instead, Athenian freemen sought to cultivate their minds and souls (and those of their sons1) for the benefit of the city-state, hence the explosion of education at all levels. A minority of Athenian citizens were wealthy; by law, they were required to use their wealth to erect government buildings, pay for festivals, and field armies and navies in

---

[1]Girls were educated at home rather than in school. Those from families with some means were taught art, music, poetry, cooking, sewing, and household management. Those of lower status probably were trained solely in household tasks.

time of war—expenditures that frequently sent families and entire clans into bankruptcy. Poor citizens lacked the means to provide these benefits to the city, so their contributions came in the form of government service—a happy compromise that saved the ruling elite from revolution while maintaining their general status. Such service, however, required more and better education, greater skill as a speaker, and more democracy. Therefore, all of these factors combined to create an environment that was ideal for the teaching and practice of rhetoric. When the Sicilian handbooks arrived in Athens, circumstances ensured an enthusiastic reception.

Rhetoric and the Greek Philosophers

Initially, rhetoric was grounded in law and politics, which led to the development of what are termed *forensic* and *deliberative* rhetoric, respectively. The goal of those who taught rhetoric and of those who studied it was to succeed in the courts and the assembly. Thus rhetoric was very pragmatic from the beginning. But just a few years after the handbooks of Corax and Tisias appeared in Greece, rhetoric began to change under the influence of various philosophers. Greek philosophers generally were not concerned with pragmatics. Instead, they were interested in the concept of reality and in exploring the nature of truth, virtue, and knowledge. They emphasized rhetoric as a *theory of knowing*. Nevertheless, the demand for teachers of rhetoric was high, and many philosophers earned a good living by training students to speak in the courts and before the governing assembly.

The Sophists

The first philosophers to influence rhetoric are known collectively as *Sophists*, a term that comes from *sophia*, the Greek word for wisdom. Little is known about the Sophists because they did not produce much writing and because what survived the centuries consists largely of fragments embedded in the works of others. We do know, however, that many of them came to Athens from Asia Minor. Although we refer to them as a group, they held only a few views in common, which increases the difficulty of reaching any generalizable conclusions about them.

Kennedy (1980) described the Sophists as "self-appointed professors of how to succeed in the civic life of the Greek states" (p. 25). In addition to legal and political rhetoric, however, they also professed to teach *areté*, or civic virtue. The ancient Greeks were the first people we know about who recognized that they had the ability to govern themselves. The development of democracy was a huge conceptual leap because it was contrary to the traditional notion that government was based on divine rights, with the king being a representative of the godhead, if not actually a god himself. In this tradition, the king might disseminate and enforce laws, but the laws themselves were given by god. One of the more well-known examples of this principle appears in the Bible, where God writes his laws (The Ten Commandments), on stone tables and directs Moses to give them to the Israelites.

The Greeks were sophisticated people and understood that certain prohibitions, such as the prohibition against killing, probably did not come from Zeus but reflected a principle of nature. They also recognized that many laws, such as those protecting property, had no natural foundation but were exclusively the work of men who wanted to live together harmoniously. Thus the Greeks differentiated between the laws of nature (*physis*) and the laws of man (*nomos*). They also saw that these laws frequently were in conflict, making it difficult to know how to behave for the good of society. Laws of nature might move people to punish criminals as a form of retribution for past actions. Laws of man, on the other hand, might move people to punish criminals as a way of discouraging them from future criminal actions. In this case, laws of nature move citizens in one direction, whereas laws of man move them in another, and it can be difficult to know which path is better overall. The Sophists claimed to be able to provide this knowledge.

In doing so, they set themselves against the Greek aristocracy, which maintained that *areté* could not be taught because it was innate, at least among members of their class. Beck (1964), for instance, wrote that the Sophists believed "in the power of knowledge to improve human character. This implies both a theory of the disciplinary value of certain studies and the rejection of the aristocratic theory of 'virtue' as a matter of innate gifts and divine descent" (p. 148).

Although we know little about the philosophies the Sophists taught in conjunction with rhetoric and *areté*, we do know they tended to be relativists, believing that the truth concerning any issue depends on one's point of view. Three of the most well-known Sophists, Protagoras (approximately 490–420 B.C.), Gorgias (approximately 480–375 B.C.), and Isocrates (approximately 436–338 B.C.) argued that truth was relative, although they differed in other respects. If a question arises regarding the truth of a matter, each person involved is right, because each sees one facet of the truth. Rhetoric for the Sophists, then, was a tool for examining the various sides of an issue. Because each side holds an element of truth, in the sophistic view, people who practice rhetoric are obligated to explore that truth fully in order to understand it. By understanding multiple aspects of truth, or rather by understanding all sides of an issue, one acquires wisdom. Thus, to the Sophists, the person who mastered rhetoric also mastered knowledge and could view reality more clearly than someone limited by a single perspective.

Examining the views of the three Sophists mentioned—Protagoras, Gorgias, and Isocrates—can shed more light on these ideas. It also helps to better understand some of the tensions that arose early in the development of rhetoric, tensions that exist today.

Protagoras.   In keeping with the Sophists' relativistic views of truth and knowledge, Protagoras taught his students to take each side in a legal case. This approach was based on a view of knowledge that was contrary to tradition, which maintained that one side always was right and the other wrong; Protagoras proposed that there was no such thing as falsehood.

According to Guthrie (1971), Protagoras taught his followers that "a man was the sole judge of his own sensations and beliefs, which were true for him so long as they appeared to be so" (p. 267). This view had a significant influence on Greek rhetoric, moving it farther in the direction of language being used as a means of persuasion. If no objective reality exists, but only personal beliefs exist, a skillful speaker can create truth and reality in the minds of an audience—quite useful in court or government. However, this view also was a strong affirmation of the value of *nomos*, and it set Protagoras at odds with the Athenian aristocracy. Traditionally, laws of nature had been held to be absolute, whereas those of man were merely matters of convention and convenience. Patterson (1991) suggested that antidemocratic forces frequently appealed to laws of nature to support their arguments for oligarchy and against democracy. These forces pointed out that, in nature, the strong rule the weak through inherent superiority; because democracy treats men equally, it is unnatural.

A fragment from Protagoras' lost work entitled Truth demonstrates how strongly he disagreed with such notions: "Man is the measure of all things, of the things that are, that they are, and of the things that are not, that they are not" (Guthrie, 1971, p. 183). Jarratt (1991) concluded on the basis of this fragment, that Protagoras deemed "phenomena outside individual human experience" to be insignificant, but perhaps the idea that Protagoras was a humanist who placed mankind at the center of life is more accurate (p. 50). Patterson's (1991) work supported this humanistic reading when he wrote: "Implicit in this [statement] is a momentous shifting of the focus of thought from people in their relation with god to people as the basis for all judgment about the world" (p. 149). In this regard, Protagoras was following a tradition that started with

Homer, which led Patterson to conclude that Protagoras "finally humanized the Delphic injunction 'Know thyself'" (p. 149).

The ideas expressed in this fragment also represent a movement away from an emphasis on the divine toward an emphasis on individualism and democracy. Athenians probably understood Protagoras' assertion not just in a philosophical sense but also in a practical one. It was an affirmation that did more than shift the focus from Mount Olympus to the agora, the marketplace; it shifted the focus from the divine right of kings to the statutory rights of citizens. It was an assertion of manmade law over natural law.

Gorgias.   Gorgias continued this line of thought in a treatise titled *On the Nonexistent*, which has survived in outline form. Gorgias stated that truth and ideas do not have any essential existence; if they did they would not be knowable to man; even if they were knowable they could not be communicated to anyone. Usually, Gorgias' views are interpreted philosophically to mean that the world always is changing, so any essential existence is impossible. If it is possible, people would not be able to understand its nature because they are part of the ever-changing reality, which limits their ability to perceive anything outside or different from their changing universe. However, they can also be interpreted as an attack on traditional views that held that truth (often in the form of laws) came from the gods and was articulated by their representatives. In Gorgias' statement, there is a declaration that such truth is meaningless because it is incomprehensible. It would be easy to conclude on this basis that manmade laws are fundamentally superior to natural laws.

In addition, as Enos (1993) suggested, the philosophy inherent in Gorgias' statement is related to a view of rhetoric and reality that understands individual concepts as being comprised of "dichotomies." Enos noted, for example, that "the nature of rhetoric [for Gorgias] depends upon the proportion of 'truthfulness' or 'falsehood' it exhibits at any given time" (p. 78). Gorgias' philosophy suggested a chaotic view of the world that is contrary to the pragmatic goals of legal rhetoric and leads to what has been called *sophistic rhetoric* (see Enos, 1993; Kennedy, 1980).

Sophistic rhetoric did not deal with truth but dealt with the complex interplay of dichotomies, with the uncertain mixture of truths and falsehoods that made up reality. The only course available to the sophistic rhetorician, therefore, was to argue probability. However, the chaotic world view was not entirely incongruent with the workings of Athenian courts, in which eyewitness testimony was suspect owing to the prevalence of bribery and influence peddling. In lieu of such testimony, those presenting their cases (remember, there were no attorneys) commonly relied on argument from probability, not from fact. In most instances, there exists a range of probabilities from which arguments can be constructed; therefore, in this account, rhetoric becomes not only a means of persuasion but also a means of discovering probable arguments based on what normal people do under normal circumstances. Gorgias' *On the Nonexistent* took this notion to its logical conclusion.

Yet perhaps he was more famous for his rhetorical style than for his philosophy. Gorgias favored an ornate style filled with parallel constructions, attention to clause length, and striking images. When he arrived in Athens from Sicily in about 427 B.C., Gorgias became wildly popular, attracting fans much in the way that a rock star does today, and he apparently earned large sums of money by giving demonstrations. Gorgias was infatuated with the power and beauty of language, and he unabashedly claimed to be able to turn any argument around. He apparently argued a point vigorously in his demonstrations and then argued the opposite just as vigorously.

Eventually, the ornate style Gorgias practiced and promoted drew much criticism (even though it continued to be taught in many schools of rhetoric throughout the Roman period). His emphasis on style necessarily subordinated substance, and it frequently resulted in highlighting the cleverness of the speaker. As a result, critics began to disparage rhetoric that aimed simply to entertain audiences through linguistic acrobatics or that obviously aimed to play on the audiences' emotions.[2] These features came to be viewed as tricks that were dishonest and ultimately meaningless, which led to the expression, "empty rhetoric" that we frequently hear today. People began to view the Sophists negatively soon after Gorgias arrived in Athens. In his play *The Clouds*, produced in 423 B.C., Aristophanes lampooned the Sophists and their ability to confute creditors and spin nonsense.

Isocrates.   We can credit Isocrates with developing rhetorical study into a coherent system. Earlier Sophists, such as Gorgias, traveled from city to city giving demonstrations. Even when they remained in one city for years, as Gorgias did after arriving in Athens, they largely taught rhetoric by using an apprenticeship method. A few young men would follow their teacher around while he gave demonstration speeches. They would meet more or less informally at someone's home to receive instruction. Isocrates, however, established a school of rhetoric in Ath-

---

[2]Because so many Sophists came from Asia, the ornate style came to be known as *Asian rhetoric*.

ens around 390 B.C., which gave his teaching a sense of stability and formality that was lacking among other teachers. Here, he lectured on philosophy and the structure and nature of rhetoric. Thus the apprenticeship method continued, but in a more formal setting.

Isocrates' school provided a model for all others in the ancient period, and it influenced formal education throughout Western history to such an extent that Isocrates occasionally is referred to as the founder of humanism (Kinneavy, 1982). Some features of the curriculum can be seen even in our own schools, such as the inclusion of music, art, and math. Isocrates was also the first rhetorician who wrote all of his own speeches; he never delivered any through public demonstrations as his contemporaries did. We can assume that writing was an important part of the curriculum throughout the 50-year life of the school. As Welch (1990) noted, "part of the intellectual revolution of the second half of the fifth century and the fourth century B.C. involved the centrality of writing" (p. 12). In addition, Kennedy (1980) suggested that writing was an important step toward shifting rhetoric from purely oral to written discourse, a process that he described as the *letteraturizzazione* of rhetoric, or the shift in rhetorical focus from oral to written language. This process, of course, underlies our own emphasis on composition in public schools and colleges.

Finally, Isocrates proposed that there were three necessary factors to make a good rhetorician: talent, instruction, and practice. Of these three, Isocrates said, talent was the most important. He had no hesitation in affirming that his teaching was the best and that he gave students ample practice, but he admitted he could not provide anyone with talent. This view dominated Western schools until modern times, resulting in higher education that was primarily for the intellectual elite.[3] When American universities began moving toward more open admission policies in the 1960s, the role talent played in education, regardless of level, became a hot topic. It continues to be important in composition studies because so many teachers, students, and parents believe that good writing is the result of talent rather than effort.

Socrates and Plato

Although many people have never heard of the Sophists, just about everyone has heard of Socrates and Plato, even though they may not have read any of their work. They are cultural icons who exist in our

---

[3]It is worth noting that Scottish higher education took a more democratic approach until it was finally restructured in 1858, using the British model as its foundation. Scottish universities recognized the uneven preparation and abilities of their students and provided what we might think of as remedial classes for those who needed extra help.

collective consciousness, often without any clear reference. Plato was a student of Socrates, and most of what we know about Socrates comes from Plato's dialogues, especially *Apology, Gorgias, Protagoras*, and *Phaedrus*. Another notable source of information are four works by Socrates' friend and contemporary, Xenophon: *Oeconomicus, Apologia, Symposium*, and *Memorabilia*. Separating the historical Socrates from the literary figure is not easy, but several characteristics emerge that most scholars agree on. Like the Sophists, Socrates was concerned about the nature of truth, reality, and virtue. He considered wisdom to be the greatest good, and he advocated soundness of mind and body through philosophic inquiry, exercise, and moderation in food and drink, although (reportedly) he was quite overweight.

Rather than give public speeches and lectures like the Sophists, Socrates used a question-and-answer approach—or *dialectic* approach—that has come to be known as the *Socratic method*. Apparently, Socrates never committed anything to writing, and in two of Plato's dialogues, *Gorgias* and *Phaedrus*, he displayed outright hostility toward writing, arguing that it dulls the senses and destroys the memory. Furthermore, Socrates distrusted democracy; he decried the growth of democracy in Athens, but he was not directly involved in politics.

Unlike the Sophists, Socrates did not consider himself to be a teacher, although he had many students who held him in the highest esteem. Instead, he was a social critic who disapproved of the changes that Athens had undergone during his lifetime in the areas of education and politics. He saw his role as being that of a gadfly ever ready to challenge the increasing pride and self-satisfaction of his fellow citizens. In *Apology*, for example, Plato (1937) had Socrates describe his role in Athenian society in the following terms: "And so I go about the world, ... and search and make inquiry into the wisdom of any one, whether citizen or stranger, who appears to be wise; and if he is not wise, then ... I show him that he is not wise" (p. 406).

On the whole, Socrates and Plato contrast the Sophists. In fact, these two philosophers apparently disliked just about everything associated with the Sophists, although the reasons are not entirely clear.[4] In *Protagoras*, Socrates suggested it was because they charged fees for their teaching, which hardly seems probable because teachers had been charging fees for many years. Moreover, Plato charged students at his school—the Academy.

Numerous writers proposed alternative explanations for the animos-

---

[4]Having previously mentioned *The Clouds*, it's worth noting that Aristophanes identified Socrates as a Sophist, which seems to be a deliberate misrepresentation designed to enhance the humor of the play.

ity toward the Sophists (e.g., De Ste. Croix, 1981; Dodds, 1951; Havelock, 1982; Ober, 1989). For example, the Sophists were foreigners in a land where all non-Greeks were called "barbarians," and it is possible the underlying prejudice against foreigners became stronger than the Greek fascination with the rhetoric they employed. Gorgias' rhetorical flourishes were admired by many, but they also left many confused and dazed. His style of rhetoric emphasized the cleverness of the speaker rather than the discovery of truth and led to cynicism with respect to human values. Such cynicism not only was contrary to accepted notions of justice, philosophy, and rhetoric but also was contrary to the primary emphasis of Socrates and Plato.

Another explanation that may be easier to defend is based on disagreements over politics and philosophy. The Sophists generally supported democracy and argued that *nomos* was superior to *physis*.[5] Ostwald (1986) suggested that the two positions developed together: "Norms which before ... [the democratic revolution in Athens] were thought of as having existed from time immemorial, now came to be regarded as having been enacted and as being enforceable in a way similar to that in which statutes are decided upon by a legislative agency" (p. 50). This change in perception placed more authority in the hands of people and less in the hands of the gods; on the day-to-day level, less authority was held by a ruling aristocracy claiming divine rights. Given the tendency of the Sophists to wander from city to city, it is easy to understand how they linked the supremacy of *nomos* to relativism. They could observe that social norms and laws differed from place to place.

Unlike the Sophists, Socrates and Plato proposed that everything was absolute and that change occurred only at a superficial and ultimately trivial level. In their view, there was an absolute truth, an absolute virtue, and so on. There was also an ideal rhetoric, the question-and-answer process of dialectic, and Plato used it to great effect in his dialogues. He argued that language in this ideal should be used as a tool to separate truth from falsehood—that is, to determine the true and absolute nature of reality. Consequently, those who claimed truth and reality to be relative concepts and used language to argue this point were deceivers who should be censored.

---

[5]An exception was Isocrates, who had close connections to courts of various tyrants. Isocrates was critical of democracy, which put him in a difficult position when armed conflicts between forces supporting democracy and forces supporting tyranny clashed for several years during the middle of the 4th century B.C. Bluck (1947) argued that Isocrates published *Antidosis* in the hope of defending himself against democrats who were angry about his associations. Enos (1993, p. 84) concluded, on the basis of a brief reference to Isocrates in Plato's *Phaedrus*, that Isocrates was at one time Plato's student. This would explain much about Isocrates' attitudes toward democracy, but Enos' conclusion appears to go far beyond any evidence present in *Phaedrus*.

Socrates and Plato were not much concerned with legal rhetoric, although Plato was involved in writing laws and a constitution. Moreover, Plato claimed that the rhetoric the Sophists taught was used to trick audiences into believing that the worse argument was the better, which he maintained was inherently evil because it masked the truth and hindered justice. As already suggested, Plato may have distrusted rhetoric (legal or otherwise) because it was intimately linked to the rise of democracy; he was a conservative aristocrat who characterized democracy as the rule of the mob. Not surprisingly, Plato viewed the Sophists' advocacy of nomos over physis as a profound mistake that threatened society with chaos because it elevated uncertain man-made law over natural law. Given the connection between democracy and rhetoric, it is revealing to note that Plato and his students frequently visited the courts of tyrants, behavior that the democracy-loving Athenians probably did not appreciate. When Sparta defeated Athens in 404 B.C., the Spartans chose a group of 30 men from the Athenian aristocracy and installed them as rulers. Plato supported the "Thirty Tyrants," as they came to be known. He was also intimately involved in a messy coup attempt in Syracuse that temporarily replaced a relatively benevolent tyrant, Dionsyius II, with the austere and haughty tyrant Dion, who was one of Plato's students.[6]

From a political perspective, it's easy to see how Plato's conservative views brought him to oppose the Sophists and rhetoric. The Sophists' rhetorical instruction gave anyone with the means to pay the fee the ability to influence others. The power of language, as already noted, came to replace the power of the sword and to a certain degree the power of money and position. However, the power of the word in the hands of someone lacking virtue was relatively weak in a society that placed great weight on personal character and honor. The Sophists overcame this fundamental problem by claiming that they could teach *areté*, or civic virtue. This was a brilliant move that threatened the existing power structure, moving all citizens closer to political equality. Anyone who believed in natural superiority and social stratification would resist these ideas as an act of self-preservation.

Aristotle

Aristotle exerted more influence on rhetoric than any other person in history. He was born in 384 B.C., and in 367 he traveled to Athens to study with Plato. The curriculum of Plato's Academy included philoso-

---

[6]In a letter to Dion's supporters, Plato (1961) lamented that, under the democracy that overthrew the Thirty Tyrants, Athens "was no longer administered according to the standards and practices of our fathers" (Letter VII, 325d).

phy, political theory, math, biology, and astronomy. At the time of Aristotle's arrival, rhetoric may have been taught as an object of study rather than as a subject; that is, students may have studied what the Sophists taught, but they did not practice giving oral presentations. After completing his studies, Aristotle stayed on as a teacher for almost 20 years. Kennedy (1991) suggested that, along with other classes, Aristotle began teaching rhetoric of some kind in the late 350s: "The course seems to have been open to the general public—offered in the afternoons as a kind of extension division of the Academy and accompanied by practical exercises in speaking" (p. 5). When Plato died in 347, Aristotle left Athens and taught in various places before returning in 335 to start his own school—the Lyceum. Aristotle was a prolific writer, producing works on natural science (which includes astronomy, meteorology, plants, and animals); the nature, scope, and properties of being; ethics; politics; poetry; and rhetoric. Kennedy (1980) indicated that rhetoric was not a major interest for Aristotle and that he "taught it as a kind of extracurricular subject" (p. 61). If rhetoric was merely a hobby, it was one that Aristotle actively pursued. He produced *Gryllus* around 360 B.C., a lost work that examined the artistic nature of rhetoric. Another lost work, *Synagoge Technon*, was a lengthy summary and analysis of the rhetorical handbooks that Aristotle knew. The work that survived, *The Art of Rhetoric*, analyzed rhetoric in great detail and offered views that continue to be useful today.

Aristotle called rhetoric an art because it can be systematized and because it results in a specific product, not because it was related to literature or painting or because it drew on some romantic notion of inspiration. Unlike Plato, Aristotle accepted the practical nature of rhetoric and was not overly concerned about the prospect that speakers might use it for ignoble ends. However, he did criticize the Sophists because, in his view, they advocated an irrational approach to language that focused on style and emotion rather than substance. In the first part of *The Art of Rhetoric*, for example, Aristotle defined rhetoric as a theoretical system for discovering the available means of persuasion on a given topic. He then used this definition to dismiss sophistic rhetoric because it did not provide a theory of knowing and because it did not deal systematically with the *proof* necessary for persuasion to occur.

Proof is a central feature of Aristotle's rhetoric; consequently, it's important to avoid a common tendency—confusing our modern notions of scientific proof with what Aristotle meant when he used the term. In Aristotle's rhetoric, proof does not consist of factual evidence that leads to an incontrovertible conclusion. Instead, it consists of the reasons that speakers give their audiences; these reasons enable audiences to accept the point of view or position of the speech. Over the centuries, factual evidence has become far more available than it was in Aristotle's time, but the centrality of reasons has not diminished a bit. Reasons have come to be recognized as "rhetorical proofs" that are fundamental to rhetoric. Legal arguments, for instance, continue to revolve around rhetorical proof even when factual evidence is strong. One of the more graphic examples in recent times is the O. J. Simpson murder trial, in which the jury discounted solid DNA evidence that linked Simpson to the crime and accepted the defense team's emotional reasons for acquittal.[7]

Aristotle outlined several different kinds of rhetorical proof in *The Art of Rhetoric*, but he deemed three to be so important that he devoted about 20 chapters to them. They are *ethos*, *pathos*, and *logos*. *Ethos* is usually translated as "character." A speaker or writer has to project a good character to audiences, a character that is kind, considerate, intelligent, and so forth. A good character is simply more believable than one who is not, and audiences want to accept what he or she has to say. Consider the following two modern examples that illustrate the operation of ethos: citations in academic texts like this one and athletes' endorsements. At work is the principle of association. Citations associate writers' ideas with those of published scholars; this makes those ideas seem more credible. They also have the effect of displaying writers' intelligence and knowledge because of the projected implication that the writers have read all the works they cite. Something similar happens in advertising. When athletes appear on cereal boxes or when they endorse a brand of sneakers, consumers of those products feel as though they are associating with (perhaps even being like) their sports heroes, even if it is in the most marginal way.

Pathos is usually translated as "emotion." Emotion can be a powerful proof in language because it circumvents reason. Advertising and sales offer ready examples. Ads soliciting donations for children's aid programs commonly picture woe-begotten children who tug at our heart strings. Many car salespeople urge prospective buyers to take a test drive to "feel the excitement" of the new car. They know that a test drive bonds people emotionally to the car, making it harder to walk away from the purchase. It is easy to adopt a negative view toward such blatant emotional manipulation. However, emotion does not have to be negative. A positive use of emotion is exemplified in Martin Luther King, Jr.'s "I Have a Dream" speech, which decades after it was delivered still has

---

[7]Pragmatic rhetoric in ancient Athens dealt with questions that needed a quick decision, either in court or in government. A speaker had to propose a decision and persuade others to accept it. A typical argument might have had a basic structure similar to the following: "We should build a road to Corinth, and here are the reasons why." Little has changed in the intervening centuries, as the Simpson example illustrates.

the power to move audiences to tears.

Logos, Aristotle's third rhetorical proof, is usually translated as "reason" but may be better understood as "analysis" or "information." It often consists of facts, common knowledge, specialized knowledge, or statistics. Consider a continuation of the earlier example about the road to Corinth: Building such a road would make it easier to transport goods to and from Athens, which would benefit trade.

After treating proof extensively in *The Art of Rhetoric*, Aristotle took up the psychology of the audience, examining not only the range of psychological states that a speaker might encounter but also how to identify them. In each case, Aristotle identified the associated emotion, the state of mind that leads to it, and the focus or direction of the emotion. This discussion of psychology is the earliest one known, and it is particularly important in understanding how rhetoric from the beginning was linked to the characteristics of particular audiences. This connection has become a central feature of current rhetorical theory.

JOURNAL ENTRY

Classical Greek rhetoric was inextricably linked to the development of individualism and democracy. Reflect on the relationship that you see among rhetoric, individualism, and democracy; what factors strongly link them? Then reflect on our society, giving special attention to what you know about the current state of rhetoric, individualism, and democracy. Are there any similarities between the relationship in the past and the relationship in the present?

ROMAN RHETORIC

As Rome grew from a small village to a major power, it begrudgingly adopted much of Greek culture and civilization, including rhetoric. The Romans perceived the Greeks as weak and effeminate, a people too attached to unproductive intellectual pursuits like philosophy. The Greek influence, however, was unavoidable: Most of Sicily and nearly all of southern Italy had been colonized by Greeks and was dotted with prosperous, well-populated cities. With regard to rhetoric, Sicily was considered to be its birthplace, and southern Italy became an intellectual center because teachers from both Greece and Sicily opened numerous schools of rhetoric there. The growth of Rome naturally attracted Greeks from these southern cities, including teachers of rhetoric.

Rhetoric in Rome was different from rhetoric in Athens, however, because the cities had different sociopolitical agendas. Like Athens, Rome shifted to a slave economy fairly early, and it experienced many of the same difficulties, particularly the threat of revolt by freemen displaced when they could not compete in the new economy. Yet the outcomes were quite different. In Athens, laws and customs required citizens of means to contribute to the city's infrastructure. This amounted to a tax that essentially kept the wealthy on the brink of bankruptcy. Consequently, when the poor and displaced threatened revolt in Athens, the ruling aristocracy was not in a position to appease them by redistributing wealth. They chose, instead, to redistribute power, which resulted in a more democratic government.

There were no similar laws or customs in Rome, and by the time the poor threatened to revolt, a state of continual warfare and expansion was channeling the wealth of the Mediterranean into the coffers of the ruling elite, who were able to buy off the rabble through an elaborate system of doles and entertainment that quickly came to be viewed as entitlements. Thereby, they preserved their power. Meanwhile, the poor and displaced seemed quite willing to give up any demands to participate in government as long as their entitlements were not threatened. As Grant (1992) stated, "The very root of Roman society was the institution of a relatively few rich patrons inextricably linked with their more numerous poor clients, who backed them in return for their patrons' support" (p. 50).

In this climate, rhetoric could not have a significant link with democracy because democracy never existed. The ruling elite, in fact, viewed rhetoric with such great suspicion that the Roman Senate twice banned the teaching of rhetoric and closed all the schools, first in 161 B.C. and then again in 92 B.C. (Enos, 1995). Although these efforts were in part motivated by strong anti-Greek sentiments among the Romans, it is clear that the major motivation was to eliminate a powerful tool for democratic change. As Enos stated, underlying the Senate bans was fear that rhetorical education would enable the poor to "express attitudes contrary to patrician interests" (p. 47).

The bans, however, could not last as long as Rome invested the court system with some measure of justice and fairness. The pragmatic need for rhetorically trained legal advocates was so strong that the bans were lifted and, for a time, rhetoric flourished, producing such great rhetoricians as Hortensius, Cicero, and Quintilian. In addition, entitlements reduced the threat of revolution, and schools modified their methods to make them more congruent with Roman, rather than Athenian, values. The result was a renaissance of Roman rhetoric that began toward the latter part of the republic. Space constraints make it impossible to look closely at Roman rhetoricians, but we cannot leave this important period of classical rhetoric without looking at the greatest of them—Cicero.

Cicero

Although Aristotle was known to the Romans, Cicero (106–43 B.C.) was held in higher esteem. After the Empire collapsed, Aristotle was lost to the West until the 13th century, and throughout this time Cicero was considered to be the greatest rhetorician. Many of his speeches have survived, as well as more than 900 letters and several works on rhetoric, such as *On Invention (De Inventione), On Oratory, (De Oratore),* and *Brutus.*

Cicero's parents were of modest means, but they nevertheless managed to provide their son with a good education. He studied rhetoric with various Greek tutors and was apprenticed to the most important lawyer of the time, Mucius Scaevola. Cicero enjoyed quick success as a trial lawyer, which opened the door of government service. For a time, he was in charge of public works, then he became a magistrate (praetor) and consul. At one point, he served as the governor of Cilicia, a town in Asia Minor. He was exiled in 63 B.C. because, when serving as consul, he executed (without trial) a group of men charged with conspiring to overthrow the government. Cicero himself was executed in 43 B.C. after he tried to stir opinion against Mark Antony, who assumed authority in Rome after Julius Caesar was assassinated.

On Invention is a technical handbook that focused on discovering ideas and topics. In many respects, it reflected a contemporary emphasis on form that had its roots in the early Greek handbooks. *On Invention* also seemed to be consistent with how rhetoric was being taught in the Roman schools, where little consideration of philosophy, psychology, or truth existed and where rhetoric was not deemed to be a theory of knowing. By Cicero's time, rhetoric had been divided into five "offices": *invention*, analyzing a topic and finding material for it; *disposition*, arranging the speech; *elocution*, fitting words to the topic, the situation, the speaker, and the audience; *delivery*; and *memory*. *On Invention* described these offices and thereby reflected much of the rhetorical teaching of the time, which tended to reduce rhetoric to a rigid system for producing certain kinds of discourse. *On Invention* presented a rhetoric that consists of form without content, in spite of its stated aim of helping readers discover ideas and topics.

On Oratory, on the other hand, is much closer in spirit to Plato and Aristotle, so much so that many modern evaluations criticize it for being derivative. The work—a dialogue—begins with a discussion among friends about the value of rhetoric. Crassus, one of the key speakers, stated his view that rhetoric is the foundation of government and leadership because without it government has no direction. In addition, Crassus proposed that the ideal rhetorician was a philosopher states-man. After being challenged to elaborate on these claims, Crassus outlined a course of study for the rhetorician that included information on such topics as the duties of the rhetorician; the aims of speaking; the subjects of speeches; the division of speeches into invention, arrangement, style, memory, and delivery; and rules for proper language use. Following Isocrates, Crassus noted that talent, an appropriate model, and practice are necessary qualities for a person to become an orator and that talent is the most important requirement.

Although *On Oratory* offers interesting insights into Cicero's (1970) views on Roman rhetoric, views that probably were representative, it contains little original material. Cicero borrowed extensively from Plato and Aristotle, as well as from the Sophists. In Book I, XIII, for example, Crassus noted that "the accomplished and complete orator I shall call him who can speak on all subjects with variety and copiousness," an observation that is strikingly similar to the view of Gorgias (*De Oratore*, 1970, p. 20). Cicero acknowledged his debt to the Greeks throughout the work, but in Book I, XXXI, he also suggested that there was nothing new in *On Oratory*. Crassus stated "I shall say nothing ... previously unheard by you, or new to any one" (p. 40). However, Cicero did explore style more than earlier writers. He identified three categories—grand, middle, and plain—and discussed their use in detail. Cicero exerted tremendous influence on rhetoric throughout the Middle Ages, but, as a result of this lack of originality, his value today may lie largely in his speeches, which provide important historical information and also illustrate an excellent practitioner at the height of his craft.

THE EARLY CHRISTIAN PERIOD

Enos (1995) argued that Cicero's death marked the end of rhetoric as a "political force" in Rome, but this evaluation is based on the perception that the courts of law were arenas in which litigants fought political, not just legal, battles. Such battles were not possible under the Roman Empire, so there was little need for the sort of rhetoric that Cicero practiced. In this environment, the focus of rhetorical study shifted. Schools increasingly concentrated on technical matters of form (and less on pragmatic applications). Students studied texts, such as Cicero's speeches, and wrote analyses that defended an interpretation. Kennedy (1980) described this shift as moving from *primary* (oral speeches intending to persuade) to *secondary* (written interpretations of texts) rhetoric (pp. 4–6).

In this context, there was another shift that was growing more powerful and influential every year—Christianity. Although Hollywood depictions of this period usually portray the early Christians as peasants, downtrodden by the nobility and the government, history offers a different view. Brown (1987) noted that the majority of Christians in Rome were members of the middle and upper classes, well educated, and imbued with a sense of morality that was entirely compatible with Christianity. They were sophisticated and cultured to such a degree that the pagan stories of the gods borrowed from the Greeks failed to satisfy their spiritual needs. One such citizen of Rome, St. Augustine, born in North Africa, not only exerted a tremendous influence on the development of the Church but also on the development of rhetoric.

St. Augustine

St. Augustine significantly accelerated the shift to secondary rhetoric. His work led scholars to concentrate on interpreting the Bible and on debating their interpretations with one another in an effort to establish biblical truth. St. Augustine was born in 354 A.D., in what is now Algeria. He studied rhetoric and became a professional rhetorician, but he also had a philosophical inclination that was stimulated when he read one of Cicero's works, *Hortensius*. Under the influence of his mother, St. Augustine considered becoming a Christian early in life, but he did not find it particularly congenial because of the strictures it placed on behavior. He expressed the source of his reluctance years later when he wrote his autobiography, which came to be known as *The Confessions of St. Augustine* (1962): "Make me chaste and continent, but not yet" (p. 174).

Not all Christian sects were equally strict, however, and St. Augustine experimented with several of them. Then, in 383, St. Augustine left Carthage for Italy, eventually taking a position as a teacher of rhetoric in Milan. There he met the bishop of Milan, St. Ambrose, whose presence and intellect attracted him once again to the Church. After much prayer and reflection, he was baptized by St. Ambrose in 387. He returned to North Africa and was ordained in 391; he became bishop of Hippo (now Annaba, Algeria) in 395, an office he held until his death.

Although nearly 400 years had passed since the Crucifixion, the Catholic Church was hardly the bastion of doctrine and faith that it is today. Various sects vied for followers and power in the newly Christianized West, such as the Pelagians, who denied the doctrine of original sin, and the Donatists, who believed that the sacraments were invalid unless administered by priests who were without sin—a requirement that had the unfortunate consequence of bringing religious services to a complete halt. Manichaeism offered a special challenge because it was a sect that St. Augustine himself had belonged to before his conversion. It was founded by Mani, a 3rd-century Persian from southern Iraq who proclaimed himself the last prophet in a succession that included Zoroaster, Buddha, and Jesus. The fundamental doctrine of Manichaeism was its dualistic division of the universe into contending realms of good and evil. God ruled the realm of light, whereas Satan ruled the realm of darkness. God and Satan were believed to be in perpetual conflict, and out of this conflict mankind was created. Human life, in fact, was a microcosm of the great struggle between good and evil, for the body was seen to be material and evil, whereas the soul was seen to be spiritual and good.

Paganism, however, appears to have presented the greatest challenge. Countless people continued to cling to pagan beliefs, in spite of vicious persecution by the Christians (see Brown, 1987; Chauvin, 1990). Even more problematic was the fact that pagan ways of thinking permeated the lives of Christians, bringing them into frequent conflict with Church values. For example, upper-class Romans generally were highly moral, a characteristic that made Christianity attractive to them, and they viewed sex as a civic duty imposed on married couples for the express purpose of begetting children for the empire (Brown, 1987). However, this solidly Christian antipathy toward sex was seriously compromised by the widespread pagan belief that only "a hot and pleasurable act of love" experienced by both the male and the female could guarantee conception of a child with a good temperament (pp. 304–311).

St. Augustine also faced two other challenges (one from within his own ranks). First, various pagan leaders and philosophers criticized the Bible as an inept work that showed no evidence of divine inspiration. Indeed, before his conversion St. Augustine had the same sentiment. Second, many church leaders began attacking rhetoric and the schools throughout Italy for espousing pagan ideals (Murphy, 1974). "The wisdom of man is foolish before God" became a favorite expression of those who sought to discredit Roman education and learning. Matters reached a crisis point when the Fourth Council of Carthage in 398 issued a resolution forbidding bishops from reading pagan texts.

In this context, Augustine set about defending the Bible and rhetoric, although he approached the latter with an ambivalence caused by his training in rhetoric on the one hand and Christian distaste for anything pagan on the other. *On Christian Doctrine (De Doctrina Christiana),* completed in 477, reflects his efforts at reconciling these opposites. In this work, Augustine argued that rhetoric could be put to use in preaching and, more important, in interpreting the Bible. In addition, he proposed that rhetoric was a critical tool for discovering scriptural truths and explaining them to the misinformed and the unenlightened, thereby possibly gaining new converts. He also used rhetoric to analyze the Bible in ways that illuminated its literary merit.

St. Augustine's success on all fronts can be measured by the fact that, over a relatively short time, texts other than the Bible became the subject of much rhetorical analysis. Furthermore, a vast array of pagan myths and writers was assimilated into the Christian cosmology. The most notable example is Plato, whose work came to be embraced as a precursor of Christian values, with the result that Plato's influence on the Middle Ages was greater than Aristotle's until the 13th century (Artz, 1980).

St. Augustine lived at a time when the Roman world was in turmoil and decline. The imperial armies had been defeated by Teutonic barbarians, and the Vandals controlled North Africa. Schools of the middle and late Roman Empire (300 and 600 A.D., respectively) could not realistically prepare students to use forensic or deliberative rhetoric, which no doubt motivated changes in curricula, changes that signaled a departure from the tradition established by Isocrates and Aristotle. Students increasingly concentrated on declamations—set themes—as rhetoric became more literary. The content of these speeches became ever more abstract and irrelevant; what was important was style and delivery.[8] As Bonner (1977) noted, "Many teachers of rhetoric ... under the Empire did not have ... [Cicero's] practical experience, but were content to transmit the precepts [of rhetoric] in stereotyped and compact form, and to make their students learn them by heart" (p. 288). Bonner also pointed out that these declamations became "more bizarre and artificially contrived, [and] the exercise was especially associated with the *scholasticus* or 'school-man,' and was called a 'scholastic theme'" (p. 309).

Although St. Augustine condemned sophistry, the rhetoric he espoused was grounded in literature, or more accurately, the Bible. A literature-based rhetoric is ineluctably tied to matters of style, a fact that made Augustine's condemnation of sophistry ring hollow. Furthermore, this rhetoric emphasized the search for biblical truth, which was deemed to be universal but which also was highly abstract. These factors combined eventually with others to create, for the first time since Plato, significant interest in dialectic. This interest grew as the West moved into the Dark Ages and opportunities for primary rhetoric diminished. In time, the focus on literature and the concurrent emphasis on style led to the gradual reduction of rhetoric, until Ramus stripped it of all but two of its traditional offices—style and delivery.

---

[8]Most historians refer to this period as the *Second Sophistic*, indicating a connection with the sophistic rhetoric of ancient Greece. Although in most respects there is little connection, it is the case that both forms emphasized highly ornate style and rhetoric as a demonstration. *Lives of the Philosophers*, by Eunapius (ca. 345), provides numerous interesting insights.

JOURNAL ENTRY

Ancient Greece and Athens have influenced greatly who we are today, and some of those influences are examined in the previous pages. Consider some other ways we have been influenced by these ancient cultures, such as education.

FROM THE MIDDLE AGES TO THE 19TH CENTURY

The Middle Ages strike many people as being dull and relatively uneventful. When the empire fell near the end of the 5th century, what Poe (1831) referred to as the "grandeur that was Greece and the glory that was Rome" (p. 23) faded from the world scene, along with the sense of purpose and direction that had characterized Western civilization for 1,000 years. Although the Roman Empire was plagued by internal conflicts throughout its history, it nevertheless manifested a political unity and a civilizing influence that were profound. Both disappeared with the last emperor, Romulus Augustulus. In his place emerged a hodgepodge of petty dictators and self-proclaimed kings who engaged in warfare so relentless that war, along with religion, became the cultural signature. The now separate parts of what had been the Western Empire began developing their own histories, not just because they were ruled by separate groups of barbarians but also because the universal culture that had defined the Roman Empire was shattered. In a remarkably short time, Latin evolved into the Romance languages—Spanish, Portuguese, Italian, French, Romanian—each distinct and each mutually unintelligible. Even handwriting, which had been uniform under the Roman Empire, evolved into independent forms: Visigoth script, Beneventan script, and Insular script, as well as numerous scripts peculiar to various monasteries—each essentially unreadable to anyone untrained in that form.

In this environment, rhetoric became, in certain respects, more complex than ever before, which makes it difficult to address the many developments that occurred during the Middle Ages. However, two fairly distinct trends in rhetoric were visible, trends that persist even today: Aristotelian and Platonic. Many of Aristotle's ideas about rhetoric survived through translations and commentaries on Cicero. One of the more important was Aristotle's emphasis on the practical nature of rhetoric.[9] Plato had not fared well among the Romans; he was too philosophical, and his rejection of practical rhetoric in favor of dialectic simply did not meet Roman needs. Only one of his works, *Timaeus*, was widely known,

---

[9]Aristotle and Cicero, however, differed in other respects. For example, Aristotle emphasized argument and proof, whereas Cicero emphasized eloquence.

but the church fathers had so thoroughly assimilated Plato into Christianity by the Middle Ages that he was, as Artz (1980) indicated, the spiritual and philosophical "guiding star" of Catholicism (p. 181).

Plato's popularity led to a general reevaluation of dialectic, most notably in the work of the philosopher and statesman Boethius. In his most important work, *Topics (De Differentiis Topicis)*, Boethius (ca. 523) set out to explain the work of Aristotle and Cicero, but what he ended up with was a treatise on the relation between rhetoric and dialectic. Dialectic played little role in rhetorical education or practice until the Second Sophistic, but Boethius argued that dialectic was prior to and inherently superior to rhetoric. He based this argument on the perception that rhetoric deals with the immediate concerns of daily life whereas dialectic deals with universals. As Conley (1990) noted, this distinction led Boethius to conclude that "rhetorical topics derive their force from the abstract propositional rules provided by dialectic. Dialectic therefore governs the genus of argumentation, and rhetoric becomes a subordinate part of dialectic because it is a species of that genus" (p. 80).

During the years after Boethius, rhetoric continued to change in ways congruent with the needs of the church, particularly the monastic influence that always had been strong. For example, Cicero came to be admired not as much for his work in rhetoric as for his eventual withdrawal from public life, which was congruent with the monastic goal of disengagement (Conley, 1990). Two new strands of rhetoric emerged: the art of letter writing (*ars dictaminis*) and the art of preaching (*ars praedicandi*). Grammar and logic became important as fields of study. In fact, logic increasingly connected to dialectic, which Bishop Isidore of Seville described in the 7th century as that discipline "which in the most exacting controversies distinguishes the true from the false" (quoted in Murphy, 1974, p. 74). By the 9th century, the study of grammar replaced the study of rhetoric, leading the writer Rabanus to define grammar as the science of speaking and writing correctly. By the end of the 12th century, most schools in Europe were not teaching rhetoric at all but were teaching grammar and dialectic (Murphy, 1974).

Interest in rhetoric revived significantly in the 13th and 14th centuries, when numerous classical texts were discovered and made available to scholars. Gerardo Landriani, bishop of a small town just outside Milan, found the complete text of Cicero's *On Oratory* in a cellar. Poggio, who happened to develop the font that came to be known as Roman, discovered Quintilian's *Instituto Oratoria* in the basement of a monastery. As these manuscripts became widely disseminated, Renaissance readers grew curious about the Greek authors that texts cited so regularly. Their curiosity was more easily satisfied after 1453, when

Constantinople fell to the Turks; Greek scholars fled westward in droves and were able to teach Greek throughout Europe.

Soon, classical texts were systematically integrated into higher education, which had the inevitable effect of motivating scholars to analyze and criticize the rhetorical precepts of Aristotle, Plato, Cicero, and others. It appears that these criticisms were grounded in a significant change that was altering the way Europeans looked at the world. The ancient Greeks and Romans interacted with the world on a qualitative basis and did not concern themselves much with exact measurements. Although they used hours to calculate duration, they did not use minutes. In addition, they divided a day into 24 hours, but they assigned 12 hours to day and 12 hours to night, although the lengths of daylight and night vary with the seasons and geography. During the Middle Ages, people throughout Europe became increasingly concerned with accuracy of measurement, and the end result was that, as a group, Europeans shifted from a qualitative to a quantitative world view. In rhetoric, this view finds expression in the emphasis on grammar and logic; these are more quantitative than the general rhetorical principles of Plato and Aristotle.

Peter Ramus was one of the more influential scholars who benefited from adopting a more quantitative approach to rhetoric. In the mid-16th century, he declared that most of what the ancient writers proposed about rhetoric was wrong, and he offered his own model as a replacement. The result was a significant departure from classic notions of rhetoric, a departure whose influence has extended even into modern times.

Ramus removed all of the offices from rhetoric except style and delivery. He argued, for example, that syntax was the proper domain of grammar and that invention, memory, and arrangement were part of dialectic. In addition, Ramus argued that dialectic should subsume other features of discourse that in the past had been part of rhetoric. Dialectic was not merely a means of determining truth and falsehood; in Ramus' view it was also the art of speaking decisively on matters that were in question. However, real-world applications never figured into Ramus' consideration; in his view, neither rhetoric nor dialectic was related to law or politics and both primarily involved writing, not speaking. In making this shift, Ramus expanded the role of dialectic to include forensic and deliberative language. The demise of primary rhetoric was virtually complete, and as a result of Ramus' work, Plato's notions of rhetoric and dialectic came to dominate the schools, especially in Germany (Conley, 1990). As Kennedy (1980) noted, there were no Aristotelian rhetorics developed during this period (p. 204).

The belles-lettres movement of the 18th and 19th centuries built on the work of people like Ramus, and in many respects it represented the natural evolution of the program of literary exposition that St. Augustine had given so much impetus. Following Ramus, Hugh Blair, for example, argued in the late 18th century that invention was beyond the scope of rhetoric. The consequences of this view are important. Invention, after all, was the process of discovering things to say about a topic. Since ancient times, invention had provided the content of discourse. What was left if there was no content? About a hundred years later, Alexander Bain provided the answer when he took Blair's view to its logical (but ultimately damaging) conclusion. Bain (1866) argued that content was also beyond the scope of rhetoric, leaving nothing to teach or learn but style. In one respect, Bain brought rhetoric full circle, back to the worst of the Sophists, who taught form without content.

Bain also proposed that rhetoric was composition. The emphasis on writing had been building since St. Augustine, but Bain was the first to equate one with the other. His book *English Composition and Rhetoric* (1866) was remarkably popular and went through numerous editions in the United States. Part of its appeal may have been Bain's attempts to provide a psychological foundation for rhetoric and style (Bain was a psychologist), but most of the appeal no doubt resided in the way in which his views simplified teaching. From classical times, teachers stressed the role of talent in rhetorical training; where there was no talent, there could be little education. Plato, for example, complained about the lack of talent he saw in the young tyrant Dionysius II of Syracuse. Teaching students how to think is so difficult that not even someone of Plato's genius could get ideas to germinate in barren soil. Bain implicitly provided a rationale for not trying: If the content of rhetoric, or composition, is irrelevant, and if all that remains is style, instruction can focus on imitation. Therefore, the rich (and demanding) education Cicero described in *On Oratory* became irrelevant.

THE NEW RHETORIC

It is difficult to pinpoint the birth of the *new rhetoric*—the term that has been used to describe the reemergence of modern interest in rhetoric and composition—but the early 1960s is probably an accurate estimate. A number of important works emerged that fueled the imaginations of scholars and motivated them to begin reexamining rhetoric and composition. In 1963, for example, Braddock, Lloyd-Jones, and Schoer published *Research in Written Composition*, a seminal book that traced several lines of research in composition and suggested new areas for investigation. A year later, Hunt (1964) published *Differences in Grammatical Structures Written at Three Grade Levels*, a work that sought to identify the factors related to maturity in student writing. Also in 1964, Bateman and Zidonis published *The Effect of a Knowledge of Generative Grammar Upon the Growth of Language Complexity*, a study of the relationship between grammar and writing that was to have a significant influence on later efforts of using developments in linguistics to help students improve their writing.

These works challenged many of the notions about rhetoric and composition that had emerged during the 19th century and that continued to influence writing instruction in the 1960s. Together, these 19th-century notions came to be referred to as the *current–traditional approach* to composition because they are rooted in long-standing conventions but are applied in a contemporary context. They are also referred to as the *product model* because they concentrate on stylistic features of finished essays. For example, teachers who use the current–traditional approach typically edit student papers as though they are preparing manuscripts for publication, with one notable exception: Students never have the opportunity to correct mistakes. The errors are usually deemed to be the result of students' deficiencies in grammar, so teachers spend a great deal of time drilling their classes on subject–verb agreement, punctuation, sentence construction, and so forth.

The basis for this pedagogy can be traced back in time to rhetoricians like Peter Ramus and teachers like Alexander Bain who separated form from content and then linked form to grammar and logic. Experience should have made it clear to everyone that grammar instruction did nothing to improve writing, but in this case experience was a poor teacher. The belief was unshakable. Indeed, it persists even today. Braddock et al. (1963), however, took an important step forward when they tackled this issue without trepidation, declaring, "The teaching of formal grammar has a negligible or, because it usually displaces some instruction and practice in actual composition, even a harmful effect on the improvement of writing" (pp. 37–38). These sentiments were substantiated in Bateman and Zidonis' work.

More important, and the fundamental reason that the works previously mentioned deserve special attention, was that these writers rejected the belief that there was nothing to teach in composition but style. In *Research in Written Composition*, Braddock et al. (1963) asked a question that defined new rhetoric: "What is involved in the act of writing?" (p. 53) Answering this question took scholars down numerous paths; some led to classical rhetoric, others to linguistics, philosophy, and psychology. Researchers also adapted empirical designs and methodologies from the social sciences to tackle the many thorny problems inherent in studying writing. Even with the many diverse approaches, however, the new rhetoric was unified by two desires: *discovering what differentiated good writers from bad ones and helping bad writers become better*. Therefore, the new rhetoric was, in part, an expression of the growing democratization of American society and higher education that marked the period following World War II (Jencks, 1972). It was also firmly situated in the classical tradition that linked rhetoric and democracy.

The Early Influence of Linguistics

The influence of linguistics was evident early, no doubt owing to the work of Noam Chomsky, who redefined linguistics with his development of transformational-generative grammar. Drawing on Chomsky, Hunt determined that as children become older the length of their clauses, or what he termed *T-units*, increases. Mellon (1969) saw in this finding an opportunity to shorten the process by teaching students transformational grammar rules that combine short sentences into longer ones. Because short sentences generally have just one clause, the effect of combining them is longer clauses, which is indicative of more mature writing. Mellon taught these rules to a group of students over a period of several weeks, until they could perform the required operations easily. Then he asked them to write essays.

In theory, this program should have worked, but it did not. The essays the students produced were not any better than those they wrote before the study; some were actually worse. O'Hare (1972), however, saw a flaw in Mellon's approach. He recognized that students do not need to have a formal knowledge of grammar to combine short sentences into long ones because every native speaker of English already knows the grammar implicitly. Teaching students grammar raises tacit knowledge to a conscious level in ways that interfere with the efficient language processing necessary in writing. In other words, students probably were thinking more about the grammar rules than they were about writing, with deleterious effects. O'Hare altered the focus of Mellon's research so that students did not spend any time studying rules but simply focused on combining sentences. The results were impressive. At the end of the study, students produced essays that were judged as being far better than the ones they had written before training. Thus, sentence combining was born. It became, in just a couple of years, a pervasive technique for improving student writing, and teachers and students from coast to coast began combining sentences.

Finding Rhetoric in the New Rhetoric

The term *rhetoric* was absent from the publications of researchers such as Hunt, Mellon, O'Hare, and others. One reason was that the scholars involved were from university English departments, where hostility toward rhetoric had been strong since the 19th century, finally leading rhetoricians to pack their bags and move to speech communication departments around 1915 (Miller, 1982). Consequently, there was a knowledge gap that made it difficult to see how the work of classical rhetoric was applicable to modern composition. This situation changed in 1971, when Kinneavy published *A Theory of Discourse*, a complex but clear analysis of the relation between composition and classical—specifically Aristotelian—rhetoric.[10]

A Theory of Discourse affected the field in several ways. For example, it suggested that anyone who was serious about composition needed to go back to its roots and study the classics, particularly Aristotle, and it provided a historical and theoretical rationale for viewing composition as part of a 2,500-year-old rhetorical tradition. In doing so, *A Theory of Discourse* helped legitimize composition as a field of study. Scholars (particularly those in literature) denigrated composition for generations, but they could not denigrate the classics as easily, and *A Theory of Discourse* effectively illustrated how composition and classical rhetoric were intertwined.

In addition, the book's subtitle suggested rich associations. Classical rhetoric was pragmatic and closely tied to concerns of audience, but these features disappeared from composition; student essays were school exercises that generally focused on literary analysis or personal experience. Using a "communication triangle" that included "reality" as one of its points, Kinneavy reminded readers that people generally use language for good reasons and that good reasons should underlie school writing. (This triangle is reproduced in Fig. 1.1, with minor modifications.) Finally, *A Theory of Discourse* also connected composition to important work in the philosophy of language, where scholars like Austin (1962) and Searle (1969) described language as an action. (See Witte, Nakadate, & Cherry, 1992, for a book-length discussion of *A Theory of Discourse's* influence on composition.)

---

[10]It is worth noting, however, that hostility toward rhetoric and composition remains strong in university English departments nationwide. Those who teach literature have intense negative feelings about the service features of modern composition, and large numbers of them reject the empirical basis of some of the more important research. Postmodern rhetoric aligned itself with literature and literary criticism, ostensibly, in the beginning, in an attempt to attenuate the hostility. This attempt was soon replaced by efforts among postmodernists to shift the agenda of rhetoric and composition from pragmatics to politics.

From Theory to Practice

If Kinneavy provided a theoretical grounding for the new rhetoric, Emig provided the pedagogy. The same year Kinneavy published *A Theory of Discourse*, Emig published *The Composing Processes of Twelfth Graders* (1971), a work that marked the end of the product model among forward-thinking scholars and teachers. North (1987) called Emig's work "the single most influential piece of ... [composition] inquiry" (p. 197). Many others in rhetoric and composition share this assessment because Emig showed that effective teaching must be concerned with process rather than product.

The process model that Emig was instrumental in creating is discussed in chapter 2. Nevertheless, a few remarks are pertinent here. It has become commonplace that social contexts provide the soil necessary for ideas to germinate and flower. Understandably, then, thinkers often come up with similar ideas and associations. Although *The Composing Processes of Twelfth Graders* is in many respects completely different from *A Theory of Discourse*, both works are linked to classical rhetoric. In the process model, teachers do not concentrate their efforts on error correction; instead, they work to change students' behaviors with regard to composing—helping them identify and then emulate the behaviors of successful writers. This model entails a great deal of close contact among students and teachers; it is individualized and collaborative, with teachers commonly joining groups of students to show them how to solve rhetorical problems. The degree of contact resembles the apprenticeships that existed in classical times among students and teachers, such

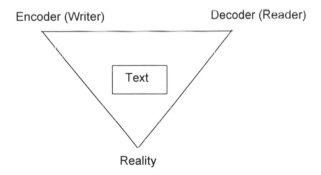

FIG. 1.1. Kinneavy's communication triangle. From Kinneavy (1971). Copyright © 1971 by Norton. Reprinted with permission.

as Isocrates and Aristotle. Thus both the theory and the pedagogy of new rhetoric were linked to classical rhetoric at the outset.

Nevertheless, there is a certain irony associated with Emig's work. Through her study of high school students, she altered the way composition specialists thought about how we teach writing, but the practical consequences were felt primarily in university writing programs. Teachers in public schools were generally slow to learn about process pedagogy and even slower to adopt it. Although a new generation of public school teachers made process pedagogy more widespread than ever, the majority of the nation's schools have not made this transition. Writing instruction continues to focus on grammar drills and exercises, and it continues to emphasize mechanical correctness rather than content.

Rhetoric and Cognition

Berlin (1990) traced the early developments in new rhetoric not so much to the classics, but to what, at the time, were recent developments in cognitive psychology. The National Defense Education Act of 1958 made improving public-school performance a high priority. Educators held numerous conferences over the next several years to develop strategies that would enable them to meet challenges presented by this act, and an influential leader in these efforts was Jerome Bruner, one of the foremost psychologists in the country. Drawing on the stage developmental theories of Jean Piaget, Bruner articulated curricula that emphasized using process to master the core knowledge of academic disciplines, and his ideas took root. (Efforts to base classroom instruction on psychological principles are often linked to what is known as the *progressive education movement*, which generally attempted to focus attention on schools' role in giving students the cognitive tools to lead a well-balanced and productive life.) Berlin's evaluation of Bruner is worth quoting at length:

> [Bruner stressed the] role of discovery in learning, arguing that students should use an inductive approach in order to discover on their own the structure of the discipline under consideration. ... The student was to engage in the act of doing physics or math or literary criticism, and was not simply to rely on the reports of experts. ... The implications of Bruner's thought for writing instruction are not difficult to deduce. Students should engage in the process of composing, not in the study of someone else's process of composing. Teachers may supply information about writing ..., but their main job is to create an environment in which students can learn for themselves the behavior appropriate to successful writing. The product of student writing, moreover, is not as important as engaging in the process of writing. (p. 208)

From these observations, Berlin argued that Emig's work emerged from the cognitive context that Bruner in particular and progressive education in general encouraged. It is easy to note that Kinneavy's work also emerged from this context because, as mentioned in regard to Aristotle, any discussion of discourse aims necessarily must consider the psychology of the audience.

Cognition offered fertile lines of research for scholars, and between 1975 and 1985, the majority of influential studies in composition examined psychological dimensions of writing (Hillocks, 1986). Flower and Hayes (1981), for example, developed a cognitive model of the composing process that was one of the more frequently cited studies throughout the 1980s. Matsuhashi (1981) simultaneously published an important assessment of pausing and planning during writing, suggesting that effective writers use pauses during composing to adjust their plans. Williams (1985) studied micromovements of the articulatory musculature, which becomes active during mental activities, and concluded that good writers think more during pauses. Nevertheless, many people in composition and rhetoric were uncomfortable with the cognitive approach. Conducting such research required serious training in statistics and research methods and design; reading and understanding it demanded equally serious training. The people conducting this research, however, came largely from university English departments, which generally view empiricism with disdain. Furthermore, composition and rhetoric scholars were developing graduate programs that were attracting bright students who otherwise might have elected to study literature. These students began writing dissertations that literature-trained graduate studies committees found hard to understand and inappropriate for English departments. A backlash was inevitable as established literature faculty, joined by some manqué compositionists, sought to reassert traditional values.

ROMANTIC RHETORIC

The first signs of backlash manifested themselves through what has come to be known as *romantic rhetoric* (Winterowd & Blum, 1994). *Romantic rhetoric* is linked to *romanticism*, a movement in literature that lasted from about 1750 to 1870 and that is characterized by reliance on the imagination, subjectivity, freedom of thought and expression, idealization of the individual, a search for individual truth, and rejection of rules. In most respects, romanticism emerged as a reaction against *classicism*, a term used to characterize art governed by conscious restraint, form, and rationality. However, it also was a reaction against *rationalism*, a system of thought that maintained that reason is the basis for knowledge, and *empiricism*, which maintained that all knowledge is based on experience. One of the chief proponents of romanticism was French philosopher Jean Jacques Rousseau, who expressed many of the movement's tenants when he made a play on René Descartes' famous statement of rationalism— "I think, therefore I am"—by declaring, "I felt before I thought." Romantic rhetoric, then, is concerned with individual feelings and a search for personal truth.

Winterowd and Blum (1994) argued that romantic rhetoric developed as a reaction to current–traditional composition, and there is much truth to this view. But other factors were also involved, particularly the volatile mix of culture and counterculture that dominated American society during the late 1960s and early 1970s. Colleges and universities in the United States faced significant changes in response to challenges to traditional curricula as well as demands that administrators make higher education more personally meaningful—more relevant. Furthermore, the Civil Rights movement and the Vietnam War created a flood of internal refugees pouring into higher education. Students who, in the past, never would have sought admission to a university because they lacked the money or the motivation suddenly had both as the Civil Rights movement prompted the U.S. Congress to make financial aid available to large numbers of minorities. In addition, the war prompted even larger numbers of working-class young white men to seek safe havens in college, where they could get a draft deferment as long as they were enrolled.

It is an understatement to say that the majority of these new students were inadequately prepared for university work. Their reading and writing skills were particularly weak, and teachers and administrators scrambled to find ways to reduce the failure rates (see Coulson, 1996; Shaughnessy, 1977). Then Labov (1964, 1966, 1969, 1970, 1971, 1972a) published a sequence of influential works that recast scholarly thinking about language and literacy. Labov showed that Black English vernacular (BEV), which had commonly been characterized as a bastardization of standard English (Dillard, 1973), was a separate and largely independent dialect, with its own grammar and logic.[11] Suddenly, the meaning of standard was not as clear as many had always thought. Also, because dialects are unconsciously acquired from birth, they are difficult to modify, and they do not readily lend themselves to instruction. Validating individual voices regardless of how well they approxi-

---

[11]Standard English is the prestige dialect in the United States, although readily identifying those who speak standard English is difficult. Standard English is the dialect that most closely approximates written English. For more on dialects and standard English, see chapter 5.

mate existing standards is one way to deal with the situation, and in the late 1960s there were nationwide calls for what was termed "students' rights to their own language"—calls that were intended to provide that validation. School districts responded by jettisoning traditional curricula. Reading and writing were particularly hard hit. Composition courses in many schools were replaced with creative writing; in many other schools, writing disappeared altogether. Chronicling the consequences, Goodlad (1984) reported (a decade and a half later) that the nation's high school students were writing an average of 300 words a year.

Meanwhile, the angst of a generation drove students, iconoclasts at odds with institutions, to demand more freedom and more voice in the way schools operated. Protests and demonstrations became commonplace as college students sought to assert their right to be individuals, who they wanted to be. High schools faced protests against dress codes, tracking (which grouped students in classes on the basis of ability), discipline, and homework. In unprecedented numbers, politicians and academic leaders acquiesced to these demands and developed curricula based on what students wanted at the time rather than on any academic principle, educational theory, or vision of the future.

The confluence of these factors encouraged a view of language that dismissed ideas of "correctness," which many began labeling a form of elitist repression of the underclass (see Lunsford, Moglen, & Slevin, 1990), and that ultimately dismissed content. Other changes were less visible outside university English departments, but they were significant insofar as they shaped the will and ideas of those opposed to the new rhetoric. For example, building on the work of Hunt, Mellon, and O'Hare and drawing deeply from Chomsky's work on grammar, Christensen (1967) provided a perspective on literary style that exhilarated some and exasperated others. Christensen proposed that traditional definitions of style were useless because they were subjective. Hemingway may have a "manly" style, and Steinbeck may have a "tedious" one, but what do such assessments actually mean? They do not mean much because they vary from reader to reader. Christensen used grammar to describe style in terms of operations performed on sentences to obtain quantifiable stylistic effects. For many literature scholars, these efforts to quantify art were worrisome. The social sciences, particularly psychology, seemed staged to force traditional notions of language and literature into what was, for most university English department faculty, hostile territory.

In this context, Macrorie (1968, 1970) and Elbow (1973, 1981) developed the foundational texts of romantic rhetoric. Macrorie set the tone in his 1970 work, *Telling Writing*. In the Preface, he wrote:

> [The New English movement] allows students to use their own powers, to make discoveries, to take alternative paths. It does not suggest that the world can best be examined by a set of rules. It does not utilize the Errors Approach. It constantly messes around with reality, and looks for strategies and tactics that work. ... The program gives the student first, freedom, to find his voice and let his subjects find him; and second, discipline, to learn more professional craft to supplement his already considerable language skills.
>
> And for both teacher and student, a constant reading for truth, in writing and commenting on that writing. This is a hard requirement, for no one speaks truth consistently. (pp. vii–viii)

Many teachers were sympathetic to these views for several reasons. A curriculum based on romantic rhetoric asks students to explore their feelings and thoughts through what is called *self-expressive composing*, which makes classroom writing tasks marginally congruent with works of literature. Self-expressive writing is also thought to motivate students to write because it rests on something they know well and are presumably interested in—their own experiences. At the same time, a curriculum based on romantic rhetoric is fundamentally at odds with the educational principles inherent in the cognitive approach advocated by scholars such as Bruner. These principles encourage self-expressive assignments at the beginning of the curriculum, but they quickly move on to more demanding tasks; romantic rhetoric does not. In addition, the cognitive approach stresses using process to master the core knowledge of disciplines. By their very nature, self-expressive tasks do not deal with academic content. These factors made romantic rhetoric widely popular in the public schools, so much so that today most of the writing that students do in public schools is self-expressive writing.

On yet another level, romantic rhetoric offers a safe solution to the problem presented by students who, for one reason or another, cannot meet academic standards of literacy. This issue became increasingly important in public schools in the early 1970s as administrators sought to reduce the high failure rates among minority groups. There is no "right" or "wrong" in self-expressive writing; there is only the expression of true feeling. Students who cannot reason sufficiently to write analytical papers or who cannot spell or punctuate nevertheless can receive high grades because assessment becomes determining whether the writing seems "real." Elbow (1981) captured the essence of this characteristic of romantic rhetoric when he wrote: "That writing was most fun and rewarding to read that somehow felt most 'real.' It had what I am now calling voice. At the time I said things like, 'It felt real, it had a kind of resonance, it somehow rang true'" (p. 283). Romantic rhetoric therefore gave the appearance of solving the problems associated with illiteracy. In the parlance of the times, it required only that students "Get real, man."

Romantic rhetoric was especially appealing to university writing teachers because it denied the feasibility of designating composition as a "service" course that aimed to help students perform better in other courses. It was congruent with the counterculture agenda, being subtly subversive with respect to higher education's institutional mission. Moreover, many university composition teachers resented (and continue to resent) the suggestion that writing courses were service courses. At the Penn State Rhetoric Conference a few years ago, for example, a group of presenters described how they insist that their composition students explore "alternative forms" as a means of gaining new personal insights. The presenters explained that their students write poetry and stream-of-consciousness journal entries rather than essays. When someone asked how writing poetry helped students write better in subjects such as biology and history, the presenters said that they were not concerned with what students did in other classes because they did not believe it was their job to help students write better; their job was to help students explore who they are.

In their assessment of romantic rhetoric, Winterowd and Blum (1994) noted that one of the biggest problems with this approach is that it is predicated on the idea that writing has only one purpose—self-exploration. However, in reality it has multiple purposes. Anyone who becomes a better writer must be able to negotiate these multiple purposes. Winterowd and Blum also suggested that this approach does students a disservice because they need and want to learn how to write better. Unfortunately, there is no evidence that indicates the romantic approach leads to better writing (Hillocks, 1986).

POSTMODERN RHETORIC

The ultimate backlash against the new rhetoric is postmodernism, whose adherents have jettisoned traditional theories of rhetoric in favor of literary criticism. In 1985, at the Conference on College Composition and Communication (CCCC), presenters argued that new rhetoric lacked any viable theory, and they advocated that composition should adopt the theoretical position of critics such as Stanley Fish. Raschke (1996) recently defined *postmodernism* as everything that "cannot be compressed in the term *modern*" (p. 2). Consequently, understanding the nature of postmodern rhetoric and its effect on composition theory, research, and teaching demands some understanding of what constitutes modernism.

More than a set of fixed ideas, modernism implies an attitude, a method of thought. On a broad level, the attitude can be described as an abiding self-confidence in the steady progress of Western civilization; the inherent superiority of Western science, technology, social structures, and political systems; the value of formal education; and the value of high culture, represented in standard works of literature, classical music and opera, and art. The method of thought in modernism is dominated by empiricism and rationalism, with special status given to the scientific approach. Although modernism's roots extend to the 18th century, it gained impetus during the early 1900s until, as Docker (1994) noted, it "flowered into a great aesthetic movement, challenging and transforming every received art form, from literature and music to painting and architecture" (p. xviii).

The new rhetoric is situated squarely inside the framework of modernism. For example, both modernism and new rhetoric are preoccupied with the problems of creativity and composition (Raschke, 1996). In addition, new rhetoric inherently values writing, not only as part of formal education but also as a means of discovery and self-definition. Writing is commonly linked to ideas of personal growth and progress. New rhetoric also values analysis and argumentation for their own sake and as ways to master the content knowledge in a variety of disciplines. Furthermore, because new rhetoric focuses on academic writing, which involves formulating a claim (or hypothesis) and marshaling evidence to support that claim, the associated method of thought is fundamentally scientific.

Two other factors are equally important, however. The first is the implicit assumption in the new rhetoric that words have meaning, individually and collectively. Words signify something. A paper on *Romeo and Juliet* might argue that the play is primarily about the misfortunes that follow when people cannot control their emotions and that it is not primarily about romance. In this framework, the word *romance* signifies a certain meaning; likewise, all the words together signify that the paper is an argument, that the argument reaches a certain conclusion, that the writer advocates this conclusion, and so forth. The second factor is that effective writing can and should be taught. It is a learnable skill with both inherent and pragmatic value.

Postmodernism offers different attitudes and methods. It rejects high culture in favor of popular culture, eschewing *Hamlet* for *Roseanne*, Mozart for Michael Jackson, Socrates for Bart Simpson. If in modernism all the world's a stage, in postmodernism all the world's a spontaneous carnival, but much less fun (see Eco, Ivanov, & Rector, 1984, for a discussion of the festive elements of postmodernism).

Although often predicated as "play" (Raschke, 1996), postmodernism has a cutting edge. Raschke (1996) noted, for example, that "Postmodernity is the transcendence, 'overcoming,' of all archaic or 'legendary' orders of significance that have underwritten cultural discourse" (p. 2). In other words, an important goal of postmodernism is to overturn established values, principles, and ways of thinking, which are held in contempt (Norris, 1993; Seidman, 1994).

Nowhere is this goal more evident than in the postmodern perspectives on politics and language. The politics of postmodernism borrow heavily from Herbert Marcuse, a philosopher who advocated leftist politics and who was a severe critic of Western (especially American) society.[12] Marcuse blended Marxism with Freudian psychoanalytic theories and reached the conclusion that Western society is corrupt and repressive. In *Eros and Civilization: A Philosophical Inquiry Into Freud* (1955) and *One-Dimensional Man: Studies in the Ideology of Advanced Industrial Society* (1964), he argued that in the West the "ruling classes" have established scarcity in lands of plenty by deliberately withholding resources, goods, and services from "subject populations" so as to keep them deprived, downtrodden, and miserable.

Western society—insofar as it is defined as the prevailing traditions and institutions that are deemed to be of historical significance—is fundamentally evil, according to Marcuse, and must be overturned by any means necessary. For example, in 1965, he argued that only those with left-wing views should be afforded the right of free speech. This right should be denied to those with incorrect thoughts by invoking the "natural right" of "oppressed and overpowered minorities to use extra-legal means" (p. 17) to silence opposing points of view. Therefore, the carnival of postmodernism is tightly supervised and controlled by those with correct thoughts—who have turned out to be the campus protesters from the 1960s, many of whom now hold important university and government positions. As Seidman (1994) indicated, "the idea of ... postmodernity has been advanced largely by western, mostly academic, intellectuals, many of whom are connected to the social rebellions of the sixties and seventies" (p. 2). The efforts to silence opposing points of view resulted in policies at numerous universities and public schools restrict-

---

[12]Seeking refuge from Nazism, Marcuse immigrated to the United States from Germany in 1934. Although later he often seemed to urge the overthrow of the American government, he worked, ironically, for various intelligence agencies during World War II. Postmodern thought is deeply indebted to Marcuse, who introduced the ideal of *transcendence* into his social theory in *Reason and Revolution: Hegel and the Rise of Social Theory*, published in 1941. He argued that *personal liberation* involved transcending the archaic social traditions that keep people alienated and unhappy, a thought that has become doctrine in postmodernism.

ing free speech by classifying certain types of language as "hate crimes."[13] They also resulted in what is known as *radical pedagogy* among many writing teachers. Radical pedagogy advocates that teachers have an obligation to "shout down" students who express views that are not congruent with leftist ideology (see Lunsford, Moglen, & Slevin, 1990; Williams, 1992).

Postmodern Language: Against an Objective Reality

In his book *Of Grammatology*, French philosopher Jaques Derrida (1976) argued that the question of meaning in writing was itself meaningless because there is no connection between reason and what words signify:

> The "rationality" ... which governs a writing thus enlarged and radicalized, no longer issues from a logos. Further, it inaugurates the destruction, not the demolition but the de-sedimentation, the de-construction, of all the significations that have their source in that of the logos. Particularly the signification of *truth*. (p. 10)

Herein lies the basis for a persistent postmodern attack on traditional notions of language and rhetoric. In this passage (and throughout the book), Derrida is denying the existence of an objective reality, a reality that exists independent of individual acts of mentation. In one respect, it recalls Gorgias, who stated that truth and ideas do not have any essential existence; if they did, they would not be knowable to man; and if they were knowable, they could not be communicated to anyone. Generally, the Sophists denied that communication could be an end in discourse (Murphy, 1974). In Derrida's view, if words do not signify anything, determining what they mean is impossible (see Putnam, 1975, and Quine, 1960, for further discussion of signification).

This indeterminacy goes beyond replacing objectivity with subjectivity because denying a link between language and *logos* suggests that not even the speaker or writer of given words can know what they mean. As the term *deconstruction* indicates, the result is an attitude that denies the value of creating, of writing. In its place is reading. Deconstructive reading, however, cannot focus on what words mean because meaning is indeterminate. Instead, it must focus on what words do not mean.

A perspective that denies meaning, even a subjective one, is hardly conducive to teaching students how to write better, and one of the biggest

---

[13]In every case that has been challenged in court, these policies have been struck down as unconstitutional. Nevertheless, they persist at many schools and in many districts where they have not been challenged legally.

differences between new rhetoric and postmodern rhetoric is that the latter largely has abandoned concern for what differentiates poor writers from good ones. Indeed, it has abandoned any attempt to help improve the writing of students. In place of this legitimate pedagogical concern is an abiding interest in politics, as manifested in the neo-Marxist writings of Berlin (1992a, 1992b) and others. Owens (1994) for example, argued that freshman composition, as a venue for teaching academic discourse, should be abandoned because such discourse imposes "debilitating restrictions" on writers (p. 225). Fitts and France (1995) opposed "'writing' in general" and argued that it should be replaced with "cultural studies" that focus on "cultural critique, even ideological transformation" (p. 324).

Such publications illustrate just how significant the shift away from new rhetoric has been. Even a superficial survey of works published in rhetoric and composition journals during the past 10 years shows it has been pervasive. Although most of the ramifications of postmodernism are found in university writing programs, it seems inevitable that they eventually will be felt in the nation's public schools.

Perhaps no one better exemplifies just how influential postmodernism has become than Mike Rose. Trained as an educational psychologist, Rose (1984) earned early praise for his examination of writer's block, which applied standard empirical techniques to questions of writing performance and which followed the psychological research paradigm. Then, in 1988, he published an article, "Narrowing the Mind and Page: Remedial Writers and Cognitive Reductionism," that blasted the very psychological approaches he had used in the past. Rose called them "reductionistic" and claimed that they led to "social distinctions that have important [and negative] consequences, political as well as educational" (p. 268). Not only was the psychological research paradigm flawed, but it was also racist.

The gist of Rose's article was that psychological approaches to the study of writing are inappropriate because they look at complex behaviors through the lens of constructs that describe unitary dimensions of cognitive processing. In the stance he adopted in his article, these approaches focus so narrowly on discrete facets of cognitive processing that they cannot possibly reveal anything worthwhile about the big picture. Playing naive, Rose ignored the fact that most scientists are reductionists. As Kelso (1995) recently noted, scientists follow the "time-honored thesis of classical physics, namely, that macroscopic states can be explained through microscopic analysis" (p. 53).

More troubling is the fact that his critique was frequently inaccurate or simply wrong. For example, one of the constructs Rose (1988) examined was *cognitive style*, which describes preferred ways that people have of processing information. Some people are *field dependent*; they tend to process information relative to a field or context. Other people are *field independent*; they tend to process information independent of a field or context. Rose suggested that cognitive style is not a valid construct because tests measure only field independence, which has the effect of determining field dependence "by default" (p. 272). However, personality psychology has many such constructs, such as ego resilience, that identify their opposites by default. It is common for researchers in personality to develop a construct and, in the process of testing, to recognize its opposite. Many fields assign classifications this way without risk to their scholarly integrity. In medicine, blood tests look for specific pathogens linked to certain diseases. If a test does not find those pathogens, the person is healthy by default. Thus it seems that the reprobation leveled against cognitive style is highly selective and at odds with practices in established disciplines.

Rose (1988) then turned to one of the more detailed studies of cognitive style and writing, conducted by Williams (1985), purported to examine its results, and argued that the writing of field-dependent and field-independent writers should be of similar quality although of a different nature. According to Rose, "the discourse of field independents would be more analytical and impersonal while field-dependent discourse would be richer in social detail" (p. 271). The problem, Rose claimed, was that Williams merely reported that "papers written by field-dependent students are simply poor papers, and along most dimensions—spelling, punctuation, and sentence structure" (p. 271). Furthermore, he suggested that Williams and others engaged in psychological investigations of writing that unfairly labeled minority students as remedial, concluding that if these approaches are not "racist, sexist, or elitist," then they are riddled with "cultural biases that are troubling" (p. 295).

However, the Williams study did not report correlations between cognitive style and writing mechanics. It reported on the relation between cognitive style and coherence, specifically addressing three variables: identification of topic; identification of intention, or thesis; and role-taking ability of writers. Spelling and punctuation were not discussed. Furthermore, the Williams study did not discuss race, labeling, or remediation. These terms did not even appear in the study because subjects were not classified by race at any point. The study only reported that the writing of the field-independent subjects was judged to be more coherent than the writing of the field-dependent subjects, and it made no effort to generalize beyond the data.

From a postmodern perspective, Rose was justified when he failed to deal with the reality of such studies and when he insisted on rewriting them to support his claim that empirical research is racist—there is no objective reality. He was also effective. This article struck a chord with large numbers of teachers and scholars and is frequently cited by those who argue against applying social science to composition as proof of its perversity. Confronted with a paradigm that seems destined to reveal more about human development and cognition than most people want to know, many readers undoubtedly sympathized with the views Vaillant (1977) expressed when he wrote that lives are "too human for science, too beautiful for numbers, too sad for diagnosis, and too immortal for bound journals" (p. 11).

The problem is that from the postmodern perspective—where objective reality does not exist—distortions are facts, inaccuracies truth. As Plato might say, that is both the power and the danger of postmodern rhetoric. To writers like Rose, the lack of an objective reality appears comforting because they are able to create their own reality at will. But there is a price to pay. Recasting empirical composition research as racism simply shuts down research in composition studies, which students with weak writing skills cannot afford. As Charney (1996) stated, "Critics making such sweeping generalizations about science often exhibit their own propensity to dehumanize the Other, imputing bad motives to anyone who uses experimental and other quantitative methods" (p. 571). It also shifts the focus of research to other disciplines. Since about 1990, most of the significant research in writing has come out of schools of education and departments of psychology while composition studies has been struggling with the question of whether students should even be taught how to write academic prose (see, e.g., Zebroski, 1990).

Students at risk suffer most; they need help to become competent writers, help that they just are not getting. A shrinking pool of students, who for whatever reasons can write fairly well without extensive instruction, will continue to succeed, but the gap between them and their less fortunate cohorts will increase (Berliner, 1996). If unchecked, the result will be a return to the kind of elitism that characterized education prior to the end of World War II.

EXPLORING KEY IDEAS

1. This chapter defines rhetoric as something people study and something they apply. This leads to an interesting question: Are writing teachers rhetoricians? Why or why not?

2. Although Athens and Rome experienced similar social problems—an economic shift that resulted in large numbers of displaced farmers and a growing reliance on slaves—they solved
them in different ways. What effect did the solutions have on
rhetoric?

3. Many people tend to compare our society with ancient Athens
because of the emphasis on democracy, but where rhetoric is
concerned, we seem much closer to ancient Rome than Athens.
Why is that?

4. The Sophists claimed they could teach civic virtue. What is civic
virtue, and what might its value be today?

5. The differences between *nomos* and *physis* were important to
ancient Athenians, but are they important to us? Are there any
conflicts or controversies in our society about the superiority of
manmade or natural laws?

6. Why did Aristotle call rhetoric an art? What are some modern
connotations of the term *art*?

7. Teachers do not reflect much on the Eurocentric focus of historical rhetoric. Are there any implicit messages in this focus that
non-European students might object to?

8. Romantic rhetoric is quite popular in public schools. What are
some of the benefits and costs to students of an over-reliance on
self-expressive writing assignments?

9. What might be some consequences of shouting down students in
the classroom?

10. Postmodern rhetoric can be seen as an attack on individualism
and democracy. If these are what postmodern rhetoric is against,
what might it be for?

2

Models for Teaching Writing

OVERVIEW

This chapter describes the major models of composition instruction—the *product* (or current–traditional) model, the *process* model, the *social-theoretic* (or social construction) model, and the *writing-across-the-curriculum* (WAC) model. It also examines the pedagogical consequences of each. The *product model* developed out of the decline of oral composition and the increasing emphasis on belles-lettres during the 17th and 18th centuries. Most of the factors, or conventions, that govern writing in this model—such as audience, aims, and form—are related to two types of writing: journalism and literary criticism. Style is a major concern, and for this reason the pedagogy associated with the product model tends to focus on error correction and telling rather than showing. As a result, it involves little true writing instruction.

The *process model* emerged in the early 1970s as teachers and researchers began evaluating the factors that distinguish good writers from poor ones. As the name suggests, the emphasis is on writing as a process rather than on product. This model therefore aims to improve writing by helping students master a range of behaviors associated with effective composition. It restructures the current–traditional classroom into a writing workshop where students collaborate on drafts of assignments in small groups. When ideally applied, the process model emphasizes group activities geared toward discovering things to say about a topic (*invention*), drafting, pausing, sharing work in progress, revising, and editing. As students work on drafts of assignments, teachers circulate among the groups, offering advice and suggestions through formative rather than summative evaluation.

The *social-theoretic* model developed when teachers saw that process was limited in some important ways. For example, the process model focuses on writers and their psychological states. Although it addresses audience needs, it offers little insight into the relationship between writers and audience. Especially absent is any recognition of how

45

audience determines numerous significant features of text. In other words, the process model generally invests writers with control over their work that does not exist in real situations. In addition, invention, which designates a search for things to say about a given topic, was modified in the process model to focus on finding topics. In most real writing situations, however, writers have little if any control over topics. These factors motivated many scholars to consider the ways in which society affects writers. A concept that became increasingly important in this consideration was *discourse community*, which signifies a group of people who share language, views, and values. Everyone, it was understood, exists in various discourse communities that determine, to a large extent, what and how people write.

The *WAC model* and the social-theoretic model are alike in most respects. The difference is not based on theory but on aims and methods. The WAC model draws teachers together from many disciplines and engages them in helping students become better writers in specific content areas. It is predicated on the idea that good writers are not people with a monolithic skill that is transportable to any situation. Instead, good writers are people with a repertoire of skills that they draw on as situations dictate. Consequently, instruction focuses on mastering the conventions of writing in subject areas related to science, social science, and humanities.

Although this range of models suggests great variety in regard to teaching writing, several factors work to constrain what goes on in the classroom. For example, perhaps the majority of teachers, administrators, parents, and politicians nationwide believe that mastering writing involves learning grammar, and the expression "back to basics" dominates much of the talk about writing instruction. The product model is most congruent with back-to-basics sentiments, and it continues to dominate writing classes across the country. Nevertheless, the other three models are winning converts.

THE PRODUCT MODEL OF COMPOSITION

The product model gets its name from the fact that the focus of instruction is on students' finished products, whatever those products might be. In a typical product-oriented classroom, teachers describe the various features of an essay in general terms, pointing, for example, to the introduction, body, and conclusion. They do not mention the fact that different kinds of writing are required for different situations or that different disciplines have different conventions and standards for correctness. Instead, instruction proceeds from the perspective that one type of writing, the literary–journalistic essay, is suitable for all situations.

After they receive an assignment, students write their papers at home and turn them in. Their teachers collect the papers; take them home; read them while using red ink to note errors in spelling, punctuation, word choice, and so on; write a final, or "terminal," comment; and assign a grade. Teachers then return the papers to students, spend a few minutes commenting on what students did wrong, urge them to do better next time, and go on to the next activity. As this summary suggests, very little real writing instruction occurs in this approach. Teaching writing is viewed primarily as teaching mechanics: punctuation, subject–verb agreement, spelling, and correct usage. Class time designated for writing is typically devoted to drills and exercises on mechanics or grammar. The underlying rationale is that good writing is correct writing. In other words, the product model perpetuates the 19th-century dichotomy between form and content.

This summary also suggests a key feature of the product model: It puts teachers at the center of class activities. They do nearly all of the talking during class time, even during discussions. For this reason, the product model is considered to employ a *teacher-centered pedagogy*. A teacher-centered classroom has some advantages for teachers. It tends to create an orderly, controlled environment; students raise their hands for permission to speak—otherwise they tend to be quiet or to talk out of turn. It gives the impression of teacher control, which administrators appreciate, and it allows teachers to display their knowledge. However, this pedagogy also discourages independent thinking among students, as well as risk taking, because students recognize that they must adhere to the values and perceptions of the teacher. It also fails to introduce students to the group interactions that tend to characterize writing outside of school.

Writing in the Product-Oriented Classroom

Product-oriented classrooms concentrate on literature and reading, not writing. In many elementary language arts classrooms, for example, students have two reading assignments per week but only have two writing assignments per year. Even in schools where teachers seek better balance between reading and writing, students receive far fewer writing activities than reading activities. In addition, the models of effective writing that students study are from literature, and classes devote a great deal of time to discussing these models as works of literature. A high school class might read Shakespeare's *Romeo and Juliet*, discuss the play over several days, and then write an analysis of it.[1] Students never see any examples of literary analysis, however, which puts them in the difficult position of having to guess what the paper is supposed to do and how it is to be structured and organized.

For decades, assignments that asked students to write about their personal experiences were about as popular as literary analysis. Many years ago, most teachers began the school year by asking students to describe what they did during summer vacation, and the responses formed the basis of writing activities for the rest of the year. But the rise of new rhetoric resulted in serious criticism of this assignment, and it has been mocked so thoroughly during the last 20 years that it is less popular than it used to be. Nevertheless, romantic and postmodern rhetoric have encouraged teachers to continue to use it in a different form. One result is that the personal-experience essay is no longer limited to the product-oriented classroom. For example, Andres (1993), reflecting a common romantic stance, argued that teachers should develop a writing curriculum around a single image from students' home lives, which would enhance their ability to convey their thoughts and emotions. In other words, personal-experience assignments today are more varied than they used to be. They are also more pervasive insofar as many teachers focus all writing tasks on self-expression, whereas in the past there was movement toward analysis and argument. Typical assignments ask students to recount an event that changed their lives or to describe a person who helped shape who they are rather than describe their summer vacations.

The rhetorical task, however, remains unchanged. These assignments are literature-based in that they call for narration and description. They also have a tendency to ask students to reveal personal information that teachers may not have any right to request. Some of the more egregious assignments actually require students to recount events that reveal their secret fears or personal pain. For example, an assignment that was popular with numerous high school teachers several years ago asked students to describe their most humiliating experience and to explain what they learned from it. Many students understand that such assignments are an invasion of privacy and consequently invent experiences that meet the requirements of the task but that are totally fictional.

---

[1]Until the late 1960s, Shakespeare was standard reading for nearly all high school students. Curriculum changes in response to social changes, however, significantly diminished Shakespeare in the high school curriculum. In many schools, Shakespeare is reserved for Advanced Placement students.

Some Consequences of Using the Product Model

One of the more obvious consequences of using literature-based assignments and personal-experience essays is that they do not give students practice with the kinds of writing they will be expected to produce in college or on the job. There just are no employers who have a need for employees who can write personal-experience essays. In addition, the inability of high school graduates to meet the writing demands of college has created a great deal of tension between college composition teachers and high school English teachers, who have been fighting skirmishes for many years over student writing skills.

The majority of college freshmen received good grades in their high school English classes and seem to have had teachers who told them that they were the best writers they had ever seen. Nevertheless, nearly all of these students are required to take composition because of their low SAT scores.[2] Their resentment is high, and it quickly escalates because the majority receive average to below-average grades on their first few papers. They complain to their high school teachers, who in turn call up directors of college writing programs and ask why the composition classes are staffed with incompetents who cannot recognize good writing when they see it. The college teachers, for their part, want to know why high school teachers are not doing their jobs and teaching students how to write.

This cycle of accusations does not address the real problem, which is that college composition classes tend to require students to analyze, interpret, and argue, whereas writing in the majority of high school English classes focuses on grammar, literary criticism, and self-expressive, personal-experience essays. As a result, most freshmen start college without the basic writing skills they need not only for composition but also for their other courses, with the possible exception of the one or two literature classes that are a part of general education requirements. From this practical perspective, "basic writing skills" consist of the ability to analyze, interpret, and develop a formal argument and these are skills that few language arts classes teach.

In spite of these problems, it is important to stress that the reasons for teaching students how to write are not entirely pragmatic. Anyone who thinks otherwise is mistaken. Language in general and writing in particular are linked to individual conceptions of the self. People use

---

[2]SAT scores have been declining nationwide since about 1967. Recently, the College Board revised the SAT and rescaled the scores, which had the effect of increasing individual scores by 150 points. Critics charged that the revision was politically motivated. The decline in scores meant that even better high schools were having trouble placing their students in the best universities. Adjusting the scale solved this problem but created others.

language to discover who they are and how they fit into society. Writing tasks that help students in this endeavor have an inherent value far beyond the pragmatic. Moreover, personal-experience writing, when appropriately balanced with other types of writing, provides students with important opportunities to reflect on life and its many puzzles. Such reflection is crucial to the process of self-discovery. It also takes students down pathways of thought that they might not travel without this stimulus, engaging them in complexities that are the hallmark of cogent reasoning. Students who reflect on life's complexities are more likely to provide a complex analysis, a complex argument, and a complex interpretation. Therefore, balancing personal-experience writing with the other kinds of writing that students need to master appears to be the real problem.

Some Assumptions of the Product Model

The product model is based on a number of assumptions that many writing teachers and scholars have come to reject over the last few years. One of the more obvious is the link between good writing and knowledge of grammar. A range of studies shows that knowledge of grammar does not result in good writing (e.g., Bateman & Zidonis, 1964). Foreign students, especially those from Asia, provide one of the more visible repudiations of this assumption. Many of these students come to study at American universities and know more about English grammar than most teachers, yet their writing is almost always below the standard of their English-speaking counterparts.

The product model also assumes that there is a positive correlation between being able to discuss a published piece of writing (identifying the thesis, tone, organizational features, etc.) and being able to write a well-organized essay with a clear thesis. It assumes that students can look at the editing marks their teachers put on papers and learn how to avoid similar mistakes on the next assignment. Research and experience, however, indicate that these assumptions are wrong (Mansfield, 1993).

An approach that concentrates on telling writers they have errors and that then expects them to eliminate those errors in the next essay represents faulty thinking. Pointing out the mistakes in a paper after it has been graded is about as useful as mentioning to beginning cooks that their soufflés did not rise because they left out the eggs. Because writing an essay is more complex than baking a soufflé, there is a great likelihood that the next time around the writers will be so busy juggling all the various elements of the process that they simply will forget the comments on the earlier paper or they will not know how to fix the errors.

Equally likely is that students will not even be aware that they are repeating the same errors from one paper to the next.

There is no question that all teachers must be fundamentally concerned with the final product of writing instruction. Similarly, there is no question that students should spell and punctuate accurately, but good writing consists of more than accurate spelling and punctuation. Experienced teachers are very familiar with the error-free student essay that says absolutely nothing—form without substance.

The idea that form, or style, is all that matters in student writing is congruent with the 19th-century view of rhetoric, which held that content was outside the domain of composition, but this view has become unacceptable in a society that places ever-increasing demands on its citizens for high levels of literacy, thought, and understanding. Perhaps the largest problem with the product view is that by focusing attention on the results (rather than the means), it asks us to believe we can teach writing simply by telling students what writing is about. In contrast, work over the last two decades suggests that effectively teaching writing has two crucial requirements: teachers provide students with situations in which language can be used meaningfully, and teachers focus attention on and emphasize the act of writing itself, not finished essays.

THE PROCESS MODEL OF COMPOSITION

In the 1960s, composition scholars began reassessing the effectiveness of the product model (see Braddock et al., 1963; Rohman & Wlecke, 1964). Work in grammar, psychology, anthropology, and other fields combined with significant changes in the demographics of college students to stimulate interest in what differentiated good writers from poor ones. Behaviors associated with composing appeared to be crucial, which resulted in more attention to examining and understanding the actions that give birth to writing and less to product. By the 1970s, there was an intellectual shift in many fields toward process, a shift grounded in *process philosophy*—a world view that identifies reality with pure process. Perhaps the most vivid examples come from art, where process began emerging as a new voice in artistic expression. In 1976, the artist Christo made headlines when he ran a nylon ribbon 18 feet high and 24 miles long across a California hillside. The artistry did not reside in two dozen miles of nylon, the art critics noted, but in the process of erecting the ribbon in such an unlikely place.

When writers such as Elbow (1973), Emig (1971), and Moffett (1968) advocated a move away from an emphasis on product, they were in many respects reflecting the spirit of the times. What emerged was one of the more comprehensive reevaluations of writing and writing instruction in the last 100 years (North, 1987). It is important to recognize, however, that postmodernism had a strong influence on the notion of process (Faigley, 1993). In many fields, including rhetoric and composition, it led to the redefinition of process as performance. The difference is significant; whereas *process* connotes communication, *performance* connotes dramatics. In a postmodern performance, communication in the usual sense is not even a goal. As Raschke (1996) recently noted, postmodernism's aim is to tear down the notion of "language as social interaction" (p. 3). To accomplish that aim, it has redefined "logic as 'aesthetics,' . . . message as medium, communication as dramatics . . . [and] truth as embodiment" (p. 2).

A performance is intended to draw attention to the performer, and in language, the result has been a loss of emphasis on content. Recently, the mayor of Chicago announced that tenants of a public housing project were going to be relocated temporarily while the city tore down the old buildings and built new ones. A local political leader denounced the plan, even though it would result in better housing for the tenants. He stated that the plan to relocate the tenants was equivalent to *ethnic cleansing*—the wholesale massacre of tens of thousands that the Serbs conducted against the Bosnians in what was once called Yugoslavia. From the modern perspective, this statement demeans those who lost their lives in a brutal civil war. From the postmodern perspective, the dramatics of the comparison make it bold; its embodiment in words makes it true. Nevertheless, few reasonable people could take this comparison seriously. It succeeded, however, in putting the speaker in the news. It succeeded as performance. In this postmodern climate, process is struggling to survive. Therefore, teachers who embrace process are careful to guide students in ways that help them avoid performance.

Writing in the Process-Oriented Classroom

The process model does not focus on the completed essay but on helping students through various stages of composing. Classrooms become writing workshops in which students share their work with one another and teachers regularly intervene as students develop compositions through several drafts (see chap. 3 for a detailed discussion on workshops). The workshop has become a central feature of writing in the process-oriented classroom. Teachers divide each class into groups, usually of five members each. These groups become collaborative teams in which students help one another succeed. The teacher's role in the workshop is largely one of coach or facilitator.

The emphasis in a process-oriented classroom is on process rather than on product. Students attempt to master the behaviors that characterize good writers, with the teacher offering advice and suggestions. Activities focus on writing, discussing drafts, and rewriting. Consequently, an important difference between the product- and the process-oriented classroom is that students do much more writing in the latter.

Since the workshop concept became popular, many public school teachers have pointed out that their language arts classes are not composition classes. They must engage students in many different activities in addition to writing. This point is well taken, but it does not detract from the effectiveness of workshops. Workshops can form the foundation of a class, regardless of the lesson or unit. The key is to maintain focus on a student-centered environment. In addition, because all education involves language, teaching writing should be an integral part of all instruction, regardless of the subject.

Teacher as Coach

As with most other complex skills, people bring any number of bad habits or poorly learned techniques to the writing process. Weak writers, for example, have a tendency to assume that the only reader of their essays will be the teacher, who already knows what the topic is, so they fail to identify the topic explicitly in their text. Many of these writers learned a variety of myths associated with writing that hinder them whenever they compose. For example, they may believe they cannot begin a sentence with a coordinating conjunction: *and, but, for, nor, or, yet*. They may believe they cannot use the personal pronoun *I*, end a sentence with a preposition, or use contractions. When more knowledgeable teachers try to help them overcome these myths, the writers may resist.

In most cases, students adopt more effective writing behaviors when they are encouraged on the spot. Advocates of the process model therefore propose that effective teachers think of themselves as coaches in a workshop environment. Coaches intervene regularly in the learning process, immediately correcting those things students do wrong and praising those things they do right, giving reinforcement when it is most useful and most beneficial. When teaching writing, the same principles apply. In practical terms, such intervention requires that teachers ask students to produce multiple drafts of an assignment. Class time is devoted to revising drafts on the basis of feedback that the teacher, as well as fellow students, provides.

In *Research on Written Composition: New Directions for Teaching*, Hillocks (1986) reported that the process model leads to better writing among students, but the available research literature since Hillocks

conducted his study is not entirely clear. The National Assessment of
Educational Progress (NAEP) report, published in 1994, indicated that
writing skills among students at all levels continued its 25-year decline.
Given the number of classrooms that have adopted the process model,
this finding should be startling. In any event, it raises an important
question: "Will the process model turn students into brilliant writers?"
The NAEP data suggest that it will not. However, it will allow teachers
to make more effective use of class time, which in turn may translate
into improved skills.

Stages of the Composing Process

The process model proposes that a finished paper is the result of the
complex interaction of activities that include several stages of development: prewriting, drafting, pausing, reading, revising, editing, and
publishing (see Table 2.1). Not every writing task passes through every
stage, however. In some situations, a writer may not have an opportunity to do much planning, or a professional editor may do the editing.
Nevertheless, these stages are believed to reflect in a general way how
successful writing develops.

Prewriting

Prewriting activities help writers generate ideas, strategies, information, and approaches for a given writing task. They are processes that
engage the mind with the writing task at hand. From this perspective,
prewriting, in its broadest sense, is the thinking good writers do before
they start composing.

   The sections that follow describe some of the more effective ways to
stimulate student thinking about a topic. It is important to stress that
there is not one best way to go about prewriting. What works well for
some students does not work as well for others; what works well for one
assignment will not work well for another. Some writers use various
combinations of prewriting activities, whereas others are only committed to one. Students should experiment to determine what works best
for them.

   Discussion.   Discussion provides multiple points of view on a given
topic. Teachers usually initiate the discussion by asking the class questions regarding how to proceed. Discussions tend to be most helpful
when they do not start immediately upon receipt of an assignment but
a short time after. The time in between allows students to begin formulating a plan they can modify and enrich through the discussion.

TABLE 2.1
Stages of Writing

Writing Process	Definition	Description
Prewriting	Generating ideas, strategies, and information for a given writing task.	Prewriting activities take place before starting on the first draft of a paper. They include *discussion, outlining, freewriting, journals, talk–write, and metaphor.*
Planning	Reflecting on the material produced during prewriting to develop a plan to achieve the aim of the paper.	Planning involves considering the rhetorical stance, rhetorical purpose, the aim of the text, how these factors are interrelated, and how they are connected to the information generated during prewriting. Planning also involves selecting support for a claim and blocking out at least a rough organizational structure.
Drafting	Producing words on a computer or on paper that match (more or less) the initial plan for the work.	Writing occurs over time. Good writers seldom try to produce an entire text in one sitting or even in one day.
Pausing	Moments when writing does not occur. Instead, writers are reflecting on what they have produced and how well it matches their plans. Usually includes reading.	Pausing occurs among good and poor writers, but they use it in different ways. Good writers consider *global* factors—how well the text matches the plan, how well it is meeting audience needs, and overall organization.
Reading	Moments during pausing when writers read what they have written and compare it to their plans.	Reading and writing are interrelated activities. Good readers are good writers and vise versa. The reading that takes place during writing is crucial to the reflection process during pausing.
Revising	Literally "re-seeing" the text with the goal of making large-scale changes so that text and plan match.	Revising occurs after the first draft is finished. It involves making changes that enhance the match between plan and text. Factors to consider usually are the same as those considered during planning: rhetorical stance, rhetorical purpose, and so on. Serious revising almost always includes getting suggestions from friends or colleagues on how to improve the writing.
Editing	Focusing on sentence-level concerns, such as punctuation, sentence length, spelling, agreement between subject and verb, and style.	Editing occurs after revising. The goal is to give the paper a professional appearance.
Publishing	Sharing the finished text with its intended audience.	Publishing is not limited to getting a text printed in a journal. It includes turning a paper in to a teacher, a boss, or an agency.

DISCUSSION CHECKLIST

- Who is the audience for this paper?
- What am I trying to do in this assignment? Interpret? Explain? Analyze? Compare and contrast? Am I writing a term paper that reflects everything I learned during the semester? Am I writing a paper that applies a single principle studied during class? Am I writing a research paper that demonstrates my ability to identify and interpret leading work in the field?
- What effect am I trying to produce in those who read my paper? Am I writing as an inside or an outsider? Do I want to show the audience that I understand the topic? Do I want the audience to understand the topic better? Do I want the audience to accept my point of view?
- What point or message do I want to convey?
- How should I begin?
- Where will I get information about my topic? Through library research? Through experience? Through background reading?
- When explaining a point in the paper, what kind on examples should I use? How will the examples work to make my paper more readable, informative, or convincing?
- If I make a claim in the paper, how do I support it? On the basis of experience? By citing authorities? On the basis of reason? On the basis of emotion?
- What is the most effective way to organize the paper, to make sure that the various arts fit together well?
- What should the conclusion do?

Teachers should urge students to listen as well as contribute and perhaps to jot down notes.

Above is a checklist of questions students can use to stimulate and guide discussions; although they are not comprehensive, the questions illustrate the kind of thinking that is part of an effective discussion.

Outlining.   Outlines can be a very beneficial prewriting device if used properly. Too often, however, the focus is on the structural details of the outline rather than its content. That is, students spend much effort deciding whether an A must have a B; whether a primary heading begins with a Roman numeral or an upper-case letter; whether a secondary heading begins with a lower-case letter, a lower-case Roman numeral, or an Arabic numeral, and so on. Such details are not important. Outlines begin when writers list the major points they want to address in their papers without worrying much about order. They become more useful when they acquire more features. In other words, outlines start with general points and shift to specific ones. The outlines that follow illustrate these principles. It is worth noting, however, that outlines appear to work most effectively when writers use them to generate ideas about topics and theses that they have already decided on.

The first outline was produced by Misty Q. as she started working on a psychology paper:

Blocking (talk-write notes)
　Big Blocks
　　sub blocks
—open w/ the situation of Candy Johnson—propose the question—mental home or police custody?
—give opinion—keep for evaluation

- *How do Candy's actions, mannerisms & body language help her cover up her internal nervousness & fear—does she consciously use this as a tactic?*
　　—feet in chair, chips, hair down, shoes off
　　—she keeps professing her respect for the doctor verbally but physically she insults him w/her informal posture & slang vocabulary—she believes she can use him

---

background info, home, status, employment

Proposal: the problems stem back to her childhood
- *inflicted by mother (increased withdrawal)*
- *father driven to drink by mother*
- *boarding school, "split" at 15*
- *on her own since 14*
- *married at 16*
- *drug abuse*

Present psychiatric problems—is there really a Billy? Is there any proof of truth anywhere?
- *very evasive about his whereabouts & well-being except for his illness*
- *makes him sound like he is her world—possibly in response to her neglected feelings as a child*
　　—if he was her world would she have abandoned him?
- *her bad luck w/ guys could go back to her problems w/ her mother & the way mother treated father (whom she perceived to be a good man)*

refuses to see or admit to guilt
- feels she did what she had to do
- no remorse
- her life of hard knocks gave her subconscious justification for writing the bad check? ? ? ?
- Benney's idea

Reasons for my opinion
 —possible hope for her future if the childhood hostilities are lessened
 —drug addiction finished (stopped)
 —how would this benefit society?

The next outline was written by Bruce B. as he started working on a history paper. Bruce B. takes a more formal approach to outlining than Misty, but note again that structural details are not as important as content.

I. Introduction
 A. Significance of Civil War to America.
 B. Most people think Civil War was about slavery.
 C. Claim: Civil War wasn't about slavery; it was about different ideas of government.
II. Body
 A. Trace history of federalism and republicanism (Aristotle? Madison?).
 1. Note shift from Articles of Confederation to Constitution in 1789.
 2. Is it the case that the South never fully accepted the federalism inherent in the Constitution? (Need more research on this.)
 B. Examine evidence of Northern emphasis on federalism, Southern emphasis on republicanism.
 C. Present evidence from Johnson showing South's belief in state's rights.
 D. Present evidence showing that Lincoln didn't come out against slavery until well into the war.
 E. Are there underlying factors, such as industrial economy vs. agricultural economy, that influenced federalism vs. republicanism? (Talk to Prof. J. about this.)
 F. What factors made the South believe that it was being dominated (dictated to) by the North?
 G. South did not want to grant Washington power or control over states. J. Davis argued that federal government got its power from the states. (Get reference.)
III. Conclusion
 A. Cause of the Civil War was opposing views of government. South would not accept federalism preferred by the North. Felt oppressed by DC. Believed only solution was war.

Experienced writers are sometimes able to begin expanding outlines like Misty Q.'s and Bruce B.'s into coherent writing immediately. They also commonly organize their work mentally, without the aid of an outline. Most people, however, benefit from supplying some specific information for each point in the outline.

Freewriting.   Freewriting, developed by Elbow (1973), draws on the perception that, when present too early, concerns about audience, aims, organization, and structure can keep writers from fully exploring potential ideas and meanings for topics. Freewriting is intended to force writers to set such concerns aside while they consider potential ideas. The main goal is to discover things to say about a topic rather than to plan the paper.

This technique involves writing nonstop for 5, 10, or 15 minutes. During this period, students keep generating words, even if they cannot think of anything meaningful to say. The rationale is that, eventually, they will begin producing ideas that they can develop later into an effective paper. Sometimes freewriting is combined with an activity called *looping*, in which students stop freewriting after 5 minutes and reread what they have produced. If they find a good idea on the page, they use it as the basis for another freewriting period, repeating the process for about 15 minutes.

The following freewriting sample was produced by Amy B., a high school student who had to write a history paper about the Civil War:

1   I have to write a paper about the civl war, but I do not know much about the civl war yet. I'm only a sophomore so how am I supposed to know anything about it? But the teacher says I have to write the paper and that I can find out information about the war in the library. I hate going to the library—it's so full of books! I feel helpless. How can anyone expect me to know as much as the people who wrote books, for goodness sake. Maybe I can fake it and not really go to the library. This is dumb. I'd much rather be at the lake, but what does my teacher care. He is not interested in how hard it is to write and how boring the civl war is. I mean, who cares? Seems to me that the whole thing was a mess, so many people dying. Hey, how did I remember that? Oh, yeah, my teacher talked about the civl war in class one day. What did he say? Something like 600,000 people died in the war, more than in any other war in American history.

2   Hmmm. I wonder about that. I mean, everyday I hear about how the country is so racist and everything, but if America is such a racist place, why did so many white soldiers fight and die to end slavery? That does not make sense, does it?

3 That might make for an interesting paper, though. I remember grandma telling me that her grandfather fought in the war. I wonder if I could work that in. See, I just do not know enough! I guess I have to go the library after all.

Journals.   Journals are like diaries: Each entry has a way of helping students reflect on their experiences. They are places in which students can filter and process ideas in private. One of the more effective ways to help students plan writing tasks is to have them keep a reading journal in which they record their reactions to all the reading they do, assessing texts, summarizing their main points, linking them to one another and to ideas. Many teachers encourage students to use their journals as the starting place for writing because they contain not only a wealth of information but also their reactions to and interpretations of this information, which are central to success as a writer.

    The following is an excerpt from a journal that a student (Steve R.) kept for a high school English class in which students were reading Moby Dick.

1 Ok, I've read so much of this book and it's tough. People do not talk this way. These sentences go on forever. Why in the world do I have to read this thing? How could anyone think this book is a great work? And the teacher said that the whale was symbolic. Symbolic of what? I guess that's what I'm supposed to figure out. Well, the whale is pretty evil. It ate Ahab's leg and now Ahab wants to kill it no matter what. It's like he's a force for good or something, out to destroy evil. Yeah. And Melville made the whale white to confuse people because white usually is linked to good. But in this case it is linked to evil.

Talk–Write.   Another prewriting activity is based on the perception that speaking, listening, reading, writing, and thinking are intimately related and mutually reinforcing. It is also based on the idea that if students can explain a concept or an operation to someone, they probably understand it pretty well.

    Talk–write involves asking students to construct a plan mentally and deliver an oral composition to the class. The goal is to have students develop a plan that is as complete as possible, with minimal reliance on writing. Generally, they have a short time for planning—about 20 minutes. They may jot down a few notes initially, but when they deliver the oral composition, they must do so without using any notes. After they finish, classmates provide suggestions and comments designed to help improve and elaborate the plan. The next step is for students to begin writing, using what they learned from their presentation to develop a first draft of the assignment.

An advantage of talk–write as a prewriting activity is that it forces students to develop fairly elaborate plans very quickly and to internalize their details. The writing itself is usually easier as a result, and it also tends to be more successful. Researchers account for this consequence in fairly complicated terms that come down to a simple principle: A person has to understand a topic to explain it to others. A valuable fringe benefit is that making such oral presentations is likely to increase self-confidence about speaking in public (see Zoellner, 1968).

Metaphor. The last prewriting activity discussed here is one that is not often considered in examinations of prewriting. *Metaphor* is a description in which one thing is compared to another. The following are some simple metaphors that illustrate how the comparison works:

- The car was a lemon.
- The party was a bomb.
- Fred was a real animal.
- The outgoing governor was a lame duck.
- Rita sure is a hothead.

Many discussions of metaphor suggest that it is merely a figurative use of language that helps writers create special images. In this view, metaphor is a feature of style. However, metaphor can be a powerful model-building device that helps students generate ideas and information. Metaphor includes comparisons such as those just mentioned, but it also includes *metaphorical language*, that is, statements that use imagery without the formal comparison associated with true metaphors. For example, consider the following sentences:

- The day I came home from my vacation, several science projects greeted me when I opened the refrigerator.
- It was raining cats and dogs.
- Fritz insisted that he was not thin, really, but when he stripped to his swim trunks at Macarena's pool party, I decided that Webster's Dictionary needed to add a new entry under the definition of *toothpick*.
- Historians have described American Indians in one of two ways—as noble tribesmen living in harmony with nature or as vicious brutes caught up in perpetual warfare with their neighbors and then the white settlers—and neither is quite correct. In reality, American Indians were examples of evolution in action, people driven to the brink of extinction when faced with social and technological changes that they could not understand, could not even grasp.

The novelist Richard Wright left a valuable record of how metaphor can work as a prewriting technique. Shortly after he published *Black Boy* in 1945, he was asked to write a short essay discussing how other autobiographical narratives influenced his life and work. In the first draft of this essay (see Peterson, 1985), Wright listed a number of books that influenced him, and then he stated that "these books were like eyeglasses, enabling me to see my environment."[3] In the second draft, Wright expanded this metaphor and changed it from "eyeglasses" to "eyes." He stated, for example, that the books that influenced him were "eyes" through which he could see the world as the authors saw it, enabling him to "understand and grasp" his own experiences. This metaphor continued in the third draft, but again there were changes. The paragraphs that show Wright's revisions illustrate how the writer used the metaphor to develop his thoughts.

By the time Wright got to the final draft, however, he shifted the metaphor again. Books were no longer "eyes" but "windows." The change is significant, in part, because it allowed Wright to become the agent of seeing rather than the beneficiary of others' sight.

Planning

Successful writers do a lot of planning before they start writing. Unlike unsuccessful writers, they usually have more information at hand about their topic because they've spent more time researching, thinking, and talking about it. Successful writers benefit from a period of reflection during which their ideas are incubating. At the end of this period, they have a fairly flexible initial plan for the text, and they are ready to write a draft. Planning, however, isn't finished. Successful writers pause regularly as they compose. During these pauses, they read the text and compare it mentally to their initial plan. They assess how well the words on the page match the plan, and on the basis of this assessment they change the plan or the direction the draft is taking. They revise both the plan and the text as they work.

Unsuccessful writers provide a telling contrast. They commonly have too little information about a topic, or they haven't thought much about the information they have—which forces them to deal with superficial ideas that show little reflection. Unsuccessful writers may do no planning before writing, or they may do very little, limiting it in various

---

[3]Technically, Wright uses a *simile* when he writes, "these books were like eyeglasses." *Similes* are a certain kind of metaphor that normally use the preposition *like* to make a comparison. Differentiating metaphors from similies does not appear to provide many benefits, so the term *metaphor* is used here for both.

ways. For example, they may consider nothing but length and where to put references to research material. Or if they are writing in response to an assignment, they may use the assignment itself as their plan. Two pitfalls await them when they do. Many assignments aren't very specific and can lead to vague plans and texts. More troubling, many teachers view a paper that merely responds to the assignment as being, in the best of circumstances, a minimal achievement.

Inadequate planning has several consequences, one of the more common being that unsuccessful writers begin drafting without knowing what their paper is supposed to do. During composing, unsuccessful writers don't read their drafts as much as successful writers, and they don't use their reading in the same way. They don't read to assess the match between their plan and the words on the page; they read to check for mechanical problems, such as spelling and punctuation. Any revising they do while composing therefore tends to focus on correcting surface errors that have nothing to do with the content of the work. The finished product typically is a patchwork of loosely related ideas that never come together to convey a message or make a point.

Drafting

After students have generated some ideas about topics and developed a working plan, the next step is to begin writing a first draft. Several factors influence a successful drafting process. Discipline is perhaps one of the more important, so students need to be encouraged to budget their time and plan ahead. Flexibility is another factor. The downfall of many student writers is their belief that their first draft should be perfect; they spend far too much time fiddling with sentences and punctuation rather than concentrating on getting their ideas on paper. Some writers, in fact, get a good idea while writing a draft and worry so much about how to express the idea that it slips away or becomes strangely less appealing as the frustration level mounts. Students need to understand that early drafts do not have to be neat or well organized, or even highly readable. A first draft simply should chart the territory of the topic. It should be like a road map, marking the general direction the paper will take.

In addition, students should be encouraged to use a computer for all their writing, including drafts. Computers make drafting easy for several reasons. Most people can type faster than they can write by hand, and the work is easier to read. Moreover, computers can check for spelling errors, so writers are freed from the worry of whether they are spelling something incorrectly. Having a typed draft is particularly important if the class is divided into work groups. People read more intelligently and efficiently when they have a typed paper rather than one that is handwritten. As a result, they are able to give better feedback about what works and what does not. Perhaps the greatest benefit, however, is that computers allow writers to move text around at will, cutting, pasting, and rewriting with ease.

In the 1st century B.C., a Greek author named Longinus recommended that writers who were serious about their work should set a draft aside for 9 years before going back to it and making changes. His idea was that the passage of time would allow writers to see their writing more clearly and to determine whether it was worth improving. Longinus was a bit extreme in recommending a wait of 9 years, but the principle he advocated was right on target. All writers, but especially students, need to allow some time to pass before making changes.

How many drafts should students produce before a paper is finished? There is no answer to this question. Every paper is different; every paper has its own context and requirements. Sometimes a single draft will be sufficient, other times a paper may require 5, 6, or even 10 drafts.

Pausing and Reading

Matsuhashi (1981) examined what happens when people write and saw that the *scribing* of her subjects (the time that they actually applied pen to paper) was interrupted frequently by pauses. Williams (1985) examined pausing in more detail and suggested that pauses are linked to thinking during writing. His data indicated that good writers use pauses to think about factors such as audience and aim, whereas poor writers use them to think about punctuation and word choice. In addition, good writers use pauses to read what they have written; reading enables them to assess how effectively their work is following their plan, how well it matches the audience, and so forth. Poor writers reported doing little reading, and what they did was limited largely to word choice, which should have come later, during the editing stage, not during writing.

Studies like these suggest that pauses serve an important role in the writing process. In many respects, pauses continue the planning that begins before students start writing. Good writers appear to use pauses for reviewing their plan and for making changes in it. Poor writers, on the other hand, appear to stick rigidly to their initial plan, with bad results. A key to improving student writing therefore may lie in helping them to use pauses more effectively.

Revising

Revising is an important part of writing well, yet students generally have an unclear perception of what revising is about. They may concentrate on sentence-level concerns, changing individual words or reorganizing sentences. Actually, revising occurs on different levels and at different times. The level just described, fiddling with sentences and punctuation, perhaps more accurately should be called *editing*, which is discussed later in some detail. *Editing* deals with the surface features of writing and is generally performed after a paper does what writers want it to do. *Revising* is more properly what writers do to the writing before a paper does what they want it to do.

As the previous section indicated, good writers appear to revise mentally during pauses in composing, and they tend to focus on *global changes* that are intimately linked to their audience, purpose, and stance. Revising, then, requires that writers consider their role, as well as that of their readers, in regard to the topic. In addition, effective revising depends on having knowledge about an audience's motivation for reading a paper. It requires that writers be critical readers (Johnson, 1993). They must be able to look at writing that has taken time and effort to produce and see it as it is, not as they wish it to be. They must be willing to cut sentences and paragraphs that do not work. They must be willing to shift sections from one place to another to enhance the overall organization of the composition. Shifting the focus of writing activities to the classroom workshop makes these difficult tasks easier to perform because it is a relatively risk-free environment in which making changes in drafts is a given.

Editing and Publishing

During the prewriting stage, writers generate ideas and organization, and when planning, they reflect on how these ideas match the goals of the paper. During the drafting stage, they put these ideas into some rough order. Then, during the revising stage, they hone organization and expression. Finally, during the editing stage, they deal with sentence-level concerns such as spelling, punctuation, and usage.

In some respects, editing is one of the harder parts of writing. Writers generally have trouble spotting surface errors in their own work. One reason is that they read for content rather than form, so they will not see an error in, say, spelling, but will see the correct form. Asking students to edit one another's papers in class is an effective way to help them improve the quality of their papers while giving them needed practice in attending to surface details.

After a paper is edited, it is ready for the final stage. *Publishing* is used in composition to refer to the act of making a finished paper public. It does not suggest that a paper is printed in a journal or book, although many public school teachers often bind student papers into a book because it is motivating for students. Making a paper public may involve simply sharing it aloud with other students or posting it on a bulletin board or some other place where people can read the work. There is a popular but mistaken perception among students that writing is private. An important part of teaching writing is helping students understand that writing is a social action and that their work is inherently intended for others to read.

JOURNAL ENTRY

Consider the writing classes you have taken. What model did they follow—product or process? Looking back on those classes with the benefit of what you have read so far in this chapter, what were some strengths and weaknesses of the instruction you received?
It is important that writing teachers be writers themselves. Reflect on your own writing process. How do you go about writing papers? Can any of the information in this chapter enhance your writing?

A Phase Model of the Composing Process

One of the difficulties inherent in the concept of stages is that they seem to be discrete. That is, stages create the impression that students cannot begin drafting until they have finished prewriting; they cannot begin revising until they have finished drafting, and so forth. Thus, in the minds of many teachers, the stages of the composing process are part of an algorithm—a step-by-step procedure—that should ensure effective writing. We know, however, that composing does not consist of discrete stages and that, in fact, there are no such stages.

A more effective way of conceptualizing the various activities associated with successful composing is through a *phase model* rather than a stage model. Phase models occur most commonly in science. Water, for example, when described with a phase model, has three dominant states—liquid, vapor, and solid—and it can be understood to be always in a state of flux between states. Thus water in a liquid state is turning into vapor through evaporation; water in a solid state is turning into both vapor and liquid. The composing process can also be thought of as having dominant states (prewriting, drafting, revising, etc.) but these states can be understood to be always in a state of recurrent flux. Thus students revise as they draft; they prewrite as they edit; and so forth. A phase model therefore has the advantage of describing the simultaneous and recurrent nature of the composing process; prewriting, drafting, and editing may occur more or less simultaneously and in a recurrent manner. The stage model does not readily account for or describe either the co-occurence or the recurrence.

THE SOCIAL-THEORETIC MODEL
OF COMPOSITION

The *social-theoretic model* of composition recognizes that people belong to a variety of groups, each with its own requirements for membership and participation, its own core body of knowledge, and its own values and ways of looking at the world. It also proposes that writers produce texts in response to the social demands of these groups, not in response to an innate need to communicate or express themselves. It describes writing as an interaction between writers and their environment. Some scholars refer to this as *social construction*. The problem with this term is that it is easy to confuse the model with *social constructivism*, which is a stage-based model of cognition and development that rejects innate processes. In this model, children are blank slates who are shaped entirely by society. *Social theory* avoids this potential confusion and has the added advantage of avoiding the Marxist connotations that adhere to social construction.

The groups writers belong to consist of people with shared interests and goals who will use the finished text in some pragmatic way. Cooper (1986), in an important article that was the first fully articulated presentation of the social-theoretic model, characterized this environment as the "ecology" of composing. In this view, groups define their members, giving them an identity and insisting on adherence to certain behaviors and language. Attorneys must use the language of the law, accountants the language of accountancy, teachers the language of education, and so forth. Members also define themselves on the basis of their membership in the group, but they simultaneously define the group through their participation in it. The social-theoretic model proposes, as a consequence of these factors, that the texts people produce are governed comprehensively by the writers' membership and participation in a particular group (see, e.g., Allen, 1993).

The development of the social-theoretic view can be understood in two ways: as an extension of or as a reaction against the process model. From the first perspective, process forms the foundation for expanding the notions of collaboration and audience from work groups to society. The social-theoretic model is based on process pedagogy, but it provides a necessary correction to a model that overemphasizes the psychology of individual writers. This model, then, builds on the process model, providing a more accurate and applicable description of how people produce texts.

From the second perspective, however, process was inextricably linked to new rhetoric, which made it susceptible to two major criticisms and which led many teachers and scholars to seek something better. The first criticism was that the process model failed to describe adequately the way writers work in real situations. For example, its emphasis on the writer and on changing the writer's behavior suggests that writers have some innate desire to express themselves and that writers are largely in control of what they produce. In real situations, however, there are very few people who write because they want to; most write because they have to. Moreover, they have very little control over any aspect of the task. If an accounting manager needs a financial statement, he or she assigns someone to produce it. The person who receives the assignment normally gathers a team to assist on the project, and the team members have considerable influence on the finished product. In this scenario, the writer has little choice regarding what he or she writes and has even less choice regarding how to write it (the accountant realistically could not decide to produce the financial statement in verse). Also, the collaboration ensures that the finished product reflects the input of several voices, not just one. Although the process model's workshop classroom has students work together on their individual projects, their collaboration is different from what occurs in real situations, in which a team works on a single project.

The second criticism of the process model arose from the neo-Marxist ideology implicit in postmodernism. The process model may not describe adequately the way writers work in real situations, but it is well suited to helping students master the kinds of writing expected in school because it is closely linked to academic discourse. From the postmodern perspective, the result is a form of social engineering perpetuated on students by teachers who, according to writers like Courts (1991), are the unwitting servants of the "military-industrial complex" (p. 66). Courts, as well as Berlin (1992a, 1992b), Mack and Zebroski (1992), Petrosky (1990), and many others implicitly endorsed the social-theoretic view because of its proposal that language and thought are influenced by social forces. For those who are ideologically oriented, the social-theoretic view captures what (for them) is the paradoxical danger and salvation of language and education: It can be used by capitalists to maintain the political status quo in America, or it can be used by revolutionaries to tear down the status quo and build anew.[4]

Discourse Communities

A key to understanding the proposed interaction between writers and groups is the notion of *discourse communities*. Members of discourse communities share not only values and views but also language and language conventions. For example, professional groups both implicitly and explicitly agree to use language in certain ways. Jargon usually is implicit, but matters pertaining to writing usually are explicit. English teachers agreed at some point that they would use the format specified in the *MLA* (Modern Language Association) *Guide to Writing*. Psychologists, on the other hand, agreed at some point that they would use the *Publication Manual of the American Psychological Association* (the APA guide). Each guide offers a list of expectations regarding writing for members of these groups. The guides are different in many ways, but one is not more correct than the other. However, it is generally unacceptable for an English teacher to write a paper for fellow English teachers using the APA format, just as it would be unacceptable for a psychologist to use the *MLA Guide to Writing*. They would be violating the conventions of their respective discourse communities if they did so.

The practical as well as the ideological features of the social-theoretic model have been reinforced by the work of Lev Vygotsky, a Russian psychologist whose research from 1924 to 1934 provided interesting insights into the relation between thought and language (Vygotsky, 1962). Vygotsky proposed that thought and language have similar roots, and he set about exploring their origins. He developed the view that thought originates in children as internalized, or inner, speech that is shaped and influenced by the language of adults. In this account, language, which is fundamentally social, influences cognition. But because language itself is a social phenomenon, language and thought ultimately are *social constructions*. The process model offered little insight into the role discourse communities play in writing.

To a significant degree, mastering the language of a given group is a basic requirement for admission. People who want to become attorneys have to be able to use the language of law, and those who want to become psychologists have to be able to use the language of psychology. Obviously, more is involved than merely knowing which terms to use.

---

[4]This view is nearly identical to Plato's, which suggts the neo-Marxist position is unintentionally conservative. McKowski (1993) made this point forcefully and argued that the neo-Marxism that permeates postmodern rhetoric is academically conservative and is antithetical to true postmodernism.

Students have to understand the core knowledge of the discipline and the way members of the discipline view reality. But these factors are intimately related to language. Slang is one way young people, particularly teenagers, use language to join groups: It easily identifies who belongs to the group and who does not. The urge to belong, to be the same rather than different, is so strong that it even affects accents: Children who move to the West Coast from the South quickly lose their southern accent so they will fit in with their peers at school. A similar motivation operates among high school students, who commonly invent expressions for certain actions or things, expressions that have meaning only for them and the members of their group. In all these instances, an underlying pattern is visible—language differentiates insiders from outsiders.

Writing in a Social-Theoretic-Oriented Classroom

From the perspective of the social-theoretic model, writing is a social action. It does something. Consequently, people write for a reason. In the workplace, people write because they must produce a report that conveys information, a business letter that acknowledges an order, a memo that communicates a new policy, or a proposal that aims to bring in new business. In school, students write because they must demonstrate that they have learned course material, that they can interpret information using what they have learned in class, or that they can work independently or in a group.

Underlying each instance is an individual reason for writing, which is called *rhetorical purpose*. *Rhetorical purpose* includes the writer's personal goals for producing a text. These goals are not the same as the aim of a text, which may be to inform, argue, or persuade. Rhetorical purpose is about the writer, whereas the aim of a text is about the audience and the effect the text should have on readers.

The range of individual purposes is broad but not limitless. Within professional groups, there are three categories of rhetorical purpose: *traditional, innovative,* and *confrontational. Traditional rhetorical purpose* is to maintain the accepted point of view of facts of a group; *innovative rhetorical purpose* is to share new knowledge or a view of reality; last, *confrontational rhetorical purpose* is to overturn an established point of view, using confrontational language—writers are insiders, but they often distance themselves from the group to attack it. It is common to think of scientists, for example, as people who typically write to disseminate new facts. Those scientists who do have an innovative rhetorical purpose. Many scientists, however, replicate experiments to validate work others have performed. When they publish their findings, these writers have a traditional rhetorical purpose, to the extent that their research confirms established conclusions. Scientists who attempt to overturn established conclusions may have a confrontational rhetorical purpose.

The Problem of Discourse Communities in the Classroom

The social-theoretic model is elegant and powerful because it accurately describes the various factors associated with real writing. People participate in discourse communities, and these communities determine, to a significant degree, the "what" and "how" of writing. The problem, however, is that the composing students do in school is usually far removed from real writing, so the notion of discourse community applies to students only in a marginal way. Students belong to several communities, the most obvious one being that of "students," but these groups are amorphous and inclusive, whereas the discourse communities described by the social-theoretic model are discrete and exclusive. Students also have the opportunity to identify a discourse community that they would like to gain entry into, but few take advantage of that opportunity. Fewer than half of all incoming freshmen at the nation's colleges and universities know what they want to major in, and half of them change majors at least once during their first 2 years at school. The suggestion, therefore, that many public school students might know what they want to be cannot be taken seriously.

Some teachers have attempted to solve this problem by proposing that the classroom itself is a discourse community. However, this proposal is based on a misunderstanding of the social-theoretic model, specifically that a discourse community is merely a group of people sharing common experiences (the class). As the previous discussion indicated, communities are complex and are defined by more than the shared experiences of their members. The only theoretically congruent efforts at building a discourse community in the classroom are those that engage students in role playing. For example, a class might take on the role of a business, with groups of students assigned specific roles within that business, such as marketing, accounting, and personnel. But this sort of role playing does not work very well at the public school level because it requires a commitment on the part of students to participate. High absenteeism and daily discipline problems in the public schools work against such efforts.[5] Equally problematic is the fact that role-playing activities seldom account for a key factor in the social-theoretic model—individual motivation to become a member of a given discourse community.

---

[5]Nationwide, about 25% of students are absent from middle and high schools every day.

Making Writing Meaningful

Perhaps the greatest benefit of the social-theoretic model is that it provides a goal that writing teachers can strive for with their students. The majority of students may not be able to see themselves as historians, musicians, accountants, or whatever, but at least they may stop seeing themselves merely as students and start seeing themselves as writers. Teachers are responsible for helping them attain this vision, and in most situations they can do so by making certain that every writing task be related to the real world. In practical terms, a real-world emphasis means that students' compositions will do something in the tangible sense of performing a social action.

The following anecdote suggests one way the pragmatic view may be translated into practice. Robert, a credential candidate with a degree in history, began his student teaching by asking his eighth-grade class for a writing sample. He felt very strongly that all teachers, not just those in language arts, should be dedicated to helping develop children's language. The class had been studying U.S. government, and one of the students, Joey, submitted the following:

> The US consitution is an importent dokument. It give us many rites. Like speech and freedom. Witout the Consitution we might as well be rushans. What our president Raygin call the "evil empire." But sometime it seem that the consitution give us to much freedoms. Many time crimnals do not go to jail for doing bad things when they should go to jail. Thats not right and the consitution should change it.

In a conference 2 days later, Robert asked Joey to recall the things he had been thinking about when he wrote this paper. The purpose was to gain additional insight into Joey's composing process. Joey's response, which Robert recorded, was typical for a student who has come to believe that product is all important and who has come to see writing as a nonfunctional enterprise: "I was thinkin' I do not spell so good and was wonderin' if I had written enough."

Robert knew his work was cut out for him. According to the course guide, the next major study unit dealt with U.S. involvement in Southeast Asia. He asked his class whether they would like to have some pen pals from the Philippines who could give them some firsthand knowledge of life in one part of Southeast Asia. The students were enthusiastic, and a letter to a school principal in Manila began an exchange of letters that continued long after the unit on Southeast Asia was concluded.

Students on both sides of the Pacific were interested in learning more about the culture and lifestyle of their counterparts, and for the

American children, the letters from Manila seemed to reinforce significantly what they were learning about history and government. Just as important, they suddenly had a purpose for writing. Written language had become meaningful. Composing the letters was always a collaborative project, with children working together in small groups, sharing letters they had received from abroad and also sharing the letters they were writing. The children were encouraged to include pertinent class experiences in their letters. Robert circulated among them as they composed, offering suggestions when necessary and answering questions when asked.

Giving these students a real reason to write had a very positive effect on their work. All the students improved, as the following letter shows. Like the previous sample, it was written by Joey, just over a month after the paper about the Constitution, at a time when Ferdinand Marcos, former dictator of the Philippines, was still in office:

> Dear Emilio,
> Thank you for your last letter. Since I got it we have been studying more about your country. And I have been thinking about what you said about how nice it must be to live in America. We seem to have more freedom than you and its easier for us to make money and buy the things that make life comfortable. I think things would be better for you if you did not have martial law. Then maybe the government would not have all the money. It must be tough with the army and the police telling you what time you have to go to bed and stuff. ... I do not know why our president helps keep your president in power. I think he do not want to lose the navy base that keeps alot of our ships on one of your islands ... .

What we see here is that when written language becomes meaningful, writing performance improves on all levels. For example, Joey's concern over the impression his spelling might have on Emilio motivated him (perhaps for the first time) to write with a dictionary close at hand.

THE WAC MODEL

Writing across the curriculum (WAC) is the name used to identify the effort teachers and administrators have been making since the mid-1970s to give writing a more prominent role in classes other than English.[6] To a large extent, WAC preceded the social-theoretic model by

---

[6]It is important to note that WAC is not really a completely new approach to composition. Colgate College established such a program in the early 1930s, and University of California at Berkeley did the same in the 1950s (see Russell, 1987). The current approach is different in that it is more widespread; WAC programs exist at the public school level as well as at the college level.

a full decade. WAC recognizes writing is situation specific and that good writers are people who can apply different conventions to different writing conditions. WAC also recognizes that writing is a vehicle for learning and self-definition. It is therefore tempting to conclude that the social-theoretic model is a fuller articulation of WAC, but this conclusion would miss some subtle distinctions between the two, such as the underlying political component that has come to underlie much related to social theory.

The most popular approach to WAC in junior and senior high schools involves designating selected classes as *writing intensive*. Writing teachers serve as resource persons for other faculty, providing suggestions on how to use writing more effectively in content areas. They may give workshops on teaching writing, offer help on how to structure assignments, how to conduct conferences, and how to evaluate papers. The goal is to make teachers in fields outside English better writing instructors.

The writing-intensive courses then use writing as a vehicle for learning, usually taking advantage of the workshop environment. Rather than lecture on American history, for example, a teacher might have students write papers that immerse them in the material to be covered for a given lesson. A math teacher, on the other hand, might have students write problems or situations that call for application of a newly learned mathematical principle. Students in these classes just do not do more writing. They do writing that is focused in ways that help them master content and the conventions associated with writing in given disciplines.

At the elementary level, WAC has to be applied differently because one teacher usually is responsible for teaching all subjects at given grade levels, but the principles are the same. Teachers engage students in writing tasks in ways that help them master content and writing. Elementary teachers actually have more flexibility than middle and high school teachers. They are able to build integrated units that link science, social studies, math, and language, in which reading and writing activities work together to build skills.

For example, during art lessons, some elementary teachers have children work in teams, as in the workshop approach. After finishing their artwork, the children write stories for one another's pictures and then bind them into "books." Also at the elementary level, science lessons provide rich sources of writing opportunities. Lee (1987) related how several different writing tasks were linked to a unit on garden snails. In an assignment that called for description, students were asked to "Write an account of a day in the life of a snail." For narration, they were asked to "Write a story in which ... [they] speculate or fantasize about how the snail got its shell." Then, for exposition, he offered the following: "Suppose that the sun is moving closer to the earth each day. Using the theories of natural selection and survival of the fittest, project what physical changes might occur in the snail as it attempts to cope with its changing environment" (p. 39).

In each of these tasks, students interacted cooperatively in their work groups, but the latter assignment better utilized the potential of collaborative learning. Illustrating the inquiry method in action, this hypothetical situation prompted students to brainstorm ideas as they examined the potential effects of the sun's shift. The writing assignment became a stimulus for learning, the social interaction of the work group became the vehicle for learning, and the resulting papers represent students' formulation of their learning.

Those schools that implemented WAC have generally seen students improve all skills above the norm. Unfortunately, the majority continue to offer curricula that have few opportunities for writing (Ackerman, 1993, Walvoord, 1996b). The situation is especially bad at the elementary level, in which it is common for students in Grades 3 through 6 to have only one or perhaps two real writing assignments all year. Instead of helping students practice analysis and description, teachers in these schools waste students' time by forcing them to practice cursive writing, a 19th-century skill that has no viable place in a 21st-century society. Finding instances of cursive outside the classroom is almost impossible. No text appears in any public forum in cursive; all text appears in print. In addition, cursive is usually introduced in third grade, just when students have started to master printing. The result is confusion and frustration, especially among boys, whose fine-motor skills lag behind those of girls. Nevertheless, teachers have students spend countless hours practicing swirls and loops, as though computers and printers do not exist.

Implementing WAC

It is relatively easy to implement a WAC approach at a public school because the small staff keeps coordination simple. WAC commonly begins when two or more teachers decide they want to find ways to improve the reading and writing skills of their students (Walvoord, 1996a). Their informal discussions usually lead them to contact a composition specialist at a local university for information, and then they take a proposal to the school principal. A few meetings and a workshop or two later, and all the teachers at most schools are ready to proceed.

These efforts are often initiated by English teachers, who must keep in mind that the conventions that govern the typical English essay are seldom applicable to other disciplines. Science reports, for example, have a structure that is quite different from a humanistic essay. If good writers are flexible writers, students stand to benefit from experience with a variety of composition requirements; they stand to benefit from mastering the conventions that underlie writing in different disciplines. To suggest, even implicitly, that only the belles-lettres essay has any value is to undermine the very foundation of WAC.

Above all, successful implementation depends on reaching consensus among colleagues about the role of writing in students' lives and in their education. Ideally, those involved would consider the role of writing in the light of pragmatic concerns associated with academic performance in public school and beyond, as well as society's needs for a literate citizenry. The role most definitely should not be limited to considerations of self-concept and personal growth through self-exploration. Such a consensus *should* be easy to achieve, but it can be difficult because writing has been and continues to be a widely neglected part of most curricula. In every school that I have visited or reviewed—and the number is in the hundreds—reading, math, computers, science, and social studies always take precedence. The reasons are both historical and political, but the point is that any given school will find it difficult to develop a WAC program if teachers fail to agree that writing should be at least on the same level as these other subjects.

The Argument Against WAC

Although WAC has been successful and remains one of the more popular models for composition, it has come under attack in recent years as being an unacceptable approach. Kirscht, Levine, and Reiff (1994) suggested that hostility toward WAC is the result of incompatible views of what writing and education are supposed to do. They noted that some teachers see WAC as a means of improving learning, whereas others see it as a means of mastering discourse conventions specific to given disciplines. Consequently, writing to learn just does not mean to English teachers what it does for those outside English. In the first case, writing to learn is related to personal, social, and political growth; in the second case, it is related to the sort of knowledge the academy makes available to students. Those who hold these different views supposedly now form two camps, and the hostility toward WAC emerges out of disagreements about the nature of learning.

This analysis, however, misses the mark. The real problem is that during the past 10 years or so, academic writing itself has come under attack by numerous composition scholars, such as Berthoff (1990), Bizzell (1992), and Elbow, Berlin, and Bazerman (1991). WAC happens to be a highly visible means by which students are taught how to write academic prose. The argument, perhaps most forcefully articulated by Elbow (1991), is that academic writing leads students to adopt the thoughts and views of corporate America, as well as to "detachment." As a result, they are unable to become "liberated" but instead are pawns in what Courts (1991) characterized as the "military-industrial complex." WAC, therefore, is seen to perpetuate the status quo, so it is at odds with postmodern ideology—at odds with *liberation pedagogy*.

Parents and people in other disciplines have a hard time understanding the argument that students should not learn how to write academic prose, and they have an even harder time accepting the premise that underlies the argument: Students are oppressed and need to be liberated. They have a hard time believing that their lives are repressed and controlled by some military-industrial complex. Nevertheless, the seriousness with which so many leading composition scholars make this argument suggests that it should be acknowledged. What remains inescapable, however, is that formal education inherently is a process of preparing children to take their place in society. When schools fail, and many of them have, society begins to fall apart. Liberation pedagogy therefore strikes many as being antithetical to the best interests of both children and society.

WAC grew out of the perception that students can more effectively learn to write when they have a purpose for composing and when they have exposure to the types of writing that people in identifiable communities actually produce. It is difficult to see any overt political agenda in the work of pioneers in the WAC model. It is easy to see, however, great concern for the pragmatic question of how to help students become better writers.

Exploring Key Ideas

1. Some people suggest that the product model continues to dominate language arts classrooms because teachers are fearful of giving up total control over what students do. Assuming that there is some truth to this idea, how might you prepare yourself to be more flexible, more willing to experiment with ways of teaching that may not be familiar to you?

2. A fundamental feature of the process model is the idea that everyone has his or her own process, yet very often implementation in the classroom seems based on the idea that there is only one process

that everyone must follow. What could be influencing teachers as they implement the process model?

3. A major difficulty of the social-theoretic model is that it is hard to implement in public schools because it requires getting students to identify themselves as would-be members of a specific professional group. What are some ways to overcome this difficulty?

4. One of the largest criticisms students have about education in general and language arts classes in particular is that they do not seem relevant. This criticism seems particularly apt when writing assignments have nothing to do with the world outside the classroom. Building on suggestions in this chapter, how might you make your writing assignments more meaningful?

5. A growing number of schools are implementing WAC, some as early as third grade. What do you believe are the biggest rewards and challenges in implementing the WAC model?

6. The idea of discourse communities provides a powerful tool for teaching—the classification into insiders and outsiders. It seems that one's desire to become an insider is the most important factor in improving writing, but for the majority of young people the concept of insider is limited to peer groups. What are some ways you can expand students' interests?

3

The Classroom as Workshop

OVERVIEW

The process model brought about significant changes in the way teachers interact with students. One of the more important of these changes was restructuring the classroom to allow for a workshop environment that shifts the focus of the writing class from teacher to students. In a workshop classroom, students sit in groups of three to five rather than in rows. Ideally, all activities begin and end with these groups. There is very little lecture; instead, students are working and talking among themselves, focusing their attention on drafts of assignments. Students read one another's drafts in their groups, offering comments and suggestions for revision. Sometimes, they work on projects together, as a team. In many respects, these work groups require the sort of collaboration that characterizes what takes place in natural writing situations. Students take on more responsibility for their own learning and for their own achievement. They also engage in cooperative problem solving that can enhance critical thinking skills.

Teachers who use the workshop find that their roles change. They move freely about the room to offer advice on papers that are still in draft form. Students can use this advice immediately to improve their revisions. Teachers, in this environment, serve as coaches for their students, intervening when their help is needed most and when it is most effective.

STRUCTURING A CLASSROOM WORKSHOP

Most writing intended to be read by others is a collaborative effort. In the workplace, reports and proposals are commonly written by teams. Before academicians send their papers out for publication, they ask friends to read the manuscript and offer suggestions for improvement. Sometimes they use the suggestions in their revision and sometimes they do not, but they always feel grateful to their friends for taking the time to offer constructive comments.[1] Recognizing these realities, the process model led to an important change in the structure of writing classrooms. It transformed them into writing *workshops.*

In a workshop, students sit in groups of three to five. Nearly all of their work begins and ends in the group. For example, a teacher who intends to ask students to write an analysis of a reading assignment might begin with some freewriting on the assignment. The freewriting then might form the foundation for group discussions and group brainstorming to help develop ideas for the writing task. Students might use the information from these activities to begin drafting their analysis. Drafts can be read by groupmates or by members of other groups, but they eventually return for revision. As students are revising, the teacher circulates among them and offers constructive comments on their work. He or she may see that several students need intervention for, say, punctuation problems. The teacher interrupts students, gives them brief instruction on punctuation, and then has them return to their work so that they can apply the lesson immediately. These sorts of interventions led many in composition to view the writing teacher as a coach.

Although it is natural to focus on how teachers in workshops respond to errors or problems in students' drafts, it is a mistake to ignore the opportunities that workshops provide for teachers to offer individual words of encouragement and praise for what students do well. Effective teachers balance advice with encouragement, and they regularly ask students to stop working for a moment so they can read to the entire class part of a work that is particularly well written. This technique makes everyone feel better about writing, strengthens the bonding in the class, and motivates students to work harder.

Building Community

Because students read one another's drafts and then offer constructive comments, they need to feel comfortable working together. However, one of the biggest obstacles to the success of a workshop is the high level of discomfort students feel when asked to offer meaningful comments on their peers' papers (Bleich, 1995; Bruffee, 1993). Therefore, an important first step toward developing a viable atmosphere for a workshop is to allow students to get to know one another as well as possible during the first several days of class. Each student needs to come to think of

---

[1]Feedback of this sort, used to help revise a paper still in draft form, is often referred to as *formative evaluation* (see Huff & Kline, 1987).

the class as a group of friends who can be counted on for help, advice, and support. This kind of relationship takes more than a few sessions to develop, of course, but the goal is clear: Students need time to get acquainted so they can respond candidly to one another's work. However, they also need some guidance regarding how best to provide constructive comments, and this should emerge from the teacher's comments as he or she is circulating among students. Teachers need to model the behavior they expect from their students.

Workshops are relatively noisy places. Students are reading papers aloud, asking one another questions about their writing, and offering comments. If a workshop is quiet, it probably is not working. Students are allowed to assume a great deal of responsibility for their own learning, which means not everyone will be doing the same thing. Some students may be working alone writing a draft, others may be discussing ways to improve a student's paper. Still others may be getting advice from the teacher in a short conference.

Writing workshops may seem chaotic to teachers who have been trained to think of composition pedagogy in a traditional way. Some teachers are initially threatened by the seeming lack of structure and control. But a successful workshop actually requires more structure and planning than a traditional classroom, because students must be kept busy, as well as focused, without being made to feel that the teacher is hovering over them.

Setting Up Work Groups

After students have had time to get acquainted, many teachers attempt to make some evaluation of their writing abilities. The aim is to identify strong and weak writers so as to balance the work groups. It is not a good idea to have all the strong writers in one group and all the weak ones in another because collaboration thrives on input from different voices. Teachers often ask students to respond in class to a selected topic, after making it clear to them that the essays will not be graded. They then evaluate these responses and use their analyses to group students according to ability.

In most classes, some students have had richer experiences than others, and the wealth of background material they can draw on puts less fortunate students at a disadvantage when it comes to writing this initial essay. Making the task text-based can help level the playing field; students read a short, selected passage and then use it as the basis for their writing. They do not necessarily write about the reading selection, but the selection is relevant to their writing; it forms the background for the response. For example, a writing prompt might ask for an argument for or against the idea of having students in public schools wear uniforms; the associated passage might be a published article that describes instances in which one student harmed another and stole his or her designer-label clothes.

Many teachers refer to this initial writing task as a *diagnostic essay*, but this seems to be a particularly inapt term, given its medical connotations. Teachers are not physicians working with diseased patients in need of healing; they work with normal students going through the normal process of mastering the language.

Although writing samples can be useful in forming work groups, they should be used with a high degree of caution. A variety of studies noted that impromptu writing tasks do not assess student skills with much accuracy (Belanoff, 1991; Haswell & Wyche-Smith, 1994). Sometimes those who produce the worst impromptu responses turn out to be the best writers in a class and vice versa. Teachers should use these initial writing samples as one piece of data and should balance them with others, such as grades from the previous year, comments by other teachers, and their own observations.

When work groups are balanced, the strong writers are able to help the weak ones. Sometimes group balance is a factor of the social network in the class rather than writing skills. As a result, many teachers find it desirable to have students respond to a questionnaire that helps identify the social network. Such a questionnaire typically asks students who is the smartest person in the class, who is the best leader, who is easiest to get along with, and so forth. Even very young students probably have some awareness of the existing network, and because the questionnaires are filled out anonymously, the responses are generally candid.

Before groups can function effectively, members must go through a bonding process that unites them in a common purpose. Once the bonding is completed, the group works as a collaborative unit. For these reasons, groups should stay together for an entire term. Moving students from group to group appears to offer greater variety in regard to feedback on drafts, but the advantage of variety is significantly offset by the lack of bonding that results from shifting students around. For the true cooperation that characterizes effective work groups, bonding is essential (see Huff & Kline, 1987). Without it, student feedback on drafts rarely rises above a superficial level.

The size of a group affects how well it functions. In groups of three, two members may take sides against the third. In groups of four, the group may split evenly whenever decisions are called for, so little gets accomplished. The ideal number is five, because it avoids these difficulties and allows for better interaction among members.

Over the last decade, fewer and fewer schools have desks bolted to the floor, and the advantage to group work is significant. With movable desks, students can arrange their seats into small circles that make working together easier. Bolted desks require arranging students in small semicircles facing the front of the room. Group members sit in adjoining rows, with two students in one row and three in the next. This seating pattern enables students to see each other as they interact, and it allows them to observe the teacher when he or she needs to address the whole class. Finally, it is always a good idea to have an empty desk or two separating the groups (if at all possible). Such separation not only leads to a greater sense of bonding within each group, but it also creates a sense of privacy. Both are important.

Students may form their own groups, but more often than not this creates problems as friends cluster and end up talking about everything other than class work. In addition, if left to themselves, younger students commonly group themselves by gender. In some classes, students group themselves by race or language. None of these membership patterns is desirable.

A key factor in creating successful workshops lies in devising plans that move students through different activities during each lesson. For example, a typical lesson lasts 1 hour. Students may spend 10 minutes analyzing a writing sample at the beginning of the hour, 25 minutes writing or rewriting, and then the final 15 minutes talking about the work they just finished. They may use the first 15 minutes in role playing to enhance audience awareness, with the remainder of the hour devoted to writing and rewriting. In any case, the writing activity should be a part of every day's lesson. No matter what they do, students should write for at least 20 minutes a day, especially at the elementary level. Hour-long writing activities, however, usually are not very productive because students lose their attentiveness. Nesting writing between two brief, related activities helps keep students focused on the task. Some schools are shifting to 2-hour blocks for language arts, but the entire period is seldom devoted to writing. Nevertheless, these block schedules offer teachers greater flexibility, for they can adjust how they divide the time given to writing.

Obstacles to Work Groups

Legislated curricula and district-imposed programmed instruction often thwart even the best teacher's intentions. Many districts, for example, limit writing instruction in English classes to 1 day per week, or less.

The other 4 days are reserved for literature and traditional grammar instruction. At the elementary level, English instruction is commonly limited to reading, spelling, grammar, and handwriting exercises. Although there is no question that reading skills are crucial to children's education, the absence of writing is remarkable, especially in view of the fact that writing about reading assignments enhances comprehension and critical thinking. Many parents measure the success of elementary English instruction by their children's scores on spelling tests, and they never question the pervasive lack of writing assignments. But the role spelling plays in most elementary classrooms is highly questionable. Students learn lists of words that have no context. One result of this is that many do not know what the words mean or how to use them. Another is that students receive the lists on Monday, take a spelling test on Friday, and forget the words by Sunday.

Grammar instruction is usually just as devoid of context. The typical English text at all grade levels provides lists of sentences that students use to identify nouns, verbs, modifiers, and so forth. Students use these books to complete exercises that never call for any writing. Instead, they underline and circle words in a workbook, which leads them to believe that writing and grammar are totally divorced from each other. Without a context for grammar, most students rapidly forget what little these books teach.

It is important to keep in mind that curriculum guides are not the absolute arbiters of what teachers do in the classroom. In many cases, they are not even written by teachers, so they do not reflect much awareness of the dynamics of instruction. Newly credentialed teachers often feel compelled to follow their guides religiously, never deviating one bit; others simply follow the guides because it is easier than teaching creatively. Guides should be viewed as a map for taking students from Point A to Point B, which leaves ample room for meeting the needs of individual students, classes, and schools. If a guide does not specifically call for including writing activities in each day's lessons, teachers need to use their own professional judgment to provide them. Likewise, if a guide does not specifically call for using work groups in the classroom, the teacher should, on his or her own initiative, implement them. There may be some subjects that cannot be enhanced through the incorporation of writing activities, but none comes readily to mind.

A more problematic obstacle has recently emerged that attempts to undermine the concept of collaboration and work groups. A number of scholars argued that work groups are discriminatory (see Clark, 1994; Halloran, 1993; Harris, 1989; Kent, 1991; C. Miller, 1993; and Young, 1990). They base their argument on the fact that workshops are predicated on democracy, which depends on agreement and cooperation. Students and teachers have to agree on a wide variety of values: what constitutes good writing, a meaningful response to an assignment, acceptable behavior in the classroom, the goals of writing in particular and education in general, and so forth. Democracy is not viewed positively, however. According to these scholars, agreement (and consequently democracy) inevitably silences expression of values contrary to those accepted and endorsed by the majority. As Clark (1994) noted: "The problem is that a discourse of pluralism [such as exists in a workshop environment] … maintains connection and cooperation by excluding the most divisive forces of difference" (p. 64).

This argument is flawed in a basic way. It always involves these underlying premises: Differences are more valuable than similarities and agreement is inherently bad. But the argument fails whenever a reader rejects the validity of the premises; it can stand only when there is agreement. For anyone who denies the legitimacy of the premises, the argument is absurd. Moreover, those who argue against cooperation unwittingly create an inescapable paradox. If agreement is inherently bad, then there is no rationale for the argument because accepting the argument—agreeing with it—puts readers in the impossible position of doing what they have just accepted as being inherently bad. It is a situation that requires agreement, in order to accept the value of disagreement. In other words, if readers accept the argument against agreement, they logically must reject the argument to be consistent with the argument.

In anything other than the most superficial analysis, the idea that democracy and cooperation silence voices at odds with the majority reflects a poor understanding of both democracy and society, suggesting as it does that the majority use some hegemonic form of agreement to keep the minority repressed and that it imposes some social reality that works to the detriment of students. A more cogent analysis would at least consider the role cooperation plays in the foundation of society. As Searle (1995) convincingly argued, social institutions and social facts require collective intentionality for their very existence. Institutional facts, such as money, marriage, property, and even education, cannot exist without agreement. For example, there is nothing intrinsic in the piece of paper that we use for a $20 bill that makes it count as money. Two factors give this piece of paper value and allow it to function as money: (1) the social agreement that there is such a thing as money and that these pieces of paper will count as money, and (2) the collective behavior that we demonstrate in using this piece of paper as money. Stated another way, money is whatever we agree to call and use as money. Its existence is a self-referential social reality (Searle, p. 32). In some far-fetched circumstances, a few people might decide that, to be different, they will not accept the pieces of paper that collectively society has agreed will stand for money, but that decision has no effect on the social reality of money or on the status of the pieces of paper that our collective behavior designates as money.

In the context of education, there is nothing intrinsic in the person of a teacher that gives him or her the authority to ask students to agree on what constitutes good writing, meaningful responses, and so on. Rather, this authority has been bestowed on the teacher through a licensing procedure and certain performative acts that are part of a broader social agreement pertaining to education. Both the procedure and the performative acts are designed to ensure, to whatever extent possible, that those who are licensed as teachers reflect a range of values and behaviors that are consistent with the institutional fact of education and the institutional reality of being a teacher. Although describing these values and behaviors is problematic, we can assume, fairly reasonably, that they include such factors as love of learning, desire to help others, fondness for children, dedication to freedom, and so forth. They do not include such factors as marital status, sexual orientation, fondness for gambling, or a variety of values and behaviors that are deemed personal rather than professional—and which in any event are excluded from the classroom both by convention and fiat. The questions that arise, therefore, are these: Just what values might students bring to the workshop environment that would be contrary to those accepted and endorsed by the majority? Just what are the "divisive forces of difference"?

Within the postmodern paradigm used by writers like Clark (1994), the divisive forces of difference are neo-Marxist forces at odds with individualism and democracy. History has shown, however, that the alternatives to democracy and agreement are not very palatable when they move from naive intellectual abstraction to the reality of everyday lives, as illustrated by China's Cultural Revolution. When diversity is equated with divisiveness and contrarianism, as in Clark, it erodes the polity that holds a society together and leads to educational chaos. Given free rein, the divisive forces of difference must inevitably result in students who refuse to complete their assignments—refuse even the most minimal cooperation—on the grounds that they are different from and in conflict with their teachers. Some might conclude that these divisive forces already have been unleashed in many schools.

Those teachers who believe that their job is to prepare young people for successful lives in a functioning society have little difficulty recognizing that cooperation and collaboration have social and educational benefits that make work groups an important part of the classroom experience. The act of sharing drafts of writing in progress helps students understand that mastering composition consists, in part, of becoming aware of how others respond to the work. Another part consists of revising the work on the basis of these responses. In fact, the very nature of group work builds revision into the act of writing, so that young students are more inclined to see revision as a reformulation rather than an indication of failure. In this respect, work groups can be particularly important for very young writers, who, as Scardamalia and Bereiter (1983) showed, just do not revise on their own.

Summarizing the Benefits of Work Groups

The benefits of work groups are significant; as a result, many teachers have reoriented all their teaching activities—not just writing—around groups (see, e.g., Spear, 1993). The cooperation required in group activities appears to lead students to work harder and to discover more than they do when they perform tasks on an individual, competitive basis (Crawford & Haaland, 1972). In addition, work in groups tends to improve motivation. Students who are not strongly motivated to perform are encouraged by those who are, and for all students the level of motivation seems to remain higher when participating in group work (Garibaldi, 1979; Gunderson & Johnson, 1980; Johnson & Ahlgren, 1976). Groups also provide an effective environment for interaction among mainstream and non-mainstream students (Johnson, Johnson, & Maruyama, 1983).

Work groups emphasize what too often is ignored in the daily routine of classroom assignments: Writing is a social action. This assessment in no way undermines individualism because, as a social action, writing involves the consensual engagement of writers and readers. Groups provide students with frequent opportunities to interact with one another through writing and talking about their writing, allowing for collaborative learning in the richest sense. A key to improving students' writing skills does not lie in simply having them write. They must write and receive meaningful feedback on work in progress, and then they must use that feedback to revise.

It seems difficult to overestimate the importance of peer interaction in a positive learning environment. Johnson (1980) noted that such interaction contributes significantly to "internalization of values, acquisition of perspective-taking abilities, and achievement" (pp. 156–157). Working through problems in rough drafts together and discussing ways to make writing clearer and more meaningful lead group members to internalize values and to expand their role-taking ability. Expanded role-taking ability lies at the heart of cognitive growth because it enables the formation of a repertoire of alternative mental models (Flavell, Botkin, Fry, Wright, & Jarvis, 1968; Johnson-Laird, 1983). Applying these models helps students become better, more critical readers of their own work, which in turn helps them become better writers (Hawkins, 1980; Huff & Kline, 1987).

As mentioned earlier, collaboration on projects provides students with an element of realism when they write, and there is evidence that they may actually learn more when collaborating than they do when working alone (Crawford & Haaland, 1972; Laughlin & McGlynn, 1967). Huff and Kline (1987) reported that "students working together on assignments have more success in completing them, remain motivated longer, build a sense of group purpose that provides additional motivation, tend to continue into other, higher tasks in the same subject area, and view the instructor more and more favorably as learning and success rates improve" (p. 136).

JOURNAL ENTRY

It is often said that teachers teach the way they were taught. Consider for a few moments your own experiences with working as part of a group or your lack of such experiences. How might your own training as a student influence your use of groups in your teaching?

SHARING STUDENT DRAFTS

The act of sharing drafts in progress among work group members can present certain problems. The easiest method is to have students make photocopies of their papers and pass them around to their groupmates. After every group member has read a particular draft, the group talks with the writer about the paper's strengths and weaknesses. Unfortunately, many parents resist paying for this, even though the total cost per child seldom exceeds $10 per year.

Teachers whose schools have large photocopying budgets and a relatively reliable copier can make the required copies, but few schools have such budgets. During the last few years, many schools nationwide have started imposing user fees for certain extracurricular activities, such as athletics and band, and even more recently, some have started collecting similar fees for science and computer labs. As voters continue to place limits on property-tax increases or actually reduce such taxes, the amount of money available for schools will decline, and user fees may eventually provide for photocopying. Short of paying for photocopies out of their own pockets, which could run into several hundred dollars and is not advisable, teachers have fairly limited options.

One such option involves having each writer read his or her draft to the group. This method has the advantage of aiding both reading and listening skills, and writers are often surprised at how their writing actually sounds. During a reading, they commonly discover errors in logic, support, wording, and punctuation. The problem with this method is that it is difficult for group members to offer advice for improving a paper when their percep   of it is limited to hearing it read aloud. At some point, they really need to see the paper, which allows them to reflect on it and offer better comments. When photocopies are not available, the only way to allow students to look at papers is to pair them up and have them exchange drafts. Then they make comments directly on the paper.

SOCIAL BONDING IN WORK GROUPS

Collaboration troubles some students and parents because the traditional educational model proposes that real learning is something people do on their own. Working with someone else is often seen as cheating. Nothing can be farther from the truth; teachers nevertheless have to be prepared to help students overcome perceptions and beliefs that they have formed from previous experiences in school.

In addition, it is not easy to be candid about a classmate's work when there is a fear of hurt feelings. Helping students feel more comfortable with one another eases these fears, and teachers need to emphasize that neither comments nor revising is a signal of failure. Both goals are linked to three distinct stages of development that mark collaborative learning: the *bonding stage*, the *solidarity stage*, and the *working stage*. The teacher's job is to help students through the first two stages and then to keep them on task throughout the third.

Before bonding can occur, two things need to happen more or less simultaneously. Students have to identify themselves with their particular group, and they have to feel that they are not competing with fellow group members. Establishing this group dynamic requires a degree of skill and ingenuity because, in many cases, students in writing classes are reluctant to work together in a constructive fashion. The myth of writing as a solitary act is pervasive, and students may also worry about individual grades. They need opportunities early on that will promote social bonding and a spirit of cooperation.

During the *bonding stage*, group members are adjusting to the idea that they will be working together closely for the entire term. They are trying to get to know one another, trying to establish a sense of community. During the *solidarity stage*, the group establishes a social network in response to the dominant and subordinate personalities of the members. Students recognize their strengths and weaknesses relative to their cohorts and make the adjustments necessary for effective feedback during the composing process. For example, some students may have poor organizational skills but may be excellent editors. The result is a natural division of responsibility, with members sharing equal but different tasks. Also during this stage, students experience a growing sense of confidence in their abilities to evaluate one another's papers, which makes them feel more comfortable with their roles in the work groups. During the *working stage*, students come to see fellow members as a true support group whom they can rely on for positive advice that leads to a better essay. Students often identify with their groups to the extent that individual success on an assignment tends to be viewed as group success. However, it may take most of a semester for students to reach this stage.

One technique that many teachers use to enhance the bonding process during the first stage involves asking group members to complete projects that require the participation of all members. The members are essentially forced to work together. Such projects can take the form of reports, where students investigate a topic on their campus or community and write a group report; they also can take the form of panel presentations, where members research a topic and then share what they learn with the entire class. Although most teachers think such presentations are appropriate only for older students, this technique actually is quite effective with elementary-age children, who approach it with a level of enthusiasm that middle and high school students rarely muster. Periodic checks on student progress ensure that each group member is taking part in the project and that no one is neglecting his or her responsibility to the other members.

Another effective technique involves competition. In all but a few esoteric cultures, competition serves as a healthy vehicle for bonding when it makes groups of people feel they are engaged in a mutual effort for a common cause. Thus one effective way to achieve group identity and bonding is to make it clear that the various work groups are competing with one another to produce the best possible writing. The prospect of competing with other classes tends to enhance the group dynamic even more.

In academics, unlike sports, the sheer joy of winning does not often work as a motivator, perhaps because of the higher level of abstraction involved. Grades are universal and strong motivators, but they generally fail to solidify the social bonds necessary to make collaboration succeed. In addition, there is evidence suggesting that competition between groups has little or no effect on achievement (see Johnson, Maruyama, Johnson, Nelson, & Skon, 1981). Generally, grades are individual rewards for achievement that can actually work against bonding. Therefore, for the bonding stage, it is important to consider alternative rewards that motivate students to compete seriously as groups. Ingenuity is invaluable here because the rewards vary, depending on the personal inclinations of individual teachers and the degree of freedom allowed by districts and principals.

One potential motivator worth considering, devised many years ago by Staats and Butterfield (1965), is a *token economies system*, which has been used very successfully (often with modifications) in numerous classrooms. Students earn tokens of different values for their work; these can then be used like cash to buy items provided in the classroom. This system seems to lead to significant improvements in both motivation and performance. It is also readily adaptable to work groups. Rather than individuals earning tokens, groups earn them on the basis of the quality of their projects. In classrooms where students have access to computers but where computer time is generally short owing to the number of students who have to share terminals, the most popular "item" for groups to spend their tokens on is computer time. Addison and Homme (1965) developed a system similar to the one advocated by Staats and Butterfield, but tokens were used exclusively to purchase free time, during which students could engage in a play activity. Computers and educational software, of course, now allow students to turn play activities more easily into learning activities.

Token economies seem to be extremely effective as motivators and thus probably would prove quite valuable in establishing a reward system to enhance group bonding. Yet some parents and administrators frown on token economies. They feel uncomfortable with the idea of encouraging competition among students and with the idea of linking education to what they view as classroom consumerism. In addition, token economies tend to provide extrinsic motivation to achieve, and it is widely recognized that real commitment to learning is largely the result of intrinsic motivation. Some teachers therefore avoid token economics while nevertheless using competition and rewards to solidify group identity. For example, several high school writing teachers in Los Angeles take work groups with the best records out for ice cream cones at the end of each semester. The biannual gatherings have become something of a ritual, and students work hard to stretch their limits, not so much for the ice cream but for the honor of being among a select few. Many elementary teachers get similar results with homework slips.

They give these slips to students who have done exemplary work; then on any given day, the students can use a slip to skip a homework assignment by writing the specific assignment on the slip and handing it to the teacher. The delight elementary children feel when they can skip, say, a math assignment after doing well in a writing workshop is wonderful to see.

COMPUTERS AND WORK GROUPS

Advances in technology have given teachers some amazing tools that enhance group work. Many schools have computer networks that allow students and teacher to view work in progress, which eliminates the need for photocopies. In such a network, each group member has a computer linked to the teacher's terminal. Members can work on their individual essays, but at the press of a key or a mouse they can see any one of the group's essays on all their screens. Not only can they then read the draft together, but they also can offer suggestions for revision through their own terminals so that changes appear immediately in the draft, where they can be further evaluated to determine their effectiveness. Of course, work in one group does not interfere with work in any of the other groups. Several companies, such as Lotus and Houghton Mifflin, market software that allows teacher and students to place comments in the margins of drafts they are reviewing.

In other schools, a similar network is connected to a beam projector that puts individual essays onto a large screen in the classroom. Although not quite as effective as the other system—because only one group (or the whole class) can use the screen at a time—it still offers a powerful means of sharing and commenting on drafts.

JOURNAL ENTRY

Many teachers are uncomfortable with computers and will not accept papers written on a computer. Consider you own feelings about the role computers play today in writing and how you will deal with students who want to use a computer for their work.

GRADING GROUP PARTICIPATION

Some teachers believe that students need a rubric to work effectively in groups, so they provide revision guides for each assignment. Students respond to the guide's questions after reading a draft and then return both the draft and the guide to the writer. Revision guides can take many forms, but the following sample seems typical.

Revision Guide

YOUR NAME:
PERIOD:
DATE:
AUTHOR'S NAME:

Use the following guideline to direct your reading of the rough drafts for this assignment. Answer each question fully so that the writer can use your comments to help his or her revising. Write on the back of this sheet if you need more space.

1. What point is the writer trying to make?
2. What specific details and/or support help the writer make a point?
3. Does the writer respond to all parts of the assignment? If not, what is left out?
4. Does the writer have an identifiable thesis? If so, what is it?
5. Is the paper interesting? Does it teach you anything? If so, what?
6. Is the paper well organized and easy to read?
7. Are the mechanics, like grammar and spelling, reasonably correct?
8. What do you like best about the paper?

Revision guides can be very useful. Their structure helps accustom students to working in groups by giving them concrete tasks and clear-cut goals. Also, because work groups are doing different things at different stages of a paper's development, revision guides serve to direct appropriate feedback at each point, such as idea generation, initial draft, second draft, final revision, editing, and proofing. Separate guides should be tailored specifically to each stage of a paper's development, thereby ensuring that group members make the most of each workshop.

A problem with revision guides is that they tend to constrain discussions of papers. Students are inclined to respond in writing to the questions on the guides and to say very little more. Experience shows that even when directed to use the questions as a starting point for discussion, students fail to develop a true dialogue concerning drafts.

Also, many teachers assign grades for students' participation in their work groups, and they rely on revision guides to quantify student involvement. These cases reflect an unfortunate misunderstanding of the process approach to teaching writing. The reasoning is that if the instructional emphasis is to be on process rather than product, then process ought to be graded in some way. Thus one gives a grade for each completed revision guide, for each rough draft, for each conference, and so on. In other words, formative evaluations become final, or summative, evaluations (Huff & Kline, 1987).

Although group work is extremely important to improving student writing performance, the idea of grading group participation, or more abstractly, process, can be counterproductive. Writers need high-quality feedback from group members, but grading revision guides or rough drafts emphasizes quantity. The task focus shifts significantly from having a thoughtful draft to having a draft. Because grades are generally considered individual rewards for achievement, not effort, students are likely to treat work groups as meaningless busywork if they are graded on participation. As a result, the effectiveness of group work is seriously compromised.

When students are working well in their groups, when they are engaging in critical readings of one another's drafts and then following through with revision, their finished essays will show it. It therefore seems reasonable to suggest that the grades teachers give finished essays reflect group participation better than any separate or intermediate evaluation. They should serve as sufficient indicators of group involvement. In other words, students in effective work groups should be writing better papers than those in ineffective groups. The motto in the classroom ought therefore to be: "Teach process, grade product."

The idea of student collaboration bothers some teachers who worry about authorship, but there is really no reason to be concerned that essays will no longer be the work of individual students. Real writers simply do not produce in a vacuum; they receive assistance from people whose contributions serve to make the finished piece better than it would have been otherwise. There is really little danger that the group will take over any given paper. In fact, teachers are far more likely to appropriate a student essay, giving so much guidance that the paper becomes something that a student can no longer claim as his or her own. Increasing the amount of group feedback and decreasing the amount of your feedback helps avoid appropriating students' texts.

TEACHER INTERVENTION

Writing workshops are structured to allow students to work together on their compositions, but they also are structured to allow teachers to intervene frequently during the composing process. Such intervention gives guidance during the development of an essay, which is when it is most needed.

Intervention—interrupting the writing process to provide assistance—is an important part of workshops. It normally involves circulating among the work groups as students write and revise initial drafts. Of course, it is necessary to regulate the level of intervention according to students' needs. With some students, teachers may simply want to listen to the group discussion of individual papers. Where appropriate, teachers may add their own suggestions to complement those of the students. Groups also may call the teacher over for advice or to listen to a passage that is giving them problems. With other students, teachers may want to ask to look over a draft, do a quick reading, and then offer suggestions. The aim in this method is to make fast evaluations and to provide concise, positive advice on how to improve the writing. If something is wrong with a sentence, a paragraph, or a whole paper, teachers need to point it out, but then they need to give the student concrete suggestions on how to fix it rather than simply saying, "This needs more work" or "This needs revision."

When circulating around the classroom and conferring with work groups, teachers need to be aware (at all times) of their position relative to the entire class. They should make certain to situate themselves in ways that allow them to talk to one group while monitoring the others. There is no need to be obtrusive about this, of course, but merely keeping the class in line of sight discourages students who might be tempted to become disruptive when they see the teacher's back is turned. Moreover, when talking with students about their papers, it is helpful if the teacher pulls up a seat or squats to be on an equal level. As noted earlier, the teacher in a workshop takes on the role of coach, and advice is easier to take when it comes from someone seated nearby rather than from someone towering overhead.

CLASSROOM CONFERENCES

Classroom conferences with students represent the single most effective tool available to writing teachers. Conferences usually are with individual students, but occasionally it may be necessary or desirable to confer with as many as three in a tutorial, if they happen to have similar problems. The goal in conferences is to draw out of students what their intentions are, how they hope to realize them, and what techniques they are using to do so. Teachers should listen to students talk about their papers, then read them to judge how successfully the draft matches what the students have said. Chances are that the match will not be perfect, which leads to the next step—focusing student attention on difficulties and how to overcome them.

Two factors are crucial to successful conferences. First, students have to do most of the talking. Whenever teachers talk more than students, they usually are appropriating the text. The more students talk about what they are doing, the better they will understand it. Second, students get discouraged when teachers recite a list of errors after looking at their papers. Effective writing teachers commonly focus students' attention on just a couple of points, even though much more may need work. If a student has a draft that lacks support for an argumentative claim, has no transitions between paragraphs, has numerous spelling errors, and lacks sentence variety, it is a mistake to ask him or her to tackle everything at once. Each student should work on a couple of errors until showing marked improvement. In another draft or perhaps on another assignment, the student can deal with other problems. It is also important to keep in mind that writing takes many years to master fully. Every writing teacher should remember that it takes time for anyone to become a good writer and that one conference or even one class will not change this fact.

Telling students about the rhetorical problems in their papers is one way to conduct a conference, but it may not be the most effective. What seems to work better is an approach that focuses on using questions to direct students' attention to features that need improvement. For example, if a paper lacks an easily identifiable thesis or purpose, the teacher might ask the writer to state what he or she wants to do in the paper. More often than not, students have an aim that just does not come through.

After listening to an oral statement of purpose, a teacher can ask the student to indicate where the equivalent statement is in the text. If it is not there, the student will recognize at that moment that an important part of the paper is missing. Because the writer has already formulated an oral statement of purpose, the teacher then can offer advice on just where it might best appear.

Using an approach in conferences that emphasizes questions rather than statements has the advantage of prompting students to think for themselves about what they are doing. It engages them in the processes of critical inquiry and problem solving that are essential to continued improvement in writing performance because they are discovering things about their writing for themselves. As a result, the revisions they make are their revisions, not the teacher's. In essence, this approach involves students in learning by doing, and that is the best kind of learning.

Another factor to consider is that conferences should be short. Some teachers try to limit them to 5 minutes, but that seems overly brief for most students. Ten to 15 minutes is perhaps more realistic. Even at 10 minutes per conference, it takes several class periods to meet with every student. Consequently, few elementary and high school teachers try to conduct more than three conferences per student per term, even though the benefits are so significant that they would like to conduct more.

Conferences necessarily raise questions about classroom control. Students may be tempted to drift into socializing or horseplay if they sense that their teacher's attention is focused elsewhere. For this reason, it is best to begin conferences several weeks into the term, after students have adjusted to their work groups and are used to the workshop environment. Another useful technique is to plan some structured group activities during conference days. For example, groups can exchange drafts, and then they can read one another's papers and write evaluation summaries of what they read. The papers and comments are returned at the end of the hour. Equally effective is to schedule 5-minute breaks between each conference; the breaks allow opportunities to circulate around the room and monitor group activities.

Finally, in spite of the potential difficulties alluded to in this chapter, it is important to remember that most students are kind, generous young people. Most are eager to please, and eager to do well. Most are very responsible, whenever they are asked to be. What they often lack are chances to demonstrate their responsibility. This is just as true of underachievers as it is of college-bound students. For the majority, workshops and group activities are opportunities to experiment with adulthood and to assume more responsibility.

EXPLORING KEY IDEAS

1. Sometimes, after you have set your work groups, you find that one is not working well. What should you do in this case?
2. Many students, perhaps a majority, are initially shy about sharing their writing with others. What is a key factor in helping students become more open about their work?
3. A slogan among many who orient their language arts classes around work groups is "Teach process, grade product." Nevertheless, many students will not produce a draft of an assignment if they know that the draft will not be graded. How might you deal with this situation?
4. The revision guide on page 95 offers some sample questions that students can use when reading one another's drafts. What are some other questions that you might find useful?

5. The link between critical reading and workshops is one that is not strongly articulated in most discussions of the benefits workshops provide. Why is critical reading important? How does it influence writing performance?
6. The suggestions to facilitate classroom conferences on pages 95–97 do not exhaust the possibilities. What are some other ways you can facilitate conferences without losing control of the class?

4

Reading and Writing

OVERVIEW

When children grow up in an environment that provides many encounters with written language, they frequently have an easier time learning how to read and write. Successful reading is a major factor in writing development, so major, in fact, that students who cannot read, or cannot read well, cannot write. Because students learn to read before they learn to write, understanding the mechanisms that underlie reading development is crucial to understanding writing performance.

Two views dominate the field of reading: One advocates that reading is a *bottom–up* process, the other that it is a *top–down* process. The first view usually finds application through phonics instruction, which focuses on teaching students decoding skills. Phonics approaches reading from the perspective that textual meaning is merely the sum of its visible parts: letters, syllables, and words. It emphasizes letter recognition, word accuracy, and attendance to form, with repeated error correction as the main pedagogical technique. The second view finds application through *sight–vocabulary* techniques that link whole-word recognition to context-dependent experiences. It argues that reading involves more than simply decoding letters into words and that reading is a complex activity in which readers use textual cues to generate a mental representation of meaning. Ultimately, however, reading development involves both bottom–up and top–down processes.

Schools teach students reading before writing, but over the last several years increasing numbers of teachers have recognized that reading and writing are reciprocal skills. In a growing number of elementary classrooms, teachers have given up the traditional sequence of instruction. Rather than beginning reading instruction with published texts, children write their own stories and use these as a source of reading materials. Learning how to read is thereby intimately linked with learning how to write, and the children's discourse becomes a vehicle for learning. The availability of microcomputers and printers has facilitated such programs, making it possible for students to "publish" their own texts.

At the junior high and high school levels, the relation between reading and writing remains largely traditional. For years, teachers have used works of literature as models for their students to imitate. The rationale is that by studying a model, students are able to incorporate the characteristics of professional writing into their own compositions. One of the strongest expressions of this idea is the *reading hypothesis*, which maintains that good writers are not only active readers but also at some point were self-motivated, intensive readers. A range of evidence indicates that the reading–writing relation is far from simple, and it seems certain that reading alone may not lead to improved writing performance.

THE PSYCHOLOGY OF READING

One of the more fascinating things about children is their ability to grasp complex linguistic relations without much effort, simply by experiencing them. By the time most children are about 3 years old, for example, they have made a remarkable discovery: Abstract "pictures" can represent words and convey meaning. With this discovery, they have taken the first step toward reading, and it is not long before they are able to match individual written words with the things these words signify. This is indeed no small accomplishment, given the level of abstraction involved in making the connection between symbols and the world.

A dominant characteristic of children's first efforts with language is that they use it to identify specific objects in their surroundings: "Momma" and "Dadda," of course, but also balls, pets, toys, keys, and so forth. Thus many of their first utterances are names of things.

The special significance of names is related to children's efforts to understand and control their environment. Communication requires a background of shared knowledge, and sharing names for things is fundamental to establishing such a background. Infants in the pretoddler stage are very good at conveying their wants and needs through gestures, but once they reach the toddler stage parents expect them to begin communicating through speech, and gestures are no longer as readily accepted as communicative acts. Wants and needs also become more complex. Children use the name of an object to designate the topic of the communicative act and then use gestures to convey related information (Foster, 1985). For example, a child may utter the word *ball* and reach toward it, indicating that she wants the ball.

Moreover, to know the name of something is to give it an existential reality that adults frequently take for granted but that children experience quite profoundly. "I name, therefore it is" does not seem too far-fetched in light of the fact that a world full of unknown and unidentified objects must appear chaotic. Naming begins to impose order. Most children, therefore, are excited to discover that names themselves have an existential reality in written form. The visible nature of writing confirms the identity of things in the child's world in a way that speech cannot.

Children are naturally very curious about their own names, and not long after making the connection between words and symbols, they take great pleasure in seeing their names in writing. They frequently ask their parents to write their names for them. Soon, however, they become eager to take up pen and paper themselves and, with a little help initially, write their name or even the name of a pet or a friend over and over.

Although printing their own name or that of a friend may represent a child's first true act of writing, several investigators suggested that writing begins earlier, in the form of drawing or making squiggles on a piece of paper (Graves, 1975, 1979; Gundlach, 1981, 1982, 1983; Harste, Burke, & Woodward, 1983; Vygotsky,1978). Graves (1975), for example, argued that young children use drawing as a rehearsal for writing, and certainly it is not unusual for preliterate children to combine pictures with scribbles as they compose notes for friends and relatives. When asked what a note says, they are quite happy to "read" it aloud, as though they recognize that their writing is not yet at a stage where it can be read by others. Having observed her son engage in this kind of writing activity, Bissex (1980) suggested that he used writing as an extension of both speech and drawing to help himself name and organize his world:

> As a five-year-old he was still absorbed in naming, in knowing his world by naming its parts; through his signs and labels and captions he extended this process in writing. In the next year or two, as his reasoning developed and his need to know and control the world around him [increased] ... this process was reflected in ... charts and other organizational writing. (p. 101)

Observing young children having their first experiences with the printed word can tell us quite a bit about how reading and writing develop. It appears that the ability to read and write manifest themselves at about the same time, but usually not at the same pace; language production always seems to lag behind language comprehension, even in adults.

Children have the ability to develop rudimentary reading and writing skills before starting kindergarten. Scollon and Scollon (1979) and

Heath (1981, 1983) demonstrated that parents in many cultural groups engage their children in reading activities at quite an early age, often as young as 1 month old. Parents frequently begin with picture-labeling games and bedtime stories, and it is not unusual for 2-year-olds with such experiences to manifest simple word-recognition skills.

Based on findings like these, Smith (1983) stated that "children do not learn by instruction; they learn by example, and they learn by making sense of what are essentially meaningful situations" (p. 9). On this account, he argued that children should not be taught phonics but should be taught individual words in context through a *sight–vocabulary approach*. At a supermarket, a parent might use a shopping trip to teach such words as *soup* and *shampoo*. It is Smith's belief that if a child cannot read and write by the time he or she begins school, the problem lies not in the child but in the parents, who have failed to provide meaningful reading and writing experiences. Unfortunately, this view fails to take into account the abilities and motivations of children, which range from high to low. It also implies that children are blank slates without their own unique personalities and that they are capable of any accomplishment given the right exposure. However, no matter how many meaningful reading and writing experiences devoted parents provide, children with low abilities and/or low motivation will not be reading in any substantive way by kindergarten. Even very bright children who lack motivation will not begin to show significant gains in reading until sometime in the second grade. Writing normally will not begin to develop until sometime in the third grade.

In large part, the slow pace of reading and writing skills in these early grades is developmental in nature. Rumelhart and McClelland's (1986) work in neural networks suggested, fairly convincingly, that language learning involves neurophysiological changes. As a child learns a new word, the brain constructs a neuropathway that connects the new word to other, similar words, which exist in the brain as changes in cell structure. These pathways do not emerge instantly, fully formed, but rather require an indeterminate number of repeated exposures. In the case of reading, it seems certain that the brain must develop pathways that link the sound of a given word to its symbolic form on the page as well as to the instantiations tied to experiences with the word in everyday settings.

It is also important to note that motivation to read and write in the majority of young children seldom is high. Friends and play usually are their first priorities. The brightest child will chose playing with a friend over reading an exciting book. Successful teachers recognize and accept this situation as being natural, yet they nevertheless work to make reading and writing more meaningful to children. Many teachers build free reading time into their class schedules, but few build in free writing time. Ideally, children should be able to do both.

JOURNAL ENTRY

All indicators show that reading for pleasure begins to decline when children reach middle school, and by the time they reach high school, most students just do not read for pleasure. Yet we know that reading is a crucial factor in writing well. The question is, how will you stimulate your students to read?

PHONICS

For many years now, there has been a debate regarding how people read and thus how children learn to read. The issue is *phonics*, or the sounds for which letters stand. On the one hand are writers like Flesch (1955), Fries (1962), and Mathews (1966), who argued that the best way to teach reading is through the systematic teaching of phonics. In this view, success in reading depends on accurately identifying words and the sounds of words. On the other hand are writers like Gibson and Levin (1975), Goodman (1967, 1973), and Smith (1972, 1983), who argued that successful reading is more complicated than phonics advocates recognize and that it entails predicting and synthesizing meaning on the basis of a broad range of cues, such as syntax, context, intention, and purpose.

The issues in this debate are important with respect to writing because the writer is his or her own first reader. Revisions and editing are inextricably linked to the writer's role as reader, and, quite simply, students who cannot read have no hope of writing. (This latter problem is particularly pressing in middle and high schools, where it is not unusual to have eighth-grade or even twelfth-grade students reading at a second- or third-grade level.) In addition, the phonics approach to reading has much in common with the product view of writing. All these factors suggest that how one reads affects how one writes (Beach & Liebman-Kleine, 1986; Self, 1986).

According to advocates of phonics, reading begins with the print on the page. Readers look at individual letters, combine those letters into syllables, the syllables into words, the words into phrases and clauses, and the phrases and clauses into sentences. Meaning, in this account, is determined from the meaning of individual words; these individual meanings are then summed to form the meaning of an entire sentence. In addition, individual word meanings are derived on the basis of sound.

This suggests that there is not only a direct spelling-to-sound correspondence for words but also a direct correspondence between the sound of a word and its meaning. This conceptualization of reading—going from letters to meaning— is usually referred to as an example of a *bottom–up* model of information processing.

Arguments Against Phonics

One of the most obvious shortcomings of phonics is the notion that the meaning of individual words can be derived simply on the basis of spelling-to-sound correspondences. The meaning of individual words often depends on syntax and context, not on spelling, as the word *house* in the following sentences illustrates:

1. The *house* needs new paint.
2. The *House* refused to pass the minimum-wage bill.
3. The officials asked us to *house* the refugees.

Also, there is significant research that suggests the bottom–up processing model does not depict actual language endeavors correctly (Abbott, Black, & Smith, 1985; Fodor, Bever, & Garrett, 1974; Kintsch & van Dijk, 1978; Malt, 1985; Schank & Abelson, 1977; Warren & Warren, 1970). Comprehending a sentence like (2), for example, involves knowing not just the meanings of the individual words but also something about how government operates. The meaning of *house* in this case depends on this knowledge. Thus meaning comes not from combining letters into the word (from bottom–up) but from applying knowledge of the world to this particular word (from top–down). Writers like Johnson-Laird (1983), Sanford and Garrod (1981), and Smith (1983) concluded on the basis of sentences like (1) through (3) that reading is primarily a *top–down* process.

It is reasonable to propose, in fact, that language, in general, operates primarily through top–down processes. Johnson-Laird had this proposal in mind when he suggested that top–down information processing relies on the development of mental models that describe how the world functions. Readers can distinguish the three different meanings of the word *house* in the previously mentioned sentences because they are able to construct separate mental models for each sentence. These models, developed from and elaborated through experience, necessarily are relatively general because the experiences of any two people rarely, if ever, match exactly. With a sentence like "The house needs new paint," even when the house is visible to the person producing the sentence, as well as to the person processing it, their mental models of the house may differ. Consider a scenario in which the house in question is up for sale and a potential buyer tells the owner, "The house needs new paint." The mental models for buyer and seller include a component related to money saved for the former and money lost for the latter.

In spite of the nonspecific nature of mental models, people comprehend one another because their disparate mental models are sufficiently alike that key features match across participants in a language event. Sometimes there is no match, but when this happens, the audience rejects its initial mental model and tries a different one until a match is achieved or until it gives up and classifies the discourse as incomprehensible. Smith (1972) called this process "the reduction of uncertainty" (p. 18), but perhaps a more descriptive and useful expression is *hypothesis testing*. A reader formulates certain hypotheses regarding the meaning of a text and then tests those hypotheses against the text itself.

A similar, although more complex, process occurs during the course of reading sentences, paragraphs, chapters, and so forth. When a sentence begins with the subject, readers hypothesize that a verb construction will soon follow. Likewise, the topic sentence of a paragraph prompts readers to formulate hypotheses regarding the content of the rest of the sentences in the paragraph. In the event that a verb construction does not soon follow the subject or the paragraph does not elaborate the topic sentence, readers' modeled expectations are defeated; comprehension is then very difficult.

The concept of hypothesis testing suggests that words, sentences, and longer units of discourse have significance only because readers already know a great deal about what the words and sentences mean. In this regard, most people, at one time or another, have tried to read a chapter or an article in a subject they know very little about. For some it might be physics or economics, or even something more mundane, like an insurance policy. They know the meanings of the individual words in the individual sentences, but they cannot figure out what the sentences mean. Drawing on this observation, Sanford and Garrod (1981) concluded that writing consists of supplying "a series of instructions which tell the reader how to utilize the knowledge he already has, and constantly modify this knowledge in light of the literal content of the discourse itself" (p. 8). Thus a successful writer provides appropriate instructions; an unsuccessful writer does not.

Another argument against phonics is its typical emphasis on error. Most beginning reading in the classroom is done aloud because it allows the teacher to monitor student progress. Such monitoring can be valuable if used properly; the teacher can observe a child's reading strategies and then work individually with him or her to improve comprehension. Too often, however, reading becomes merely a process of accurately pronouncing words, with the teacher correcting children when they make mistakes.

Understanding the consequences of such error correction requires noting that successful reading relies a great deal on two strategies: (1) utilizing the cues provided by syntax, context, purpose, and so forth, and (2) speed. Cues operate in a relatively straightforward fashion. Knowledge of English syntax allows native speakers to predict word functions and meaning. In a sentence that begins, "The policeman," native speakers can predict that what immediately follows probably will be a verb.

Speed, however, is often overlooked as a reading strategy, even though it is a very important part of comprehension. If reading proceeds too slowly, comprehension becomes extremely difficult. The reason lies in how the mind processes and stores information.

Cognitive psychologists currently propose that memory consists of three components: *short-term memory, working memory,* and *long-term memory*. In regard to reading, *short-term memory* is where information is stored momentarily while a person decides what to do with it. If one has no need to retain the information, it is discarded after a few seconds and it cannot be retrieved. If one decides to retain the information, however, it goes into *working memory*, which is believed to act as a processing buffer between short-term memory and long-term memory. According to most models, one part of working memory stores a limited amount of information for a limited time, while the other part processes the information for meaning. Once processing is completed, meaning is stored in *long-term memory*, often indefinitely.

Reading speed therefore is crucial to comprehension because it is related to information processing. When proficient readers read a sentence, they break it into phrases that shift very rapidly from short-term memory to working memory. The phrases are held momentarily in working memory, where they are processed into propositions that are stored in long-term memory (Shankweiler & Crain, 1986). (A proposition may be considered to be the meaning conveyed in a construction; see Lyons, 1977.)

Because short-term memory has a limited capacity, it is easily overloaded. Few people can hold more than seven bits of information in short-term memory without some deterioration. Consequently, if reading proceeds on the basis of words rather than phrases; if attention is on words rather than meaning, each word will be held in short-term memory until its capacity is reached, at which point an incoming word will displace one of those being held. This sort of overload has been demonstrated to severely impair comprehension (Clark & Clark, 1977; Malt, 1985).

To prevent an overload, information must be transferred to working memory at a rapid pace, which can be accomplished only if readers process clusters of words (phrases or clauses). Generally speaking, poor readers do not work with phrases; they work with single words. They process words one at a time, soon overloading short-term memory and thus prohibiting integration into sentence or discourse meaning (Smith, 1972). Although poor readers may be able to pronounce every word in a passage, and if queried can provide the meaning of the individual words, they are quite unable to summarize the meaning of what they have just read. They are processing words, not meaning. In this regard, Shankweiler and Crain (1986) argued that reading problems are actually working-memory problems.

Something similar occurs when children read aloud and a teacher interrupts in order to correct an error. The child's attention becomes so focused on individual words that comprehension is sacrificed to accuracy. As a result, reading speed slows, making comprehension even less likely because short-term memory becomes overtaxed, which in turn results in working-memory dysfunction.

Reading aloud without practicing the passage in advance is quite difficult. Even experienced readers make errors of various sorts, errors that Goodman (1973) termed *miscues* (also see Watson, 1985). Miscues can be classified into the following four types, listed in descending order of frequency of occurrence and with corresponding examples:

Type	*Printed Text/Uttered Text*
(1) substitution	the beautiful woman/the pretty woman
(2) omission	a cold, rainy day/a rainy day
(3) insertion	gave her a kiss/gave to her a kiss
(4) scramble	the girls left/they all left

When children read aloud, miscues are commonly seen as evidence of unfamiliarity with a word, so the child is corrected and asked to reread it. Several studies have shown, however, that most such miscues preserve the meaning of the passage, as in (1) such error correction seems of limited value (see Gibson & Levin, 1975; Weber, 1968). Gibson and Levin, for example, reported that 90% of substitution errors preserve the meaning of the text. If meaning is preserved, there seems no reason to make a correction. In the event that the miscue does not preserve meaning, some evidence suggests that children will stop and reread the passage, making the correction themselves given the chance (Smith, 1983).

In some respects teachers' corrections of reading are similar to parents' error corrections of children's speech. The two are related not only in their intent but also in their effectiveness. Clark and Clark (1977) offered an example that illustrates the typical result of a parent's attempt at correcting the speech of her child:

CHILD: My teacher holded the baby rabbits and we patted them.

MOTHER: Did you say your teacher held the baby rabbits?

CHILD: Yes.

MOTHER: What did you say she did?

CHILD: She holded the baby rabbits and we patted them.

MOTHER: Did you say she held them tightly?

CHILD: No, she holded them loosely. (p. 333)

Phonics From Another Perspective

Most of the arguments against phonics are relatively sound, and certainly they are grounded on solid research. For example, there is little question that language in general operates primarily—although not exclusively—through top–down processes rather than bottom–up. The difficulty is that the research does not appear to have been interpreted accurately with respect to children's language processing. It is not at all clear that young children rely primarily on top–down processes. Evidence against a primary reliance comes from work on language change. Children are largely responsible for language change, but until recently the mechanisms were hard to understand. It was recognized that change occurred most frequently on the level of sound (*phonemic level*), yet there was, and is, some controversy regarding the nature of the change. Is change tied to individual words, or is it tied to individual *phonemes* (sound units) without regard to lexical items (Hayes, 1992; Hoenigswald, 1978; Labov, 1980)?

In a lengthy investigation, Labov (1994) argued that change is broad based. He stated that "Sound change is a change in the phonetic realization of a phoneme, without regard to lexical identity" (p. 603). Nevertheless, the realization occurs on a word-by-word basis as children are acquiring language. As Williams (1993) and others suggested, language acquisition involves "an elaborate, interactive matching procedure that connects linguistic input and output with internalized models of reality" (p. 557). When children hear a new word uttered by their parents, they commonly repeat it aloud as they try to match their articulation with that of their parents'. Parents, in turn, commonly correct children's pronunciation to facilitate the match. Many times, however, children and parents alike have to be satisfied with an approximation, or "best fit," because the child's articulation does not exactly match that of the parents'. The principle of behavioral efficiency precludes an indefinite give and take with respect to any one word or even any set of phonemes, thus opening the door for slight variations in phonetic realizations. Once parents stop correcting errors in pronunciation, a child will accept his or her phonetic realization of a phoneme as a match and then will generalize it across lexical items.[1] The process is bottom–up. Furthermore, this process accurately describes language acquisition in general (Rumelhart & McClelland, 1986).

From this perspective, the sentences on page 104 that illustrate the operation of top–down processes are of limited value because they are not generalizable, except insofar as they show the role context plays in language and meaning, which does not have much bearing on the question of teaching phonics. Consider the following real-life scenario: A father and his 3-year-old child are seated at a park when a sea gull flies overhead. The child has never seen a *sea gull* before, but he has seen other large birds, such as eagles, ducks, and geese. Moreover, he has never heard the expression *sea gull* before. The father points to the gull and says, "Look at the sea gull." The child attempts to match the relevant utterance and produces "See girl." Both *see* and *girl* are in the child's lexicon; they are quite close phonetically to *sea gull*, so this is a reasonable attempt at achieving a match. The father corrects the child by repeating "sea gull," stressing the vowel in *gull*. The child makes another attempt and comes a bit closer. After a couple more attempts, the parent accepts the child's utterance, even though it is not an exact match. It nevertheless is a best fit that becomes established as a modified cell structure in the child's brain.

Williams (1993) suggested that meaning and language processing involve "linking words with mental representations" (p. 557). In the previous scenario, the child's phonetic representation of *gull* was linked by experience to his mental representation and to his father's mental representation. This point is key to the question of meaning because the child's best-fit articulation of *gull* was meaningful for him and for his father. Furthermore, as Labov (1994) suggested, people and language adjust to "preserve meaning in general" (p. 596). They do so by allowing

---

[1]Social factors also influence this mechanism. Children, more so than adults, are highly motivated to bond with peers, which involves a process of identification, largely through language. Hence, individual variations in phonetic realizations of phonemes will gravitate toward a mean established among peers.

a certain degree of flexibility in syntax and phonology, with the result, for example, that speakers of West Coast dialects and speakers of Southern dialects are generally able to understand one another, even though their phonetic realizations for most words are quite different.[2]

After the link is established between a mental representation and its corresponding phonetic representation, meaning is conveyed whenever the phonetic representation is invoked. Thus the articulation of *gull*, even if it does not exactly match a more generally accepted articulation of that phonetic representation, counts as signifying the appropriate mental representation in speaker and hearers. Additional encounters with utterances of *gull*, furthermore, will modify the child's existing phonetic representation, shifting it closer to the adult representation (although in some cases it will never match exactly). In the case of a word like *house*, which has more complex levels of meaning, there will be a primary mental representation signified by certain semantic features associated with a building of a certain kind used for certain purposes. The other meanings of the word must develop over time and are unlikely to be part of any child's mental representations because children below the age of, say, 10 years old, do not have any meaningful experiences with bicameral forms of government or with situations in which the noun is used as a verb. Nevertheless, when children see the words *gull* and *house* without a context, they are able to assign a meaning to these words, although the meaning is linked to the associated mental representations, which are the most generic meanings available—what Langacker (1990) referred to as *prototypical forms*. In this case, the meaning of individual words does not depend on syntax and content per se, but exists as mental representations that are drawn on to match the demands of syntax and content. Finally, the concept of hypothesis testing mentioned earlier, on this account, does indeed depend on the knowledge and experiences people bring to any language event, but all this ultimately means, is that well-read adults are capable of making richer interpretations of texts and of better exploring their complexities than are children.

A similar process is at work with respect to error corrections. Clark and Clark's (1977) report of an attempt to correct a child's tense error was discussed earlier, and the implication was that error correction fails to provide any meaningful input. In their example, the child applied the past-participle suffix to the irregular verb *hold*. Clark and Clark, like many others, argued that this example illustrates a characteristic of child-language development, in which children consistently attempt to

---

[2]Consider, for example, that the word *have* has one syllable in most West Coast dialects, but it has two syllables in many Southern dialects, so that it is pronounced as "hey-ave."

regularize irregular verbs. However, Rumelhart and McClelland (1986) showed that this error is far from consistent. Sometimes children use the regular and irregular forms correctly. Over time, with additional input, errors become fewer, indicating that some form of error correction, largely implicit modeling, has a positive effect. Excessive error correction, of course, is not desirable because it induces performance anxiety. Some error correction, on the other hand, appears to be a natural part of language—and therefore literacy—development, especially when it takes the form of natural modeling characteristic of language acquisition.

In addition, the arguments against phonics instruction fail to account adequately for the real need students have for a method of decoding words for which they have not yet established mental representations of sound-to-symbol correspondences. Teachers who rely on sight–vocabulary approaches or learning in context, as though these provide students with all the tools they need, are not recognizing the role bottom–up processes play in reading development. Indeed, any approach that relies on everyday experiences for word mastery is severely limited by the fact that such experiences do not provide a transportable decoding method on which students can depend—phonics does. Furthermore, such approaches fail to account for the numerous function words that are part of all reading activities. A trip to the supermarket is unlikely to provide any contact with the word *because*, yet a child encountering *because* in a text must be able to decode it or reading comes to a stop. Asking the teacher to prompt the word is not effective because children eventually have to read on their own (at home) to become proficient, and the teacher will not be there.

In the end, it seems that the great divide that separates phonics advocates and opponents is based on politics. Effective teachers usually use both phonics and whole-word approaches because they understand that most children need as many tools as they can get when they start reading.

CONNECTIONS BETWEEN READING SKILL AND WRITING PROFICIENCY

Teachers have long speculated on the relation between people's reading habits and their ability to write, perhaps because classroom experience shows us that good writers usually are good readers. Various scholars have attempted to explain the relation, and one of the more interesting efforts came from Krashen (1981a, 1985). He approached the question from the perspective that composition skill is similar to second language skill: Mastery requires comprehensible input over an extended time. In his view, writing skill develops on the basis of the psycholinguistic principles that govern language acquisition.

Acquiring language is different from learning it. *Acquisition* involves the unconscious assimilation of language, whereas *learning* involves the conscious mastery of knowledge about language. In the early stages of language development, children infrequently repeat sentences they hear; they tend to generate their own expressions. This phenomenon suggests that children do not learn a particularly large set of expressions or phrases that they repeat back under appropriate conditions. Instead, they seem to internalize the features of language that enable them to produce unique utterances. The process is unconscious and is based on comprehensible and meaningful input, from which a child makes generalizations regarding form, function, intention, and meaning.

Krashen (1985) proposed that writing ability is acquired through reading rather than through listening. In his view, we gain competence in writing by the same way we gain competence in oral language—by comprehending written discourse and by internalizing, after much exposure, the numerous conventions that characterize texts. He stated, for example, that "if second language acquisition and the development of writing ability occur in the same way, writing ability is not learned but is acquired via extensive reading in which the focus of the reader is on the message, i.e., reading for genuine interest and/or pleasure" (p. 23).

Krashen (1981a) called this proposal the *reading hypothesis*, and he argued the following: (a) "all good writers will have done large amounts of pleasure reading"; (b) "good writers, as a group, read and have read more than poor writers"; and (c) "reading remains the only way of developing competence in writing" (p. 9). Drawing on self-report reading surveys, he further argued that good writers are not only active readers but are also self-motivated readers who read intensively during adolescence.

The reading hypothesis is an elegant way of explaining the differences in students' writing abilities and it is entirely accurate, insofar as it proposes that reading is a crucial factor in internalizing the various conventions of written discourse. However, reading may be a necessary factor in writing skill, but it is not a sufficient factor. Many extremely well-read people are poor writers. In fact, some of the very worst writing comes from university professors, all of whom are well read. Teachers should encourage students to read and should help them discover the joy in reading and acquiring knowledge through reading, but it is a mistake to assume that in doing so they are directly helping students become better writers.

MODELS AND WRITING

Students have been studying models of good writing since the days of ancient Greece, when grammar school teachers introduced students to literature to help them improve their own language and to provide moral edification. Currently, the use of models in writing instruction remains very popular in spite of a shift over the last several years to a process approach that emphasizes students' own writing rather than that of professionals (Johnson & Louis, 1985). Models therefore figure significantly in writing instruction in junior and senior high schools, as well as in colleges.

There is no question that students must study models to become successful writers. Without models, they have few means of understanding the conventions that govern written discourse. Determining what constitutes an effective model, however, is a point of real controversy (Lindemann, 1993a; Tate, 1993). It is not surprising that most writing teachers assume that literary models are best; after all, they are trained in literature and have an intrinsic love of great books. But, even in ancient Greece, the models were largely literary, at least at the initial levels, with Homer esteemed above all others. Historically, the rationale for using literary works has rested on the notion that literature represents the very best writing that exists, which automatically makes it ideal for teaching good writing. More recently, some teachers have justified literary models on the grounds that the study of literature entails high-level critical thinking that is transportable to a range of intellectual activities. Others have suggested that literature introduces students to humanistic values, whatever they might be, that are necessary for a civilized life (see Green, 1992).

These rationales ultimately are unsatisfactory. The goal of getting students to imitate works of literature in any explicit way has failed. If it had not, written language would not have changed, and readers would have a hard time differentiating between the writing of, say, Melville and Hemingway because both would use similar language. Although works of literature generally convey solid values, their civilizing influence is questionable. Compulsory education and near universal teaching of literature in the Western world has done nothing to reduce crime rates, child abuse, or war.

A more viable rationale for using literary models is rooted in motivation. Many years ago, Mano (1986) reported a case study of a teenage boy—a mediocre student and poor writer—who went to see *Star Wars* and it changed his life. He saw the movie again and again, and he determined that he wanted to write screenplays just like *Star Wars*. He began using the library to get books about writing, and he wrote on his own. His grades improved, as did his writing. Literary models work in much the same way; they have the potential to touch students in ways that make them want to produce writing that has a similar effect on others (see Albano, 1992). The resulting motivation is remarkably strong. Unfortunately, the number of students who are touched in this way proves to be quite small, which makes the reliance on literary models pedagogically unsound.

In addition, there is a tendency among those who use literary models to confuse object with artifact. Students and teachers talk about the model, discussing such features as theme, character, setting, plot, and so forth. One result is that the focus of the class or the lesson is on reading rather than writing. Students clearly need to practice reading and writing, not just reading. Moreover, at the end of the discussion teachers ask students to write a paper about the work, and a few days later they collect an assortment of essays. What is missing is a model of an effective literary analysis paper and any meaningful instruction in how to go about writing literary criticism. The work of literature—the artifact—has become the object, although the true object of instruction should be the critical essay. The piece of literature should simply be a tool for helping students focus on the object. On this account, the attention to the literary model could be justified only if students were being prepared to write something similar to the model, which (with the possible exception of some poetry) is never the case.

Criticisms such as these prompted numerous advocates of process pedagogy to abandon professional models entirely and replace them with students' own writing. There were other factors underlying this shift: an effort to distance the new rhetoric from literature and literature faculty; an effort to validate and empower students; an effort to strengthen the sense of community in individual classes; and an effort to focus on writing rather than reading. These are worthwhile goals, but this approach was always open to criticism as well—the most damaging, perhaps, being the assertion that asking students to use one another's writing as a model is the equivalent of asking the blind to lead the blind. Almost as troubling was the level of student resistance to the effort. Models show students what they should do, but they also show what they should avoid, and the negative comments that inevitably arise during a discussion of any given model are hard for students to take. As a result of these criticisms and of the pressure postmodern rhetoricians have exerted to shift composition back to literary moorings, large numbers of teachers who had used student models during the height of the new rhetoric period returned to professional, and usually literary, models. This is an unfortunate turn of events insofar as students have few opportunities to study a variety of genres. Where in literary models are interpretations and argument, the very basis for most writing beyond public school?

Integrating Reading and Writing

If one were to use a single word to describe literacy instruction in most schools, it would probably be *sequential*. Traditionally, students work on developing oral skills, then go on to reading, which forms the foundation for writing. Following the sequence, beginning writing instruction has tended to use a bottom–up approach: Students practice writing the alphabet, then words, then sentences, then paragraphs, then essays.

Although a sequenced approach may be orderly, it is not pedagogically sound because it assumes that the language modes are distinct and different. Yet all language activities are essentially similar; utterances and texts are alike in a fundamental way. Speech may tend to be interactional and writing may tend to be transactional, but both are actions and both are used to make requests, supply information, make assertions, and ask and answer questions.

Functional similarity suggests a reciprocal relation, that improving students' skills in one area affects their skills in another. In regard to language, it is indeed the case that students with good oral skills tend to be good readers and writers (Loban, 1976). But improving skills in one area has a chance of improving skills in another only if children are given opportunities to practice both skills in conjunction. Separating speech, reading, and writing into a sequence greatly limits these opportunities.

As more and more teachers have recognized the importance of an integrated approach to language instruction, there has been a shift—admittedly modest in some districts—away from the traditional language arts sequence. An emphasis on a process approach to composition has made teachers aware that reading what one has written has a positive influence on both activities. In many classrooms, teachers have abandoned language arts sequencing for a more integrated curriculum, in which activities draw on students' own experiences and their linguistic and rhetorical knowledge. Through big book programs and whole-language programs, students have opportunities to benefit from effective integration of activities.

JOURNAL ENTRY

Reflect on ways you might integrate reading and writing activities in a
language arts class.

READING AND WRITING WITH COMPUTERS

Integrated approaches to reading and writing instruction have been
enhanced by the growing availability of computers, the software that
makes them function as word processors, and printers. Often working
in small groups, children develop oral narratives that they then type
into a computer or word processor. If the classroom also has a printer,
students can "publish" their papers with ease, thereby making it possible to share their writing in a meaningful way. With more sophisticated
equipment, students can even add illustrations to their work, a feature
that younger children especially appreciate.

Another advantage to computers is that they allow writers to edit
their drafts with ease, inserting or deleting words, sentences, and
paragraphs at the touch of a button. Word processors also allow writers
to reorganize without much effort; any element of the text can be moved
and inserted elsewhere. Students can run spell check, which helps them
learn correct spelling.

When word processors initially became widely available in classrooms, few teachers saw their potential for integrating reading and
writing; they were regarded primarily as a means of improving writing
through drafting and revision. At secondary and college levels, computers continue to be viewed exclusively as a means of making revision less
onerous.

By and large, the early expectations teachers had concerning improved revision and improved writing have not been fully realized. A
range of studies showed that the mere act of using a computer to produce
a text did not affect the quality of students' writing, except insofar as a
printed text is much easier to read than one produced by hand (Beesley,
1986; Gilbert, 1987; Hawisher, 1987). In addition, many teachers will
not accept student papers that are not written in cursive, and they
actually force students to copy a printed paper by hand. The reasoning
in these instances is unclear, but the consequences are not: The affected
students are certain to resent the teacher and are equally certain to have
a negative view of writing.

Currently, teachers and administrators have shifted their attention
to the Internet, claiming that if students do not have access, they simply

will not have an adequate education. So far, however, the Internet is little more than a gigantic catalogue where everyone from universities to car dealerships hawk their wares, and it is difficult to determine what value it has to children who cannot read and write. The ease with which priorities get confused is illustrated in numerous inner-city schools that have a million dollars in computer equipment but that do not have enough textbooks for students.

EXPLORING KEY IDEAS

---

1. During the last decade, reading scores in California have plummeted, and many critics blame the widespread adoption of whole-language learning in context in the state's schools. Is there any controversy in your community about how to teach reading? If so, what are people saying?
2. Reading aloud seems to improve both reading and writing skills. Given the information in this chapter, can you suggest some reasons why?
3. If, as indicated, extensive reading is such an important factor in becoming a good writer, how do we account for the fact that so many people with extensive reading histories are poor writers?
4. You know that you cannot have your tenth-grade students read Shakespeare and then write a paper about *Romeo and Juliet* without a model of an effective literary analysis. The question is, where are you going to find one that your tenth-graders can understand?
5. What is the ever-present danger inherent in using models?
6. At many schools, students use computers for math and reading lessons, and increasingly, they use them for research on the Internet. Nevertheless, large numbers of teachers and their principals will not allow students to write their papers on computers but instead require them to write them by hand. As a new teacher who believes in technology, how might you respond to your colleagues who take this position?

5

Grammar and Writing

Grammar is a system for describing language. Some people believe that it also constitutes a theory of language. This chapter provides a brief discussion of some of the characteristics and goals of different grammars and offers an analysis of the relation between grammar and writing. The aims are twofold: to help teachers gain a better understanding of what grammar is about and to enable them to evaluate the role of grammar instruction in their writing classes.

Perhaps the majority of parents and teachers believe that teaching writing entails teaching grammar. Consequently, grammar has played a significant role in language classes for generations. The grammar taught in most schools is *traditional grammar*, which has roots in ancient Greece but is largely based on Latin. Traditional grammar is fundamentally prescriptive; its principal concern is the question of language correctness. It operates on the assumption that literary language is better than spoken language, and thus its focus often is literature (see Lehmann, 1983; Leiber, 1975; Lyons, 1970; Scargill & Penner, 1966). Because everyday language differs from the language of literature, traditional grammar necessarily views speech as inherently inferior to writing (Lyons, 1970).

Around the beginning of the 20th century, a number of language scholars began to recognize that traditional grammar failed them when they tried to describe the language of certain American Indian tribes. They were forced to develop a new grammar to meet their needs—a grammar based on phrases rather than on parts of speech, a grammar that was descriptive rather than prescriptive. The new grammar was named *constituent analysis*, but it later became known as *phrase-structure grammar* (Bloomfield, 1933).

In the mid-1950s, a young linguist named Noam Chomsky argued that phrase-structure grammar failed to account for a variety of language features, such as passive sentences, and in 1957, he published a

118

book titled *Syntactic Structures;* it was revolutionary in scope and developed a new grammar that Chomsky called *transformational-generative grammar.* Chomsky's grammar had a significant impact on every facet of language study, and as chapter 1 indicated, it also had a significant influence on rhetoric and composition.

Although these three grammars are different in many respects, they have an important characteristic in common. Each is based on the assumption that language is governed by a system of rules. In fact, these rules form individual grammars. However, work in cognitive science over the past decade or so suggests that language is not governed by rules at all, but rather it is an associative process. Examining the consequences of an associative, as opposed to a rule-governed, model of grammar and language provides interesting insights into some of the factors that influence writing.

Throughout these explorations of grammar, it is important to keep in mind that all principled studies on the relation between grammar instruction and writing have shown that teaching grammar has no measurable effect on writing performance. Such findings seriously call into question the role grammar currently plays in writing classes.

WHY IS GRAMMAR IMPORTANT?

Most English and language arts instructors are required to teach grammar at some point, yet few credential programs require them to take a grammar course as part of their degree. As a result, large numbers of newly credentialed teachers have to rely on what they remember from their own days in elementary or junior high school for their grammar lessons. The situation is made more acute by the fact that administrators and parents often judge what students are learning about language on the basis of what they consider to be "the basics": nouns, verbs, prepositions, adjectives, and adverbs.

The combination of expectations and curriculum requirements makes a compelling case for the importance of grammar, but there are other factors. When students are discussing writing (as well as reading), their work is far more efficient if they and their teachers share a common vocabulary. Punctuation, for example, is easier to understand when teachers can explain that a comma and a conjunction combine two independent clauses. Students who do not know what a conjunction and a clause are, however, will be at a disadvantage.

It is also worth remembering that who people are and what they do are largely determined by language. People define themselves and are defined by others through language. Daily interactions are based on language, as are careers. All class work involves language. Knowing as

much as possible about something so integral to our lives may not help
anyone have better interactions or a more successful career, but it can
provide insight into the mechanisms at work, which in turn can offer us
greater understanding of ourselves and others. Language is highly
complex, and it is an area of endless discovery and exploration. Even
seemingly simple sentences, such as "It is me," present complexities that
few people consider but that can be fascinating. Grammar is the tool
people use to explore the complexities of language, and without that tool
they are limited to superficial analyses of what is nothing less than the
foundation of human culture.

PRESCRIPTION AND DESCRIPTION

Grammar is commonly thought of as "the parts of speech" or "rules for
putting sentences together correctly." Yet such expressions are characteristic of traditional grammar and are not particularly relevant to other
grammars, which tend to focus on theoretical concerns of language or
on how best to describe language. On a fundamental level, grammar
supplies terms for labeling the various components of language, such as
nouns, verbs, and adjectives; this is the *categorical level*. Grammar also
provides a means of describing relations among sentence components,
such as subject, predicate, and object; this is the *relational level*. We are
not bound by terms like *subject*, however. We could reasonably develop
a variety of different grammars with different component labels. Case
grammar, developed in the late 1960s, exemplifies some of the possibilities. Rather than *subject*, it uses the term *agent* to describe one set of
relations between a noun that initiates the action of a sentence and the
verb. In "Reina ate the sandwich," for example, Reina is the agent.

   Arguments for correctness are often tied to the relational level.
Many years ago there was a popular television commercial that depicted
a ruggedly handsome man putting up a billboard with the slogan
"Winston tastes good like a cigarette should." Just as he finished, a frail,
stodgy fellow, wearing a bow tie and probably looking a bit like a college
English professor, approached and voiced his outrage at the "ungrammatical" slogan. In a scathing tone, the "professor" told the billboard
man: "That should be 'Winston tastes good *as* a cigarette should!'"

   The grammatical aspect of the commercial escaped many people
because informal English dominates most lives. In the slogan, the word
like, which is a preposition, was used as a subordinating conjunction; in
this case, it was substituted for the conjunction *as*. The fellow in the bow
tie was faulting the use of a preposition as a subordinating conjunction.

This usage generally does not occur in formal English, especially writing, although many people make this substitution in informal conversations. As the language situation becomes more formal, those who know the distinction between *like* and *as* are inclined to shift to a more formal level (or register) of discourse, not because it is better but because under such conditions it is more appropriate. The situation influences speakers to use prepositions as prepositions and subordinating conjunctions as subordinating conjunctions, without mixing.

This observation is commonplace in linguistics, a field in which scholars believe that the ability to describe language use is fairly important. From a linguistic perspective, the sentence from the commercial is not ungrammatical at all. It does, however, illustrate a widespread pattern of *usage* characteristic of people in certain situations or from certain educational or socioeconomic backgrounds. No value judgment is assigned to this usage because the focus is on describing the way people actually use language.

But not everyone accepts differences in circumstances as being grounds for variation in register. For such people, there is a value judgment: "Winston tastes good like a cigarette should" is simply incorrect grammar and is a corruption of the language. They see grammar not only as a way to describe relations among sentence components but also as a way to prescribe how those components ought to fit together to form sentences.

The underlying tension between descriptive and prescriptive approaches to language has its source in different perceptions of language and grammar. Those people who prescribe have internalized a standard or model of correctness by which speech and writing (and thus the speaker and the writer) are judged. This standard necessarily is fixed, and the goal is to prevent deviations. By the same token, those people who describe are committed to change and diversity. An absolute standard is replaced with a scale of appropriateness conditions on which a given utterance or a given piece of writing is weighed in relation to its context. Any analysis of the cigarette commercial therefore seems to evoke different theories of language.

JOURNAL ENTRY

What was your experience with grammar in public school? Chances are that you are an English or an English Education major, and if you are going into teaching, you will be asked to teach grammar. But just how much grammar do you know? Have you taken a grammar course since public school?

TRADITIONAL GRAMMAR

School grammar is traditional grammar, which focuses on prescription and which is based on Latin. It is concerned primarily with correctness and the categorical names for the words that form sentences. The idea is that students who speak or write expressions such as "He don't do nothin" would modify their language to produce "He does not do anything," if only they knew a bit more about grammar. Grammar instruction may begin as early as third grade and may end as late as twelfth grade, but for many children it is limited to one or two classes in middle and high school. Regardless of the students' grade level, the instruction follows the same routine, with students using workbooks or handouts to complete exercises that ask them to identify nouns, verbs, adjectives, adverbs, and so forth.

Handbooks and exercises are not recent phenomena. Chapter 1 mentioned the role handbooks played in popularizing rhetoric during the classical period. In the Roman Empire and in the late Middle Ages, grammatical treatises became manuals on how to write, and great Latin masters such as Virgil were used as models of correctness because Latin was considered the normative language. Thus the prescriptive nature of traditional grammar has a long history. However, during the Middle Ages (again as noted in chapter 1), scholars made a significant shift in rhetoric when they connected grammar and logic. The aim was to make language more orderly by linking it to the rules and principles established for logic. Violation of these principles was seen as not only incorrect but also illogical.

During the 18th century, two other factors increasingly influenced work in grammar: prestige and socioeconomic status. This change resulted largely from the spread of education and economic mobility, which brought large numbers of people from the middle class into contact with the upper class. In England, for example, although both upper-class and middle-class people spoke the same language, there were noticeable differences in pronunciation, form, and vocabulary—what we term *dialect*—much like the differences we notice in the United States between speakers from Mississippi and California. Because the upper-class dialects identified one with prestige and success, mastering the upper-class speech patterns became very desirable, and notions of grammar became more normative than ever.

Language scholars during this time suffered from a fundamental confusion that clearly had its roots in the notion of linguistic decay first formulated by the Greeks. They noted that well-educated people wrote and spoke good Latin, whereas the less educated made many mistakes.

Failing to see that reproducing a dead language is essentially an academic exercise, they applied this observation to modern languages and concluded that languages are preserved by the usage of educated people. Those without education and culture corrupt the language with their deviations from the established norm. Accordingly, the discourse forms of books and upper-class conversation represented an older and purer level of language from which the speech of the common people had degenerated (Lyons, 1970).

From this analysis, a significant part of traditional grammar is the distinction between what some people do with language and what they ought to do with it. The chief goal appears to be perpetuating a historical model of what supposedly constitutes proper language. Prescription, however, demands a high degree of knowledge to prevent inconsistency, and few people have the necessary degree of knowledge.

One of the more interesting examples of widespread inconsistency involves the verb form *be* and *case*, that feature of nouns and pronouns that marks them as being subjects (nominative case) or objects (objective case). English no longer changes nouns according to their case, but it continues to change pronouns, as in the following:

1. *I* stopped at the market.
2. Fritz asked *me* a question.

I is the subject of Sentence 1, and it is in the nominative case, whereas *me* is an object in Sentence 2, so it is in the objective case. Traditional grammar therefore labels as ungrammatical any instance in which an objective case pronoun is in the subject position or in which a nominative case pronoun is in the object position, as in the following sentences:

3. * *Me* stopped at the market.
4. * Fritz asked *I* a question.

Sentences 3 and 4 rarely, if ever, occur among native speakers, but a variety of factors make people confused when there is more than one noun or pronoun in any given construction, with the result that sentences like the following occur regularly, even among well-educated people:

5. Fred handed out invitations to Fritz, Macarena, Raul, and *I*.
6. Fritz, Macarena, Fred, and *me* went into the city to see the new art exhibit.

Now consider a common situation in which *be* serves as a *linking verb*, a special kind of verb that links the subject to either a noun phrase or an adjective phrase, as in:

7. Fritz was *the winner*.
8. Fritz was *tired*.

In sentences like Sentence 7, the word *was* is the equivalent of an equals sign, a fact that led those who espoused a relation between grammar and logic to propose that such sentences can be expressed symbolically as $x = y$, where x represents the subject and y represents the noun construction after the linking verb. The logical equality of x and y requires that they share the same case, which means that both *Fritz* and *the winner* are in the nominative case.

This creates a problem for an everyday expression:

9. It's me.

The pronoun is in the objective case, and traditional grammar therefore labels this sentence as being both ungrammatical and illogical. Nevertheless, the number of people who actually use the correct form is quite small:

10. It's I.

The point here is straightforward. Teachers who criticize sentences—similar to Sentence 6—for being ungrammatical need to make certain that they do not produce sentences like Sentence 9. If they do produce such sentences, they are inconsistent and are giving mixed signals to students.

Perhaps one of the foremost difficulties with traditional grammar is that it does not fit English very well. English is a Teutonic language and is not based on Latin. English tenses illustrate part of the problem. Even in the most accurate discussions, traditional grammar proposes that English has three tenses: past, present, and future. However, English has only two: past and present. The future in English is usually signified through the auxiliary *will*.[1] On the other hand, Latin and Latin-based languages such as French and Spanish indeed have all three tenses. Although published by major companies such as St. Martin's Press, Prentice-Hall, and HarperCollins, the handbooks that teachers use to study grammar are written by English teachers rather than linguists, and they manage not only to perpetuate traditional grammar but also to get concepts like tense totally confused, with predictable consequences. These books offer a great deal of useful information, but they nevertheless fail to differentiate between *tense*—a change in the verb

---

[1]The future (in English) actually can be signified in several different ways. Consider the following sentences: "Macarena is jumping tomorrow"; "Fritz can leave in the morning"; "Raul is going to go to the mountains next week"; and "Fred swims on Saturday." Each has a different verb form, but each indicates a future action.

stem to mark the time at which an action occurred—and *aspect*—a verb form that indicates the duration or ongoing nature of an action, as in progressive and perfect. Consider the verb *jump*. The present tense is simply *jump*, whereas the past tense is *jumped*. The future verb form is *will jump*. *Is jumping* and *has been jumping*, progressive and perfect forms, respectively, do not signify different tenses, however, but different aspects. Nevertheless, handbooks treat progressive and perfect forms as tenses, with the result being that they manage to multiply tenses prodigiously. Although there are only 3 possibilities of tense in any language, handbooks propose as many as 16 for English.

JOURNAL ENTRY

Has anyone ever corrected your language? If so, how did it make you feel? Is there any lesson in your experience that you can apply to your students?

PHRASE-STRUCTURE GRAMMAR

Until the 19th century, Latin grammar was deemed universally applicable to all languages, not just to English and related European tongues. Contact with exotic languages such as those spoken by Native Americans, however, presented insurmountable problems for traditional grammar that led scholars to replace it with a new grammar that was descriptive rather than prescriptive and that focused on phrases rather than individual words. This new grammar came to be called *phrase-structure grammar*.

The Native American tribes were more or less ignored after the period of the great Indian wars, but during the last years of the 19th century, they became the focus of scholarly attention as anthropologists like Franz Boas came to recognize that the distinctive characteristics of these indigenous people were quickly vanishing. Researchers began intensive efforts to record the details of their cultures and languages.

Some records already existed, made years earlier by missionaries, but it became increasingly clear during the beginning of the 20th century that these early descriptions failed to record the languages adequately. In fact, in his introduction to the *Handbook of American Indian Languages*, Boas (1911) stated that the descriptions were actually distorted by the attempt to impose traditional grammar on languages for which it was simply inappropriate.

The issue of tense again provides an interesting illustration. English grammar distinguishes between past tense and present tense, but Eskimo and some other related languages do not. In Eskimo, "The husky was running" and "The husky is running" would be the same. As more data were collected, the number of such incompatibilities grew. Within a few years, it became apparent that the goal of traditional grammar, prescription based on a literary model, was out of place in the study of languages that lacked a written form.

Led by Boas, and later by Bloomfield (1933), anthropologists and linguists abandoned the assumptions of traditional grammar and adopted the view that every language is unique, having its own structure and grammar. Known as the *structuralist view*, this approach and the grammar that grew out of it saw the objective and scientific description of languages as a primary goal.

Phrase-structure grammar dominated American language study for many years. Students completing their doctorate in linguistics, for example, commonly spent time on reservations studying aspects of tribal languages as part of their graduate work. Moreover, it remains in wide use around the world, although in the United States it was supplanted in the early 1960s by transformational-generative grammar, which is discussed in the next section (Harris, 1993).

A detailed analysis of phrase structure is beyond the scope of this book, but it is important to note that its emphasis on description means that questions of correctness, in keeping with arbitrary grammar rules, are not germane to analysis. What matters is usage. On this account, grammaticality judgments are linked to attested utterances; this has the effect of focusing on word order in naturally occurring expressions. Native speakers seldom violate word order in any egregious way. In English, the dominant word-order pattern is subject–verb–object (SVO). Other languages have different dominant patterns. Hebrew, for example, follows a verb–subject–object (VSO) pattern and Japanese follows subject–object–verb (SOV). To violate acceptable word order in English, a person generally would have to produce a sentence such as:

11.   Dog man the at barked.[2]

This perspective means that according to phrase-structure grammar, Sentences 12 and 13 are grammatical, whereas according to tradi-

---

[2]Less serious violations occur with some regularity. For example, English allows for movement of particles from their verb to a position behind the object noun phrase, as in the following sentences in which *up* is the particle:
- Macarena looked up the number.
- Macarena looked the number up.

Movement behind the object noun phrase is optional. However, if the noun phrase is a pronoun, the movement is obligatory. Thus, "Macarena tied him up" is grammatical, whereas "Macarena tied up him" is not. Nevertheless, speakers occasionally utter sentences like the latter, violating this particular word-order pattern and producing an ungrammatical sentence. The mechanisms underlying this error are discussed later.

tional grammar, Sentence 13 is ungrammatical:

12.   I saw Harry last night.

13.   I seen Harry last night.

Phrase-structure grammar developed a notation system for writing grammar rules that makes it easier to describe sentences and their constituent parts. This system is based on the perception that sentences have subjects and predicates, subjects consist of noun phrases, and predicates consist of verb phrases. Thus the first rule of phrase-structure grammar states that a sentence, S, can be rewritten as a noun phrase (NP) and a verb phrase (VP) (as indicated), where the arrow means "is rewritten":

$S \rightarrow NP\ VP$

This grammar rule, along with supplemental rules for the components of noun phrases, verb phrases, and so forth, allows for a detailed description of the language. For example, noun phrases consist of nouns plus determiners (such as *the, a,* and *an*) and any adjectives. Verb phrases consist of verbs plus any modifiers and any noun phrases that represent objects. For a sentence such as Sentence 14, phrase structure provides the following grammar rules to describe the structure of the sentence:

14.   The woman kissed the man.

$S \rightarrow NP\ VP$

$NP \rightarrow det\ N$

$VP \rightarrow V\ NP$

$det \rightarrow the$

$N \rightarrow (man,\ woman)$

$V \rightarrow kissed$

Each level of this analysis is called a *phrase-structure rule,* and the result is a grammar for this particular sentence. To make the rules more general so they can describe more sentences, it is necessary to make changes in the rules, expanding them to include prepositional phrases, additional determiners and other function words, and modifiers. Thus the range of nouns and verbs would include all nouns and all verbs, not just *man, woman,* and *kissed.*

Phrase-structure grammar is superior to traditional grammar because it is not prescriptive and because it provides a more accurate analysis of language. In addition, phrase-structure grammar developed conventions that allow most people, especially students, to understand better how the various parts of a sentence work together. Traditional grammar relies on Reed-Kellogg diagrams for analyzing sentences. These are horizontal figures with various types of lines whose shape indicates the functional relation of any given part. Thus subjects are identified by one type of line, predicates by another, and subordinate clauses by yet another. Students commonly spend so much effort figuring out what the lines mean and then remembering them that they have little mental energy left over for understanding the construction of any sentence they have to analyze.

The diagramming convention in phrase-structure grammar draws on the generalization just noted—that the basic sentence pattern in English is noun phrase plus verb phrase. It involves using a *tree diagram* to depict how phrases are related within a sentence. Using Sentence 14 as an example, the tree diagram is depicted in Fig. 5.1.

This diagram gives us more information than a traditional diagram. It shows graphically that the sentence is composed of two constituents, the noun phrase and the verb phrase. It also shows which elements compose these constituents. Moreover, the object of the sentence is dominated by the verb phrase that forms the predicate. Not only is this system more descriptive, but most students also find it more logical.

Another superior feature of phrase-structure grammar is related to the fact that natural languages (i.e., English), as opposed to artificial languages (e.g., mathematics and symbolic logic), are inherently ambiguous. That is, they convey two or more possible interpretations simultaneously, as in Sentence 15:

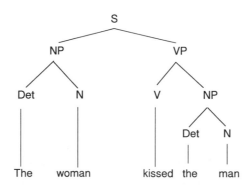

FIG. 5.1. Tree diagram for *The woman kissed the man.*

15. Fritz put the toy in the box on the shelf.

There are two possible interpretations of this sentence. In one, the toy is already in the box; in the other, it is not.

Sentence 16 illustrates another sort of ambiguity:

16. Old men and women are interesting conversationalists.

In one interpretation, the adjective *old* modifies both *men* and *women*; in the other, it only modifies *men*.

In Sentences 15 and 16, the linear sequence of the words does not determine the phrase structure of the constituents. That is, simple word order does not indicate what goes with what, whether the toy is already in the box or not, whether both the men and the women are old or not. However, traditional grammar is based on linear order and cannot disambiguate Sentences 15 and 16 or those that are similar. Yet phrase-structure grammar can, through what is known as the *bracketing convention*.

Phrase-structure bracketing is based on mathematical bracketing and operates in the same way. In the expression $a\ (b + c)$, for example, the sum of b and c is multiplied by a. That is, a applies equally to both b and c. On this basis, Sentence 15 has two bracketed phrase structures, each corresponding to the respective interpretations possible in this sentence:

15a. (Fritz) (put (the toy in the box) (on the shelf.))))
15b. (Fritz) (put (the toy) (in the box on the shelf.))))

This analysis shows that linear structure—simply categorizing as it does the parts of the sentence—is not necessarily a reflection of phrase structure, which captures relations important to understanding meaning. Because traditional grammar lacks this ability to disambiguate, linguists generally have concluded that phrase-structure grammar is more powerful than traditional grammar when it comes to description and analysis.

The tree diagrams in Figs. 5.2, 5.3, 5.4, and 5.5 illustrate the analysis of several different sentence types.

TRANSFORMATIONAL-GENERATIVE GRAMMAR

Transformational-generative grammar is synonymous with Noam Chomsky, who proposed it as an extension of and an alternative to phrase-structure grammar in his book *Syntactic Structures* (1957). Since 1957, transformational-generative grammar has gone through many changes, and the current version, known as Extended Standard

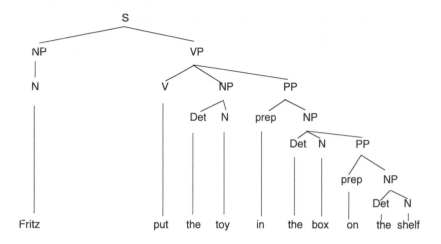

FIG. 5.2. Tree diagram for *Fritz put the toy in the box on the shelf.*

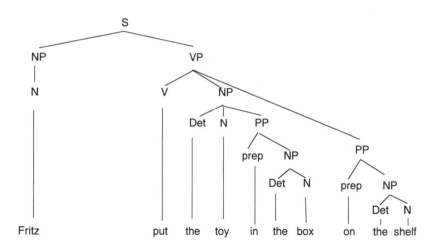

FIG. 5.3. Another interpretation of *Fritz put the toy in the box on the shelf.*

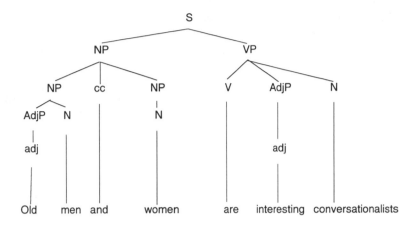

FIG. 5.4. Tree diagram for *Old men and women are interesting conversationalists*.

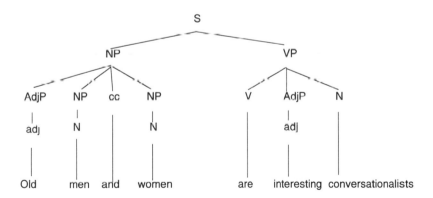

FIG. 5.5. Another interpretation of *Old men and women are interesting conversationalists*.

Theory (EST), has only a few features in common with the original (Chomsky, 1957, 1965, 1972, 1975, 1979, 1980, 1981, 1986, 1988, 1992). It is difficult to overestimate Chomsky's influence on modern language study. His work in linguistics is generally considered revolutionary. In *Syntactic Structures*, Chomsky argued that phrase-structure grammar was inadequate because it failed to explain and describe simple sentences and because it failed to provide a theory of language. In other works, he explored a wide range of linguistic features, particularly the connection between language and mind, but underlying it all is his abiding interest in grammar.

Chomsky's idea that a grammar should provide a theory of language is important, and in many respects it was novel. A *theory* is a model that attempts to describe a given phenomenon regardless of situation. For example, the theory of gravity proposes that gravity is a force associated with the mass of objects; the more mass an object has, the stronger its gravitational attraction. This theory describes equally well the operation of gravity on Earth and the operation of gravity on the Moon; it is not limited to earthly observations. Phrase-structure grammar was based on a body, or corpus, of sentences for a particular language. The corpus typically was collected through field studies in which structuralists spent time observing the speakers of a language and recording a wide range, although finite number, of its sentences. The emphasis on observation and on methods for compiling a corpus reflected the structuralist orientation away from notions of universal grammar. Stated another way, the focus was on languages rather than language. Consequently, phrase-structure grammar is highly situation-specific, a result, in part, of structuralists' negative experiences with traditional grammar.

Although trained as a structuralist, Chomsky disagreed with many of the principles of structuralism, but the orientation toward empiricism and the rejection of any notion of a universal grammar were particularly problematic for him because they led to a general lack of theory.[3] It should be noted that structuralists never were particularly concerned with theory, so when Chomsky criticized phrase-structure grammar on this ground, he was being a bit unfair. Nevertheless, in his view, reliance on a corpus was fundamentally unsound because it limited what one could know about language. He argued that the number of possible sentences in any language is infinite because language allows for endless expansion, much in the way that math does. There is no largest number because no matter how high one counts, it is possible to add

---

[3]The scope of Chomsky's influence is evident even in the term *phrase structure*. Structuralists called their grammar *immediate constituent analysis*. Chomsky renamed it *phrase-structure grammar*, and the new name stuck (Harris, 1993).

another number to it, thereby making it even larger. It is likewise possible to add a modifier to a noun or a verb and create a new sentence with a new meaning, so that any corpus can never be complete. Chomsky argued that a grammar that concentrates on describing simply a list of attested sentences, even a very long one, will be concerned with only a small portion of the language. The grammar will account for only the sentences in the corpus, and it will not account for all the possible sentences a speaker of the language can produce. It is the equivalent of having a theory of gravity that applies only to the earth.

By criticizing the structuralist reliance on method, Chomsky laid the foundation for a powerful argument: A viable grammar is only one that provides universal rules that describe the sentences people produce and all of the sentences that they potentially can produce. It must have a "generative" component, which Chomsky (1957) characterized as "a device of some sort for producing the sentences of the language under analysis" (p. 11).[4] Thus Chomsky proposed a break with structuralists and a return to some of the principles that underlie traditional grammar. Grammaticality, he argued, cannot be determined merely by asking native speakers to make a judgment (the structuralist approach), but must be determined on the basis of an utterance's adherence to the rules of grammar.[5]

In addition, Chomsky argued that phrase-structure grammar could not adequately explain language, even with respect to simple sentences. He noted that phrase-structure grammar assigns different analyses to certain sentences that intuitively seem closely related, such as actives and passives (see Sentences 17 and 18) and that its lack of an apparatus to illuminate their relatedness was a serious weakness.

17.   Macarena kissed Fritz.
18.   Fritz was kissed by Macarena

Transformations

To meet the theoretical, explanatory, and descriptive requirements he deemed necessary to a grammar, Chomsky proposed a new set of rules that operated in conjunction with phrase-structure rules. He argued that each sentence uttered or read has a history, so the new rules must

---

[4]What Chomsky meant by "producing" has been a matter of significant debate. As Harris (1993) noted, "Chomsky proposed his grammar to model a mental *state,* but many people took it to model a mental *process*" (p. 99).

[5]It would be a mistake, however, to link transformational-generative grammar too closely with traditional grammar. Chomsky's concern for universal rules was part of a goal that traditional grammar never considered and that phrase-structure grammar never seriously articulated.

allow an analysis that reveals that history. Sentences 17 and 18 are useful in illustrating what this means.

Intuition indicates that these sentences are related, but the grammar, according to Chomsky, should explain the nature of their relatedness. He therefore proposed that all sentences have two states, an *underlying form* (or "deep structure") and a *surface form* (or "surface structure").[6] Pinker (1994) wrote that "Deep structure is the interface between the mental dictionary and phrase structure," which reflects Chomsky's early view that transformation rules are a bridge between the mind's representation of related propositions and the ultimate articulation of those representations in a grammatical sentence (p. 121). In early versions of the grammar, the underlying form always is an active sentence, which is reasonable because most sentences that people construct are active rather than passive. In this case, the underlying form of Sentence 18 is Sentence 17. Stated another way, all passive sentences begin in the mind of the speaker or writer as active sentences. The question Chomsky had to answer, therefore, was how sentences like 18 are derived from sentences like 17.

In the early versions of the grammar, Chomsky proposed a transformation rule that changed actives to passives. He proposed a variety of other transformation rules that dealt with other types of sentences. Some of the rules were obligatory, whereas others, like the one for passive sentences, were optional. These rules used phrase-structure notation, but they were by nature more general. For example, a phrase-structure analysis of Sentence 17 could take the form:

$$S \rightarrow NP_1 \ V \ NP_2$$

where the verb is in the past tense, NP_1 is *Macarena*, and NP_2 is *Fritz*. An analysis of Sentence 18 could take the following form:

$$S \rightarrow NP_2 \ \text{be} \ V \ \text{by} \ NP_1$$

with a past-tense marker eventually turning *be* into *was*.

The transformation rule is essentially a statement of conditions: Any sentence that has the structure of $S \rightarrow NP_1 \ V \ NP_2$ can be transformed into the structure of $S \rightarrow NP_2 \ \text{be} \ V \ \text{by} \ NP_1$. The rule itself would look something like this:

---

[6]For many years, linguists wrestled with the concept of deep structure because it appeared to contain the meaning, or semantic content, of a sentence. The question of meaning became so problematic that many linguists eventually rejected the very notion of deep structure. The term used here, *underlying form*, is intended to acknowledge the shift away from deep structure and to avoid some of the connotations inherent in the word *deep*. Chomsky, reluctant to give up a concept that is central to his psychological view of language, currently uses the term *d-structure*.

Passive: NP_1 V NP_2 (optional)

              NP_2 be V by NP_1

One effect of this rule is that an analysis of any passive sentence requires an analysis of its corresponding active form.[7] The analysis therefore delves into the history of the sentence. With Sentences 17 and 18, the surface structure and the underlying structure are different; in other instances, however, they will be the same, as in Sentences 19 and 20 below[8]:

19.   Fred ate the peach.
20.   Fritz left the book on the table.

A consequence of the distinction between surface and underlying forms is that transformational-generative grammar involves two phrase-structure trees for analyzing transformed sentences. The first tree shows the structure of the underlying form whereas the second shows the structure of the transformed sentence, or surface form. Figure 5.6 illustrates the procedure for Sentence 17.

Grammar, Language, and Psychology

Chomsky's argument that grammar was a theory of language opened avenues that linguists had not explored in great detail. Psychologists like Vygotsky (1962), Piaget (1955, 1974), and Skinner (1957), on the other hand, had studied language fairly extensively. Although Chomsky disagreed vehemently with the stimulus–response model of language that Skinner proposed, he nevertheless declared that the study of grammar and thus language necessarily involved the study of psychology.

Chomsky's rationale for this view was linked to his interest in linguistic universals. From his perspective, the obvious differences in languages masked underlying similarities. All languages have subjects, verbs, objects, modifiers, and function words. All languages are based on phrases. In addition, children learn language in about the same way and at about the same pace in every culture. They acquire it easily on

---

[7]The rule described for passive here has been replaced by a much more general rule that is beyond the scope of this text.

[8]Some versions of transformational-generative grammar propose that even sentences like these have underlying structures different from their surface structures. The surface structure in Sentences 19 and 20 shows a tensed verb; a more detailed analysis would show that the underlying form contains an untensed verb and a separate tense marker. A transformation then attaches the tense marker to the verb, yielding the surface form. Because this chapter cannot examine such details, it seems permissible to overlook this minor difference between surface and underlying forms and state that the two are essentially the same in certain cases.

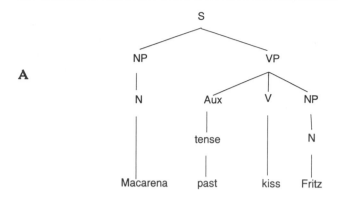

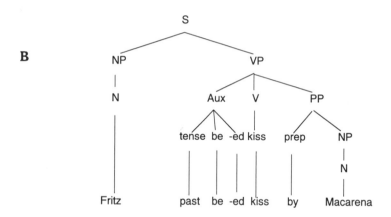

FIG. 5.6. Tree diagrams showing the underlying form (A) and the surface form (B).

the basis of relatively little input. Adults use language fluently and efficiently to convey information and ideas and as a means of social bonding and cultural dissemination. All languages make use of logical implications, such as "If I fall into the water I'll get wet."

These facts long suggested that language is organized in keeping with how the brain is structured or with how it operates. A viable theory of grammar—and correspondingly a viable theory of language—would have to address the relation between the brain and language. Chomsky turned to rationalism as a foundation for his argument that language is innate—genetically determined. Work by Broca (1861) and Wernicke (1874) lent support to this argument. Their investigation of language among patients with brain injuries revealed that specific areas of the brain are responsible for different types of language processing. This high degree of cerebral specialization made a strong case for the idea that the brain evolved centers whose sole task is language processing.

More recent research involving people with severe brain injuries has confirmed the concept of innateness (Lenneberg, 1967; Restak, 1979; Wittrock, 1977). The brain is divided into two hemispheres, and mental and physical functions tend to be dominated by one hemisphere or the other. Physical movements on the right side of the body involve primarily the left hemisphere; movements on the left side involve primarily the right hemisphere. In most people, the left hemisphere controls language, so when adults suffer damage to this part of the brain, language is almost always permanently impaired. This phenomenon suggests that an innate, physiological basis for language exists, that the left hemisphere is genetically programmed to control language function much in the same way that the occipital region of the brain is genetically programmed to control vision.

Yet in cases of preadolescent children who experience damage to the left hemisphere, the uninjured right hemisphere in most instances somehow manages to take over language function intact without measurable impairment. Although this phenomenon does not invalidate the innateness proposal, the effect weakens it because language takes on characteristics of learned behavior. Moreover, it suggests the existence of a critical period during which brain function and language development are plastic and can shift readily from the left hemisphere to the right. The idea of innateness required evidence that some features of language are specifically and nontransferably located in the left hemisphere.

Such evidence was found in studies of children who at birth were diagnosed as having one diseased hemisphere that would lead to death if left alone. The children were operated on within a few days of birth (Day & Ulatowska, 1979; Dennis & Kohn, 1975; Dennis & Whitaker, 1976; Kohn, 1980). In some cases, the entire left hemisphere was removed; in other cases, the entire right hemisphere was removed. (This procedure causes serious intellectual deficits, but children who undergo the operation develop normally in many ways.) The children were studied as they matured, with particular attention to language development. Tests of vocabulary and comprehension showed no significant differences between those with right hemisphere or left hemisphere removed. Both also seemed equally able to carry on a normal conversation.

Closer examination, however, revealed several important differences. Dennis and Kohn (1975) found that children with the right hemisphere removed could process negative passive sentences, but those with the left hemisphere removed could not. Dennis and Whitaker (1976) found that children with the left hemisphere removed showed an inability to deviate from subject–verb–object word order. They could not understand or produce what are called *cleft sentences*, such as, "What the teller wanted me to do was deposit more money." They also could not process sentences that use *by* in any way other than indicating location. Thus they could understand, "The book was by the lamp" but not, "The cake was made by my sister." On the basis of such evidence, most scholars have concluded that some grammar-related features of language are indeed exclusively part of left-hemispheric function. Chomsky's intuition about linguistic innateness was substantially correct.

Language Acquisition

One consequence of the innateness hypothesis was that the question of how children acquire language became a matter of understanding cognitive development. Chomsky observed that young children are not taught grammar, yet they manage to produce grammatical sentences at a fairly early age on the basis of often distorted input ("baby talk"). Moreover, their sentences cannot be viewed merely as parroting of adult speech, because their utterances are not repetitions of what they hear. Chomsky maintained that such facility with language would be impossible without some innate *language acquisition device* (LAD) that induces grammatical rules from very little data.

The standard account of language acquisition proposes that children begin receiving linguistic input at birth. (For an alternative to the standard account see pages 144–147.) This input is severely limited because of the nature of parent–adult linguistic interactions. Adults just do not speak to infants the same way that they speak to other adults. Their baby talk, or *motherese*, deletes function words, focuses on nouns, and commonly abuses normal word order. Nevertheless, children begin producing intelligible speech within 1 to 2 years of age, speech that conforms in significant ways to adult language.

In this account, the LAD is considered to be a subsystem of the language mechanism, with the sole role of inducing the grammar rules of the child's home language. Fodor (1983), Johnson-Laird (1983), and others argued that these rules are explicit but inaccessible; they can be described but not consciously altered. The LAD hypothesizes the rules on the basis of input, and the hypotheses are accepted or rejected on the basis of their ability to enable processing of the sentences children hear. Hudson (1980) and Slobin and Welsh (1973), noting that children face a major problem because they must induce accurate rules on the basis of inaccurate and distorted data, argued that the LAD has an innate knowledge of the possible range of human languages and therefore considers only those hypotheses within the constraints imposed on grammar by a set of linguistic universals.

In support of the standard account of language acquisition, many scholars (Clark & Clark, 1977; Krashen, 1980; Pinker, 1994) have turned to an overgeneralization phenomenon involving regular and irregular verbs. During their early stages of language development, children use only a small number of past-tense verbs, but they often use present-tense verbs to indicate a past action. Most of the past-tense verbs they use are irregular and high frequency. For example, a child's lexicon of past-tense verbs might consist of *ate, got, shook, stopped, did, went,* and *kissed.* Because the lexicon includes regular as well as irregular verbs, there is no evidence that the child is using a past-tense rule. The regular and irregular verbs simply appear to be separate items in the lexicon.

Many observers have noted that a change occurs at about 2.5 years of age. Children start using more past-tense verbs. The number of irregular verbs grows, but not significantly. However, in the standard account, two new linguistic behaviors emerge. First, children develop the ability to generate a past tense for an invented word. If a parent (or researcher) can persuade a child to use, say, the word *bloss,* they will say *blossed* to describe whatever action this might be when it occurred in the past. Second, children now incorrectly attach regular past-tense endings to irregular verbs that they used correctly earlier. As Clark and Clark (1977) noted, children add *ed* to the root, as in *comed* or *goed,* or they may add *ed* to the irregular past-tense form, as in *wented.*

After about 8 months, the regular and irregular forms come to coexist. Children begin to use the correct irregular forms of the past tense and to apply the regular form correctly to new words they learn. These developments have led many to view the process as strong evidence for the successful induction of grammar rules, for children appear to be using the rules to compute the appropriate output for both regular and irregular verb forms. The rules operate more or less automatically from that point on, in a manner that Fodor (1983) characterized as a reflex. Thus it is widely accepted in linguistics that children's overgeneralization of tense formation is representative of the entire range of grammar rules.

The grammar rules that the LAD induces, of course, are transformational-generative rules, and the suggestion that such rules are internalized led early researchers to attempt to determine whether they had a psychological reality. The research question was simple: If language users actually apply transformation rules to underlying structures, do they take longer to process transformed sentences? Miller (1962) attempted to answer this question through what came to be known as the *click experiments*. He compiled a list of sentences, gave subjects a device that made a click sound, and then directed them to use the device as soon as they understood each sentence. Passives and actives were of particular interest because the passive transformation has such a significant effect on the structure of the active form. Miller's data indicated convincingly that transformed sentences like passives took subjects longer to process (see also Miller & McKean, 1964). Only much later did it become clear that other factors may have caused the longer processing times. Passives, for example, generally are longer than their corresponding actives, which influences time.

Competence and Performance

The standard account of language acquisition raised a problem. If the LAD induces correct grammar rules, why is human speech full of errors? People have many slips of the tongue that jumble up their language. They often use prepositions incorrectly, saying that someone "got in the bus" rather than "on the bus," and so forth. Many utterances are ungrammatical, as in the case of a person who fails to shift a particle behind a pronoun, illustrated in Sentence 21:

21.   Macarena tied up him.

Sometimes speakers are aware of the flaw and stop midsentence and begin again, repairing the problem. Other times they may not be quite as attentive, and the flaw will slip by undetected.

As Chomsky formulated the grammar, however, it does not produce ungrammatical sentences under any circumstances. Thus the generative component of transformational-generative grammar was not congruent with actual language use. To account for the apparent inconsistency, Chomsky distinguished between the sentences generated by the grammar and the sentences actually produced by language users. The terms he used to make this distinction are *competence* and *performance*. *Linguistic competence* may be understood as the inherent ability of a native speaker to make correct grammaticality judgments. *Performance* is what people actually do with the language, subject as they are to fatigue, distraction, and all the many psychosocial factors that prevent optimal language production. All native speakers possess linguistic competence, but only an ideal speaker, a mental construct, would be able to translate competence into error-free performance.

The competence–performance distinction was deemed to be quite useful because it accounts for the occurrence of ungrammatical sentences and also for the occasional inability of listeners to analyze

grammatical sentences. Such difficulties are due to errors of performance, errors made somehow between the application of the rules and the
articulation of an utterance. They are not due to errors in the grammar.

During the 1960s, many people reasoned that the competence–performance distinction could be turned into an instructional agenda: One
need simply provide students with the means for turning tacit knowledge on the level of competence into explicit knowledge on the level of
performance. Numerous efforts were therefore made at teaching transformational-generative grammar to raise performance to the level of
competence (see Gale, 1968; Mellon, 1969; O'Hare, 1973; R. White,
1965). Although not terribly successful in a direct sense, these efforts
had an indirect and substantial impact on studies of style (see Bateman
& Zidonis, 1966; Mellon, 1969; O'Hare, 1973; Winterowd, 1975). The
stylistic device of sentence combining arose out of attempts to increase
writing maturity by teaching students transformational-generative
grammar.

Many people were confused by the notions of competence and
performance. They reasoned that if students already knew everything
about language, teachers had nothing to teach. Others could not understand—as writing skills deteriorated more every year—how students
who presumably had such extensive knowledge of English could write
so terribly.[9] The problem was (and is) that competence is a slippery term.
In everyday language, the term has two meanings: It refers to skill level
or to potential ability. In the first case, a person may be a competent
pianist if he or she can play a tune on a piano. In the second case, a
person may be competent to play the piano if he or she has arms, hands,
fingers, legs, and feet. The person may not be able to play at all but is
competent to do so. Moreover, there is no promise that this level of
competence has any real connection to actual performance. Even with
training there is no assurance that a person will ever be competent in
the first sense of the word.

When composition studies adopted the competence–performance
distinction, the tendency was to ignore the technical definition of competence in favor of the popular one related to potential ability. Matters
were confused further by notions of innateness, until *writing competence*
came to mean (for many teachers) something along the lines of *the innate
ability to write*. So for many teachers, competence suggested a classroom
environment in which students have ample opportunities to write, and
have the chance to practice what they already know how to do (Berthoff,
1981, 1983; Elbow, 1973; Graves, 1981; Murray, 1982; Parker, 1979). In

---

[9]Whitaker (personal communication, November 17, 1984) expressed the puzzlement of
many when he compared the writing of college freshmen to the speech of aphasics.

a peculiar twist, transformational-generative grammar served to support the agenda of romantic rhetoric.

JOURNAL ENTRY

Reflect on your feelings about language and students' abilities to draw on some innate potential to produce correct language. How do those feelings compare with the earlier discussion?

COGNITIVE GRAMMAR

Transformational-generative grammar became popular for many reasons, but two stand out. It was simple and elegant, and it promised new insights into the psychological mechanisms that underlie language. As the grammar matured, however, it lost its simplicity and much of its elegance. The role of meaning in transformational-generative grammar always had been ambiguous. In *Syntactic Structures*, Chomsky (1957) noted that his grammar "was completely formal and non-semantic" (p. 93). Nevertheless, discussions of deep structure suggested that it represented the meaning of a sentence, which led many people to suspect that Chomsky was really interested in meaning after all. A flurry of activity followed, during which scholars attempted to develop a way to bring grammar and meaning together successfully in one theory, a move that Chomsky alternately supported and opposed for many years (Harris, 1993). But the theories of grammar kept changing, and, moreover, they kept becoming more abstract and in many respects more complex, until they no longer were easily accessible to anyone without specialized training in linguistics.

Cognitive psychology deals with human knowledge and how people use it (A. Clark, 1993; Glass, Holyoak, & Santa, 1979; Kelso, 1995), and cognitive psychologists were among the earliest supporters of transformational-generative grammar because they saw it as a means to better understanding the mind. A certain irony was inevitable. Chomsky was (and is) notoriously anti-empirical, whereas cognitive psychology is grounded in empiricism and experimental method. Nevertheless, psychologists ignored the irony, largely because the grammar was congruent with the computational, rule-governed model of mind that had dominated psychology for decades. In this model, explicit, inaccessible rules compute input and output of all types: logic, decision making, reading, and so forth. With respect to language, computation, in part, involves combining small units to create larger ones.

As noted earlier, one of the first attempts to apply experimental methods to Chomsky's theory was made in 1962, when George Miller set out to evaluate the psychological reality of transformation rules. Miller hypothesized that transformed sentences would require longer processing times than nontransformed sentences, and he developed an experiment to measure the differences in processing rates. If the rules were psychologically real, if they truly existed in the brain, then transformed sentences indeed would take longer to process. Negatives would take longer than positives, passives longer than actives. Sentences with multiple transformations would take even longer.

Miller's results confirmed his hypothesis, and initially psychologists and linguists alike were excited to have empirical validation of Chomsky's intuition-based model. For several years, the psychological reality of transformation rules was deemed to be a given. But problems began to emerge when some researchers noted that passive sentences generally are longer than their corresponding active form and that sentence length could have accounted for Miller's results. Then a range of studies that took into account such factors as sentence length and subtle changes in meaning showed that transformations had no effect on processing time (Bever, 1970; Fodor, Bever, & Garrett, 1974; Fodor & Garrett, 1966; Glucksberg & Danks, 1969). Neither transformations nor deep structure seemed to have any psychological reality whatsoever, and transformational-generative grammar failed to lend itself to empirical validation.

Chomsky was unfazed. After all, he developed transformational-generative grammar, in part, as a rationalist reaction against structuralism and its empirical basis. Cognitive psychology, however, is rooted in empiricism, and psychologists generally saw the lack of experimental validation as a mortal blow for the grammar. Transformational-generative grammar became widely viewed as an interesting theory that had no measurable support, and by the late 1970s, most cognitive psychologists had abandoned it. Because language is a fundamental component of cognitive processing, psychologists began searching for a new theory that was experimentally verifiable. What emerged is known as *cognitive grammar* (Langacker, 1987, 1990).

A characteristic of rule-driven systems is that they consistently produce correct output. They are deterministic, so after a rule is in place, there is no reason to expect an error. For example, after a person has induced the rule for passive transformations, whenever he or she intends to produce a passive sentence, the rule is invoked unconsciously, and it necessarily must produce the same result each time. However, the frequent errors in speech suggest that the rules, in fact, do not produce correct output, which is why Chomsky's concept of competence and performance is so important to transformational-generative grammar. Without it, the grammar fails to describe or explain language in any principled way.

Cognitive grammar simplifies matters immensely by rejecting the rule-governed model of mind and language, replacing it with an association model based on the work in cognitive science by Rumelhart and McClelland (1986) and others working in an area known as *connectionism* (see also Searle, 1992). Although an in-depth analysis of connectionism is not possible here, the model is fairly straightforward. Connectionism describes learning in terms of *neural networks*. These networks are physiological structures in the brain that are composed of cells called *neurons* and pathways—*dendrites* and *axons*—that allow neurons to communicate with one another. This basic structure is illustrated in Fig. 5.7. When a person learns a new word or concept, the brain's cell structure changes, literally expanding the network to accommodate the new knowledge. (Sometimes, the network contracts.) The more a person learns, the more extensive his or her neural network becomes.

Rule-governed models like Chomsky's assume that mental activity or thought is verbal—any given sentence begins as *mentalese*. Some of the early versions of transformational-generative grammar attempted to capture the nature of mentalese in the underlying structure. Sentence

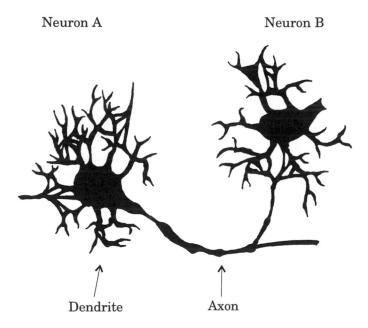

Neuron A   Neuron B

Dendrite   Axon

FIG. 5.7. Neurons, dendrites, and axons. Each neuron has numerous dendrites that connect it to other neurons via connecting pathways called axons. From Carlson (1994). Copyright © 1994 by Allyn & Bacon. Adapted with permission.

22 illustrates a simple example:

22. Fritz loved the woman who drove the red Porsche.

This surface structure contains an independent clause ("Fritz loved the woman") and a relative clause ("who drove the red Porsche"). The sentence has an underlying structure that consists of the following:

22a. Fritz loved the woman. The woman drove the red Porsche.

This underlying structure is how Sentence 22 supposedly exists as mentalese, only to be altered through the application of a transformation rule.

Connectionism, however, suggests that it is a mistake to assume that cognitive activities are verbal just because everyone reports hearing a mental voice when thinking. Instead, it proposes that mental activities are primarily (though not exclusively) *imagistic*—based on images. This point is important for a number of reasons, but one of the more relevant is that it allows language processing to be understood as a matter of matching words with mental representations and internalized models of reality. No rules are involved. Instead, language is governed by patterns of regularity (Rumelhart & McClelland, 1986).

These patterns begin establishing themselves at birth (see Kelso, 1995). As Williams (1993) noted, when children encounter the world, their parents and other adults provide them with the names of things. They see dogs, and they immediately are provided the word *dog*, with the result that they develop a mental model related to "dog-ness." On a neurophysiological level, this model consists of modifications to the cerebral structure: Cells change; the network grows. A child's mental model for "dog-ness" includes the range of physical features that typify dogs, and these features are connected to the mental representation as well as to the string of phonemes that form the word *dog*. Rumelhart and McClelland (1986) argued convincingly that the connection is via neural pathways. Over time or owing to some other factors, such as interest, the connection becomes stronger, like a well-worn path, until the image of a dog is firmly linked to the word *dog*. From this point on, the child is able to process the image of "dog-ness" and the word *dog* simultaneously. Stated another way, "Hearing the word [dog] or deciding to utter it triggers an association between one set of patterns of regularity, the string of phonemes, and another set that contains subsets of the various features related to 'dog-ness'" (Williams, 1993, p. 558).[10]

---

[10]Although the emphasis here is on intentional activities, clearly other factors can have a similar effect. Most people have the experience of encountering a certain fragrance or hearing a certain song that evokes detailed images from the past. The process of association is similar, if not identical, to the account here.

In rejecting the rule-governed model of mind, cognitive grammar also rejects the idea that language is computational and rule governed. Conventions still play a significant role, but rules do not because syntax is determined by the patterns of regularity that develop in childhood. (To an extent, cognitive grammar is quite congruent with social-theoretic views of language.) The number of acceptable patterns in any given language is relatively small and is based on prevailing word order. In English, for example, the two dominant patterns for sentences are SVO and subject–verb–complement (SVC). All other sentences are essentially variations of these patterns. Production consists of selecting a given pattern and then filling it with words that match the mental model of the proposition that the speaker wants to convey. On this account, the grammar itself has no generative component—it is purely descriptive. The high degree of creativity observed in language is the result of an essentially limitless supply of mental propositions as well as the flexibility inherent in English word order. The grammar involves no special rules to explain the relation between, for example, actives and passives because it simply notes that these two sentence patterns are alternative forms available for certain propositions. The forms themselves are described as being linked psychophysiologically in the neural network, coexisting simultaneously.

In this view, grammar is a system for describing the patterns of regularity that are inherent in language; it is not specifically a theory of language or of mind. Because mental activities are deemed to be imagistic rather than verbal, cognitive grammar does not need an underlying grammatical form for sentences. The free association of images makes the question of underlying structure irrelevant. Surface structure is linked directly to the mental proposition and corresponding phonemic and lexical representations. A formal grammatical apparatus to explain the relatedness of actives and passives and other types of related sentences is not necessary because these patterns coexist in the neural network. The role of the grammar is merely to describe surface structures. Phrase-structure conventions are best suited to this role.

Another advantage of cognitive grammar and the cognitive theory that it is based on is that they explain errors in language without recourse to notions of competence and performance, which at best are highly artificial, ad hoc. Errors occur because each person has other, similar patterns of regularity with many overlapping features. For example, cats and dogs have four legs, tails, and fur. They are pets, require a great deal of care, shed, and so forth. When an association is triggered, the connecting pathways become excited. Thus whenever a person's intention causes a phoneme or phoneme sequence to become active in a particular utterance, all the words in the lexicon that are similar to the target word become active as well. These words compete with one another on the basis of their connecting strengths to their corresponding mental representations. Normally, the target word has the greatest connecting strength; there is a match, and the person's intention is realized. Sometimes, however, on a probabilistic basis, an incorrect match or error will occur. When it does, the person may replace the word *dog* with the word *cat*, or using an example that parents are very familiar with, a child may call *Mommy Daddy*, or vice versa. Figure 5.8 illustrates a schematic rendering of a developed neural network.

Age increases the connecting strengths within the network, so as people grow older, they produce fewer errors. However, this model predicts that, statistically, errors always will occur on a random basis regardless of age. This prediction is born out by the fact that everyone produces errors of one type or another while speaking. Analysis shows that people produce similar errors while writing. In addition, the model provides a more accurate explanation of the phenomenon of tense overgeneralization. Contrary to the standard account of language acqui-sition, children do not apply the past-participle affix to irregular verbs consistently. Sometimes they use the regular and irregular forms cor-rectly, sometimes incorrectly. As Williams (1993) noted, this "inconsis-tent behavior is almost impossible to explain adequately with a rule-governed model" (p. 560). However, this behavior is easily under-stood in terms of competing forms: The connecting associations related

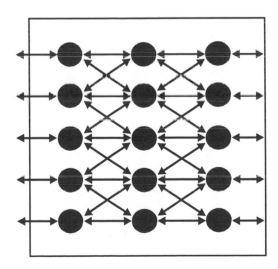

FIG. 5.8. Schematic of neural network. This schematic representationally shows neurons and their corresponding pathways. Note how the neurons are interconnected.

to past-tense forms are insufficiently developed to allow one form to dominate.

Although cognitive grammar provides explanations of language that are simpler and more elegant than any other grammar, it faces strong opposition from orthodox linguistics, where there is a powerful vested interest in preserving transformational-generative grammar. For a time during the late 1980s and early 1990s, those working in cognitive grammar attempted to share ideas and theories with those working in mainstream linguistics, with disappointing results. Rumelhart (personal communication, July 22, 1990) indicated that orthodox linguists, as a group, finally turned away from cognitive grammar and connectionism and wanted nothing more to do with it. Many years later, it appears as though the situation has not changed.

GRAMMAR IN THE CLASSROOM

Most language arts teachers do not have many opportunities to explore the fascinating intricacies of grammar in their classrooms, but nearly all of them have to teach grammar. The most pressing questions they face are: "What role does grammar play in writing performance?" "And how does one teach grammar effectively?"

Although grammar has been taught to generations of writing students (and continues to be taught), reliable evaluations of the connection between studying grammar and writing performance are fairly recent. In 1963, Braddock et al. summarized early research when they stated:

> In view of the widespread agreement of research studies based upon many types of students and teachers, the conclusion can be stated in strong and unqualified terms that the teaching of formal [traditional] grammar has a negligible or, because it usually displaces some instruction and practice in actual composition, even a harmful effect on the improvement of writing. (pp. 37–38)

Even after this assessment, various researchers continued to investigate grammar instruction and writing performance, in part because the assumption of a connection was so strong. Whitehead (1966), for example, compared a group of high school students that received no grammar instruction in writing classes with one that received instruction in traditional grammar, with an emphasis on sentence diagraming. The results showed no significant difference in writing performance between the two groups. White (1965) made his study more complex, using three classes of seventh graders. Two of the classes studied grammar, one traditional, the other transformational, and the third class spent the same amount of time reading popular novels. At the end of the study, White found no significant difference in terms of writing performance.

Gale (1968) studied fifth graders, dividing them into four groups: One received instruction in traditional grammar, one in phrase-structure grammar, one in transformational-generative grammar, and one did not receive grammar instruction. The students who studied phrase-structure and transformational-generative grammar were able to write slightly more complex sentences than students in the other two groups, but Gale found no measurable differences in overall writing ability.

In a much longer investigation, Bateman and Zidonis (1966) conducted a 2-year study that started when the students were in ninth grade. Some of the students received instruction in transformational-generative grammar during this period; the remaining students did not receive grammar instruction. Students who studied transformational grammar were able to write more complex sentences than those who did not study grammar, but there was no significant difference in overall writing performance.

Elley, Barham, Lamb, and Wyllie (1976) began with a relatively large pool of subjects ($N = 248$) that they studied for 3 years. Because some critics of the earlier studies suggested that the lack of any measurable differences might be the result of different teaching styles, researchers were particularly careful to control this variable.

The students were divided into three groups. The first group—composed of three classes—studied transformational-generative grammar, various organizational modes (narration, argumentation, analysis, and so on), and literature. The second group—also of three classes—studied the same organizational modes and literature as the first group but not transformational-generative grammar; instead, they studied creative writing and were given the chance to do additional literature reading. The two classes in the third group studied traditional grammar and engaged in reading popular fiction.

At the end of each year of the investigation, students were evaluated on a range of measures to determine comparative growth. These measures included vocabulary, reading comprehension, sentence complexity, usage, spelling, and punctuation. Furthermore, students wrote four essays at the end of the first year and three at the end of the second and third years; these essays were scored for content, style, organization, and mechanics. The students were also asked to respond anonymously to questionnaires designed to assess their attitudes toward the various parts of their English courses.

No significant differences on any measures were found among the three groups at the end of the first year, with one notable exception. The students who had studied transformational-generative grammar seemed to like writing less than students in the other two groups. At the end of the second year, the students who had studied traditional grammar produced essays that were judged to have better content than the students who had not studied any grammar, but raters found no significant difference between the traditional grammar and the transformational-generative grammar groups. In addition, other factors, such as mechanics and sentence complexity, were judged as being similar for all groups.

The results of the attitude questionnaire at the end of the second year indicated that the students who had studied transformational-generative grammar not only continued to like writing less overall than their counterparts, but they also felt English as a whole was more difficult. Nevertheless, in regard to expository writing and persuasive writing, the students who had studied transformational-generative grammar and those who had studied no grammar had a significantly more positive attitude than the traditional-grammar students. They also seemed to enjoy literature more.

At the end of the third year, the various factors related to writing were evaluated a final time. A series of standardized measures showed that the students who had studied grammar performed better on the usage test than those who had not. No significant differences on the other measures were found. On the final attitude survey, the transformational-generative grammar students indicated that they found English to be "repetitive," which is understandable considering that each year they studied the same grammatical principles. The traditional-grammar group indicated that they found their English program less "interesting and useful" than the other two groups.

More significant, however, is the fact that even after 3 years of work and effort, the actual writing of the students who studied traditional grammar or transformational-generative grammar showed no significant differences in overall quality from that of students who had studied no grammar. Evaluations of the three groups' essays failed to reveal any measurable differences at all. Frequency of error in spelling, punctuation, sentence structure, and other mechanical measures did not vary from group to group. As far as their writing was concerned, studying grammar or not studying grammar simply made no difference.

Such studies make it clear that grammar instruction has no demonstrated positive effect on the quality of students' writing. This is not to suggest that it has a negative effect, nor should anyone dismiss the possibility that grammar instruction may have some, as yet unspecified, effect on students' general language skills. Yet the data suggest that teaching students grammar has no measurable effect on writing performance.

TEACHING GRAMMAR

The studies just reviewed prompted different responses from those involved in education. Many teachers, administrators, and parents discounted the research and proceeded as though the findings did not exist, putting students through exercises and drills year after year. Others saw them as a rationale for ignoring grammar instruction. Neither response is appropriate. Students deserve an opportunity to learn about the language they speak. Given the right approach, students are as interested in grammar as they are in psychology, for many of the same reasons: Both subjects reveal much about students themselves and about those around them. The real issue is how grammar should be taught, not whether it should be taught.

When people complain about the quality of student writing, they focus on such factors as faulty subject–verb agreement, faulty punctuation, faulty word choice, errors in number, and so on. Although these flaws are labeled as grammar problems, they reflect errors in usage, not grammar. Therefore, it is crucial to differentiate between grammar and usage. As the previous sections made clear, grammar has to do with the structure of language, not with its production. Usage, on the other hand, has little to do with structure but very much to do with production.

Usage Problems

The range of usage problems in speech and writing is so broad that it cannot be addressed adequately here. People make numerous mistakes with language. In oral discourse, the message is the focus of attention, so mistakes tend to be less distracting, but the situation is different for writing because readers have more time to attend to form. Some of the usage problems that appear in writing are the result of students transporting informal speech to more formal composition. Many others, however, are rooted in a pervasive lack of reading experience among students and an even greater lack of reflection on the fundamentals of textual form.

Some errors in subject–verb agreement are linked to speech, as in Sentence 23:

23. Fritz and me was going to the ball game.

This structure is perfectly acceptable in certain dialects of English, but it is not in the standard dialect that governs writing. Thus Sentence

23 illustrates one type of error that occurs when students transport their spoken English to their writing. Sentence 24 illustrates a different problem, however:

24.   Our catalogue of courses and requirements baffle students.

The plural terms, *courses* and *requirements*, dominate the verb because of their proximity, leading to the error. Sentences of this type cannot be written correctly on a consistent basis without more reading experience and time spent reflecting on that experience than most students have.

The same can be said of the punctuation errors that cause fragments and run-on sentences and of the numerous faulty word choices that characterize student writing. Students consistently confuse *affect* and *effect* because there is no way to distinguish them in speech and because they have not read enough to note the distinction. These words have caused so much grief that many people have tried to replace both with *impact* in an effort to avoid the problem:

25.   The change in leadership had a big *impact* on us all.
26.   Our new coach *impacted* the team in unpredictable ways.

Unfortunately, this replacement has not solved anything because it creates its own usage problems. As a noun, *impact* generally means *collision*, or the striking of one body against another; this makes Sentence 25 questionable. As a transitive verb, the word generally means "to pack firmly together," which makes Sentence 26 funny as well as questionable.

Other problems abound, such as the pervasive confusion of *lay* for *lie*, *that* for *who* and *whom*, and *each other* for *one another*.[11] Although parents and educators regularly call for increased attention to grammar in the schools, there is a growing tendency among many to discount usage distinctions or to ridicule them as being elitist. Often language change is cited as a rationale for sanctioning the acceptance of *impact* in place of *affect*. The situation is paradoxical. The following sections examine several common usage problems.

---

[11]*Lay* is a transitive verb, which means that it always must be followed by a noun or noun phrase, as in "Macarena *lay the book* on the table." The past tense of *lay* is *laid*, producing "Macarena *laid the book* on the table." *Lie* is an intransitive verb, which means that it never is followed by a noun or noun phrase, as in "Fritz can *lie* on the table." Many people get confused because the past tense of *lie* is *lay*, as in "Fritz *lay* on the table all night." *Who* always is the subject of a relative clause; *whom* always is the object. The difference has confused so many people that they have tried to avoid the whole question by using the relative pronoun *that* instead of *who* or *whom*. Some purists, however, argue that *who* and *whom* designate people, whereas *that* does not; in this case,   (cont'd.→)

This and the Problem of Reference

The demonstrative pronoun *this* does not always work with a noun, as in "This book is interesting." In certain situations, it replaces an entire sentence, as in the following:

Fritz opened another beer. *This* amazed Macarena.

Here, *this* refers to the fact that Fritz opened another beer, and in this kind of construction it usually is referred to as an *indefinite demonstrative* pronoun. Because the two sentences are side by side, the relation between them is clear. Inexperienced writers often do not link the indefinite demonstrative with the word it refers to; they may have several sentences separating the two, which makes comprehension difficult. Consider the following student example:

I liked Cannery Row a lot. I especially like the part where Doc gets conned out of a quarter for a beer. Doc probably was the best educated of all the characters in the story. But that does not mean he was the smartest. All of the characters seemed smart in their own way. This is one of the funniest parts of the story.

The word *this* in the last sentence should refer to Doc getting conned in the second sentence, but it does not. The intervening sentences make the connection hard to see. Using the indefinite demonstrative in this instance is not appropriate. The sentence would have to be moved upward to be successful. Moreover, many experienced writers object to any usage of *this* in such a broad way, arguing fairly convincingly that an alternative, more precise structure is better. They recommend replacing the indefinite demonstrative pronoun with an appropriate noun.

Each Other/One Another

Each other and *one another* do not mean the same thing, so they are not interchangeable. *Each other* signifies two people or things, whereas *one another* signifies more than two.

Reflexive Pronouns

Reflexive pronouns are used in two ways: when someone does something to himself or herself or as *intensifiers*. Consider the following sentences,

---

replacing the troublesome relative pronouns with *that* simply creates another problem. Although many people use *each other* and *one another* interchangeably, they do not mean the same thing. *Each other* signifies two and only two people, whereas *one another* signifies more than two. The distinction is similar to the one that exists for *between* and *among*.

which illustrate both forms of usage, respectively:

27.   Fred cut *himself* with his razor.
28.   Macarena *herself* couldn't believe how good she looked.

Large numbers of people are confused when it comes to the case of pronouns: They do not know whether to use nominative or objective, whether to say (or write) "Fred gave the money to Macarena, Raul, and me" or " Fred gave the money to Macarena, Raul, and I." They know there is a difference because they have been taught it in school, but they really do not know what the difference is. To avoid the entire problem, at least with respect to the pronouns *I* and *me*, people will use a reflexive pronoun in either the subject or object position, as in Sentences 29 and 30:

29.   Buggsy, Fritz, and *myself* went to Las Vegas.
30.   Buggsy took Fred, Macarena, and *myself* to his new casino.

Using a reflexive pronoun to replace a personal pronoun, however, simply creates another problem because there is no reflexive action. Replacing a personal pronoun with a reflexive is a violation of standard usage.

Lie and Lay

One of the more widespread usage problems involves the verbs *lay* and *lie*. *Lay* is a transitive verb, so it requires an object; it has to be followed by a noun. *Lie*, on the other hand, is an intransitive verb and does not have an object; it is not followed by a noun. Nearly everyone is confused by this difference, with the result that they use *lay* intransitively, as in Sentence 31:

31.   I'm going to *lay* down for a while.

Standard usage uses *lie*, as in Sentence 32:

32.   I'm going to *lie* down for a while.

Subordinating Conjunctions and Semantic Content

English has lots of function words, and some of the more interesting are subordinating conjunctions. These words, such as *if, whereas, since, although, even though, because, while, until, before, after*, and so forth, link subordinate clauses to independent clauses, as in "Maria liked Raul because he was kind." Not all function words have semantic content (or meaning), at least not in the way that a word like *cat* has meaning, but most of them nevertheless do have some sort of semantic content. The semantic content of subordinating conjunctions is related to the type of information they supply to the construction they modify. For example, in the sentence, "Maria liked Raul because he was handsome," the subordinate clause, as a result of the semantic content of the conjunction *because*, supplies information of reason to the independent clause. In "Fred stopped the car when the engine started to smoke," *when* is a temporal subordinator, so the subordinate clause supplies information of time. Standard usage requires a match between the semantic content of the subordinating conjunction and the modification provided by the subordinate clause.

Growing numbers of people ignore this usage principle. In conversation and published texts, we find incongruence with respect to time, causality, and contrast, with a temporal subordinator being used where a causal and/or contrastive subordinator is required. Consider the following sentences:

33.　Macarena rode her bike *since her car was broken*.
34.　Toni Braxton wanted to wear her white jumpsuit, *while her manager wanted her to wear her white dress*.

In Sentence 33, the relation between the two clauses is one of reason, not time, so standard usage requires the following:

33a.　Macarena rode her bike *because her car was broken*.

In Sentence 34, the relation between the two clauses is contrastive, not temporal, so standard usage requires:

34a.　Toni Braxton wanted to wear her white jumpsuit, *whereas her manager wanted her to wear her white dress*.

The Reason Is Because

Finally, another widespread breach of standard usage occurs when people provide reasons for things. In remarks to the press corps, President Clinton stated, "Of course we need campaign finance reform, and I'm going to work very hard to see that we get it. The American people want action on this, *and the reason is because things are in such a mess*" (Clinton, 1997; italics added).

If we look carefully at the italicized part of these remarks, we see that it consists of a noun-phrase subject (*the reason*), a linking verb (*is*), and a subordinate clause that begins with a subordinating conjunction (*because*). However, linking verbs are only followed by prepositional phrases, nouns, and adjectives; they cannot be followed by subordinate clauses. Standard usage requires a complex noun construction called a complement clause in this particular construction, which would result in:

The American people want action on this, and *the reason is that things are in such a mess.*

Grammar Problems

Grammar errors do not occur very often because there are no competing neural connections that result in a scrambling of sentence structure. When someone wants to state Sentence 34, he or she will not just produce something like Sentence 34a:

34.   Macarena stopped at the market for a loaf of bread.
34a.   * Stopped the at of bread a for market Macarena loaf.

But from time to time, people *do* mix up words in one way or another and produce an ungrammatical sentence. Usually, the sentence goes by unnoticed, especially in speech because readers and listeners pay more attention to meaning than to structure, and these sorts of mix-ups are comprehensible, unlike Sentence 34a. Nevertheless, they violate English structure and so are ungrammatical.

A fairly common example is one already examined, in which there is failure to shift a particle behind a pronoun, as in:

35.   * Fritz looked up him.

Or Sentence 36, which came from a movie with Lucille Ball:

36.   * Turn right here left.

More frequent are structural errors that have become widespread throughout the language, even among well-educated people. *The reason is because* represents one, albeit common, type.

Another type occurs when people add words to sentences unnecessarily, as in Sentence 37:

37.   * Where is he at?

Questions of this sort are based on the understanding that the subject (*he*) is somewhere, either here or there, but the word *at* does not figure at all into this understanding. It simply appears and is unrelated to the structure or the meaning of the sentence.

Sentence 38, on the other hand, is representative of the ungrammaticality that results when people leave words out of sentences in ways that do not follow the patterns of English:

38.   * How south is it?

Ungrammaticality also occurs when people use function words in ways that English does not accept. The error usually involves prepositions and articles, and it may arise from using an unacceptable preposition or article or from having no preposition or article where one is needed, as illustrated in Sentences 39 through 42:

39.   * Fred put the shoes *in* her feet.
40.   * Macarena went the market.
41.   * *A* trouble with Fritz is that he never arrives on time.
42.   * Fritz saw dog walk across the lawn.

Most people associate this type of error with nonnative speakers, yet they nevertheless occur among native speakers with regularity.

Direct and Indirect Instruction

Students need to know grammar and usage on an explicit level because it gives them shared concepts and vocabulary for talking about language. With these at hand, they can discuss their writing more easily and effectively with their teachers and among themselves. This kind of knowledge can be taught directly, but direct instruction does not mean, in this case, the continued reliance on workbooks and exercises. Given the presence of language everywhere, such workbooks and exercises seem redundant at best. Most effective direct instruction therefore immerses students in their own language. It explains basic concepts and then asks students to use those concepts to analyze their own language, always taking care to distinguish between grammar and usage. Students usually get excited about grammar and usage when they have opportunities to apply their knowledge; activities that ask them to listen to others speak with the goal of identifying and recording variations in usage are very popular. They usually are tickled to discover that highly paid and well-educated people make numerous mistakes with usage.

Focusing on the language that surrounds them is only one part of the instruction. Students also need to master terms and functional concepts. Drills and exercises do not seem to be very effective in this regard, unless they happen to involve sentence diagraming of the sort illustrated in Figs. 5.1 through 5.6. Direct instruction works best when complemented by indirect instruction, which commonly links the study of grammar and usage to some other subject as an integral part of daily activities. Reading is particularly appropriate, and the rationale is straightforward. Discussions of reading inevitably involve questions of meaning as students and teacher explore what a given author means in a text; questions of *what* lead quite naturally to questions of *how*, which is where issues of structure and usage come in.

In this way, grammar instruction becomes part of an overall analysis of how good writers achieve the particular effects they do. Such analyses are important from any number of different perspectives, beginning with attention to detail and craftsmanship. This approach works best when teachers read with their students and periodically make a comment that focuses students' attention on a particular word or phrase. Such indirect instruction reinforces concepts in ways that direct instruction cannot. Remarking that a certain word is an "interesting adjective" draws students' attention to the word; it models the idea that some words are more interesting than others and reinforces the concept of an adjective.

Above all, grammar and usage instruction should give students tools for discovering language because language is at the center of everything people do. Grammar therefore should have an important role in the language arts. However, it is important to keep in mind that knowledge of grammar will not lead to better student writing. Indeed, knowledge of usage may not do so either because so many factors contribute to good writing. Experienced teachers are quite familiar with the well-structured paper that has nothing worth reading. Nevertheless, attention to usage can help students reduce some of the common errors that characterize the work of inexperienced writers.

EXPLORING KEY IDEAS

---

1. Teachers always seem to be caught between using grammar descriptively and using it prescriptively. Why is that?
2. If linguists have not used traditional grammar in more than 100 years, why is it still taught in the schools and where do teachers learn it?
3. Which grammar one chooses to accept as the best seems to depend on one's goals. How would you characterize the goals of the structuralists and the transformationalists? How would you characterize your goals?
4. We start internalizing the grammar of our home language at birth, speaking our first real words at about 1 year old. Why is this fact important to language arts teachers?
5. We know that neural networks like those depicted in Fig. 5.7 grow in part on the basis of stimulation. What are the implications for literacy?
6. About 35 years of research show that grammar instruction does not improve writing performance. This chapter insists, however, that it is important for students to study and master, on some level, grammar. Why?

7. Consider your own language carefully. Do you commit any of the usage errors described in this chapter? If so, what are the implications for your teaching?
8. What is it that cognitive grammar does that neither phrase-structure nor transformational-generative grammars do?

6

Style

Style has been part of rhetoric since the days of the Sophists, when speakers such as Gorgias held audiences spellbound with their flourishes. Throughout history, however, characterizations of style were highly subjective, with good reason: Discussions of style relied on metaphor. The development of new rhetoric changed matters considerably because of the link to linguistics. Although transformational-generative grammar has its share of metaphors, the phrase-structure grammar it uses as a foundation is empirical and associated with word counts, sentence length, and so forth. Linguistics gave scholars in the 1960s tools with which they could reevaluate style, which quickly came to be viewed as the linguistic choices a writer makes in the course of producing a text.

Differences between speech and writing were of special interest during this period because literacy was deemed a reflection of cognitive development. In this case, not only writing but also stylistic maturity was seen as a manifestation of reasoning ability. The presumed connection between language and mind formed part of the rationale for several studies in the mid-1960s that attempted to identify the characteristics of sentence or syntactic maturity. Hunt (1965) pioneered this work, determining that as writers mature they produce sentences with longer clauses.

On the basis of such research, theorists proposed that syntactic maturity could be increased through direct instruction. The result came to be widely known as *sentence combining*, which consists of exercises that require students to manipulate combinations of sentences, a technique that helps develop syntactic fluency. Although the popularity of sentence combining has declined considerably over the last decade, it was an important movement in new rhetoric and had a major effect on writing instruction. Whenever teachers attend to style today, they usually introduce students to sentence combining.

Substantial evidence suggested that sentence combining was effective in helping students produce longer and more varied sentences, and some evidence indicated that it had a positive effect on overall writing quality. These studies are counterbalanced by others that suggested that the effects of sentence combining were transient and by still others that indicated that the gains attributed to the technique may actually be the result of underlying rhetorical factors. The weight of the conflicting data was impressive and largely explains the decline in sentence combining's popularity.

DEFINING *STYLE*

Language is simultaneously universal and individual. It allows people to communicate across time and distance, but it also serves to define almost everything that makes a person unique. Individual differences are the result of nuances of vocabulary, sentence patterns, and organization that vary from person to person, giving each his or her own linguistic signature. It is unusual (if not impossible) to find two people who speak or write exactly alike. This commonplace observation is important with respect to writing because the written word gives people the luxury of reflecting on just how writers express themselves. Indeed, the study of literature has become an industry with authorial expression as a driving force. *Style* is the term used to identify and characterize the subtleties of language that distinguish one writer from another.

Mature readers usually have some awareness of stylistic features in discourse, even if only on a tacit level. They recognize, for example, that the writing of Tom Clancy is different from the writing of John Steinbeck, not just in subject matter but in expression as well. Each writer has a different quality of prose, a different style. If one were to ask just what that style is, however, most people would have a hard time describing it. The typical response might be "Clancy has a manly style" or "Steinbeck has a talkative style." The problem with these descriptions is that they are subjective and do not express much about what a manly or a talkative style might be. They are metaphors that reveal more about the person offering the description than they do about the writer's style.

Impressionistic metaphors dominated discussions of style until the 1960s. Then, Chomsky's work in linguistics brought about a change in perspective. Various scholars, influenced by Chomsky and utilizing the transformational-generative framework, began considering style in a new light, essentially abandoning the qualitative approach characteristic of literary studies (see Love & Payne, 1969; Turner, 1973). Qualitative analyses of texts, which previously had gone relatively unquestioned, were increasingly deemed to be simply unacceptable (Ohmann, 1969).

In the first formulation of transformational-generative grammar, any given sentence was reducible to its underlying structure, which was generally a shorter, simpler version of the surface structure. This underlying form was often referred to as a *kernel sentence*, which always existed as an active declarative, as in "Dogs bark" and "Mary kissed Juan." Scholars reasoned that because just about all writing has a variety of surface structures and is not limited to active declaratives, a writer achieves stylistic effects by performing transformations on kernel sentences, thereby creating structural diversity.

Chomsky (1957) argued vigorously that grammar was unrelated to semantics and that transformations did not affect meaning. Thus it was deemed possible to apply alternative transformations to any given kernel without significantly affecting its meaning, while nevertheless generating different surface structures. Although there are many different transformations, they perform only four different functions on kernels:

1. They add words or structures.
2. They delete words or structures.
3. They substitute one word or structure for another.
4. They reorder words or structures.

From a linguistic perspective, therefore, style seems to be a matter of the choices a given writer makes on a consistent basis for a particular type of writing in regard to the transformations applied to kernels. Thinking of style in this way—as being a writer's linguistic choices—may not make for a less problematic definition, but it is at least more concrete than Swift's proper words in proper places.

Scholars during the 1960s saw that if a writer had only four stylistic options—addition, deletion, substitution, and reordering—it was possible to quantify style. One need only analyze a piece of discourse carefully, determine what transformations were applied, add them up, and calculate how two or more writers differed. Style becomes a matter of statistics, not metaphor.

The quantification of style had two very important consequences. First, the study of style became the study of grammar. One of the more popular composition texts during the 1970s, for example, was Tufte's (1971) *Grammar as Style*. Second, the serious investigation of style, which in the past had largely been the province of literary scholars, was no longer limited to literature; it became a viable research question for scholars investigating student writing. Interest in style quickly waned among composition specialists, however. Grammar provided such a powerful tool that intricacies of style were easily revealed in terms of word counts. Furthermore, with the notable exception of sentence combining, the empirical study of style offered few insights into how to help students develop better styles. Then, as new rhetoric was swept aside by postmodern rhetoric, quantifiable analyses of style fell increasingly out of favor, replaced by deconstructionist readings that raised metaphorical descriptions of style to new levels and that motivated many people to change their notions of what a "good" style was. Rather than striving for clarity and grace, the postmodern style aims to obfuscate and distract. The techniques for studying style did not disappear, however. In a sense, they returned to their linguistic roots and reemerged as a new branch of linguistics known as *discourse analysis*, which generally does not deal with questions of style.

Finally, it is worth noting that style differs not only from writer to writer but also from one type of writing to another. This fact is a central part of most WAC programs, in which students are taught discipline-specific styles and conventions rather than one generic (and nearly always journalistic) style. For example, writing in the social sciences usually follows the convention of passive-voice constructions, whereas writing in the humanities does not. The two genres also require different word choices. Social science writing uses the verb *be* far more frequently than humanistic writing. At work are different styles. Various social and genre conventions severely limit the writer's options regarding how a discourse is structured and which styles are acceptable.

THE SOCIOLOGY OF STYLE

Much of the work in style over the last 35 years or so was conducted at universities. The implications for public schools are important because so much of this work and its influence has entered our public schools. The study of style during the 1960s was influenced by several factors in addition to the emergence of transformational-generative rhetoric. One of the more significant, although seldom examined, was the significant changes in college demographics at that time. American higher education had undergone important democratization after World War II, but until the 1960s, it still could be characterized as a domain of the elite. The Civil Rights Movement and its subsequent legislation, however, mandated equal educational opportunities; more important, it provided the funds to make the mandate real.

Blacks were not the only ones who reaped the benefits. Suddenly, the universities were inundated by a flood of internal refugees—various minority groups who, by virtue of previously unobtainable financial aid, entered higher education for the first time; working-class students who, faced with the choice between carrying a rifle to Vietnam or a book to class, enrolled in colleges by the tens of thousands (see Jencks, 1972; Shayer, 1972).

Generally, these students were unprepared for college, and colleges were largely unprepared for them. Faculty were faced with varieties of English that had long been associated with ghettos and the working class, neither of which fit into the cultivated image of ivory towerism on most campuses. The students' language was unacceptable by academic criteria, and given the lack of preparedness on the part of so many, it was relatively easy to equate nonstandard English with failure and stupidity.

One of the largest problems nontraditional students had was expressing themselves in writing.[1] Their speech was described as barely adequate, though sometimes colorful, but at least it was comprehensible. Their writing, however, was described as totally incomprehensible. This observation led to two widespread conclusions: First, the nation's public schools were not doing much in regard to literacy; second, spoken language is intrinsically different from written language. Educators and theorists proposed, for example, that "utterance is spontaneous" and "text is planned" (Dillon, 1981, p. 7).

At the heart of these emerging views was a model of language and mind that attempted to explain why certain segments of the population did so poorly in school. Known as the *cognitive deficit model*, it was based on research conducted by a number of anthropologists who investigated the cognitive development and reasoning abilities of nonliterate tribespeople during the late 1950s and early 1960s (see Goody, 1977; Goody & Watt, 1968; Greenfield, 1972; Greenfield & Bruner, 1966; Lévy-Bruhl, 1975). These scholars determined that the literate people in their studies significantly outperformed the nonliterate people on tests of reasoning ability. On the strength of these findings, many researchers concluded that cognitive development is shaped by the acquisition of literacy (Bruner & Olson, 1979; Walters, 1990), an idea that many educators still hold.

The principal component of this model in U.S. education is the idea that black children who speak what is known as Black English Vernacular (BEV), or simply Black English, come from impoverished cultural environments and have underdeveloped language skills. Because their experiential and linguistic backgrounds are assumed to be basic to their learning, and because both are deficient, their cognitive abilities also

---

[1]The term *nontraditional* is often used to describe students who have a handicap of some sort. It is used here, however, to describe students who traditionally were not served by higher education.

must be underdeveloped. The educational impact of this model was evident in the charter of the Head Start programs during the 1960s, which was organized to aid cognitive development and increase IQ levels among minorities.

Proponents of the cognitive deficit model maintained—and continue to maintain—-that learning how to write consists of acquiring the conventions of text and shedding the conventions of utterance (Dillon, 1981; Olson, 1977; Ong, 1978, 1982). This view reflects a version of *linguistic relativism*, a concept popularized by both Vygotsky (1962) and Whorf (1956) that claims language influences the nature of thought. Dillon (1981) and Shaughnessy (1977), for example, argued that the source of most difficulties in writing lies in students' failure to make a complete shift from oral conventions to written ones. Underlying this proposition is the notion that the ability to write well is linked to the ability to think well. Thus poor writers are simply poor thinkers. For anyone raised speaking a nonstandard dialect, such as Black English, the educational implications are harsh: By this account, their written discourse will be deficient in both form and content. Chapter 8 examines linguistic relativism in further detail.

The cognitive deficit model has been repudiated by psychologists since the early 1970s for a number of reasons (Cattel, 1971; Epstein, 1978; Hunt, 1975; Jensen, 1969). One of the more important is that the anthropological studies that led to its formulation were flawed. The investigators failed to develop adequate controls and ended up comparing dissimilar groups of subjects (Scribner & Cole, 1981). Nevertheless, the model continues to find favor among many educators because it provides a facile explanation for the traditionally low academic perform ance of minorities.

One could reason on the basis of linguistic relativism that if writing reflects cognitive development, *mental maturity* can be evaluated on the basis of *writing maturity*. Writing, in this view, is nothing more than thought transcribed. The logic, as far as it went, was impeccable: Good writers are good thinkers. It was this assumed relation that gave impetus and validity to the study of style. Stylistics promised to provide the long-term benefit of better understanding the mind and the short-term benefit of understanding why minorities did poorly in school.

If one were to accept the premise of the cognitive deficit model, it seems reasonable that studying style could provide such understanding. In addition, the notion of linguistic relativism (language affects thought) would predict that teachers could have students work on style and thereby directly influence mental processes and content. During the late 1960s and early 1970s, numerous teachers and scholars, in fact, accepted not only the cognitive deficit model but also the idea that stylistic exercises led to heightened reasoning abilities, even though there were no data to support either concept. Style was reinforced as the focus of writing and writing pedagogy because style was thought to have a direct impact on the way the mind operates.

STYLE AND SENTENCE COMBINING

When style and linguistics came together, it was inevitable that sentences and sentence structure would receive increased attention. Nevertheless, the outcome was more significant than perhaps anyone imagined. Out of this merging came what was called the *sentence-combining movement*, a technique for helping students become better able to control the sentences they write.

Hunt (1965) was one of the first researchers to use the transformational-generative framework to examine the relation between stylistic maturity and cognitive maturity. He studied maturation by comparing student writing at three grade levels to the writing of "superior" adults who published regularly in magazines and journals. Before Hunt's work, stylistic maturity was measured in terms of sentence length. He immediately found that sentence length was a poor standard for defining a mature style and that a much better indicator was clause length, or what he called a *minimal-terminal unit*, or simply *T-unit*—the shortest grammatical construction that can be punctuated as a sentence. Underlying Hunt's research is a hypothesized linear relation between age and style (which prompted Witte & Cherry, 1986, to ask whether there is such a thing as *syntactic senility*). Within limits, such a relationship does exist. The older and more experienced writers in Hunt's study produced sentences with longer T-units, which prompted him to link syntactic maturity with developmental maturity.

Sentences 1 through 3 illustrate this finding. A third-grade student, for example, would use two sentences to express two propositions, as in Sentences 1 and 2, producing two short T-units, whereas the adult would embed one proposition in the other in a single sentence, creating a single T-unit, as in Sentence 3:

1. The woman had red hair.
2. The woman laughed.
3. The woman who laughed had red hair.

Hunt's study suggested that competence and performance are at work in this case. Third graders can understand sentences with embedded subordinate clauses, like Sentence 3, but they do not produce such sentences very often. In fact, children under 10 years old just do not use many relative clauses. Sentence combining was seen as a way, then, of raising competence to performance. Explicit instruction in forming sentences like 3 should, in theory, lead to greater production of such sentences, which in turn should provide greater syntactic maturity. Sentence combining was therefore viewed as a method of taking a short cut through normal cognitive and linguistic development.

Mellon (1969), drawing extensively on Hunt's findings, recognized that subordinate embeddings have a transformational basis, and he hypothesized that teaching students how to perform grammatical transformations would have a significant effect on T-unit length. He gave a group of seventh-grade students intensive training in applying transformations over a period of 9 weeks and then presented them with sentences like 1 and 2, with a relative-clause marker indicating the appropriate transformation. Pretest–posttest analysis of T-units indicated a significant increase in length, from 9.98 to 11.25 words. Unfortunately, although the subjects managed to produce longer T-units, trained readers did not judge their writing to be particularly better overall.

Despite these problematic results, the theory underlying the technique of combining short sentences into longer ones seemed flawless, which created some confusion. Mellon's study should have shown improved writing among the subjects. It was O'Hare (1973) who saw a difficulty in Mellon's methodology. O'Hare reasoned that subjects did not need any formal instruction in grammar to perform transformations because such transformations were already part of their linguistic competence. Students did not need to know the formal aspects of, say, the relative-clause transformation in order to form a sentence with a relative clause.

Using 95% of the sentences from Mellon's study, O'Hare had students manipulate them to form the combinations, which they were able to do quite easily. His results showed an increase in T-unit length 5 times greater than what Mellon reported, and 23 times greater than the normal increase reported by Hunt. Moreover, trained readers rated the quality of the subjects' posttreatment writing as better than the writing of the control group. Sentence combining was born.

Christensen (1967) took a somewhat different approach to syntactic maturity. After studying the work of professional writers, he determined that they used short base (or independent) clauses to which they attached modifying phrases that added detail and depth. The following student sentences illustrate this technique. The italicized portions of these sentences are the base clauses:

4. *I danced with excitement*, winding myself around my nana's legs, balling my hands in her apron, tugging at her dress, stepping on her toes, until finally she gave me a swat across the bottom and told me to go play.

5. *I dragged a chair to the counter and climbed up*, grasping the counter edge with my hands, stretching my body, pulling up with my arms until my head was above the tiles.

Unlike other sentence-combining techniques, this one emphasizes having students start out with short base clauses; they then supply modifying detail on the basis of close observation. Modifying constructions usually are added to the end of the base clauses, producing what Christensen referred to as a *cumulative sentence*. Cumulative sentences appear with great frequency in narration and description and have an ebb-and-flow movement from the general to the specific, what Christensen called changes in *levels of generality*. His approach focused on helping students shift from one level of generality to another.

Sentence combining became popular very quickly, in part because it fit neatly into the already established focus on style in student writing. In addition, many teachers noted that students liked sentence combining; they liked figuring out different ways to join sentences together. Even more important, teachers began to see that sentence combining seemed to improve writing performance. Students who practiced it gained greater control over their sentences and were able to develop more variety in sentence types.

These classroom observations were supported by many studies showing that students who engaged in regular sentence-combining exercises increased the length of their T-units and improved overall composition quality (Combs, 1977; Daiker, Kerek, & Morenberg, 1978; Howie, 1979; Pedersen, 1978). After reviewing the major investigations related to sentence combining, Kerek, Daiker, and Morenberg (1980) stated that sentence combining "has been proven again and again to be an effective means of fostering growth in syntactic maturity" (p. 1067).

One of the major attractions of sentence combining was that it could be used effectively by students at all grade and ability levels (O'Hare, 1973; Sullivan, 1978, 1979; Waterfall, 1978). If anything, in fact, poor writers seemed to benefit most from this technique. Part of the explanation appears to be that sentence combining offers an algorithmic approach to teaching writing that many teachers and most students are very comfortable with. Moreover, it provides quick, tangible results, giving students as well as teachers a sense of accomplishment. Occasional difficulties arise with older students who have generally been told to perform just the opposite task, taking long sentences and reducing them to short ones, but these are not insurmountable.

This positive assessment of sentence combining, however, must be weighed against various studies that suggested that, over time, the gains in sentence length and writing quality attributed to sentence combining disappeared (Callaghan, 1978; Green, 1973; Sullivan, 1978). Kerek et al. (1980), in the same study that commented on the positive effects of the technique, found that 2 years after instruction, there were no measurable differences between the writing of those students who had practiced sentence combining and of students who had not. The control group had completely caught up with the treatment group, which over the 2-year period had made no further gains. If the results are transient or mitigated by time, teachers must carefully evaluate the energy and effort involved in using the technique.

In addition, it should be noted that rhetorical mode may affect measures of syntactic maturity. Studies by Perron (1977) and Crowhurst and Piche (1979) suggested that narration and description result in the shortest T-units, whereas analysis and argumentation result in the longest. Furthermore, having students write regularly in the argumentative mode seems to produce gains in T-unit length and writing quality equal to those related to sentence-combining exercises.

Ample data indicate the reality of what may be thought of as a complexity continuum for rhetorical modes (Britton, Burgess, Martin, McLeod, & Rosen, 1975; Williams, 1983). At least with regard to classroom compositions, analysis and argumentation are cognitively more demanding than description, so the frequently noted correlation between complexity of thought and syntactic maturity serves to explain the effect of mode on performance (Williams, 1983, 1987). Along these lines, Kinneavy (1979) and Witte (1980) argued that the gains in T-unit length and writing quality attributed to sentence combining may actually be the result of inductively teaching rhetorical principles such as analysis and synthesis, principles that are inherent in the process of combining. If this is the case, teaching these principles directly, through the associated rhetorical modes, probably is more efficient. In other words, it may well be that teachers can have a significant effect on syntactic maturity and writing performance simply by focusing more attention on more demanding writing tasks, such as analysis and argument.

This suggestion is an important one, because it raises a serious question not only for sentence combining but also for any approach to writing instruction that emphasizes style. The issue is this: Will students benefit more from working on isolated sentences or on whole essays?

New rhetoric came down solidly on the side of the whole essay. Writing, like reading, is primarily viewed as a top–down rather than a bottom–up process. In this view, to focus on style is to deal with the surface features of discourse, with matters of form. An emphasis on surface features tends to lead to error correction that slights the rhetorical, functional nature of discourse. Content, meaning, and purpose too often get ignored in such a learning environment, and an emphasis on style in general and sentence combining in particular may not be conducive to successful writing instruction over the long term. These considerations, combined with the studies showing no lasting gains attributable to sentence combining, deflated the movement. About 10 years after it began, sentence combining was relegated to a minor place in overall composition instruction.

STYLE AS VOICE

Today, there is increasing attention to the idea of style as voice, but the notion of linguistic choices based on grammar is absent. Certainly, it is the case that we want students to develop an individual voice in their writing, one that differentiates their work from that of others', but defining what voice is without reference to linguistic choices or quantitative measures is quite difficult. As a result, many of the discussions of style have returned to the reliance on metaphor that dominated composition prior to the 1960s. Equally problematic is the fact that many teachers, in a well-intentioned effort to give students a sense of freedom associated with voice, tell students that they can write any way they want, as long as they express themselves. Usually, this advice means that students transcribe their speech.

It is important to recognize that style and voice are not exactly the same thing. Style more often than not is a feature of genre, which means that it is influenced significantly by the discourse community for which one is writing. Voice, on the other hand, transcends style. The style of two history papers, for example, may be very similar, but they may have different voices. No one understands all the factors that contribute to the development of an individual voice. However, reading, once again, seems to be a central factor, as does the kind of feedback teachers provide when they talk to students about or write comments on papers. Students develop an aesthetic that guides them as they write, an aesthetic based on texts they have read and admired and based on the preferences of teachers they have admired. Reading was discussed in some detail in chapter 4, so no additional comments are necessary here, which leaves the role of the teacher, which cannot be underestimated.

TEACHING STYLE AND DEVELOPING VOICE

Too often, teachers engage students in talk concerning the *what* of texts without addressing the *how*. Any effort to help students develop style and voice must start with more balance between the two. There is great beauty in language, and students need help in discovering examples of it. In addition, they need help in learning how to create similar beauty in their own work.

Active modeling is one of the more effective ways to provide this help. It involves the ancient tradition of having students attempt to imitate the style of a professional writer. Teachers select a model, of perhaps 100 words, and then explain to students the features that make the model exemplary. This explanation includes metaphor, imagery, diction, and sentence construction. Students then produce a similar piece of writing on a different subject. The following are three examples that illustrate the process. The first example comes from a high-school class in which students were studying John Steinbeck's (1937) *Of Mice and Men*; the following is the studied excerpt:

A few miles south of Soledad, the Salinas River drops in close to the hillside bank and runs deep and green. The water is warm too, for it has slipped twinkling over the yellow sands in the sunlight before reaching the narrow pool. On one side of the river the golden foothill slopes curve up to the strong and rocky Gabilan mountains, but on the valley side the water is lined with trees—willows fresh and green with every spring, carrying with their lower leaf junctures the debris of the winter's flooding; and sycamores with mottled, white, recumbent limbs and branches that arch over the pool. On the sandy bank under the trees the leaves lie deep and so crisp that a lizard makes a great skittering if he runs among them. Rabbits come out of brush to sit on the sand in the evening, and the damp flats are covered with the night tracks of 'coons, and with the spread pads of dogs from the ranches, and with the split-wedge tracks of deer that come to drink in the dark. (pp. 7–8)

The following is Maria's—a twelfth grader's—imitation:

Not far from my house, through a bramble of trash pines and weeds, lies a meadow with a small stream running along its side. The meadow is flat and green, dotted with yellow and blue flowers in the spring, but the banks of the stream are tangled with blackberry bushes, tall grass, and wild holly. A narrow path, worn down by deer, winds its way through the tangle to a small sandy beach and the water, which in the spring bubbles its way over moss-cover rocks jutting up from the bed. Here and there, the rocks wall off the tumbling water and create small pools that the fish have used to lay their eggs, and in the spring they are alive with minnows. In the late afternoon, raccoons come to these pools for a snack, plunging their paws into the icy water in a flash and pulling out a minnow, which they pop into their mouths like popcorn. On a rock in the middle of the stream, caught in a ray of afternoon sunlight, an old turtle watches the raccoon through its half-open eyes, ready to drop into the depths of the stream at the first sign that the raccoons want more than a snack.

This sort of exercise, based on narration and description, can be popular among students and teachers alike and is an effective way to link reading and writing. Students usually are fairly successful in imitating the professional model, and they seem to be able to transfer the skills they learn to later writing tasks, provided that those tasks are narration and description. There is no clear evidence of transfer to expository writing tasks, although it seems reasonable to propose that, over time, some transfer would occur.

The next example also comes from a high school class, and it illustrates the use of an expository model for imitation. Although many teachers and students prefer working with narration and description, we have to recognize that students have few occasions to produce narration and description; nearly all the writing that students do in classes other than language arts, and certainly, all the writing that they will do in universities and beyond, will be expository. The professional model comes from an article by Davis (1990) titled "Natural Restoration":

By 1953, when South Korea and North Korea signed the Armistice Agreement that ended the Korean War, the 151-mile strip designated as the demilitarized zone had been devastated. Once littered with terraced rice fields, small crop plots and villages, the DMZ was bare of vegetative cover, pockmarked by bomb craters, and crisscrossed by hundreds of artillery roads. Towns and farms had been forsaken. Most of the region's forests had been razed to deny enemy North Koreans cover. Four million lives had been lost. So too had hundreds of acres of farmlands and wildlife habitat.

Today, the scarred slopes have been invaded by mixed hardwood forest. Terrace rice paddies have converted to marshland. Grass and shrubs have conquered abandoned farms. The trumpeting cries of the endangered Manchurian cranes replace the sound of gunfire; pheasants, deer, lynx, and occasional tigers roam the still heavily land-mined area. What is a military no-man's land—site of the longest cease-fire in history, only one gunshot from explosive conflict—has become a wildlife sanctuary. And it has become that with no aid from humans—other than removing our presence.

The Korean DMZ illustrates an idea many of us forget: Nature heals itself. In the midst of warnings of humans' irrevocable impact, news of an irrepressible nature sounds peculiar. But the DMZ story is not an isolated example. Plants and animals are very stubborn. Given a disturbance, an ecosystem regenerates, even without our helping hands. Put another way, ecosystems regenerate if we leave them alone. (p. 603)

After studying this model, Clarence wrote his emulation:

Cabrini Green had started out as a place where people who needed government assistance could live comfortably. Throughout the 1950s and early 1960s it provided modest but decent housing to several hundred families at little or not cost. Things began to change in the mid-1960s, and today Cabrini Green represents all that has gone wrong with public housing in America.

The population is composed largely of single mothers and their children. Many of these children are teenage and young adult males, and most of them are involved in gangs and drugs. The mothers do not want their sons to become in gangs and drugs, but for the boys it is a matter of survival. Few of these males attend school after about the tenth grade, and they cannot get jobs. Even if they could get jobs, they are not going to work for 6 or 7 dollars an hour when they can make 10 times that amount by selling crack. In the midst of the poverty of the projects, these gang members are earning as much as $1,000 a day on drugs. They have the money to leave Cabrini Green, but doing so would mean an end to they business, so they stay. Meanwhile, the police generally try to leave them alone.

What we notice about imitation with this kind of writing is that it is far harder to duplicate the style of the original. Nevertheless, there is a similarity between the two samples. The model gives students a structure that otherwise would be lacking. Such a structure is especially important for inexperienced writers because they often have something to say but worry about how to say it. The model reduces their anxiety about structure and allows students to devote more attention to content.

The final sample illustrates what can be done with poetry. The original is a poem from Wadsworth's "Over in the Meadow" (1971):

Over in the meadow, in the sand, in the sun
Lived an old mother turtle and her little turtle one
"Dig!" said the mother
"I dig!" said the one
So he dug all day
In the sand, in the sun.

The following student sample was written by John, a third grader:

There in the treetop, on a branch, have fun
Lived a little mother sparrow and her tiny baby son
"Fly!" said the mother
"I fly!" said the son
So he flew all day
Through the air, having fun.

Young children enjoy this sort of activity, and it really lends an element of fun and excitement to writing that can have long-lasting benefits, especially to boys, who tend to have less of an interest in language. Animation software that is now readily available turns this sort of imitation into a major project, with the teacher helping students use the software to create comic books on the basis of stories that the children write.

JOURNAL ENTRY

Do you have your own style, your own voice? How would you characterize it? If it is still in the process of developing, what have been some of the major influences?

EXPLORING KEY IDEAS

1. A common style exercise during the 1970s involved selecting a 100-word sample from two favorite authors and performing an analysis. The analysis consisted of determining average sentence length, average clause length, average number of clauses per sentence, average number of adverbs and adjectives, sentence openers, and so on. The result was a very concrete way of differentiating the writing of the two authors. What would such an analysis reveal about your two favorite authors?
2. One of the objections mounted against a qualitative approach to style is that it encourages students to be very conscious about the structure of their work, which detracts from their concentration on meaning and substance. What would be an effective response to this objection?
3. There are indications that students must attend consciously to sentence-combining techniques for about 1 year before the techniques become internalized and largely unconscious. If accurate, what does this finding suggest may be the greatest difficulty with using sentence combining to improve student writing?

4. There are also indications, as noted in the chapter, that after 2 years students with and without sentence-combining experience are writing at about the same level. This finding calls into question the benefits of sentence combining, but does it suggest that teachers should not use the technique? What might be a continuing benefit of sentence combining?
5. The emphasis on personal voice in so many writing classes probably is in conflict with the social-theoretic view of writing. Why?
6. In most views, that style is best that is clearest. What are some of the biggest obstacles that students face with respect to developing a clear style?

7

English as a Second Language and Nonstandard English

OVERVIEW

American society has grown increasingly pluralistic since the mid-1960s as a result of the largest wave of immigration in the nation's history. One significant consequence is that more and more students in public schools do not speak English as their native language. To meet the challenge these students present, bilingual education programs have been established across the United States with federal support. The goal of these programs is to help nonnative speakers master English. Although all bilingual education programs use English and another language, they commonly differ in structure and focus. Some offer instruction in the native language (L_1) in content classes until students show sufficient mastery of English. Others offer instruction in L_1 for content classes and provide students with an English as a Second Language (ESL) class to help them master English. Still others offer instruction in English (L_2) for content area classes and provide a supplemental ESL class. All these approaches can be described as a form of *bilingual immersion*, although they reflect different goals for bilingual education—either bilingualism or monolingualism. These goals are normally articulated in the specific orientation in a given district or state. Those schools that perceive value in helping students preserve their home language and culture adopt an approach that emphasizes *language maintenance*, whereas those that perceive value in helping students assimilate into the English-speaking mainstream emphasize *language shift*.

In addition to nonnative English speakers, today's classrooms have large numbers of nonstandard English speakers. Most of these speakers come from ethnic minorities, particularly black and Hispanic students, but significant numbers are white students from lower socioeconomic backgrounds. The combination of various language groups in individual

176

classrooms suggests that teachers need to see their classes as being both multilingual and multidialectical.

For the purposes of this text, the term *nonmainstream* is used to designate students whose first language is one other than English or whose first dialect is nonstandard English. Many times these two groups of students are present in the same class, but more important, there are numerous similarities between bilingualism and bidialectalism. Thus many of the factors related to teaching bilingual students are pertinent to teaching their bidialectal counterparts.

Traditional methods for teaching writing to nonmainstream students consist of providing drills and exercises to train them to use standard grammar and usage. Students write very little under this methodology, and what writing they do is often limited to sentences and paragraphs. Only occasionally do they write whole essays. Intuitively, it should be apparent that methods that fail to improve the writing of students who speak standard English will fail even more severely when the students involved speak ESL or a nonstandard dialect. This intuition is supported by a variety of studies that have suggested that nonmainstream students benefit most from the student-centered workshop approach characteristic of the process or social-theoretic models.

BILINGUAL EDUCATION

According to census figures, the U.S. population has grown by about 100 million since 1960, and immigration has contributed significantly to this growth. Although exact figures are impossible to determine, some estimates put the total immigration during the period from 1960 to 1995 at about 40 million. The social consequences of this mass immigration are significant, for it quite literally has altered the state of the nation and figures into nearly every question associated with public policy—from education and health care to housing and employment. For this reason, bilingual education always has been—and is likely to remain—primarily a political issue rather than a pedagogical one.

With good reason, mainstream English speakers feel some apprehension when they consider the level of immigration that has occurred since the 1960s. The status that English enjoyed after World War I as the dominant language in American society is no longer as secure as it once was. The sheer number of Spanish speakers now in the United States (estimated by census figures to be anywhere from 20 million–40 million), the majority of whom speak little or no English, is reshaping the linguistic characteristics of the nation. For example, there are now about 300 Spanish-language newspapers in the United States, more than 300 Spanish-speaking radio stations, and several Spanish television networks. In many areas of the Southwest, Spanish is the first language of the majority of the population. More than half of the states in the country, including California, have passed legislation declaring English to be the official language, and many others are considering similar legislation. Such legislation, in turn, makes nonnative English speakers feel apprehensive. The resulting tension seems to escalate each year.

The politics of bilingual education are polarized. On the one hand are those who advocate assimilation into the English-speaking mainstream. They argue convincingly that assimilation is necessary if non-English-speaking children are to have any hope of enjoying the socioeconomic benefits available to those who have access to higher education and professional jobs, for which fluency and literacy in English are fundamental requirements. Less often heard, but nevertheless salient, is the argument that language is the thread that binds diverse people into one nation and that the welfare of the country is enhanced through monolingualism. On the other hand are those who advocate linguistic and cultural pluralism. They argue convincingly that people identify who they are—individually and culturally—on the basis of the language they speak. Therefore, to ask children to assimilate into the English-speaking mainstream is to ask them to lose their identity and their cultural heritage. They also argue that the nation is enriched by the linguistic and cultural diversity inherent in bilingualism and that the country would be well served if native English-speaking children were required to learn a second language. The arguments of the two camps are convincing because both contain many elements of truth. Nevertheless, the nation's overall goal, expressed clearly in the Bilingual Education Act of 1968, is assimilation.

Typically, parents must identify the home language when they register their children for school. On the basis of these reports, the schools test nonnative English speakers just before or shortly after classes begin, using any one of a variety of available instruments, such as the Bilingual Inventory of Natural Language (BINL). Students then are classified on the basis of this test as either English proficient or limited English proficient (LEP). This classification is important because it determines student placement.

Students classified as LEP generally go into an *immersion program*. Immersion provides dual instruction in L_1 and L_2, until students are proficient in both languages. In ideal situations, *proficiency* includes literacy as well as oral skills, yet in many districts literacy in both languages remains a nagging problem that receives inadequate attention. One result is that large numbers of nonnative English speakers fail to become literate in either L_1 or L_2 (Williams & Snipper, 1990).

The goal of immersion can be bilingualism or monolingualism, and the approaches of Canada and the United States offer illustrative examples. In Canada, the goal is bilingualism, so students whose home language is English take content classes in French, whereas students whose home language is French take content classes in English.[1] The Canadian approach is intended to reduce, if not eliminate, the stigma attached to minority languages by treating both equally in the schools. A handful of American schools have experimented with the Canadian model, but resistance is strong because the goal of bilingual policy in the United States is monolingualism, not bilingualism. Consequently, immersion in this country is unilateral rather than bilateral. Nonnative English speakers take classes in English, but native English speakers do not take classes in, say, Spanish. Those schools that offer Spanish classes to native-English speakers do so as part of a foreign-language program, not as part of a bilingual-immersion program.[2]

After classification, most schools place LEP students in English-only classes that rely on bilingual aides to translate the course material; such students also attend a course on ESL. Some schools, however, place these students in content classes conducted in L_1 and provide them with a supplemental ESL class.[3] In either case, the goal of assimilation results in efforts to reclassify LEP students quickly as English proficient, so the overall approach is often described as reflecting an orientation toward *language shift*. Nearly all LEP students are reclassified within 1 year, and many of them are reclassified within 6 months.

Those educators who strongly disagree with the assumptions underlying both assimilation and language shift advocate an approach to bilingualism that strives not only to preserve but also to enhance existing skills in L_1, particularly literacy skills. This approach is usually referred to as *language maintenance*. Compared to their counterparts in language-shift programs, students take content classes in L_1 much longer, with a corresponding increase in the attention given to literacy. Teachers in all classes regularly focus on factors that reinforce students' home culture, such as celebrations of native holidays and reports of

---

[1]Students actually rotate their courses every couple of years so that they take classes in L_1 periodically.

[2]During the 1970s and early 1980s, foreign-language programs expanded in most districts to include early instruction at the elementary level. During the late 1980s and into the 1990s, budget difficulties have prompted many schools to reduce or even eliminate their foreign-language programs.

[3]Several studies show that parents and students value assimilation more than maintenance, although, as Shin (1994) reported, parents often are ambivalent about programs that keep students in L_1 content-area classes for a significant time. In addition, Luges (1994) reported that students in ESL programs view ESL classes negatively owing to their perception that such classes act as obstacles to assimilation.

important news events in the home country.

Advocates of language maintenance recognize that helping students develop better L_1 skills can have a positive effect on self-confidence, and they argue that the resulting linguistic and cultural diversity offers benefits to the whole society. Cummins (1988), for example, supports policies that would transform American monolingual society into a multilingual one and has argued for greater efforts at maintenance. Although the goals of language maintenance are worthy, Williams and Snipper (1990) correctly noted that proponents frequently fail to consider the numerous social factors that make them impractical. Because so many Americans and permanent residents speak native languages other than English, it is possible to argue that the nation is already multilingual to a certain degree, but official multilingualism of the sort envisioned by scholars such as Cummins would have to satisfy a fundamental sociolinguistic reality: People learn another language only when they have a reason for doing so. Currently, such a reason does not exist for most Americans.

Immersion and Spanish-Speaking Students

The overwhelming majority of nonnative English-speaking students in the nation's schools speak Spanish, and the majority are from Mexico and Central America. Immersion has proven stubbornly unsuccessful in helping them master English, prompting some educators to assert that immersion is more accurately *submersion*. The failure of immersion to develop English literacy and oral proficiency among native Spanish-speaking students probably contributes to the high dropout rate among Hispanics, which has hovered around 50% for decades. Some scholars attribute the failure to the proximity of Mexico and the widespread belief among many Mexican-Americans (even second and third generation) that they someday will return permanently to Mexico (Griswold del Castillo, 1984; Sanchez, 1983) Others attribute it to the size of the Hispanic community. With their own subculture of shops, newspapers, radio stations, businesses, and so on, native Spanish speakers experience less socioeconomic pressure to master English than, for example, an immigrant from Iran would feel. Because socioeconomic factors are the principal motivators in mastering another language, in this case English, the lack of such pressure significantly diminishes efforts at second-language acquisition. Still others argue that Spanish speakers have been systematically excluded from America's mainstream economic community, kept at the lowest end of the socioeconomic scale for so long that they lack hope of entry and therefore lack motivation to master English (Griswold del Castillo, 1984; Penalosa, 1980; Sanchez,

1983). Graff (1987) argued that such exclusion has been deliberate and that the nation's schools have perpetuated illiteracy among Hispanics so as to maintain for the nation a large pool of unskilled labor to perform menial tasks.

Recent research suggests that a key to improving the success of immersion programs lies in discovering ways to get the parents of native Spanish-speaking students more involved in their children's mastery of English; this is not an easy task because parents who do not speak English are often reluctant to interact with teachers who do not speak Spanish. Parator, Homza, Krol-Sinclair, Lewis-Barrow, Melzi, Stergis, and Haynes (1995) reported gains, however, when parents participated more actively in bridging the home–school environments.

THE NEED FOR BILINGUAL EDUCATION

The Bilingual Education Act of 1968 was designed to make school districts more responsive to the special educational needs of children of limited English-speaking ability. The nation's schools have responded admirably, for the most part, considering the size of the task, but it is the case that many teachers and administrators are ambivalent about bilingual education. It is costly, and the political dimension creates stress that educators would rather not face. Nevertheless, they recognize that to ignore the educational needs of such vast numbers for the 2 to 3 years required to master English is simply unconscionable.

Matters are complicated, however, by the fact that the number of nonnative English speakers continues to grow. In the school yards of the nation's larger districts, one hears a potpourri of different languages, many unrecognizable to the lay observer. In Los Angeles, for example, more than 100 languages are currently represented among students. Smaller districts are experiencing the same phenomenon; schools in Wyoming, Illinois, and Indiana now report LEP enrollments approaching 20%, with few instructors qualified to teach them.

Finding qualified bilingual teachers is extremely problematic; for some languages it is outright impossible. Though most teachers have studied some foreign language, they are far from being bilingual. Moreover, if the language they studied was French, Italian, or German, it is essentially useless in the classroom. The languages of our newest immigrants tend not to fall into the major European categories, with the obvious exception of Spanish, but are more likely to be Cambodian, Vietnamese, Korean, Farsi, Hindi, or some dialect of Chinese. As this book goes to press, nearly half of the nation's new immigrants come from Asia and Africa, and half come from Mexico and Latin America. The situation is so extreme that most districts are unable to hire enough teachers who speak the most widely distributed language—Spanish—because the demand exceeds the supply. Many schools in the Los Angeles area, for example, are 60%, 70%, in some cases, even 80% native-Spanish speakers. There just are not enough bilingual teachers to go around, even though the need is very great.

The consequences of this situation are felt by almost every teacher at the elementary and secondary level, whether one is teaching a designated bilingual class or not. Increasingly, teachers are being asked to view their classes as being multilingual because they are likely to work with nonnative English-speaking students at some point, regardless of what part of the country they teach in. The tendency to reclassify these students as English proficient before they are ready adds to the teacher's problems, because it usually places LEP students in classes with native English speakers, making uniform assignments and grading difficult. In addition, the writing teacher is confronted with linguistic patterns that he or she has not been adequately trained to handle.

BILINGUALISM AND INTELLIGENCE

For many years the two political camps in conflict over bilingual education have argued a presumed relation between bilingualism and intelligence. A variety of studies show that monolinguals outperformed bilinguals on intelligence tests (Anastasi, 1980; Christiansen & Livermore, 1970; Killian, 1971), and advocates of monolingualism used these results to argue for rapid assimilation into the linguistic mainstream. Typically, the claim is that mental processes become confused and slower when children use two languages rather than one, and often the appearance of code switching (a term used to describe shifts back and forth from one language or dialect to the other during a conversation) is cited as evidence of cognitive confusion.

Advocates of bilingualism, for their part, have soundly criticized these studies. Peal and Lambert (1962), for example, determined that researchers who found monolinguals outperformed bilinguals on intelligence tests were studying dissimilar groups. The bilinguals in the studies were not fluent in L_2, which presumably influenced their test performance. Following this line of thought, numerous researchers conducted additional studies and ensured that they used similar groups of subjects. Under these conditions, bilinguals performed as well as or better than monolinguals (Bruck, Lambert & Tucker, 1974; Cummins, 1976; Diaz, 1986; Duncan & DeAvila, 1979).

Garcia (1983), however, noted that such studies failed to account for a factor that historically has correlated significantly with intelligence—socioeconomic status (SES). He showed that, in the studies that found monolinguals outperforming bilinguals, the bilingual subjects characteristically were from lower SES levels than their monolingual counterparts. In the studies conducted with fluent bilinguals, the bilingual subjects came from higher SES levels.

Hakuta (1986) recognized the political nature of the debate when he pointed out that the majority of the studies that showed bilingualism had a negative effect on intelligence were conducted in the United States. The majority of those that showed a positive effect, on the other hand, were conducted in Canada. Hakuta interpreted his findings as reflecting the different sociopolitical agendas the two countries have with respect to language policy. Policy in Canada is oriented toward bilingualism, whereas policy in the United States is oriented toward monolingualism.

In addition, Hakuta hypothesized that bilingualism may not have any effect on intelligence. To test this hypothesis, Hakuta and Diaz (1984) and Hakuta (1984) examined intelligence and language skill in 300 bilingual Puerto Rican children but did not compare their performance on intelligence measures to monolinguals. The premise in this research was that bilingualism is a performance continuum, which means that some subjects would be more bilingual than others. This premise makes it reasonable to propose, then, that any relation between intelligence and bilingualism can be evaluated within a group. Although the design of these studies was sound, the results were inconclusive. Nevertheless, Hakuta (1986) asserted that "bilingualism ... bears little relationship to performance on [intelligence tests]" (p. 40). This conclusion is supported by additional studies. Jarvis, Danks, and Merriman (1995), for example, found no relation between the degree of bilingualism and performance on nonverbal IQ tests among third and fourth graders. At this point, it seems certain that bilingualism has no measurable correlation with intelligence.

JOURNAL ENTRY

Consider what you would think and feel if your classes were suddenly conducted in a language you do not know. Are there any lessons to be learned that you might take with you to your own teaching?

REVISITING LANGUAGE ACQUISITION

On a day-to-day basis, the question of bilingualism and intelligence, and indeed of nonstandard English and intelligence, is ever-present as a pedagogical issue in the classroom. It is especially pressing for writing

teachers, because grammatical, or surface, correctness is the criterion
by which society generally evaluates the success of written discourse.
Eliminating errors therefore takes on a sense of urgency for both
students and teachers.

With nonnative and nonstandard speakers alike, however, instruction proceeds with great difficulty. Lessons that take long preparation
and that are taught with diligence and care frequently seem to make no
difference. The Hispanic child, for example, who uses Spanish grammar
in designating the negative and produces "Maria no have her homework"
may continue to do so even after work with the English verb form *do*
("Maria does not have her homework"). Many teachers find this lack of
change extremely puzzling, and even the most conscientious teacher
may begin to doubt the intellectual ability of their nonmainstream
students. The only way to solve this puzzle is to understand that in the
process of language acquisition linguistic patterns become deeply in-
grained and therefore difficult to alter.

Language in Infants

The process of language acquisition begins shortly after birth. Halliday
(1979) reported that a 1-day-old child stops crying to attend to its
mother's voice; this response is generally viewed as a precursor to actual
language. Because the infant's response is not yet language, a more
flexible term to describe its behavior is *communicative competence*,
which specifies, among other things, the ability to make clear a topic of
interest, to produce a series of relevant propositions, and to express
ideas in a way that is sensitive to what the speaker knows about the
hearer (Foster, 1985; Hymes, 1971).

The development of communicative competence seems to be a fundamental component of the parent–child relationship. Halliday (1979)
noted that, just as a child will stop crying to listen to its mother's voice,
a mother, "for her part, will stop doing almost anything, including
sleeping, to attend to the voice of her child. Each is predisposed to listen
to the sounds of the other" (p. 171). This predisposition reflects the
innateness of language, but it also reflects the importance of early
parent–child interactions, which have a deep and powerful influence on
language development.

The complexity of these interactions is visible within a few weeks of
birth. A parent and child actively engage in an early form of conversational turn taking that consists of ongoing exchanges of attention. The
child attends carefully to the sounds and the movements of the parent,
moving with him or her in a dance of body language. To capture this turn
taking, Trevarthen (1974) used video cameras to record mother–child

interactions, which showed mother and child in animated mutual address. The child moved its entire body in a way that was clearly directed toward the mother; in addition, it moved its face, lips, tongue, arms, and hands, in what seems best described as incipient communication. At the same time, the mother addressed the child with sounds and gestures of her own that mirrored her baby's actions. The two did not appear to imitate each other; rather, the gestures and vocalizations appeared to be communicative (though nonlinguistic) initiation and response. When viewed in slow motion, the movements of the child were slightly ahead of the mother's, suggesting that he or she was the initiator, not the mother.

The amount of meaning conveyed in such exchanges is open to argument, but these gestures and movements are clearly important precursors to recognizable words and expressions that typically begin to emerge between 12 and 20 months. Prespeech exchanges may not have a propositional meaning, but they are meaningful from the standpoint of communicating attention and developing pragmatic (e.g., turn taking) competence. As a result, when children begin to produce language, they already have been engaged in meaningful communication for a long time.

Most of a young child's preverbal communication is related directly to his or her world, composed of toys, pets, parents, and so forth. Children work at communicating particular needs and desires within the context of their environment. Their first communicative efforts are highly pragmatic and functional, bound tightly to their immediate surroundings and their parents, as evidenced by the fact that parents seem to interpret their children's preverbal vocalizations accurately, whereas a stranger cannot.

By the age of 1, and perhaps even earlier, children have a broad range of knowledge about the way the world operates. They know, for example, that cups are for drinking, knives and forks are for eating, beds are for sleeping, cars take them places, knobs or remotes turn on TV sets, and so on. Moreover, their pragmatic awareness gives them an understanding that includes knowing that their environment can be manipulated. A reaching gesture made to a parent results in being lifted and held; crying attracts attention and usually results in the elimination of some unpleasantness, such as a wet diaper, hunger, or the need for a hug. Such pragmatic knowledge appears to be universal across cultures and languages, for identical behavior appears in children everywhere (Clark & Clark, 1977).

The first verbal vocalizations children make are about the world around them, regardless of the native language involved. Animals, food, and toys were the three categories referred to most frequently in the first 10 words of 18 children studied by Nelson (1973). The people they named most often were "momma," "dadda," and "baby." By the age of 18 months, children typically have a vocabulary of only 40 or 50 words, but they are able to use single-word utterances to accomplish a great deal of communication by assigning them different operational roles, depending on the communicative context and the relevant function. "Cookie," uttered in the context of a market (where the child knows, apparently, that cookies can be obtained), can mean "I want some cookies." Uttered in a high chair with a cookie on the child's plate, the same word can simply be an act of identification. Uttered in the act of tossing the cookie on the floor, it can mean "I do not want a cookie."

Within a few months of their first single-word utterances, children begin combining words into two-word utterances, such as "Jenny cup" ("This is Jenny's cup") or "Car go" ("I want to ride in the car"). In each case, these two-word phrases seem to represent a natural progression toward more complete verbal expressions. Language acquisition is a continuum, with children moving from preverbal gestures to single words, two-word utterances, and finally, complete expressions.

Home Language

The source of children's initial utterances is the family, but children do not simply repeat the language of those around them. Many utterances are novel, and they are characteristically designed to manipulate and organize the children's environment. Infants spend their first 12 months, approximately, listening to language and experimenting with sounds before producing recognizable utterances, but all research in this area indicates that first words cannot be linked to specific input provided by parents (Clark & Clark, 1977; Hudson, 1980; Slobin & Welsh, 1973). Instead, they are linked to the whole universe of discourse uttered in the baby's immediate environment and directed toward the baby, which explains why children's initial utterances include "kitty" and "dadda" but not "taxes," "groceries," and "furniture."

Nevertheless, what emerges as child language is a very close replication of the language used in the home. Children, their parents, and others in the immediate community share vocabulary, grammar, dialect, and accent. After about 5 years of age, the community exerts more influence on the shape of a child's language than the parents do (but the language children develop is still referred to as the *home language*). As a result, when parents from the Northwest move to the South, they generally do not begin speaking with a Southern dialect and accent, but their children normally do. Parents who differentiate between *lie* and *lay* discover that their children do not if the people in the neighborhood do not.

L_1 is very strong and resistant to change. The reasons appear to be psychophysiological. People define who they are through language, and most definitions are linked in one way or another to the home and family. Also, early mental patterns are more firmly established than later ones, evidenced in part by the observation that Alzheimer's patients lose their childhood memories last.

Conflicts Between Home and School

The home language is very resistant to change, and the consequences for teaching are readily apparent. Direct language instruction commonly has a modest effect on student performance, and even this modest effect is slow to develop. Direct instruction involves language *learning*, the conscious mastery of knowledge about language. It also involves cognitive processes quite different from language acquisition, the unconscious assimilation of language. When teachers strive to get ESL students to use English or when they strive to get nonstandard speakers to use standard English, they are asking students to apply language learning to supplant language acquisition.

This task is very difficult, especially for young children who cannot understand explanations of linguistic principals and therefore require teacher modeling of the target linguistic behavior. Such modeling is insufficient in most cases for two reasons: A classroom teacher cannot compose a linguistic community of the sort necessary to offer an alternative source of acquisition; and students generally have little motivation to emulate the classroom language.

Krashen (1982) argued that direct instruction in later years provides a monitor that helps bridge the gap between learning and acquisition. For example, a child who has grown up using *lay* ("I want to lay down") when standard English usage calls for *lie* ("I want to lie down") can potentially benefit from direct instruction. The teacher can point out that *lay* is a transitive verb in standard English and therefore is always followed by a noun, as in "I will lay the book on the table." *Lie*, on the other hand, is an intransitive verb and is not followed by a noun, as in "I will lie down for a nap." With this rule at their disposal, students can monitor their speech and writing to avoid the nonstandard intransitive use of *lay*. Unfortunately, application of the monitor is difficult because speakers and writers focus on meaning rather than form. Direct instruction, therefore, proceeds slowly because it requires asking students to apply conscious procedures to unconscious processes.

Although intelligence may be important in grasping and applying the content of direct instruction, it is not a significant factor in language acquisition. Even children who are severely retarded develop language and are able to use it in most social situations. Furthermore, as already suggested, motivation is an influential factor in modifying the home language. Students must have compelling reasons to change the way they speak. Most do not. Therefore, it is important to recognize that effective language instruction must proceed over several years to produce measurable results. If these results are to have any chance of becoming permanent, they must be reinforced throughout public school because of the power of L_1 to attenuate the effects of instruction. Any gaps in instruction run the risk of causing students to regress. At the end of high school, college opens new linguistic possibilities for the 65% of graduates who go on to higher education, where separation from home and immersion in a different linguistic community serve to strengthen skills in standard English.[4] Language change, like language development, requires constant stimulation and interaction, which suggests that schools should offer more courses in English rather than fewer.

JOURNAL ENTRY

Encouraging the parents of nonnative English speakers to become involved in school activities is one way to help reduce the conflict between home and school language. What are some others?

SECOND-LANGUAGE ACQUISITION IN CHILDREN

There is evidence that second-language acquisition proceeds along the same lines as first-language acquisition (Gardner, 1980, 1983; Hakuta, 1986; Hatch, 1978; Krashen, 1981b, 1982). Hakuta (1986) offered a case study that typifies the process for children who are immersed in an L_2 environment: Uguisu, the 5-year-old daughter of Japanese parents who moved to the United States for a 2-year stay. Both parents knew English, but they talked to their daughter exclusively in Japanese. When Uguisu was enrolled in kindergarten shortly after the family's arrival, she spoke no English.

Over the next several months, Uguisu continued to speak Japanese. Although she picked up a few words of English from her playmates,

---

[4]It is worth noting, however, that with respect to dialects the differences between home and university appear to be growing smaller, perhaps as a result of persistent attacks on standard English.

these were generally imitations of expressions the playmates uttered, such as "I'm the leader." The kindergarten teacher knew no Japanese and therefore was not in a position to provide formal language instruction. Thus, with the exception of classroom activities, Uguisu's exposure to English was informal and consisted of playtime with peers. It closely resembled a child's exposure to his or her first language, except for the obvious lack of parental input.

Seven months after arriving in this country, Uguisu began to use English suddenly and almost effortlessly. Over the next 6 months, English became her dominant language. She used it when talking to her parents, who continued to respond in Japanese, and when playing by herself. Hakuta (1986) stated that "within eighteen months after her initial exposure to English, only a trained ear would have been able to distinguish her from a native speaker" (p. 108).

It appears that during her initial months in the United States, Uguisu was unconsciously sorting through the linguistic data she received on a daily basis, using her innate language abilities to master the grammatical, lexical, and pragmatic patterns that govern English. Once she had grasped these patterns, she was able to begin using the language. English input from her parents was unnecessary in this case because Uguisu was, like all other 5-year-olds, linguistically mature and had already developed a high level of communicative competence in her first language.

This example indicates that second-language acquisition, like first-language acquisition, relies largely on meaningful input, not formal instruction. The primary difference between the two lies in the role of parental input: It is crucial in L_1 but incidental in L_2 because children can draw on their already developed L_1 competence. The role of peers or playmates is powerful, perhaps even more so than for the child's first language.

Contact with English-speaking peers is an important underlying assumption in bilingual education. The model of second-language acquisition is similar to the one just outlined: The children are expected to participate in the larger English-speaking community and acquire the language on their own outside the classroom. But many nonnative English-speaking children live in neighborhoods in which their primary language dominates and English is rarely heard. Schools in these neighborhoods are linguistically dominated by the minority language, so they provide little or no opportunity for children to interact with English-speaking peers. Busing is often viewed as one means of alleviating the problem; unfortunately, in the majority of schools where students are bused in from other neighborhoods, the children segregate themselves outside the classroom along racial, linguistic, or socioeconomic lines, again leaving little chance for natural acquisition to occur.

DIALECTS

Up to this point, standard English has been used loosely to describe the prestige dialect in the United States, without any effort to be more specific. A *dialect* is a variety of language that is largely determined by geography and/or SES (Haugen, 1966; Hudson, 1980; Trudgill, 1974; Wolfram, Christian, & Adger, in press). Although race appears to be related to dialect, it is not. Tannen (1990) and Lakoff (1987) showed that women use language in a way that differs from how men use it, but the variation is insufficient to count as a separate dialect. Southern dialects are recognizably different from West Coast dialects. They differ not only with respect to accent but also with respect to grammar and lexicons. A person in California, for example, is highly unlikely to utter "I have plenty enough," whereas this utterance is fairly common in parts of North Carolina. By the same token, someone from the upper third of the socioeconomic scale would be likely to utter "I'm not going to the family reunion," whereas someone from the lower third would be more likely to utter "I ain't goin' to no family reunion." A *standard dialect* is the one with the largest number of users and the one with the greatest prestige owing to the socioeconomic success of those users.

Standard English meets both criteria. It is the dialect of government, science, business, technology, and education. It is the dialect associated with success, as evidenced in part by the number of young actors and actresses in Los Angeles who take voice lessons to lose their regional dialects. It is also the language of the airwaves. More important for the purposes of this text, standard English is the language of academic and professional writing.

Nonstandard Dialects

People who do not normally use standard English use a nonstandard dialect. Although regional variations abound, nonstandard dialects are increasingly identified with SES. Wolfram et al. (in press) reported a leveling of regional differences. The reasons for this leveling are not very clear. Some scholars suggest that television is spreading standard English to regions in which it was not heard frequently in the past, but this proposal is based on the mistaken notion that people respond to the presence of language that is not interactive. An infant placed in front of a television and lacking normal contact with people using language interactively would not acquire language. The sounds from the television would be noise, not meaningful sounds. More likely, the changes Wolfram et al. reported are linked to the increased mobility of Americans. People relocate more frequently today than ever before, and the result is an unprecedented blending of various dialects, especially in the South, which has seen a tremendous population growth owing to an influx of Northerners looking for jobs, lower taxes, and better weather.

Another related factor in the issue of dialect leveling that does not receive much attention is the measurable shift of Black English toward standard English. This shift is surprising because in many respects segregation in the late 1990s is stronger than since the early 1950s. But affirmative action has been successful in increasing the educational and economic opportunities among African Americans to such a degree that Black English speakers have more contact with standard speakers than in the past. In addition, Herrnstein and Murray (1994) reported that the black middle class has been growing steadily for about 25 years, which provides a compelling incentive to shift toward standard English. Although the white middle class has been shrinking during this same period, the incentives to adopt a nonstandard dialect, to shift downward, are not strong among displaced adults. They are strong, however, among their children.

Because SES is closely tied to level of education (Herrnstein & Murray, 1994), nonstandard speakers tend to be undereducated, and they also tend to be linked to the working-class poor. Education, however, is not an absolute indicator of dialect: Some evidence suggests that colleges and universities are more tolerant of nonstandard English than they used to be, and the students' right to their own language movement has made public schools more sensitive to, if not more tolerant of, nonstandard English. As a result, it is fairly easy to observe college graduates—and, increasingly, college faculty—uttering nonstandard expressions such as "I ain't got no money" and "Where's he at." Some reports indicate that as many as 60% of all university professors are first-generation college graduates. Assuming that a large portion of these teachers came from working-class backgrounds, there is significant tension between their home dialects and the prestige dialects that were part of their university training. After becoming part of the system, tenured, there might be less pressure to maintain the prestige dialect.

Simultaneously, literacy levels in the public schools and in higher education continue to plummet. Chall (1996) and Coulson (1996) reported serious declines in language and literacy levels for students in all age groups. Chall, for example, described her experience at a community college where the "freshmen tested, on the average, on an eighth grade reading level. Thus, the average student in this community college was able to read only on a level expected of junior high school students" (p. 309). Findings like these are not limited to community colleges. Entering freshmen at a major research university in North Carolina, ranked among the top 25 schools in the nation, are tested each year for reading skill, and their average annual scores between 1987 and 1994 placed them at the tenth-grade reading level.[5]

JOURNAL ENTRY

Most people speak a dialect that moves along a continuum ranging from nonstandard to formal standard. How would you characterize your dialect? Do you think it is important to model standard English in your classes? Why or why not?

BLACK ENGLISH

For many decades, serious study of Black English was impeded by myths and misconceptions. Dillard (1973) summarized many of these misconceptions quite succinctly. He reported, for example, that until the 1960s, it was often argued that Black English was a vestige of a British dialect with origins in East Anglia (see also McCrum, Cran, & MacNeil, 1986). Black Americans supposedly had somehow managed to avoid significant linguistic change for centuries, even though it was well known that all living languages change ineluctably. Dillard also described the physiological theory, which held that Black English was the result of thick lips that rendered blacks incapable of producing standard English. More imaginative and outrageous was Mencken's (1936) notion that Black English was the invention of playwrights:

> The Negro dialect, as we know it today, seems to have been formulated by the songwriters for the minstrel shows; it did not appear in literature until the time of the Civil War; before that, as George P. Krappe shows ... , it was a vague and artificial lingo which had little relation to the actual speech of Southern blacks. (p. 71)

Mencken did not mention how blacks were supposed to have gone to the minstrel shows so that they might pick up the new "lingo," or why they would be motivated to do so.

Today, most linguists support the view that Black English developed from the pidgin versions of English, Dutch, Spanish, and Portuguese used during the slave era. A *pidgin* is a *contact vernacular*—a mixture

---

[5]During this period, students took the Nelson-Denny reading test, which was administered by the university's learning skills center. I reviewed the data in my capacity as an administrator at the school.

of two (or possibly more) separate languages that has been modified to eliminate the more difficult features, such as irregular verb forms (Kay & Sankoff, 1974; Slobin, 1977). Function words like determiners (*the, a, an*) and prepositions (*in, on, across*) commonly are dropped. Function markers like case are eliminated, as are tense and plurals. Pidgins arise spontaneously whenever two people lack a common language. The broken English that Johnny Weismeuller used in the Tarzan movies from the 1930s and 1940s (which still air on TV) accurately reflects the features of a pidgin.

European slavers developed a variety of pidgins with their West African cohorts to facilitate the slave trade. The result must have been a potpourri of sounds. Although many slavers came from England, the majority came from France, Spain, Portugal, and Holland. Their human cargo came from a huge area of western Africa, including what is now Gambia, the Ivory Coast, Ghana, Nigeria, and Zaire, and spoke dozens of mutually unintelligible tribal languages. McCrum et al. (1986) suggested that the pidgins began developing shortly after the slaves were captured because the traders separated those who spoke the same language to prevent collaboration that might lead to rebellion. Chained in the holds of the slave ships, the captives had every incentive to use pidgin to establish a linguistic community. More likely, the pidgins already were well established among the villages responsible for capturing and selling tribesmen and women to the European slavers, and the captured people began using a pidgin almost immediately out of necessity.

Once in America, the slaves had to continue using pidgin English to communicate with their masters and with one another. Matters changed, however, when the slaves began having children. A fascinating phenomenon occurs when children are born into a community that uses a pidgin: They spontaneously regularize the language. They add function words, regularize verbs, and provide a grammar where none really existed before. When the children of the pidgin-speaking slaves began speaking, they spoke a Creole, not a pidgin. A *Creole* is a full language in the technical sense, with its own grammar, vocabulary, and pragmatic conventions.

Why, then, is Black English classified as a dialect of English rather than as a Creole? True Creoles, like those spoken in the Caribbean, experienced reduced contact with the major contributory languages. Papiamento, the Creole spoken in the Dutch Antilles, is a mixture of Dutch, French, and English, and although Dutch has long been the official language, the linguistic influences of French and English disappeared about 200 years ago. The influence of Dutch has waned significantly in this century. As a result, Papiamento continued to develop in its own way rather than move closer to standard Dutch. In the United States, the influence of standard English increased over the years, especially after the abolition of slavery. Thus the Creole that was spoken by large numbers of slaves shifted closer and closer to standard English, until at some point it stopped being a Creole and became a dialect. It is closer to English than to any other language, which is why speakers of standard English can understand Black English but not a Creole.

Black English nevertheless has preserved many features of its Creole and pidgin roots, which extend to the West African tribal languages as well as to Dutch, French, Portuguese, and Spanish. The most visible of these features are grammatical, and for generations Black English was thought to be merely a degenerate version of standard English. Speakers were believed to violate grammatical rules every time they used the language. Work like Dillard's, however, demonstrated that Black English has its own grammar, which is a blend of standard English and a variety of West African languages seasoned with European languages.

There is a strong similarity between Black English and the English used by white Southerners because blacks and whites lived in close-knit communities in the South for generations, slavery notwithstanding, and the whites were the minority. White children played with black children, who exerted a powerful influence on the white minority dialect. As Slobin (1977) indicated, language change occurs primarily in the speech of children, and throughout the slave era, white and black children were allowed to play together.

Ebonics

Since the late 1960s, some educators and politicians have argued for what is known as "students' right to their own language." The focus is on Black English and its place in education (see Robinson, 1990). The argument is that BEV should be legitimized in the schools to the extent that it is acceptable for recitation and writing assignments. Some schools during the early 1970s actually issued specially prepared textbooks written in Black English rather than standard English. In 1996, the superintendent of the Oakland, California, schools issued a policy statement declaring Black English to be a separate language and giving it the name *Ebonics*, a neologism from the words *ebony* and *phonics*. The statement attributed the differences between standard English and Ebonics to genetic factors and proposed that African-American students be taught English as though it were a foreign language, while content courses be taught in Black English. Although the efforts of the Oakland administrators and teachers were well intentioned, even those who are sympathetic to the difficulties faced by students reared in a Black English environment had a hard time seeing this policy statement as anything more than political posturing.

The idea that Black English is a separate language flies in the face of the evidence that it is a dialect. More problematic, perhaps, is the fact that the media heaped unrelenting scorn and ridicule on the policy statement and Ebonics, which undermined legitimate efforts to address the challenges Black English presents to students and teachers alike.

The rationale for the argument that underlies students' right to their own language (and ultimately that led to Ebonics) is similar to the argument underlying bilingualism: The home dialect defines who each student is; it is at the heart of important bonds between children and their families. When the schools require students to master and ultimately use standard English, they are subverting students' sense of personal identity and are weakening the home bond. Arguments that standard English is important for entry into the socioeconomic mainstream are dismissed as irrelevant and are countered with the suggestion that society must change to accommodate individual differences.

The biggest difficulty with the argument that students have the right to use their own language in school is that it oversimplifies a complex problem. Schools are obligated to provide students with the tools they need to realize their full potential, and they must do so within the framework of sociolinguistic realities. It is the case that people view certain dialects negatively; indeed, Wolfram et al. (in press) correctly noted that these negative views are held even by those who speak these dialects. Such views can hinder people's access to higher education and jobs. Students who in the late 1960s went through high school using texts written in Black English, for example, had an extremely difficult time when they enrolled in college. They discovered that they could not readily read their college texts, and many dropped out. Equally important, there is no evidence to suggest that substituting Black English for standard English has any effect whatsoever on academic performance in general or literacy in particular. Those who argue for students' right to their own language today have forgotten—or never learned—this lesson from the past. In addition, actions like those of the Oakland schools, even if we were to give them the benefit of the doubt, seem, below the surface, to be disturbingly racist. There is the undeniable and unacceptable hint that students who speak Black English are incapable of mastering standard English. The suggestion that these students would learn standard English in the way that English-speaking children currently learn, for example, Spanish in our schools cannot be taken seriously. Foreign language instruction in the United States may be many things, but it is not effective.

The situation that speakers of Black English face may be unfair. It may even be unjust. But it reflects the reality of language prejudice. Language prejudice is extremely resistant to change because language is a central factor in how people identify themselves and others. Nonstandard dialects, because they are linked to SES and education levels, tend to be associated with negative traits. For this reason, many businesses may reject applicants for employment in certain positions if they speak nonstandard English. An African-American applicant for a receptionist position at a prestigious Chicago law firm may be rejected because he or she pronounces *ask* as *ax*.

The difficulty here is largely socioeconomic. Efforts to validate the use of nonstandard English in education do little to modify the status of students from disadvantaged backgrounds. They do not expand students' language skills in any way that will help them overcome the very real obstacle to socioeconomic mobility that nonstandard English presents. As Williams (1992) noted, these efforts keep "these students ghettoized" (p. 836).

It is relatively easy for those who do not have to deal with closed socioeconomic doors to focus on headline-generating political statements, but most teachers understand that education is the key to a better life and that mastery of standard English is a key to education. Consequently, large numbers of educators believe that schools must adopt an additive stance with respect to dialects, and they view mastery and use of standard English as complementing the home dialect, whatever it may be. This additive stance calls for legitimizing and valuing all dialects while recognizing the appropriateness conditions that govern language use in specific situations. From this perspective, there are situations in which Black English is appropriate and standard English is not; there are situations in which standard English is appropriate and Black English is not. The goals of schools, therefore, should include helping students recognize the different conditions and mastering the nuances of standard English. Currently, the two camps—like those wrestling with bilingual education—are unable to reach agreement on basic principles, largely for the same reason. Bidialectalism is an intensely political issue.

JOURNAL ENTRY

What is your position on Ebonics? Is your position political or pedagogical?

FACTORS UNDERLYING A PRESTIGE DIALECT

The United States does not have a monopoly on a prestige dialect. Countries like France, Germany, and Mexico have their own standard versions of their respective languages. In most cases, sheer historical accident led to the dominance of one variety of a language rather than another. If the South had won the Civil War, had then developed a vigorous and influential economy and a strong educational system, and had become the focal point for art and ideas, some Southern dialect might be the standard in the United States rather than the current Western–Midwestern dialect.

Haugen (1966) suggested that all standard dialects undergo similar processes that solidify their position in a society. The first step, and the one apparently most influenced by chance, is selection. A society selects, usually on the basis of users' socioeconomic success, a particular variety of the language to be the standard. At some point, the chosen variety is codified by teachers and scholars who write grammar books and dictionaries for it. The effect is to stabilize the dialect by reaching some sort of agreement regarding what is correct and what is not. Next, the dialect must be functionally elaborated so that it can be used in government, law, education, technology, and in all forms of writing. Finally, the dialect has to be accepted by all segments of the society as the standard, particularly by those who speak some other variety (Hall, 1972; Macaulay, 1973; Trudgill, 1974).

BLACK ENGLISH GRAMMAR

Black English normally omits the *s* suffix on present-tense verbs ("He run pretty fast"), except in those instances where the speaker overcorrects in an effort to approximate standard patterns ("I goes to the market"). It drops the *g* from participles ("He goin' home"), and it also uses four separate negators: *dit'n, not, don'* and *ain'*. Consider the following sentences:

1. Vickie dit'n call yesterday.
2. She not comin'.
3. Fritz don' go.
4. Fritz don' be goin'.
5. She ain' call.
6. She ain' be callin'.

Sentences 3 through 6 illustrate one of the more significant differences between standard English and Black English, which is called *aspect*. Standard English marks verb tenses as past or present, but it provides the option of indicating the static or ongoing nature of an action through the use of progressive and perfect verb forms. Black English grammar, on the other hand, allows for optional tense marking but requires that the action be marked as momentary or continuous. Sentences 3 and 5 indicate a momentary action, whether or not it is in the past, whereas Sentences 4 and 6 indicate progressive action, whether or not it is in the past.

Another feature of aspect is the ability to stretch out the time of a verb, and Black English uses the verb form *be* to accomplish this. Sentences 7 and 8, for example, have quite different meanings:

7. Macarena lookin' for a job.
8. Macarena be lookin' for a job.

In Sentence 7, Macarena may be looking for a job today, at this moment, but she has not been looking long, and there is the suggestion that she has not been looking very hard. In Sentence 8, on the other hand, Macarena has been conscientiously looking for a job for a long time. We see similar examples in the following:

9. Jake studyin' right now.
10. Jake be studyin' every afternoon.

Studyin' agrees in aspect with *right now*, and *be studyin'* agrees in aspect with *every afternoon*. It therefore would be ungrammatical in Black English to say or write "Jake studyin' every afternoon" or "Jake be studyin' right now" (Baugh, 1983; Fasold, 1972; Wolfram, 1969).

Been, the participial form of *be*, is used in Black English as a past-perfect marker: It signals that an action occurred in the distant past or that it was completed totally. In this sense, it is similar to the past-perfect form *have* + *verb* and *have* + *been* in standard English, as the following sentences illustrate:

11. They had told us to leave. (standard)
12. They been told us to leave. (Black)
13. Kerri had eaten all the cake. (standard)
14. Kerri been eat all the cake. (Black)
15. She had been hurt. (standard)
16. She been been hurt. (Black)

Been is also used, however, to assert that an action initiated in the past is still in effect, as in the following:

17. I have known Vickie more than three months now. (standard)
18. I been been knowin' Vickie more than three month now. (Black)

Many other grammatical features differentiate Black English from standard English. A few of the more important are as follows:

- The present tense is used in narratives to indicate past action, as in "They goes to the market."
- When cardinal adjectives precede nouns, the noun is not pluralized, as in "The candy cost one dollar and fifty cent."
- Relative pronouns in the subject position of a relative clause can be dropped, as in "Fritz like the woman has red hair."
- The possessive marker is dropped, as in "He found Macarena coat."
- Double negatives are used instead of a negative and a positive, as in "He don' never goin' call."[6]

Cultural Factors

Speakers of Black English bring more than their dialect to the educational setting—they also bring a distinct culture with values, standards of behavior, and belief systems that are different from that of the white mainstream. Delpit (1988) reported, for example, that in the black community authority is not automatically bestowed on teachers or others in positions of power.[7] It must be extracted through authoritarian rather than authoritative means. For example, a teacher who uses a forceful, direct approach—"Fritz, read the next two paragraphs"—is more likely to get a positive response than one who uses an indirect approach—"Fritz, would you read the next two paragraphs, please?" White teachers in Delpit's account are more inclined to use the indirect approach, which commonly leads to conflict because black students do not respond.

Similarly, white culture stresses students' subordinate role. Students are not expected to talk out of turn, and when they do, they are punished. The lesson is that a student should raise his or her hand when wishing to speak. Failure to do so is seen as a sign of disrespect for the

---

[6]Criticism of the double negative is made on the grounds that two negatives make a positive. On this account "I ain't got no money" means that the speaker actually has a great deal of money. Although two negatives make a positive in mathematics, they simply do not in language. No one ever, under any circumstances, would understand "I ain't got no money" to mean anything other than the fact that the speaker is broke. Furthermore, double negatives have a long history in English and are not peculiar to Black English.

[7]Whenever dealing with generalizations, it is important to remember that it is difficult (if not impossible) to generalize to particular instances. The fact that many individuals do not match the characteristics of the generalization does not invalidate the generalization.

teacher and other students. Black culture, however, does not stress turn taking of this sort but instead emphasizes a more active strategy, which leads black students to call out responses freely without waiting for permission to speak. Punishment imposes white conventions on many African-American students but not all. Many continue to call out, but many more seem deflated to such a degree that they withdraw and turn silent. The results are twofold: White teachers often view those who continue to call out as being rude and disruptive, whereas they view those who fall silent as being slow and unmotivated. Teachers who decide to accept the classroom behavior of their black students in this regard face yet another challenge. Their white, Asian, and Hispanic students determine that the black children are receiving special treatment, and many become resentful because of it.

Labov (1964, 1970, 1972a) and Heath (1983) also have shown that the environment of language acquisition can have an effect on school performance. Their research suggested that different cultural-social groups learn to use language in different ways, as determined by variations in parent–child interaction. Heath, for example, noted that the ways lower-class black children learn to use language are fundamentally different from the ways upper-middle-class white children learn to use it. The determining factor is how parents interact with their children.

In the community she studied, Heath observed that among the black subjects adults rarely spoke to children and that little of the prelinguistic interaction between mothers and offspring described in the Trevarthen (1974) investigation took place. One result was that the black children appeared to place more reliance on contextual cues for comprehension than the white children. This factor proved to be extremely problematic for them in school, where the emphasis is on language use that has no immediate audience, feedback, intention, or purpose. Heath noted another important consequence:

> [The black children] never volunteer to list the attributes which are similar in two objects and add up to make one thing like another. They seem, instead, to have a gestalt, a highly contextualized view, of objects which they compare without sorting out the particular single features of the object itself. They seem to become sensitive to the shape of arrays of stimuli in a scene, but not to how individual discrete elements in the scene contribute to making two wholes alike. If asked why or how one thing is like another, they do not answer; similarly, they do not respond appropriately to tasks in which they are asked to distinguish one thing as different from another. (pp. 107–108)

The reliance on context inevitably leads to difficulties in composition because writers must step outside the language event to avoid producing an essay that sounds like a conversation with the second party missing. They must create a context by explicitly providing some of the very factors that make conversations successful, such as audience, purpose, and intention. In addition, a holistic view of the world that is largely unconcerned with attributes and detail is at odds with the kinds of tasks children are asked to perform in school, where describing objects by listing their attributes is a common activity. It should be clear, however, that both the reliance on context and the holistic view are part of these children's linguistic processing. This is how they understand language and how they use it.

Michaels (1982) reported similar results after studying narrative patterns among black and white school children. The white children constructed narratives around a specific topic, developing a structure that included the topic at the beginning and that made reference to it throughout the paper. Black children, in contrast, mentioned a general topic at the beginning of their narratives, and what followed usually was only marginally related to that topic. For example, if the teacher assigned a narrative on the topic of "a shopping trip to the local mall," the white students might write a narrative about a specific trip that they took at some time. The black students, on the other hand, might identify "shopping" as the topic and might then develop a narrative about shopping for a Christmas tree, a new car, or even a new house. Michaels reported that the failure of the black students to meet the expectations their white teacher had for the assignment proved problematic: The teacher judged their narratives to be pointless and erratic. From the perspective of black culture, however, the point of a narrative is to tell an entertaining story, which may not be possible under the strict requirements of a writing assignment.

BLACK ENGLISH AND WRITING

The three samples that follow were written by students who speak Black English. The first comes from a sixth-grade writer, Marcy; the second comes from a tenth grader, Tawanda; and the third comes from a twelfth-grade writer, Bud. In each case, the student attended a predominantly black school in an area at the lower end of the socioeconomic scale. Marcy and her class had visited the Aerospace Museum in Los Angeles several days before the writing assignment, which asked students to describe what they liked best about the field trip. The following is her response:

My feel Trip

Lass weak we went to the natual histry museum. We seed the air Planes
an they be big. If you be standin next to one of them Planes you be lookin
real Small. they could be goin real fast if they flyin. I think it be real nice
to be flyin one of them planes. Maybe to hawae or someplace like that.
When I grow up I think I be a pilot an fly one of them big planes.

Twanda's teacher asked her class to write a paper describing their recent
field trip to the Shedd Aquarium in Chicago:

I done been to the akwearium befor so I knows somethin about it already.
They has lots of fish an some of them be bright colors. Sometime my uncle
go to the lake an ketch some fish but they not bright like dem in the
akwarium. They be good to eat tho. Sometime my momma come by
granma's house when she infatween an we cook up some them fish that
my uncle done catched. We have a real feast an my momma eat like they's
no tomora. I do to. My uncle say he gon by him a boat one these days an
when he do he take me out the lake. I laff when he do an tell him he kin
take me all the way to Canada to git me out this ol city. Then he tell me
that Canada be even colder than Chicago an that make me kinda sad.
Hard to imagin any place on earth colder than this place but I guess they
is. Maybe we take that boat right to Jamaca, "mon." Be warm there all the
time. Anyway, that's what I think about the akwariyum.

Bud and his class were approaching graduation, and their teacher asked
them to write an essay describing their plans once they were out of high
school:

I know most good job needs a college education. I would like to go to college
to git me a degree. but my grades isn't the best. It would be fun to be a
docktor or a lawyer or something like that because then I have me a big
fine car. May be a Benz. But like a says my grades is not so good and I do
not think I could be going to college. They is some good jobs in electonics
that do not take that much training. And I think that I could maybe go
into that. the important thing is to think positive. I know I can do good
work. I can work hard when I wants to. My brother got him a job doing
construction and it pays real good. The trouble is that it is not all year long
work. They git laid off alot. That might be good in a way though. Because
then you could have more time to enjoy life. I know that no matter what
kind of job I git after schools out I wants to be enjoying my self.

Oral Language Interference

Some scholars have argued that the writing of Black English speakers
is significantly influenced by *oral language interference*. Writing for

these students becomes an act of transcribing their nonstandard speech (Dillon, 1981; Olson, 1977; Ong, 1978, 1982; Shaughnessy, 1977). In this view, failure to achieve mainstream standards can be accounted for on two levels. First, the writing displays the lexical and grammatical features characteristic of Black English. Second, the lack of organization and the paucity of content is the result of linguistic deprivation and its associated cognitive deficit.

Oral language interference, however, is a description of the problem, not an explanation. Most of the problems in the previous writing samples—which are representative—are not caused by oral language per se but rather by the students' lack of reading experience. Any student who lacks extensive reading experience has no alternative but to transcribe speech, which means that features of oral language find their way into student writing irrespective of race. White students who do not read commonly write, "I could of made a good grade if I had studied," because they have not seen the contraction *could've* in print often enough to have an internalized graphemic representation of it.

In these particular examples, the surface problems speak for themselves. When Marcy writes "Lass weak" or when Tawanda writes "I laff," they are transcribing. Spelling instruction will have only a modest effect on these sorts of errors, yet spelling lists tend to be the approach of first resort. The difficulty with spelling lists is that they seldom are contextualized, so students rapidly forget how to spell the words after being tested on them. Students who manifest the sorts of surface problems shown in these examples need an intensive reading and writing program, not drills, exercises, and spelling lists.

More interesting than these surface errors, however, are Tawanda's and Bud's responses to their assignments. Tawanda was asked to describe the field trip she and her class took at the Shedd Aquarium, and the first two sentences suggest that she will respond appropriately. Yet the third sentence takes Tawanda in a different direction. Certainly, her uncle's fishing in Lake Michigan has some marginal connection to the field trip, but it still is clearly off topic. Likewise, Bud started writing about his plans after graduation but then shifted focus to his brother. These responses are characteristic of the patterns Michaels (1982) identified, in which cultural differences related to how to use language often move black students down paths that have but a ghostly relationship to the assigned topic. Students who display this characteristic face a greater challenge than those who need more reading and writing experience because their concepts of what a narrative or a description is about are at odds with those held by mainstream teachers.

Although no studies have adequately controlled for reading experience, several studies have shown insignificant effects of speech on writing. Tannen (1982) found that speech and writing share each other's typical characteristics, even though they differ in terms of level of abstraction, sentence length, sentence patterns, and vocabulary. Speech tends to have shorter sentences, to use less subordination and more coordination, and to use a simpler vocabulary than writing. Erickson (1984), studying the speech patterns of black teenagers, reported that the organizational pattern of Black English has its own structure, different from that of standard English. He found, for example, that shifts from one topic to another were not explicitly stated but were implied through concrete anecdotes. Close analysis of Black English speech patterns showed a "rigorous logic and a systematic coherence of the particular, whose internal system is organized not by literate style or linear sequentiality but by audience/speaker interaction" (p. 152).

Farr Whitemann (1981) correlated the speech of a group of Black English-speaking students with their writing and found that oral language patterns were present in the students' written language, but these patterns did not clearly reflect an attempt at transcribing speech. The most dominant characteristic of the subjects' compositions was the presence of Black-English grammatical patterns, specifically the omission of *s* suffixes and of past-tense *ed* suffixes.

Farr and Janda (1985) reported only modest oral-language interference in the writing of the black high school student they studied. They noted:

> Although features of Vernacular Black English [VBE] are part of ... Joseph's linguistic repertoire, VBE features occur relatively infrequently in his writing, eliminating nonstandard dialect influence as a major cause of his difficulty in writing. Furthermore, Joseph's writing evidenced many "literate" characteristics, i.e., devices which have been found to be typical of written English ... . What, then, is the problem with Joseph's writing? Why was he placed in a remedial writing class ... ? His writing does not appear to be language that was generated by a human being in an attempt to express or create meaning. The form is there; the functional attempt to communicate does not seem to be. (pp. 80–81)

On the basis of this research, it is tempting to suggest that the missing factor in Joseph's writing, and perhaps in the writing of students like him, is motivation to succeed at school-related tasks. However, students who lack reading and writing experience will not be able to conceptualize writing tasks as communicative efforts. Texts represent a foreign medium that is almost as meaningless as calculus is to most English teachers.

Likewise, in an extensive study of bilingual students, Edelsky (1986) found few significant oral influences on the written discourse of a group of children whose first language was Spanish. Her results repudiated many of the notions commonly associated with bilinguals and literacy. For example, she found very little code switching between L_1 and L_2. She reported that most of the switching she found was "like slips of the pen" and that it decreased significantly by the time children were in the third grade (p. 152). This finding is important because L_2 writing is widely believed to suffer from L_1 interference. Her data tend to confirm Krashen's (1980) view that second-language learners fall back on and use first-language rules, conventions, and strategies when they do not have the appropriate rule, convention, or strategy in their second-language repertoire (pp. 73–74). In other words, they use skills they already have in L_1 until they acquire the rule in L_2. Thus, rather than being prevented from acquiring a rule in the second language because they already have one in the first, they use first-language competence in a transitional way to master L_2. In this respect, Edelsky's findings echo those of other bilingual education researchers (see Calkins, 1983; Dyson, 1982, 1983; Ferreiro & Teberosky, 1982). Such findings suggest that writing instruction for nonmainstream students should focus on developing global skills rather than on surface errors.

The challenges presented by cultural differences prove to be resistant to solution for many nonmainstream students, but it is important to stress that this is not the case for all. Children are adaptable, and large numbers of nonmainstream students adjust to the linguistic and cultural demands of school quite readily. Nevertheless, it often is useful for teachers to address cultural differences candidly with students, explaining how men and women and people reared in different cultures use language in different ways. Afterwards, teachers can move forward with activities that help students understand how writing assignments provide a focus for papers that students must follow to be successful. Efforts should include helping students recognize how their backgrounds and experiences affect their academic work and on showing them ways to broaden their experiences to accommodate standard conventions.

Cognitive Deficit

The notion that literacy increases intelligence and reasoning ability has enjoyed a certain cachet since the 1960s, in spite of research findings to the contrary. No evidence has been found to support the notion of linguistic or cognitive deficit among African Americans or any other group.[8] Labov (1972a) showed that Black English is just as rich as any other dialect and that children whose dominant dialect is Black English cannot be classified as *linguistically deprived*. Writers like Dillon (1981) and Ong (1978) would perhaps claim that the problem is more accurately one of literacy deprivation, which is no doubt accurate, but their conclusions about the interaction of literacy and mind are not. They argued that facility with the written word develops cognitive abilities related to abstract reasoning; literate people think better than illiterate people. On this account, blacks, who tend to score lower than whites on tests of reading ability (Coulson, 1996), would experience deficits in thinking ability. But such a conclusion is offset by the work of Scribner and Cole (1981), who, in the most detailed study published to date on the effect literacy has on cognitive abilities, found no significant correlation between literacy and cognition. They stated, for example, that "Our results are in direct conflict with persistent claims that 'deep psychological differences' divide literate and non-literate populations.... On no task—logic, abstraction, memory, communication—did we find all non-literates performing at lower levels than all literates" (p. 251).

In addition, Farr and Janda concluded that one of the more significant problems with their subject's writing was that it was not elaborated, with inexplicit and therefore ineffectual logical relation. However, unelaborated content and weak logical relations generally are characteristic of poor writing (Williams, 1985), which again indicates that at issue is something other than the influence of Black English on cognition. The ability to elaborate content appears to be linked to reading and writing experience (Williams, 1987). Moreover, few oral language situations call for extensive use of logic. Hence, the problem with logical relations that Farr and Janda reported reasonably could be symptomatic of students who do little reading and writing.

CHICANO ENGLISH

Chicano English is the term used to describe the nonstandard dialect spoken by many second and third-generation Mexican Americans, many of whom do not speak Spanish, although they may understand it slightly (see Garcia, 1983). It is also used to describe the dialect spoken by first-generation immigrants who have lived in the United States long enough to have acquired sufficient mastery of English to be able to carry on a conversation exclusively in it (see Baugh, 1984). The fact that

---

[8]Although there is no evidence of cognitive deficit, there is evidence that some groups, such as Asians, perform better than others on intelligence tests. Herrnstein and Murray (1994) noted that "East Asians have higher nonverbal intelligence than whites while being equal, or perhaps slightly lower, in verbal intelligence" (p. 269).

measurable differences can be found between the language of relatively recent immigrants and the language of Hispanics who have lived in the United States for generations is one indication of the difficulty involved in making a concrete assessment of Chicano English.

The dialect is in many ways more complex than Black English because it is influenced by monolingual Spanish speakers, monolingual English speakers, and bilingual Spanish–English speakers, all of whom are found in a single linguistic community. The number of influences appears to further complicate children's acquisition of standard English (see Penfield & Ornstein-Galicia, 1985).

On the level of *phonology* (the sound of words), Spanish uses a *ch* pronunciation where English uses *sh*. Thus Chicano English speakers often pronounce a word like *shoes* as *choose*, which can affect how students spell English words. For example, students perceive the short *i* sound in the verb *live* to be a long *e* sound, producing sentences like the following in their writing:

19. I used to leave in Burbank but now l leave in North Hollywood.
20. Seens I been in L.A. I ain't found no job.

Other phonological differences produce additional difficulties, as the following student samples illustrate:

21. I try to safe as much money as I can.
22. When I'm a mother, I will not be as strick as my parents.

The Spanish influence is also evident on the grammatical level. Spanish, for example, uses the double negative, whereas English does not. As a result, students produce written statements like "I didn't learn nothing in this class." Other syntactic influences include those illustrated in the following sentences:

23. I asked Mary where did she live. (Chicano)
24. I asked Mary where she lived. (standard)
25. My parents were raise old-fashion, and so they do not let me date or nothing. (Chicano)
26. My parents were raised old-fashioned, and so they do not let me date or anything. (standard)

CHICANO ENGLISH AND WRITING

The few studies that examined the writing of Chicano English speakers are not particularly satisfying because they tend to focus on the sentence level rather than on the whole essay. Amastae (1981, 1984) evaluated writing samples collected from students at Pan American University in

Texas over a 4-year period to determine the range of surface errors as well as the degree of sentence elaboration as measured by students' use of subordination. Amastae (1981) found that Spanish interference did not seem to be a major source of error in the compositions but that the students used very little subordination (see also Edelsky, 1986; Hoffer, 1975). Because subordination is generally viewed as a measure of writing maturity (Hunt, 1965), its absence in the essays of Chicano English speakers could adversely affect how teachers judge their writing ability.

The problem with such studies is that they fail to examine rhetorical features like topic, purpose, and audience. The closest approximation to such research appears in Edelsky's (1986) study of bilingual, elementary-aged Spanish-speaking students. She found that when her LEP subjects wrote in English, their compositions manifested rhetorical features similar to those found among weak writers whose first language is English; that is, the rhetorical problems were largely developmental. Her students appeared to be in the process of transferring their L₁ rhetorical competence to L₂. During the transfer period, the students' rhetorical skills in English, like their surface feature skills, contained identifiable gaps that continuing development of English proficiency was likely to eliminate.

CODE SWITCHING

It is common for different dialects to use different sets of grammatical rules. In certain dialects, sentences like 27 appear regularly, but not sentences like 28:

27. I seen Harry last night.
28. I saw Harry last night.

By the same token, in other dialects sentences like 29 appear regularly, but not sentences like 30:

29. Rosie be workin at Ralph's.
30. Rosie is working at Ralph's.

Nevertheless, speakers of standard English may use certain linguistic forms that in the strict sense fall into the category of nonstandard usage. For example, people who otherwise use standard English may say "It is me" rather than "It is I," even though "It is me" technically is "incorrect." Other examples abound, such as the general confusion regarding *lay* and *lie* and the widespread disappearance of the relative pronoun *whom*, even in more formal, academic writing.

Frequently, people who otherwise use standard English produce language that violates certain formal conventions of usage. Two factors account for these occurrences. The first is simply that languages change, in spite of often vigorous efforts to prevent it, as in schoolteachers' prescriptive admonitions about what constitutes "correct" speech and writing. In this analysis, "It is me" may eventually become accepted as standard to reflect changes in usage. The second factor is that linguistic variation exists not only across dialects but also within them. Sources of variation include age, occupation, and gender. Women, for example, tend to be more conscientious about language than men. As a result, in a family whose dialect is nonstandard, the woman's language comes closer to standard English than the man's (Trudgill, 1974).

The phenomenon of linguistic variation led Labov (1969) to suggest that every dialect is subject to *inherent variability*. Speakers of a particular dialect fail to use all the features of that dialect all the time, and the constant state of flux causes some degree of variation. This principle accounts for the fact that standard English speakers periodically reduce sentences like 31 to sentences like 32:

31. I've been working hard.
32. I been working hard.

More common, however, is variation of nonstandard features to standard features, nearly always as a result of sociolinguistic pressures to conform to the mainstream. Thus people who speak nonstandard English typically will attempt to adopt standard features in any situation in which they are interacting with someone they perceive as socially superior. As a result, a student who uses a nonstandard dialect might write Sentence 32, but if asked to read his or her composition aloud, he or she might read Sentence 31. In the course of reading an entire essay, a student is likely to change many of the nonstandard features, but not all of them.

This behavior raises an important question: Why do students produce a paper with nonstandard features when they so often know a great deal of standard English? Most classroom writing assignments are decontextualized, which means, in part, that they do not conform to real language situations. Students know that only the teacher will read and grade their papers. When writing tasks lack a meaningful context, students find it difficult to take them seriously enough to use standard features.

The inherent variability of language indicates that dialects are unstable and that the language people use at any given time can be located on a continuum that ranges in some cases from formal standard written English to informal nonstandard spoken English. People move back and forth on the continuum as context demands and as their linguistic skills allow. The term used to describe this back-and-forth movement is *code switching*. In its broadest sense, code switching refers to the act of using different language varieties at different times. The varieties can be different dialects or different languages. The following example was reported by Gumperz (1982) and reflects the temporal factor often associated with code switching; the speaker uses standard English when talking with his teacher, but then he shifts to Black English when talking to a classmate:

1   Following an informal graduate seminar at a major university, a black student approached the instructor, who was about to leave the room accompanied by several other black and white students, and said:
2   Could I talk to you for a minute? I'm gonna apply for a fellowship and I was wondering if I could get a recommendation?
3   The instructor replied:
4   O.K. Come along to the office and tell me what you want to do.
5   As the instructor and the rest of the group left the room, the black student said, turning his head ever so slightly to the other students:
6   Ahma git me a gig! (Rough gloss: "I'm going to get myself some support.") (p. 30)

Code switching among bilinguals, however, seldom occurs at different times but occurs within a given language event. Labov (1971), for example, observed code switching within single sentences or utterances when studying Puerto Rican English in New York, as the following passage shows. The brackets enclose the translation of the Spanish phrases:

Por eso cada [therefore each] ... , you know it is nothing to be proud of, porque yo no estoy [because I'm not] proud of it, as a matter of fact I hate it, pero viene vierne y Sabado yo estoy, tu me ve hacia me, sola [but come Friday and Saturday I am, you see me, you look at me, alone] with a, aqui solita, a veces que Frankie me deja [here alone sometimes Frankie leaves me], you know a stick or something ... .(p. 450)

Observations like these offer evidence that bidialectical and bilingual speakers have proficiency with standard English but choose not to apply it, leading some people to argue that code switching is a reflection of linguistic laziness (Sanchez, 1987). Witnessing code switching on a daily basis, many teachers have assumed that students who speak Black English are simply being perverse when they fail to modify their speech and writing to standard English on a permanent basis. If these children can correct their nonstandard features to standard ones on some occasions, as when reading a composition aloud, then they must know standard English and are simply too lazy to use it, or so the reasoning goes.

However, most of the available research on code switching suggests that it is acquired rather than learned behavior (Baugh, 1983; Genishi, 1981; Labov, 1971, 1972a, 1972b; McClure, 1981; Peck, 1982; Wald, 1985). Wald, for example, examined the language of 46 bilingual (Spanish–English) fifth and sixth graders. The spontaneous speech of the students was sampled when they were interviewed in peer groups of four by a bilingual male investigator, when the peer groups were alone but observed surreptitiously by the investigator, and in individual sessions with a bilingual female investigator. The subjects not only switched from Spanish to English with ease, but, more important, also preserved syntactic and semantic grammaticality in both cases, as in the following: "There's una silla asi, y como sillas de fierro ... no, si, para de que se usan en de-para backyard" (There's a seat like this, and like metal seats ... no, yes, that you use in the backyard). Given the spontaneity of the responses and the ambiguous results of grammar instruction, it seems unlikely that the subjects were applying learned grammatical rules through an internal monitor.

If code switching is acquired, it is an unconscious process. The implication therefore would be that nonstandard speakers who change nonstandard forms to standard ones are unaware of the changes they make. Experience in the classroom tends to bear this point out. A student who speaks Black English and who writes, "Rosie be workin at Ralph's," but reads "Rosie is working at Ralph's," is unlikely to change the sentence during essay revision or editing. As Furr and Daniels (1986) noted, "Many students do not know how to correct nonstandard features in their writing and, even when highly motivated to learn to write standard English, are quite puzzled about which features in their writing to change" (p. 20).

Nevertheless, it is important to note that code switching is a conscious process in many situations, although the process itself may not involve any deliberation on the structural properties of the dialects or languages in question. Those who speak English as a second language tend to code switch under two conditions: when speaking with an audience they know is bilingual and when they need a word in L_2 that they do not have or cannot remember. The situation is different for nonstandard English speakers. They generally do not code switch when speaking with others who are bidialectical. Instead, they use one dialect or the other, depending on the social relationship that exists among the group and on the setting. The dominant factor, however, is the social relationship: As it becomes more intimate, there is a greater tendency to use the home dialect, even in those situations in which other speakers do not share and have a hard time understanding that dialect. As the bidialectical speaker shifts further along the continuum toward non-standard speech, the monodialectical participant may have to ask "What?" several times as a reminder that he or she is not understanding some of the nonstandard language. At such moments, the bidialectical speaker must make a conscious decision to shift in the other direction along the continuum.

TEACHING NONMAINSTREAM STUDENTS

Regardless of their subject area, all teachers are teachers of language. Consequently, they deal with universals of language, learning, and mind that transcend individual language differences. The universal factors that govern language and learning suggest that writing instruction for nonmainstream students are very similar to writing instruction for mainstream students.

Much of what effective teaching involves was explained in earlier chapters, but it is important to emphasize that research over the last few years indicates that nonmainstream students work through writing tasks in about the same way that mainstream students do (Harrold, 1995; Zamel, 1983). They develop a pretext for the discourse that includes both rhetorical features and surface features. When they write, they engage in pausing episodes indicative of mental revisions of the pretext, just as mainstream students do. They revise recursively, modi-fying their discourse plans as they go along. With nonnative speakers, planning and revising skills in L_1 transfer to L_2 (Jones & Tetroe, 1983).

Moreover, nonmainstream writers, like their mainstream counter-parts, frequently use writing to clarify their thoughts on subjects. In other words, they use writing as a vehicle for learning. Their efforts require a high degree of interaction with the text, their constructed audience, and their intentions. To paraphrase Raimes (1985, 1986), students negotiate with the text as they develop it; they engage in the sort of hypothesis testing previously described.

If nonmainstream writers are to learn to negotiate with a text successfully, they need instruction that encourages risk-taking. They need a methodology that promotes a high degree of interaction with teacher and peers, that allows them to write multiple drafts, to receive feedback as each draft is being developed, and to revise. The only environment that currently incorporates all these features is the class-room workshop.

Using a workshop approach with nonmainstream students initially seems counterintuitive. Given the types of errors that appear in their writing, there is a strong temptation to resort to drills and exercises to reduce the level of home-language or home-dialect interference. In her much admired book *Errors and Expectations*, Shaughnessy (1977) con-cluded that providing drills and exercises, along with a great deal of sensitivity to their difficulties, is about all one can do for nonmainstream students. The primary patterns they bring to school writing must be overcome, the common reasoning goes, and drill is the only way to accomplish the task. But research like Farr and Janda's (1985) has suggested that few of the errors nonmainstream writers make are the result of home-language or home-dialect interference.

Such findings do not suggest that teachers should ignore the prob-lems students have with surface features. Improving the quality of the finished product is an important long-range goal. But errors seem best addressed on the spot, as students are working on drafts in their work groups. They can be dealt with as part of the composing process through individual conferences or through a presentation to the whole class, if several students are having similar difficulties. This approach keeps the emphasis on writing. Studies like Farr and Janda's (1985) and Edelsky's (1986), set in the context of contemporary writing research, have prompted numerous teachers to reexamine composition pedagogy for nonmainstream students. The difficulties that nonmainstream students have with writing appear to stem less from linguistic features of the second language or the second dialect than from the complexities and constraints of the act of composing itself (see White, 1977). From this perspective, an emphasis on error correction is neither reliable nor effective in helping students eliminate errors in their writing. Edelsky (1986) on this account explicitly called for a literacy methodology that links reading and writing as top–down, pragmatic activities.

Speech and Writing

Linking speech and writing in a complementary way also appears to be an effective way to improve the performance of students. Videotape machines are very useful tools when introducing writing activities that include speaking and listening tasks. Many teachers bring in tapes of age-appropriate television shows and movies and let students watch the first 5 minutes of the program. Then, they turn off the sound and let students watch for another 10 to 15 minutes. The first writing task involves producing dialogue for the characters. The assignment is written collaboratively by groups because students can read their work aloud and stage a competition for the most inventive dialogue, the most dramatic, the most humorous, the most realistic, and so forth. Practicing dictation can improve students' grasp of sound-to-symbol correspondences, so some teachers replay the tape in short segments to allow students to write down the dialogue they hear. They circulate among groups to monitor the degree of accuracy between the tape and students' writing.

The differences between the students' dialogue and the original are likely to be interesting. These differences form the foundation for another writing assignment: an analysis that compares and contrasts student versions with the original. A final and related assignment asks students to summarize the story elements of the portion of the tape they viewed, then to speculate on how the story or episode actually ends. When their speculative essays are completed, they can view the entire video and compare their versions with the actual story.

A stimulating variation on these activities involves videotaping students as they act out or read the dialogues they have produced for shows. Students can comment on the reading, offering suggestions for improvement and providing feedback on language use. Seeing oneself on camera has a powerful effect on most people, and students are motivated to give complete attention to their performances. The language context in this case is so meaningful that language use tends to improve significantly on the basis of the feedback.

MORE ON WORKSHOPS

Writing workshops are structured so that students produce multiple drafts, engage in collaborative activities, and share their writing with one another. In doing so, students gain a clearer understanding of what writing entails. This understanding is especially important for nonmainstream students who may feel inferior to their mainstream counterparts. They begin to see that their problems with written discourse are similar to those that all writers have.

Language acquisition suggests that the classroom workshop provides a social dimension to school language use that is often crucial to the developing literacy of nonmainstream students. Acquisition of communicative competence in literacy requires meaningfully interacting with others who encourage reading and writing. Yet it is common to find that nonmainstream students come from family backgrounds in which literacy is not stressed: Parents may not read to their children, and they may never do any writing, which means the children lack effective models for literate behavior.

The writing workshop allows nonmainstream students to talk, but it also asks them to talk in the language of the school—standard English—as they discuss one another's work. When they collaborate on drafts, trying to make them better, they engage in problem-solving activities that enhance their critical-thinking skills. Thus the benefits of group interaction are far reaching: Students not only exercise their cognitive abilities but exchange ideas that can enhance vocabulary, clarity, and meaning. The process of working through multiple drafts and revisions has additional advantages. It provides the opportunity to experiment with language in a largely risk-free environment. Mistakes during the drafting process are allowed, perhaps even encouraged, because they are an important part of learning. Fear of failure has well-known consequences. Harter (1981) noted that students who are overly concerned with task failure withdraw, refusing even to make an attempt at a given activity. Rose (1984) suggested that fear of making mistakes is an underlying factor in writer's block. Dulay, Burt, and Krashen (1982) suggested that fear of failure and subsequent rejection prevents second-language learners from interacting with native speakers of that second language. Thus, it appears that students who avoid errors are avoiding risks, playing it safe—working with what they already know—and therefore are not learning. The workshop provides an environment that minimizes the possibility of rejection and its accompanying fear and anxiety.

The personal and pedagogical benefits of such an environment are unmistakable. As nonmainstream students take more risks, they expand their repertoire of skills, which in turn leads to greater success with standard English and to a growing sense of confidence in their writing ability (Kantor, 1985). Confidence and success are two of the more significant pillars of academic achievement, which led Diaz (1986) to argue, in regard to nonnative English speakers, that "the development of confidence in writing that can accompany the use of process techniques brings ... a powerful and important byproduct for ESL students in learning to write in English" (p. 173).

The ideal classroom would have a balanced mixture of mainstream and nonmainstream students. Where such a balance exists, the standard English speakers can work with the nonmainstream students in a buddy system that enhances the skills of both. Frequent reading of drafts written by standard speakers works to familiarize the other speakers with the rhythms and construction patterns of English. Standard speakers benefit from attempting to explain the nuances of their own language or dialect, often articulating linguistic principles they had never thought of before. For example, prepositions commonly cause nonnative speakers serious problems. In Spanish, the preposition *en* means both *in* and *on*, so a native Spanish-speaking student is likely to write something along the lines of "I got in the bus, and after we arrived I got in the car." Native English speakers' linguistic competence provides them the knowledge that we get *on* buses but get *in* cars. Yet it takes some thought to figure out the underlying principle, which is related to the size of the vehicle, that dictates the preposition to use.

Most multicultural classrooms in metropolitan areas, however, rarely have a balance of mainstream and nonmainstream students. Usually, the student body is predominantly Hispanic, Asian (Korean, Cambodian Laotian, Chinese, Vietnamese), and black. A buddy system can still work in this environment because the nonmainstream students more often than not are at various levels of English proficiency; the more fluent students can help the others.

When it comes to structuring learning activities, elementary teachers in nonmainstream classes frequently have to deal with tutorial programs that, although put together with the best of intentions, can seriously handicap instruction. In larger districts, particularly, schools provide learning specialists for many nonmainstream students. These specialists no doubt provide a valuable service, but they also complicate the teacher's job because individuals and small groups leave the class at various times throughout the day for tutoring. Teachers in this situation have to maintain the utmost flexibility in order to fit whole-class activities into those hours when all the students are present, doing group work and conferences when some students are missing.

Middle school and high school teachers face a different problem. Although collaborative learning activities have become widespread during the last decade, curriculum guidelines in many districts and private schools continue to dictate drills and exercises. Implementing a workshop may stir administrative displeasure, with the typical response being to fall back on tradition: "This is the way it is always been done, and we do not want you to try to change things." In addition, nonmainstream writing classes at these levels are commonly the dumping ground for students with discipline problems. This is not to suggest in any way that nonmainstream students are troublemakers or that they can be stereotyped as such. The difficulty is not in the students but in the nature of the classes—places where students simply sit and fill in the blanks in workbooks. Administrative thinking in this case follows a circuitous route: The idea is that the drills and exercises at least will keep difficult students in their seats. Some educators, however, believe that large numbers of such students would cease to be discipline problems if school were more meaningful and allowed young people a greater voice in their own education (Freire & Macedo, 1987). It is important to note that workshops actually enhance a teacher's ability to deal with discipline problems. With students in work groups, the troublemakers are isolated from the whole class, becoming more visible and easier to control.

At this point, it is possible to summarize the key features of an effective classroom environment for nonmainstream students. Not surprisingly, these features are very similar to those for mainstream students. It should include:

- Frequent opportunities to practice writing, with equally frequent opportunities to receive significant feedback from peers and teacher.
- Regular opportunities to confer individually with the teacher to discuss work in progress.
- Regular discussions of the differences between home languages and dialects and school language.
- Consistent validation of home languages and dialects with simultaneous emphasis on helping students master the nuances of standard English.
- A meaningful context for writing; assignments that are related to students' daily experiences and lives.
- Opportunities to practice a variety of rhetorical strategies aimed at different audiences.
- An emphasis on multiple revisions of drafts before a paper is submitted for evaluation.
- An emphasis on collaborative learning.
- Frequent opportunities to combine reading and writing as reciprocal activities.
- Major reduction in the amount of direct instruction in grammar and mechanics, with a corresponding reduction in the attention given to error correction.

EXPLORING KEY IDEAS

1. Given that the Bilingual Education Act of 1968 clearly expresses a policy of monolingualism, why is there so much controversy around the question of bilingualism?
2. The U. S. Census Bureau reported that by the year 2015 approximately 25% of the nation's population will be Latino, making it the largest ethnic group in the country. What are some of the educational implications of this statistic?

3. What are some of the factors that may account for the phenomenally high level of immigration from 1965 to 1995?
4. The English-only movement has stirred controversy for almost two decades, yet in those states where English-only legislation has been passed, the practical consequences are nil. How might you explain the controversy?
5. Americans tend to think that French-accented English is romantic but that, say, Asian-accented English is unpleasant. How might you account for the different views?
6. If bilingualism had any negative effect on intelligence, what would be a logical response toward teaching students foreign languages?
7. Why is it so hard for teachers to have an effect on students' home language?
8. What might be some objections to the additive stance toward bilingualism and bidialectalism outlined in this chapter?
9. From a political perspective, what is the value of declaring Black English to be a distinct language?
10. Many teachers who hear bilingual or bidialectical students code switching assume that their students are just being lazy when they fail to use standard English on a writing task. What is a more reasoned explanation of this failure?
11. Many schools use workshops for their successful students, but they use traditional approaches for the unsuccessful ones, often black and Latino, who are in developmental classes. What is the problem with this dichotomy?
12. Workshops frequently work better with developmental students than with very successful ones. What might be some reasons why?

8

The Psychology of Writing

OVERVIEW

The *psychology of writing* is an area of study that focuses on examining the relation between mind and language. Of particular interest is the idea that writing is related to cognitive abilities. Some people assume that writing is thinking, whereas others, in a subtle distinction, assume that thinking is writing. The first position, that cognition influences language, draws significantly on the work of child psychologist Jean Piaget. The second, that language influences cognition, relies on the theories of another child psychologist, Lev Vygotsky. This position currently dominates composition studies, where it has led to two related proposals: Writing is inherently superior to speech and abstract thought is impossible in the absence of literacy (in this context, the ability to read and write).

A close analysis of these views shows that both lack sufficient evidence to support their theoretical claims. Cognitive processes influence some aspects of language, but not many; likewise, language—specifically literacy—influences some cognitive processes but not many. Indeed, cognition and language appear to exert a modest reciprocal influence on each other.

The psychology of writing also focuses on the various cognitive processes involved in writing, with a special emphasis on the plans writers construct when they compose. Good writers appear to think more than poor ones, and they also appear to think more about rhetorical features such as purpose, intention, and audience. Thus writing can be seen as a psychosocial process. An effective writing teacher, therefore, develops activities that encourage interaction between cognitive and social processes. A realizable goal is to enable students to become more reflective as they consider issues and ideas during composing.

MIND AND LANGUAGE

People use language, specifically writing, to interact with one another and the world around them. Part of this interaction is related to learning, for writing can be used in a general way to enhance knowledge. Language provides a kind of rehearsal that helps people remember things better. As a vehicle for analysis, it can reveal a subject's complexities, and it also can help organize thoughts. Given these factors, many teachers and scholars believe that a strong relation exists between mind and language.

The nature of this relation continues to be vigorously debated. Some believe that the nature of mind influences the nature of language. Based on the work of Jean Piaget, one of the foremost child psychologists, this view proposes that language is part of the capacity to represent ideas and objects mentally (Piaget & Inhelder, 1969). Hence, cognition, in general, has structural parallels to language. Both, for example, are hierarchical as well as linear, and both are temporally ordered.

In Piaget's view, cognitive abilities developmentally precede linguistic abilities; thus the development of linguistic structures depends on cognitive abilities. Trimbur (1987) suggested that this view finds expression in composition studies as an "inner/outer" dualism, in which "the writer's mind is a kind of box" that teachers try to pry open "in order to free what is stored inside" (p. 211). This view is implicit in those approaches to rhetoric and composition that stress writing as a discovery procedure. In these approaches, writers are deemed incapable of knowing what they want to say prior to writing.

In contrast to this view, Vygotsky (1962) and Whorf (1956) believed that language influences cognition. This view is more popular in composition studies, and it serves to justify an emphasis on style and the notion that writing is inherently superior to speech. Its chief advocates, among them Dillon (1981), Hirsch (1977), Moffett (1985), and Ong (1978), argued that writing promotes the ability to reason abstractly and that without the ability to read and write, people are limited to concrete, situational thinking.

COGNITION INFLUENCES LANGUAGE

The influence of cognition on language is inherent in Piaget's (1953, 1955, 1962, 1974) model of children's intellectual development. The goal of his model was to explain children's behavior so as to determine what is common to all people. According to Piaget (1955), children go through a continuum of three developmental periods that correspond to intellectual growth and reasoning ability. During the sensorimotor period, which starts at birth and ends at about 18 months of age, children are largely governed by reflexes and cannot really think in the sense that an older child or an adult can. They are extremely egocentric and initially have little or no awareness of the world beyond their own sensations of hunger, cold, warmth, and discomfort. Objects initially have no existential reality for them, as evidenced by the observation that children at this age do not reach out for a toy that is suddenly covered by a blanket. This phenomenon is interpreted as indicating that, for the child, the toy ceases to exist once it is out of sight. Intellectual ability during this period is viewed as very limited. Children seem able to deal with only one task at a time, in a serial fashion. In addition, they seem concerned only with functional success, with performance, and generally have no abstracting ability.

The concrete operational period occurs from 18 months to about 11 years old. Piaget (1955) divided this period into two stages: the pre-operational stage, which lasts until about 7 years old, and the concrete operational stage. This period is followed by the formal operational period, which begins in early adolescence and marks the development of adult reasoning ability.

The pre-operational stage is characterized by very limited thinking ability, an inability to reason abstractly, an inability to classify appropriately, and a high degree of egocentricity that makes taking on the point of view or role of another difficult for children. They cannot, in the words of Piaget (1955), *decenter*, and as a result they are poor communicators. The concrete operational stage marks a shift in intellectual ability. When children's intellect becomes operational, they become much better at identifying changes between states and understanding the relation between those different states. For example, a toy under a blanket is understood to be simply covered up, not to have disappeared.

The relation between these stages of development and language is clear in observations of infant behavior. Infants focus their attention on their immediate surroundings and the people and objects they interact with on a daily basis. Such observations led Piaget (1955) to characterize the first stage of children's cognitive development as being concerned with mental representations of reality. These interactions begin at birth, yet language typically does not appear until children are about 1 year old, when representations of reality are already well established. As language emerges, it is object-related. Most of a child's first words are names of people and objects in the immediate environment (Bates, 1976; Bates, Camaioni, & Volterra, 1975; Macnamara, 1972; Nelson, 1973; Pinker, 1994). Thus the order of development is essentially the following: Cognition related to people and things in the immediate environment leads to language use about those same people and things. This pattern of cognitive development–language development appears to be fairly consistent from one culture to another (Bloom, 1970, 1973; Schlesinger, 1971).

As infants develop, their object-centered language shifts to actions in which they are engaged. Piaget reported that children up to about 7 years old commonly use language to describe their activities, such as "I'm dressing the dolly." Because children during this period are egocentric, Piaget (1955) referred to such language as *egocentric speech*, and he defined it as the thoughts that emerge in the minds of children; "Apart from thinking by images ... , the child up to an age as yet undetermined, but probably somewhere about seven, is incapable of keeping to himself the thoughts which enter his mind" (p. 59). Children's egocentric speech, in other words, is thinking aloud. It is important to note, however, that for Piaget, egocentric speech does not play any significant role in cognitive development; it simply marks a transition between the egocentric existence of children and the social existence of adults. After about 8 years old, it disappears as a result of further cognitive development. Piaget's analysis of egocentric speech is a cornerstone of the view that cognition influences language: Changes in cognition that are the result of maturation and development have linguistic consequences.

In composition studies, the proposal that cognition influences language is embraced on two levels. On an applied level, it informs—through Bloom's taxonomy of behavioral objectives, which are based on Piaget's insights into child development—assignment sequencing. Assignments move from the cognitively simple to the cognitively complex in keeping with Piaget's developmental taxonomy. On a theoretical level, the proposal can be seen as a reaction against Chomsky's (1965) argument that linguistic features are innate, which in its strongest form posits autonomous linguistic mechanisms outside the cognitive domain (Fodor, 1983). Along these lines, Fodor suggested that language processes such as grammaticality judgments, parsing sentences into constituents, and comprehension are essentially a reflex. Many people who study and teach reading and writing are understandably uncomfortable with this idea. If language is outside the cognitive domain, then school-related activities designed to develop critical thinking and other intellectual faculties are unlikely to have any measurable effect on language performance. The view that cognition influences language rescues the idea that teaching students how to think helps them become better readers and writers.

Problems With Piaget

Although there is no denying the importance of Piaget's contributions to the understanding of child development, research in cognitive and linguistic development has forced a reevaluation of some of his conclusions. Bates (1979), for example, engaged children in cause–effect tasks and symbolic play in order to measure cognitive development. She then compared their performance on these tasks with their performance on language tasks and found that cognitive knowledge did not always precede linguistic performance (see also Corrigan, 1978; Miller, Chapman, Branston, & Reichle, 1980). After reviewing several of these more recent studies, Rice and Kemper (1984) concluded that there is no empirical support for the proposal that children's cognitive development has a significant effect on their language, other than what may be considered normal maturational changes. They also concluded that the relevance of Piagetian sensorimotor tasks to language performance is questionable.

Part of the problem is that Piaget's analysis of children's intellectual abilities is flawed in numerous respects, which makes his formulation of the way cognition influences language highly problematic (Donaldson, 1978). The claim that children are poor communicators because they are egocentric provides an important example. The idea that pre-operational children cannot decenter is based largely on investigations involving the *mountains task* (Piaget & Inhelder, 1969), during which children are seated at a table that has a model of three mountains on it. Each mountain is a different color, and each has a different summit: One is covered with snow, one has a house, and the third has a red cross. The experimenter then introduces a doll, moving it to different positions around the table. The task becomes describing what the doll sees in each of the different positions.

This task can shed important light on the relation between cognition and language because effective language use involves the ability to take on the perspective of another. Role-taking ability is central to turn taking in conversations, and it also is central to comprehension. A speaker must be able to reason abstractly and judge from nonlinguistic cues that the listener is understanding. Children in Piaget's studies under the age of 8 years old invariably failed at this task, leading Piaget to conclude that they cannot adopt the point of view of another. He further concluded that these children generally do not understand one another, and they only understand a small portion of adult speech, principally commands. A significant part of their failure to understand was deemed attributable to their egocentricity.

Hughes (1975), however, hypothesized that children's difficulty with the mountains task was related to its content rather than to undeveloped cognitive abilities. To test this hypothesis, he altered the task by intersecting two walls to form a cross; he then changed the dolls, introducing a policeman doll and a small boy doll. The policeman doll was situated so that it could "see" two areas of the intersection, as shown in Fig. 8.1.

The boy doll was then placed in the various sections made by the intersecting walls, and the subjects were asked whether the policeman doll could see him. Few subjects had any difficulty with this, even those who were 3 years old. Next, subjects were told to hide the boy doll so that the policeman doll could not see him, and again, they made few errors. At this point, Hughes increased the complexity of the task by introducing a second policeman doll and situating him at the top of the intersection, where he has a view of Sections A and B, as shown in Fig. 8.2.

Subjects were told to hide the boy doll again, this time from both

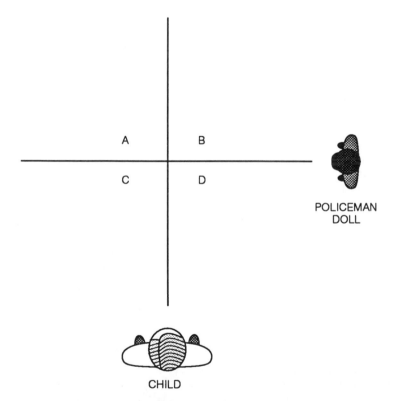

FIG. 8.1. Hughes' first modification of Piaget's mountain task. When children understood the nature of the task, they could decenter easily.

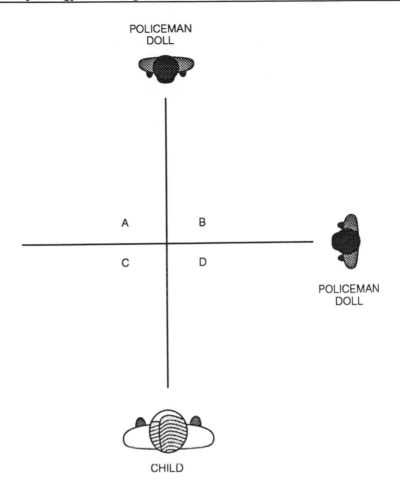

FIG. 8.2. Hughes' second modification of Piaget's mountain task. Even when the task was made more difficult through the addition of a second doll, children had no difficulty with de-centering.

policemen, which requires coordination of two different points of view. Ninety percent of the responses were correct. These findings suggest that children as young as 3 years old are as able to reason abstractly as children 2 to 4 years older, as long as they understand the task. Commenting on Hughes' data, Donaldson (1978) suggested that the findings were congruent with "the generalization of experience: they [the children] know what it is to try to hide. Also they know what it is to be naughty and to want to evade the consequences. So they can easily conceive that a boy might want to hide from a policeman if he had been a bad boy" (p. 24).

The general criticism of Piaget today is that his research failed to test children's cognitive abilities adequately.[1] The tasks he and his associates designed were removed from the world of children, and the young people they studied simply could not understand what they were being asked to do. Consequently, Piaget's interpretation of results was significantly confounded. On this basis, many scholars have concluded that Piaget's view that cognition influences language is incorrect (Karmiloff-Smith, 1992). This conclusion is reinforced by the fact that modern studies, designed to ensure that the child subjects understand what is asked of them, consistently show that children are far more capable of abstract thought than Piaget determined.

LANGUAGE INFLUENCES COGNITION

The idea that language influences cognition is very appealing to composition specialists. Known as *linguistic relativism* among linguists and psychologists, this idea emerged around the turn of the century when French anthropologist Lévy-Bruhl published *Les fonctions mentales dans les sociétés inférierures* in 1910. The English translation, *How Natives Think*, was published in 1926.[2] Although successful as a sociologist early in his academic career, Lévy-Bruhl felt that his work was too theoretical, too removed from the realities of the everyday existence of mankind. He began anthropological investigations after questioning the widely accepted view that the human mind functions the same regardless of time or culture. He then set out to study mental operations in the most remote regions of Africa to determine what, if any, differences existed between the cognition of Europeans and tribal peoples.

In *How Natives Think*, Lévy-Bruhl (1926) argued that his field studies showed great differences between the cognitive operations of the two groups. The tribal subjects he studied proved to be prelogical, which did not mean that they were incapable of logical operations but that they were indifferent to logical contradictions that arose from their failure to identify myths and mystical experiences as unreal.[3] They were, however,

---

[1]Another major criticism is that his studies of young children involved only three subjects—his own children—which is insufficient for making generalizations.

[2]This title is not even an approximation of the original, and it is enlightening to consider that a literal translation of the original title is *Mental Functions in Inferior Societies*.

[3]It is important to note, however, that near the end of his life, Lévy-Bruhl abandoned the notion of prelogical thinking. In *The Notebooks on Primitive Mentality* (1975), he concluded that the logical incompatibilities he observed were the result of mental juxtapositions of mythical reality and natural reality. As a result, positions that the European mind would find illogical, the primitive mind found logical because of the "imperceptible passage from belief to experience" (p. 13). In other words, the primitive mind does not differentiate between mythical experiences and natural experiences.

incapable of abstract concept formation above a rudimentary type associated with mystical experiences. That is, the primitives in his research might look at a tree and recognize it as a tree without any consideration of the classification of that tree as a member of a broader group of living plants.

Lévy-Bruhl was attacked soundly by other scholars for these conclusions. English anthropologists were particularly forceful in their rejection of the idea that different cultures produced different mentalities. Nevertheless, Lévy-Bruhl's work attracted the attention of enough scholars to gain a certain degree of intellectual legitimacy. More significant, his ideas received coverage in the media and led to a popular folk psychology about cross-cultural differences in cognition.

This folk psychology was reinforced in the United States through the work of Whorf (1956), an anthropological linguist who did extensive work with American Indian tribal languages during the 1920s and 1930s and who was significantly influenced by the work of Lévy-Bruhl. Whorf proposed that linguistics was ideally suited to investigating cognition, owing to his belief that all thought was verbal. Whorf noted that "the Hopi language is seen to contain no words, grammatical forms, constructions, or expressions that refer directly to what we call 'time,' or to past, present or future" (p. 57). On this basis, he proposed that the absence of time gave Hopi speakers a sense of reality far different from "classical Newtonian physics," and he linked this different reality to the sort of observations that Lévy-Bruhl made earlier about the prelogical quality of tribal cognition (p. 58). Thus Hopi, and by extrapolation all languages, creates not only a certain model of reality but also a certain way of thinking unique to that language. As Whorf stated:

> [Cognition] can only be determined by a penetrating study of the *language* spoken by the individual whose thinking process we are concerned with, and it will be found to be *fundamentally different* for individuals whose languages are of fundamentally different types. Just as cultural facts are only culturally determined, not biologically determined, so linguistic facts, which are likewise cultural, and include the linguistic element of thought, are only linguistically determined. (p. 67)

Although Whorf's work was always well known among linguists, it never stirred much interest among those working in composition studies. This role fell to Vygotsky, a Russian psychologist and contemporary of Piaget whose observations of child behavior during the late 1920s and early 1930s were unknown in America until the 1960s, when his books were translated into English. These works have provided composition specialists with a significant theoretical framework for the idea that language influences cognition. Especially influential has been *Thought and Language*, the last book Vygotsky wrote before his death in 1934.

The work of Piaget and Vygotsky has much in common. Both were constructivists who were strongly against nativism. *Constructivism* maintains that children lack any innate cognitive or linguistic structures or domain-specific knowledge. *Nativism* maintains that children have these structures, as the work of Chomsky most vividly illustrates. In Chomsky's account, language is innate. As Karmiloff-Smith (1992) noted, constructivism is similar to behaviorism because both see the child as a *"tabula rasa* with no built-in knowledge" (p. 7). Like Piaget, Vygotsky (1962) noted that at about 3 years old, young children begin to talk to themselves when doing things, as though giving verbal expression to their actions. Such talk is inherently different from the conversations they have been having for some time with others, because it seems to lack a social function. When dressing a doll, for example, children commonly utter such expressions as: "Now I'm going to put the dress on the dolly, and then I'm going to comb her hair." More often than not, children make these utterances as though no one else can hear them, so Vygotsky, like Piaget, referred to them as egocentric speech.

Again like Piaget, Vygotsky (1962) proposed that egocentric utterances mark the beginning of thought and that egocentric speech is thinking aloud. However, Vygotsky had a very different interpretation of the nature of egocentric speech. In his view, all language is social, including egocentric speech. One consequence of this view is fairly uncontroversial: Children develop the language of their community. Vygotsky took this perception to its logical conclusion and argued that the fundamental pattern of logical thought is evident in "social, collaborative forms of behavior" (p.19). The emergence of egocentric speech signals the start of an internalization process in which those social patterns of behavior take the form of what Vygotsky termed *inner speech*, or thought. On this account, not only thought but also the very processes of thought are social.

As Vygotsky (1962) noted, there is "nothing to this effect in Piaget, who believed that egocentric speech simply dies off" (p. 18). Piaget proposed a developmental sequence that began with nonverbal thought, developed into egocentric thought and speech, and then developed into socialized speech and logical thought. Vygotsky, however, proposed a developmental sequence that began with social speech, then egocentric speech, then inner speech, and then fully developed thought (p. 19). In his view, "the true direction of the development of thinking is not from the individual to the socialized, but from the social to the individual" (p. 20). Consequently:

Verbal thought is not an innate, natural form of behavior but is determined by a historical-cultural process and has specific properties and laws.... Once we acknowledge the historical character of verbal thought, we must consider it subject to all the premises of historical materialism,[4] which are valid for any historical phenomenon in human society. It is only to be expected that on this level the development of behavior will be governed essentially by the general laws of the historical development of human society. (p. 51)

In his thorough review of the language-influences-cognition question, Walters (1990) identified Goody and Watt's 1968 essay, "The Consequences of Literacy," as an important work that "influenced the discussion of literacy and its nature ... more than any other ... because of the way ... [the authors] chose to lay out the problems associated with understanding the phenomenon" (p. 174). Goody and Watt drew substantially on Lévy-Bruhl as well as Vygotsky, but as Walters explained, the focus in Goody and Watt was much more narrow than what is found in either:

Stated in its strongest form, ... [Goody and Watts'] theory claims that literacy and more particularly alphabetic literacy of the kind used for Western languages causes cognitive changes to the extent that literate people (that is, those literate in a language using alphabetic script) simply think differently—that is, more logically—than those from cultures without alphabetic literacy—an idea that many Westerners find appealing, no doubt because it "explains" what they perceive to be the superiority of Western culture. (p. 175)

In other words, Goody and Watt argued that Western culture is superior to others because it developed not just literacy but alphabetic literacy, which supposedly led to advances in cognition that other cultures have been unable to match.

It was Olson (1977), however, who perhaps most influenced composition specialists. Olson used Vygotsky's theoretical framework to explain the differences in academic achievement he observed among students from diverse linguistic backgrounds. He argued that speech is fundamentally different from writing in several important ways. In his view, they do not use similar mechanisms for conveying meaning: In speech, *meaning* is derived from the shared intentions and context of speaker and hearer, whereas in writing, *meaning* resides in the text itself at the sentence level and has to be extracted by readers. Olson

---

[4]*Historical materialism*, as defined in the writings of Marx, Engels, and Lenin, proposes that the prevailing economic system of any historical period determines the form of social organization and the political, ethical, and intellectual history of that period.

stated that writing has "no recourse to shared context ... [because] sentences have to be understood in contexts other than those in which they were written" (p. 272). He went on to assert that human history has reflected an evolution from utterance to text that has profoundly affected cultural and psychological development.

These observations were consistent with folk theories about language as well as folk psychology. More significant, however, was Olson's additional argument that writing in general and the essay form in particular account for the development of abstract thought in human beings. Olson asserted that people in nonliterate cultures are incapable of abstract thought; he claimed that writing is the key to developing abstracting ability because it forces people to comprehend events outside their original context, which alters their perception of the world, which, in turn, leads to cognitive growth. Walters (1990) noted, in this regard, that Olson "is among the most extreme of those who link the conventions of a particular literate form—in his case, the essay—with logical thought as represented in written language" (p. 177). Yet it is difficult to differentiate Olson's claims from those put forward by Goody and Watt. Following Olson's (1977) lead, Ong (1978, 1982) took these ideas a step farther. Ong (1978) claimed that "without writing ... the mind simply cannot engage in [abstract] ... thinking .... Without writing, the mind cannot even generate concepts such as 'history' or analysis" (p. 39).

These are powerful claims, and many teachers and scholars in the field have embraced them enthusiastically (see, e.g., Dillon, 1981; Hirsch, 1977; Scinto, 1986; Shaughnessy, 1977) because they create an us–them dichotomy that can be used to explain why some students do not succeed in school. Followed to its logical end, this view suggests that children from backgrounds in which written discourse is not stressed have culture-specific cognitive deficiencies that make significant academic achievement essentially impossible. In addition, these claims validate the orientation of most writing teachers. If literacy affects the quality of thought in a positive way, it logically follows that the quality of literacy would bear directly on the quality of thought. Reading great works of literature therefore has a more beneficial effect on thinking than reading a lab report or a corporate prospectus.

JOURNAL ENTRY

Reflect on your experiences with literacy and how it has affected you and those you know.

Problems With Linguistic Relativism

In Heath's (1983) research there was evidence of a strong social influence on language development that affected school achievement. To propose that the quality of mind is affected by the quality of language, whether oral or written, is to make a much stronger claim. The educational implications are clear-cut: People who do not read and write, and also probably those who do not read and write very well, must be simple-minded.

It is difficult not to find an element of elitism in this position, and some people may even see it as being ethnocentric, especially when writers like Scinto (1986) argue that written language is a "culturally heritable trait" (p. 171). Although there is no doubt that literacy provides increased opportunities for social mobility in the United States and in most Western nations, there necessarily must be some question as to the specific culture in which written language appears as a heritable trait. In this pluralistic society, it is possible to speak of American culture in the abstract, but the United States simultaneously contains numerous subcultures—black, Hispanic, Asian, and Native Americans, as well as the spectrum provided by SES and recent, massive immigration—that simply do not place the same weight on writing that mainstream, upper-middle-class, Anglo-European culture does. The task of teaching most likely would be far easier if, indeed, written language were a culturally heritable trait. In truth, however, children from mainstream and nonmainstream backgrounds alike find much school-sponsored reading and writing to be complex and baffling puzzles.

The criticism of linguistic relativism does not rest on such social and educational concerns. It is important to understand that the notion that writing exerts a cultural and psychological influence grew out of anthropological studies that attempted to explain why some cultures have reached a modern stage of development and why some have not (see Finnegan, 1970; Goody, 1968, 1972; Greenfield, 1972; Levi-Strauss, 1966; Lévy-Bruhl, 1975; Luria, 1976). In these studies, researchers gave a group of nonliterate, usually non-Western, subjects a task designed to measure cognitive abilities, then gave the same task to a group of literate, usually Western, subjects and compared the results. Colby and Cole (1976), for example, found that on tests of memory, nonliterate subjects from the Kpelle tribe in Africa performed far below the level of test subjects in the United States who were on average almost five years younger.

Similarly, Luria (1976), who was a student of Vygotsky, found that the nonliterate subjects in his study had more difficulty categorizing and sorting objects than the literate subjects. The nonliterates' method of cognitive processing tended to be more concrete and situation-bound than that of the literates'. For example, Luria presented his subjects with pictures of a hammer, a saw, an ax, and a piece of lumber, then asked which object did not belong with the others. The literate subjects quickly identified the piece of lumber, because it, unlike the other objects, is not a tool. The nonliterate subjects, on the other hand, seemed unable to understand the question. They insisted that all the objects went together because there was little use for a hammer, saw, and an ax if there was no lumber to use in making something.

From Luria's point of view, that of a psychologist trained in the Western tradition, this functional response was wrong, and he concluded that the nonliterate subjects had difficulty formulating abstract categories. This conclusion is remarkably similar to those conclusions proposed by Lévy-Bruhl. It may well be, however, that, as in the case of Piaget and Inhelder's (1969) mountains task, what was actually being tested had little to do with the ability to formulate abstract categories but had very much to do with understanding what the test was about. Lakoff (1987) and Rosch (1973) explained in great detail that there are specific cultural characteristics related to accepting the attributes objects may have in common. The often noted differences between English and Eskimo regarding the number of words used to describe snow offer an interesting example. Even in a single culture there are clusters of shared attributes that vary by gender, education, and SES. For many people in the United States, the term *car* embraces any vehicle that has four wheels and that is used principally for personal transportation. Those included are pickup trucks, station wagons, Jeeps, limousines, and sport-utility vehicles. For many other people, *car* refers only to sedans and coupes. Luria's findings therefore simply could be an instance of the nonliterate group's refusal to accept the designated category attributes, not a demonstration of an inability to establish abstract categories.

Moreover, every recorded culture, whether literate or nonliterate, has (or had) some form of religious beliefs. Such beliefs tend to be highly abstract. Also, collective terms (which are inherently abstract) are used in every recorded language to designate groups of people and things. Although not all languages have discrete terms for *brother* and *sister*, it appears to be a universal that they have a term for *sibling* (Ullmann, 1963). A culture in which it is possible to own more than one cow has some term equivalent to *cattle* or *herd*. On this account, the inability of nonliterate people to perform certain tasks, such as categorization, may not be related at all to their ability to reason abstractly.

These rather obvious difficulties beset most of the existing studies of literacy's effects on cognition. Another factor, however, is even more problematic. As Scribner and Cole (1981) pointed out in *The Psychology of Literacy*, to date the most detailed evaluation of the link between literacy and cognition, earlier researchers consistently conflated literacy and schooling. Given that it is in the nature of schooling to strip situations of their context and to emphasize nonfunctional intellectual experiences, conflating literacy and schooling may jeopardize the methodological integrity of the investigations. Thus it is impossible to look at studies like Luria's and determine any causal relations involved because there is no way to know whether the results were influenced by literacy or by schooling. Furthermore, as a consequence of this conflation, the research generally fails to compare similar groups of subjects. In the case of Luria, the groups he compared were not merely literates and nonliterates but literates with schooling and nonliterates without. These factors led Scribner and Cole to state that such studies "fail to support the specific claims made for literacy's effects. ... No comparisons were ever made between children with and children without a written language" (pp. 11–12).

To address such difficulties, Scribner and Cole (1981) were very careful to design a study that would distinguish between the cognitive effects of schooling and the cognitive effects of literacy. Their research was conducted among the Vai, a group of people in West Africa who developed an independent writing system early in the 19th century. The Vai script is used regularly for notes and letters, but there is no body of literature written in the script. At the time of this study, only about half of the people who were literate in the Vai script had some formal schooling. Thus there was a large group of literate but unschooled subjects to draw on.

Scribner and Cole (1981) evaluated more than 1,000 subjects over a 4-year period. First, the results showed that formal schooling had an effect on some cognitive abilities, but not on all. The schooled subjects were better at providing explanations, specifically explanations related to sorting, logic, grammatical rules, game instructions, and hypothetical questions. Outside the domain of verbal exposition, no other general patterns of cross-task superiority were found. Scribner and Cole suggested, on the basis of these findings, that schooling fosters abilities in expository talk in contrived situations.

As for literacy itself, only four tasks showed any influence. Literates were better able to: (a) listen to uttered statements and repeat back their messages, (b) use graphic symbols to represent language, (c) use language as a means of instruction, and (d) talk about correct Vai speech.

Given the nature of literacy, such differences would be expected, but the literates showed *no* superiority over nonliterate subjects with regard to classification, memory, deduction, and categorization. In other words, no evidence was found to suggest that literacy is linked to abstracting ability, cognitive growth, or the quality of thought. Summarizing their work, Scribner and Cole noted: "Our results are in direct conflict with persistent claims that 'deep psychological differences' divide literate and nonliterate populations. ... On no task—logic, abstraction, memory, communication—did we find all nonliterates performing at lower levels than all literates" (p. 251).

Further evidence against the idea that language influences cognition comes from studies of deaf children who have learned neither speech nor sign language. According to this view, such children either should have no thought at all or should have thought that is profoundly different from what is found in hearing children. Because it is difficult to evaluate cognitive processes without using language in some form, studies of deaf children's intellectual abilities are often less than definitive. Nevertheless, certain conclusions have been widely accepted. After conducting a series of studies into cognitive development, Furth (1966) reported that "language does not influence development [among deaf children] in any direct, general way" (p. 160). Similarly, Rice and Kemper (1984) reported that "deaf children's progress through the early Piagetian stages and structures is roughly parallel to that of hearing children" (p. 37).

The weight of the evidence against the idea that language significantly influences cognition is so compelling that its most ardent contemporary advocates have quietly retreated somewhat from their earlier positions. Goody (1987), for example, criticized his paper with Watt for placing too much importance on the alphabet as a tool for elevating culture. Olson (1987) suggested that his claim regarding the salutary effects of the essay on cognition may have overstated the case. With both the cognition-influences-language and the language-influences-cognition views discredited among psychologists, what remains?

JOURNAL ENTRY

Although the work of both Piaget and Vygotsky is suspect, they remain immensely popular—Piaget among educators, Vygotsky among composition specialists. Consider some of the factors that account for their popularity.

A PHASE MODEL OF COGNITION AND LANGUAGE

Both Piaget and Vygotsky proposed models of development that involve stages. In Piaget, children moved from the sensorimotor stage, for example, to the concrete operational stage. In Vygotsky, children moved from the egocentric-speech stage to the inner-speech stage. Neither of these models accurately reflects actual development. As children mature, their accomplishments with language and cognition are largely incremental, and they often reach behavioral milestones and then retreat from them in a recurrent ebb-and-flow movement. The same may be said of older children and even adults with respect to a range of different behaviors, particularly language. Moreover, the recurrent characteristics of development are mirrored in changes in neural structures (described in chap. 5) associated with learning, where dendrites demonstrate recurrent growth and reduction over time in response to external stimuli.

The stage models of Piaget and Vygotsky do not recognize these features of development. Instead, they posit discrete transitions from one kind of behavior and form of existence to another. As an alternative to the stage model, Karmiloff-Smith (1992) proposed a *phase model* that she referred to as *representational redescription*. In describing the difference between the two, Karmiloff-Smith noted:

> Stage models such as Piaget's are age-related and involve fundamental changes across the entire cognitive system. Representational redescription, by contrast, is hypothesized to occur recurrently within microdomains throughout development, as well as in adulthood and for some kinds of new learning. (p. 18)

In Karmiloff-Smith's model, development involves three phases. For the purposes of this discussion, these phases may be thought of as: (a) data collection, (b) reflection, and (c) reconciliation. *Data collection* encompasses gathering information from the environment so as to develop internal representations of reality. During *reflection*, these internal representations are the focus of attention to the extent that they dominate external data and thereby may result in performance errors. *Reconciliation* involves more closely matching internal representations with external data. These phases seem congruent with the model of language acquisition previously described.

Phase models have several advantages over stage models, but one of the more important is that they propose that cognition and language interact in a reciprocal process. Evidence to support this idea comes from a variety of sources (see Rice & Kemper, 1984), but one of the more elegant arises out of work with terms that indicate location. It is generally accepted that children's understanding of spatial relations follows a set pattern. First to develop are notions of *on* and *in*, followed quickly by notions of *top* and *bottom*. Other spatial concepts, such as *between*, *behind*, and *across*, develop much later (E. Clark, 1980). The development of spatial concepts is reflected in children's acquisition of the terms to identify them. Slobin (1973), however, hypothesized that linguistic variables can influence the pattern of development: The pattern may not be uniform across cultures and languages because some languages use complex grammatical features to indicate spatial relations. This complexity might make it harder for children in those cultures to formulate notions of location.

To test his hypothesis, Slobin (1973) first studied a group of toddlers who were learning both Hungarian and Serbo-Croatian. He discovered that the children learned how to express location in Hungarian before they could do so in Serbo-Croatian. Of the two languages, location is easier to express in Hungarian. His follow-up study compared acquisition of location terms in four languages: English, Italian, Turkish, and Serbo-Croatian (Slobin, 1982). Again, linguistic variables appeared to influence the development of spatial understanding. In this case, English and Serbo-Croatian proved more difficult than Turkish and Italian. As Slobin pointed out, Turkish and Italian use single words for the various spatial relations, whereas English and Serbo-Croatian have multiple terms, such as *on top of*, *next to*, and *in front of*.

The proposal that cognition and language exert reciprocal influences strikes many teachers as commonsensical, but it has two disadvantages. First, it fails to validate the study of literature as a causal factor in the improvement of mind. The argument that language arts curricula should include a heavy emphasis on literature is thereby diminished. Students of low intelligence and students with a variety of problems that make them less than ideal learners will not be transformed through Great Books programs that have students read standard works of literature. Second, it fails to provide the sort of intellectual controversy that attracts readers. In comparison to claims that anyone without literacy cannot have a sense of history, the proposal of reciprocal influences is a bit dull.

Nevertheless, the phase model that supports the notion of reciprocity is congruent with the work in cognitive science pertaining to association and neural networks, which was summarized in chapter 5. In both, language acquisition is intimately allied with experiences and internal representations of reality. The interaction of reality and internal representations of reality, when examined via a phase model, suggests that writing performance is influenced by both cognitive and social domains, which include published texts. Thus reading and immersion in a given discourse community develops internal representations of audience, rhetorical aims, argumentative structure, and so forth; instruction, likewise, develops internal representations of prewriting techniques, drafting, planning, sentence and paragraph structure, topic sentences, and theses. However, the existing stage model of composing does not explain why reading, immersion, and instruction fail to result in significant improvement in writing skill.[5] A phase model, on the other hand, maintains that the internal representations are in a steady state of flux. They are always in the process of becoming as each person strives to achieve a perfect match between those representations and external reality. Because a perfect match always remains elusive, Williams (1993) argued that:

> There is a sense in which writers, even experienced ones, must approach every writing task as though it were their first. They are faced with individual acts of creation each time they attempt to match a mental model of the discourse with the premises, paragraphs, examples, proofs, sentences, and words that comprise it. (p. 564)

When we apply the stage model to writing, there is the clear implication that students achieve developmental milestones that allow them to pass on to higher levels of achievement. This implication is valid only insofar as we recognize a general pattern of maturation in all areas of behavior. For example, a student in graduate school is better able to find materials in a library than a student in elementary school because he or she has more experience with libraries and research. Nonetheless, both have to use the same procedures and resources to locate those materials. The number of shortcuts are limited, and the procedures never become automated—they never become unconscious—to the extent that one can concentrate all energies on reaching the next stage, whatever that might be; they simply become more efficient. The early stages are always as important as the latter stages and are always omnipresent in the process.

The phase model of composing acknowledges this omnipresence without focusing on chronology. Students learn to spell before they learn to revise, and both are important in successful writing, but attention to spelling does not necessarily come before attention to revision, even though spelling was learned first. By the same token, attention to revision does not supersede attention to spelling, even though revision may be more important to the overall success of the writing. The stage model proposes a hierarchy based on importance. The phase model does

---

[5]The 1994 National Assessment of Educational Progress (NAEP) indicated, in fact, that writing performance was declining, even though classroom instruction more than ever before was grounded in process pedagogy. It is worth noting, however, that process pedagogy is linked to a stage model, as previously noted.

not. Instead, it proposes that attention to spelling and attention to revision co-occur in the act of writing and that the co-occurrence cannot be differentiated on the basis of whether the writer is experienced or inexperienced.

If we extend the phase model along the lines suggested by Rumelhart and McClelland's (1986) work in neural networks, we see that the various phases, existing simultaneously as they do, place competing demands on writers. Audience competes with message, which in turn competes with structure, which in turn competes with punctuation, and so on. This competition may serve to explain why good writing is and always has been such a premium and why education per se does not ensure that people become good writers. Instruction adds information and levels of expertise to the phases, but it does not reduce the level of competition.

PAUSES, PLANS, MENTAL MODELS, AND SOCIAL ACTIONS

With good cause, most teachers are concerned that their students treat topics superficially. They note that their students seldom venture beyond the most obvious analyses. In classes from history to science, the poorly written essay is the one produced by the student who not only has not mastered the material but also has not thought about it deeply.

Investigations into pausing and planning have shown that good writers spend more time thinking about what they write, perhaps developing and working from more elaborate mental models of the proposed text. Flower and Hayes (1981) concluded from their research on pausing episodes that good writers and poor writers use pauses in different ways. Good writers engage in global planning that incorporates rhetorical concerns such as audience, purpose, and intention. Poor writers, on the other hand, engage in local planning that focuses on surface features.

Witte (1985) suggested that when writers decide to compose, whether on their own or because of a teacher's assignment, they conceive an internal pretext that has both global and local discourse features. Planning would therefore involve a complex process of formulation, monitoring, and revision of the pretext. The physical act of writing would be largely the transcription of an already revised pretext, which would account for the observation that experienced writers frequently do less revising on drafts but still produce writing superior in quality to that of their less-skilled counterparts. Quite simply, they have performed more revision during planning. If this is the case, teaching probably should be directed toward getting students to focus more attention on planning at the global level and less at the sentence level. They need to think more during writing activities.

Empirical support for the notion that good writing is linked to the amount of thinking students do during the composing process is difficult to obtain because of the very nature of the problem. How does one measure the mind at work? The answer may lie in minute physical responses in certain muscles, such as those around the mouth and larynx, that appear to correspond with mental activity. These responses, usually called *covert*, or *subvocal, linguistic behavior*, can be measured only with the aid of special equipment, but they have been studied extensively over the last three decades. A large body of research now indicates that when people listen, read silently, solve math problems, remember, and write—that is, when they engage in almost any mental task—there is evidence of covert linguistic behavior. The more difficult the mental task, the greater the muscular response (see Conrad, 1972; Edfelt, 1960; Hardyck & Petrinovich, 1967; McGuigan, 1966, 1978; Sokolov, 1972; Williams, 1983, 1987). The link is so strong that many researchers are convinced covert linguistic behavior is a measurable manifestation of thought.

Williams (1987) found that the below-average writers in his investigation demonstrated much less covert linguistic behavior during pauses than the above-average writers. This finding suggested that the poor writers were doing less work on their internal pretext than the good writers. The models proposed by Flower and Hayes (1981) and Witte (1985) make it reasonable to conclude that it was the global, rhetorical aspects of the pretext that were being neglected. If poor writers are thinking about surface features rather than rhetorical ones, as seems indicated, it is easier to understand why they so often produce essays that lack depth and are deficient in identification of topic, articulation of intention, and specification of audience, even when these features are delineated by their teacher (see Bamberg, 1983; Williams, 1985; Witte & Faigley, 1981).

Why poor writers fail to spend much time planning their essays and thinking about their topics is unclear, but at least part of the problem is experiential and educational. Such students have not had much practice reflecting deeply on events and ideas, and they have been educated in an environment that does not consistently call for reflection. Much schooling, after all, relies on rote memorization.

Viewing the relation between mind and language as reciprocal is useful in this regard. The mind-as-a-box metaphor (Trimbur, 1987) will not work if the box is not very full, which will be the case with students who generally have been treated as empty vessels waiting to be filled.

They have not had much help in loading the box with ideas of their own. By the same token, reading and writing per se are not likely to lead to more thought. Such activities have to be part of a social context that acts on each student—through questions, differences in perspective and opinion, and demands for more detail—as he or she attempts to act on the social context through writing and sharing that writing. The idea of building new skills on old ones is implicit, but writing assignments nonetheless should be challenging if they are going to lead to cognitive growth. If children are already very familiar with object-related cognition and language, teachers should not bore them with endless object-related tasks. Because narratives and descriptions are inherently object-related, students may not be challenged by such activities after one or two essays. Challenging tasks are those that ask students to think, to formulate hypotheses concerning the way things are, and to find support for their hypotheses.

In addition, it seems clear that writing assignments should be sufficiently related to the world of students in order be understandable. A teacher who asks students to examine Marx's theory of the alienation of labor may be disappointed with the resulting essays, whereas one who asks students to examine why they attend a closed campus may not. This is not to say that our students should not know about philosophy. However, big topics often force student writers on themselves, effectively isolating them from any recognizable social factors that could help make their writing meaningful, largely because they lack sufficient subject expertise to explore such topics in meaningful ways. These topics are hard for students who do not yet see a connection between their world and the one reflected in the topic. They become like the children in Piaget and Inhelder's (1969) mountains task: They want to cooperate, they want to do well, but they just cannot understand what they are being asked to do or why they are being asked to do it.

The implications for teachers are fairly clear: They need to link writing assignments to content knowledge in ways that enhance expertise and that make the writing task meaningful. Writing just for the sake of writing does not appear to provide any benefits. However, linking writing tasks to content may be contrary to the prevalent orientation in our language arts classes that strives to avoid writing about content, but what we understand about how mind and language interact indicates that this orientation is taking students and teachers alike down a dead-end street.

EXPLORING KEY IDEAS

1. Some critics of composition studies have argued that the field's infatuation with Vygotsky reflects an infatuation with Marxism. What features of Vygotsky's model might substantiate this charge?
2. Why would teachers find comfort in the us–them dichotomy that emerges from cross-cultural research suggesting that nonliterate people cannot think abstractly?
3. Scribner and Cole showed that the real differences in thinking ability were between people with formal schooling and those without. What are the implications of this finding for America's schools?
4. What are some of the major differences between the stage model and phase model of composing? Why might teachers find the stage model more comforting?
5. If good writers perform more revising during planning, what would be an appropriate strategy for writing teachers?

9

Writing Assignments

OVERVIEW

Numerous factors contribute to successful writing assignments, but developing a sequence that allows students to incorporate skills they have practiced in previous work with new skills they are trying to master is absolutely crucial. In addition, a well-written assignment makes clear to students what they are supposed to do, how they are supposed to do it, who the students are writing for, and what constitutes a successful response.

All approaches to teaching writing include some notion of what assignments are supposed to do and be about, but few offer any principled discussion of sequencing. In both the current–traditional and the process views, sequencing is usually linked to a taxonomy of behavioral objectives and cognitive development through the various rhetorical modes. Students begin with narration and description, producing personal-experience narratives or simple firsthand descriptions. They then go on to definition, comparison–contrast, and process, until at some point, they reach argumentation (see Lindemann, 1993b). Underlying this sequence is the notion that rhetorical complexity and cognitive complexity are essentially the same thing. In the current–traditional view particularly, students are often considered incapable of coping with abstract cognitive tasks, so classroom instruction focuses on writing assignments that are deemed rhetorically concrete. However, cognitive processes and language develop interactively, each influencing the other, and they are not the same thing.

Effective teachers recognize that the distinct nature of rhetorical complexity and cognitive complexity affects the way teachers sequence assignments because the rhetorical demands of a task may be far different from the cognitive demands. For example, close analysis shows that true narration is perhaps the most rhetorically demanding of all the modes, even though it may be less cognitively demanding than argumentation. Beginning a sequence with narration therefore appears to be at odds with sound pedagogical principles. It is the equivalent of asking a child to walk before he or she can crawl.

The view of teaching composition offered in this text suggests a sequencing alternative that focuses on the functional nature of writing and on the social and intellectual demands placed on students at any given moment rather than on modes. It suggests that an effective sequence should build on students' communicative competence and should ask them to use essays to perform specific social actions of the sort found in WAC classes. We know that most of the writing students do in classes other than composition and most of what they are likely to do outside of school calls for three general skills: *analysis, exposition,* and *argumentation.* A viable sequence acknowledges the importance of these skills.

The sequence for assignments recommended in this chapter focuses primarily on argumentation—although it may include narration—because in broad application, argument can incorporate all the other discourse modes. Poetry and narrative fiction, for example, can be seen as representations of reality that a writer wants an audience to accept. The intentional component makes the writer's representation argumentative. Moving students from less difficult to more difficult tasks could be accomplished by varying the kinds and sources of information students use to support claims and/or representations of reality. Argumentation is also important because it links writing to problem solving, which enhances critical-thinking skills.

One of the advantages in this view of assignments is that it allows teachers to apply a viable theoretical framework to a curriculum often highly constrained by textbooks and district guidelines. Teachers are commonly asked to address seemingly quite disparate writing tasks, such as essay exams, analyses of literature, and research papers. Seeing all these tasks as inherently argumentative allows for greater instructional continuity because the rhetorical skills students are trying to master are very similar across tasks.

MAKING GOOD WRITING ASSIGNMENTS

When students turn in essays that have little to say and that are boring to read, teachers often blame the students for not trying. Actually, the problem may be in the assignment. There is no such thing as "the perfect assignment," but some are definitely better than others and lead to more thoughtful responses from students.

Planning

First, good assignments take time and planning. Teachers who put together a writing assignment the night before class are neglecting their students. Effective teachers generally develop assignments in advance to ensure that they are as thoughtful as possible. They also sequence assignments to provide a careful blend of the old and the new. It is generally best to start with something students already know how to do fairly well, adding just enough novelty to make the task interesting and challenging. A knowledge of district guidelines across grade levels is important to proper planning because they specify the particular skills students are expected to master from grade to grade. This knowledge allows teachers to avoid tediously repeating skill-building tasks that students have already practiced in previous classes.

The goal of sequencing is to guarantee successful learning. Therefore, sequences that help students bring their own experiences and knowledge to bear on content-related topics are particularly effective. A typical assignment sequence involving analysis might begin by asking students to write about something concrete, like a sporting event, and then go on to ask them to analyze something more complex, like a film or a story.

Most teachers find it difficult to keep a sequence in view if they develop each assignment separately as the term progresses, so they put together all the assignments before classes start. Outlining the work in advance can help a great deal, especially when the outline includes activities for each term, with due dates for all papers. Students appreciate receiving a copy on the first day of class; they then have a better understanding of what is expected of them and can begin planning their writing early. It is never a good idea to give any writing assignment orally or on the board; at least half of the class will not hear an oral assignment, and the majority of the other half will misunderstand it or forget it an hour later.

Good writing assignments are also relatively brief, although they generally provide enough information to put the task in a context and to help students discover a purpose for the writing. Some teachers mistakenly assume that the more detailed they make the assignment, the better students will respond, but this just is not the case. Overly detailed assignments lead to cognitive overload that inhibits writing performance. An assignment that consists of a single directive, however, is probably too brief because it fails to offer a context.

FEATURES EVERY ASSIGNMENT SHOULD HAVE

To write a good assignment, teachers must consider the rhetorical nature of the tasks they are setting. As Lindemann (1993b) noted, teachers must decide what they want students to do in an assignment, how they want them to do it, who the students are writing for, and what constitutes a successful response to the assignment.

Generally speaking, assignments that lack these rhetorical features are problematic because students find it extremely difficult to develop a meaningful purpose for their responses. Many teachers rely on class discussions to specify these rhetorical features, but this approach seems unsatisfactory for most writing tasks, especially those that students will complete out of class. Some students will not be listening, and others will not take notes, relying on their memory to complete a task that they will not begin until hours or even days later. Class discussions of assignments are important, but they should not be used to convey information crucial to the satisfactory completion of the task. They are excellent opportunities to start students talking about their writing, articulating not only their understanding of the assignment but also their initial conceptualization of how they plan to proceed. Such discussions are best begun in work groups, in which the give and take of ideas can be more rapid, owing to the relatively small size of the group. Group discussions can serve as a form of brainstorming, stimulating both ideas and questions that can then be shared with the class as a whole.

To summarize, good assignments generally will:

- Be part of a sequence designed to develop specific discourse skills.
- Tell students exactly what they are expected to do. The mode of the response should be clear.
- Tell students exactly how they are expected to write the assignment. If students are expected to use a formal tone, this expectation should be stated; if students are expected to use outside sources to support a claim, this too should be stated. The assignment should include practical specifics such as whether the paper should be typed, due date, length, and so on (see Tarvers, 1988).
- Tell students something about the purpose and the audience for the paper. What is the paper supposed to do? Who other than the teacher should the writer be addressing?
- Tell students what constitutes success, including some statement regarding the criteria you will use to assess the quality of the response.

JOURNAL ENTRY

Evaluate some of the assignments you have had for classes in the past. Are they part of a sequence? Do the assignments reflect a clear pedagogical purpose that can be described in terms of cognitive or rhetorical growth? If the assignments have some other pedagogical purpose, what is it? Finally, what can you learn from assignments you have worked on that will help you produce better assignments for your students?

SAMPLE ASSIGNMENTS

The following sample assignments can make these features more concrete. They were collected from teachers at various grade levels. They are presented out of the sequences in which they belong simply to make the analysis a bit easier at this point. Some sequenced samples are presented later in the chapter.

Sample Assignment 1.   This assignment was made for a group of third-grade students studying poems; the teacher was linking reading with writing:

> We have been studying poems for two weeks. Last week we wrote our own version of "Over in the Meadow." We took Olive Wadsworth's poem and put it in our own words to tell a story. Now I want you to write another poem. I want this poem to be all your own. Tell your own story in rhyme. The story can be about your dog or cat. It can be about your favorite toy, or even your best friend. Just make it your own special poem. When all the poems are finished, we will put them together in a book. Then we will make copies so everyone will be able to read your poem. We will even make enough copies so you can give one to a friend.

Sample Assignment 2.   This assignment was created for a group of ninth-grade students studying poetry; the teacher was linking reading with writing, focusing on analytical skills:

> On your last assignment, you analyzed three of Charles Webb's prose poems to get ready for his visit to class. For this next assignment, I want you to begin with your earlier analysis and then to add to it an evaluation that explains which poem you like best and why. Successful analyses will support the explanation with good reasons and illustrations from the text. We will then mail our essays to Mr. Webb, who has promised to respond to several of them.

Sample Assignment 3.   This assignment was prepared for a group of twelfth-grade students studying analysis; the teacher was focusing on relating writing tasks to situations students might encounter outside school:

> Last week we studied the brochures we received from the travel agency to decide where we would like to spend our ideal vacation. Suppose that the agency were to sponsor a contest that would send the winner wherever he or she wanted to go, all expenses paid. All you have to do to win is write an essay explaining why you want to vacation in the spot you selected and write the best essay. That is your task for this assignment. Each peer group will choose its best essay to enter into the finals, and then the whole class will choose from the final four which one is the winner. Our judging criteria should include knowledge about the vacation spot and the reasons the writer wants to vacation there.

In each of these samples, the teacher provided a background for the task, told students what they are supposed to do, how they are supposed to do it, and what she would be looking for as she evaluated responses. In Sample Assignment 2, for example, students can see that the reasons they supply to support their analyses will be a significant factor in the teacher's evaluation. The assignments are not overspecified; the teachers did not overwhelm students by providing too much detail in regard to audience, purpose, assessment criteria, and so forth.

The next set of sample assignments offer a point of comparison for the first set. They were also collected from various public school teachers, and they were not part of any identifiable sequence.

Sample Assignment 4.   This assignment was generated for a group of twelfth-grade students studying exposition; students had previously discussed film plots and had spent some time analyzing the movie *E. T.*:

> Pretend you are E. T. How would you describe your school to the folks back home? Keep in mind that you would know nothing about Earth and its customs.

Sample Assignment 5.   This assignment was given to a group of seventh-grade students studying exposition; students had recently read an essay about how to build a kite:

> Describe the process of making a peanut butter and jelly sandwich to someone who does not know how to make one.

Sample Assignment 6.   This assignment was prepared for a group of tenth-grade students studying exposition; students had just finished a unit on poetry:

> Everyone has done something they felt ashamed about later. Describe an event in which you did something that made you feel ashamed.

Sample Assignment 7.   The following was created for a group of tenth-grade students studying exposition; students had previously read a short story in which the main character enjoyed reading:

> For this assignment you will write a comparison and contrast paper. Be certain to describe each of your topics in detail. Select one from the following choices: (a) compare and contrast two types of music such that readers will understand why you prefer one to the other; (b) compare and contrast the sort of books you enjoy reading today with the sort of books you enjoyed reading five years ago, and describe how your taste has changed; (c) compare and contrast a place, such as a neighborhood, you knew as a child with how it is today.

Sample Assignments 4 through 7 are problematic for several reasons. In Sample Assignment 6, narration and description are confused; the narrative is stated in terms of describing an event. These sample assignments illustrate a further confusion: The teachers who wrote the assignments seem to mistake what students find interesting with what is personal. Outside the warm intimacy of close friendship or the anonymity of religious confession, not many people are prepared to voice their personal shame. Increasingly, parents and educators agree that teachers just do not have the authority to insist that students reveal their private lives.

In addition, there is a serious question as to the significance of some of these assignments. Under what circumstances would anyone ever be expected to explain, rather than show, how to make a peanut butter and jelly sandwich? The E. T. assignment is cute, if one likes E. T., and there is something to be said for role playing. But why that role when there are many others that ultimately are more immediate, more challenging, and more educational?

Sample Assignment 7 is especially interesting because it gives students choices regarding the exact nature of their responses. Initially, this technique may seem very appealing, but closer consideration shows that the teacher is not doing students a favor here. As is often the case when students have several choices for their responses, the question of validity arises because students are performing quite different tasks on this assignment, depending on the topic they select. Although there are several different kinds of *validity*, in this case the term refers to the idea that assessment criteria must match what is being measured. In most instances, and clearly in Sample Assignment 7, what is being measured is not simply a broad construct like writing ability but is much more specific. For example, Topics A and B call for analyses that substantiate conclusions—a weak form of argumentation—whereas Topic C calls for simple analysis. Any subsequent assessment of responses is invalid if even one student makes a selection different from the rest of the class because the assessment criteria must be different. As if this problem is not serious enough, there is also the fact that students may be confused when they perceive that they are told they can perform significantly different tasks and still meet the requirements of the assignment.

RHETORICAL COMPLEXITY

Narration is quite different from a narrative report. We can differentiate the two forms of writing on the basis of *meaning* (what is said) and *message* (what is meant). Narration has a message that demands a high level of rhetorical sophistication to convey. Even narratives noted for their entertainment value, such as *Raiders of the Lost Ark, Toy Story*, and *Star Wars*, tend to edify as well as entertain, and in this regard their rhetorical demands are great. *Narrative reports*, on the other hand, are almost entirely meaning; they present a chronology of events without comment, editorializing, or interpretation.

Narratives, however, are claims for a particular representation of reality. The goal is to get readers to accept the representation via the interactions of plot, character, and setting. In fact, one measure of a writer's narrative success is the believability or acceptability of his or her representation of reality. Argumentation also involves representations of reality, although argumentative success is evaluated on the basis of how well writers make their claims acceptable via proofs and support. In other words, when writers make claims, they are simply asserting a representation of reality that they want readers to accept, and the presentation of evidence and the manipulation of warrants (premises) are designed to accomplish this goal. On this account, narration is a special form of argumentation, special because it uses plot and characters to make and support claims in an implicit rather than an explicit manner. Other genres, such as poetry, are a special form of argumentation as well.

It is extremely difficult to write on the implicit level, a fact that many teachers ignore in their quest to make writing fun. It is so much easier to be explicit, to write, "The purpose of this paper is ... ." Good narratives do not do this, although good arguments frequently do. What this analysis suggests is that narration is more rhetorically demanding than argumentation, which may help to explain why student writers tend to produce simple narrative reports when asked to produce a personal-experience narration. If narration is rhetorically more demanding than argumentation, then any sequence that includes narratives should place these assignments at the end of the sequence rather than at the beginning. Students would thereby work on tasks that truly allow them to build on skills, moving from less demanding to more demanding activities.

DEVELOPING SEQUENCED ASSIGNMENTS

The idea of sequencing and building on skills students already have is linked to Bloom's (1956) taxonomy of educational objectives, which is based on Piaget's (1955, 1962) stage model of development. Piaget described children's cognitive development as a movement from the concrete to the abstract, and he argued that children younger than about 11 years old are incapable of abstract reasoning. The pedagogical implication of these developmental claims is fairly straightforward: Teachers should give students concrete tasks until they are old enough to work with abstract ones.

This notion had a major effect on composition pedagogy. In the majority of elementary and middle schools, students just do not work on analysis or exposition because they are deemed incapable of the level of abstract thought required to carry out the tasks. Instead, they are asked to engage, year after year, in self-expressive discourse of the narrative, descriptive, what-I-did-on-my-summer-vacation variety. In high school, the self-expressive writing continues for most students, but a few schools offer a sequence that almost always starts out with narration and description. Students then work through the various rhetorical modes of definition, comparison–contrast, analysis, and so forth, until they finally reach argumentation, if there is time left in the semester.

Both the sequence and its rationale are problematic. As noted in chapter 8, Piaget's developmental stage theory is fundamentally flawed, so using it as a basis for assignment sequencing is problematic. In addition, the idea that cognition influences language suggests that cognitive complexity is the same as rhetorical complexity—that the ability to engage in abstract cognitive tasks is the same as the ability to engage in abstract rhetorical tasks. Cognition and language, however, are most certainly separate faculties in several respects (Fodor, 1983; Glass, Holyoak, & Santa, 1979; Karmiloff-Smith, 1992; Lakoff, 1987), and it is a mistake to equate them. If they were the same, if cognitive abstracting ability and rhetorical abstracting ability were the same, we might predict that our best writers of fiction would be philosophers and physicists, but they are not. Bloom's taxonomy just does not recognize that many description and narration tasks are more rhetorically demanding than argumentation. On this account, any assignment sequence that begins with narration and ends with argumentation is likely to start students with cognitively simple but rhetorically complex tasks.

Given that the focus of language arts classes is on language rather than cognition, such a sequence is difficult to justify. Few students have the level of rhetorical sophistication necessary to convey a message implicitly, particularly at the beginning of the term. Moreover, it is worth considering Giroux's (1987) suggestion that the goal of improving student literacy is to enable young people to "locate themselves in their own histories and in doing so make themselves present as agents in the struggle to expand the possibilities of human life and freedom" (pp. 10–11). Freire and Macedo (1987), in a similar vein, suggested that realizing this goal requires students to immerse themselves in interrogation and analysis. In other words, literacy must focus on critical thinking, formulation of hypotheses, reasoning, and reflection, which are more explicitly realized in exposition than in narration.

Currently, there is no evidence that the traditional approach to sequencing accomplishes this goal. In fact, the repetitive nature of the modes approach and the unavoidably arhetorical practice of presenting modes in isolation actually have a negative effect on student perceptions of writing. The endless round of personal narratives, definitions, and comparison–contrasts fails to offer intellectual challenges to students who understand that there are few demands for autobiographies outside the walls of English class. In school and out, students are called on to analyze and to reach conclusions on the basis of their analysis. They are called on to defend their positions. A viable sequence of writing assignments helps students practice these tasks; it prepares them for the kinds of writing they actually are asked to do in other courses and in life, where analysis and argumentation are the most frequent writing activities.

Some scholars have argued that the frequency of analysis and argumentation in subjects other than English offers a rationale for focusing on narration and description in composition classes. Britton et al. (1975), for example, suggested that language learning takes place in the intimate environment of the family and that *expressive discourse*, which includes personal narratives and autobiography, should be encouraged as a means of continuing language development. The problem with this argument is fairly obvious: By the time students are old enough to write, usually around third grade, they have moved outside the narrow sphere of home language and are interacting with a variety of people and situations that call for more extensive language skills; these skills are intimately linked to the kinds of interpreting, analyzing, and arguing skills that this chapter is advocating. If students do not practice these skills in school, where will they?

Given that the rhetorical features of argumentation are relatively straightforward, dealing primarily with matching proofs to audience, a sequence that focuses on argument allows students to practice relatively concrete rhetorical skills. In middle and high schools, a sequence might begin by asking students to use personal experience to support a claim. The next step might be to ask them to develop their own data, perhaps through interviews, direct observation, or simple questionnaires, to support a claim. The final step might be to ask them to use secondary sources (e.g., books, magazines, newspapers, and so on) to support a claim. These assignments illustrate just one type of sequence and should not be viewed as comprehensive. What is important is that in this kind of sequence analysis is implicit—students analyze support to determine whether it is suitable to the task.

An immediate advantage to focusing on argumentation is that it allows teachers to deal with a range of writing tasks that otherwise would seem unrelated. In the traditional modes sequence, creative writing, essay exams, and research papers do not really have a place because they are not modes, per se. Yet these are common writing tasks. The view outlined here allows teachers to consider each of these tasks as a form of argumentative discourse in which the writer's goal is to establish an acceptable representation of reality or claim. What varies is the type of support available: In the research paper, it is documented sources; in the essay exam, it is information from the class textbook and from the teacher's lectures. Seeing these tasks as inherently argumentative allows for greater pedagogical continuity because the rhetorical skills students are trying to master are very similar across tasks.

MORE SAMPLE ASSIGNMENTS

The three assignments that follow, taken from a series of six, reflect how one teacher actually organized an argumentative sequence. They were written for a class of tenth graders.

Sample Assignment 8.

Last summer the school board met to discuss potential health hazards to students resulting from the growing number of reported AIDS cases. The question before the board was whether or not school nurses in the district should be allowed to distribute condoms to sexually active students who ask for them. Before making a decision this fall, the board wants to hear from the community to weigh the arguments for and against this proposed policy. As a student at this school, you will be directly affected by the board's decision. Based on what you know about the needs of students on this campus, write an essay that will influence the board members to support your position on the proposed policy. Successful papers will be free of surface errors, will provide detailed reasons for your position, and will recognize an alternative point of view. (After we evaluate the final drafts, we will mail the essays to the board.)

Sample Assignment 9.

In the last assignment, you drew on your own knowledge to support your claim. This assignment asks you to draw on the knowledge of others. Last year three students at this school were suspended for drunkenness on campus. Our principal is very concerned that many students may be doing poorly in their classes because they are often under the influence. In the superintendent's office there has been talk of random locker searches to cut down on the amount of drinking on campus. Many parents believe the superintendent is overreacting and are reluctant to support searches. Our principal must consider both sides of the issue before making a decision. Your task on this assignment is to advise the principal. Your advice, however, may not be very influential if you speak solely for yourself. You will therefore want to interview at least ten other students (and perhaps some teachers) to find out their views on the matter. Use their reasons for or against the searches to make your advice more informed and more significant. Successful papers will present findings clearly and objectively; they will include some background information for the reader. (After we evaluate final drafts, we will forward them to the principal for consideration.)

Sample Assignment 10.

Your last assignment asked you to use other people's views, rather than just your own, to support your position. This assignment will take you one step further in that direction by asking you to go to the library to find books, magazines, or newspaper articles that have information you can use to support your position on the following claim: *American public education is failing to prepare students for the demands of the workplace and of higher education*. Keep in mind that written arguments, unlike oral ones, are not so much concerned with "winning" as they are with getting readers to accept your view. Successful papers will be clearly documented; they will use library sources to support your view such that the tone is objective.

Sample Assignments 8 and 9 are specific to this teacher's school; they are not generic. Such specificity is characteristic of assignments designed to evoke functional responses. They engage students in the world around them as much as possible to allow writers to consider immediate experiences. Also, such assignments take advantage of the fact that much argumentation reflects a need to make a decision about some course of action. Sample Assignment 10 is far less functional, essentially being the sort of task students are often asked to do in a research paper. It is important to understand, however, how this assignment follows naturally from the other two. The distance between writer and content increases progressively from Sample Assignment 8 to 10. In addition, Sample Assignment 10 makes it clear that students are using research to support a personal belief, just as they were in Sample Assignment 8. This idea is usually absent in most research tasks, even though a majority of the research that people do when writing is conducted with the aim of supporting a personal view or representation of reality.

COLLABORATIVE ASSIGNMENTS

An important advantage to setting up work groups is that they increase the opportunities for meaningful collaboration among students. Collaboration is a natural part of the writing process because writing is a social action. Thus collaborative assignments move students closer to realistic contexts for composing and are likely to motivate students to do well.

A goal of such assignments is to get students to work together on a group project, and often groups will be in competition because they may be working with the same material. Consider, for example, the following two assignments.

Sample Assignment 11.   This assignment was written for a class of fifth graders:

> Surveys of young people show that just about everyone would like to be on television reading the evening news. Few will ever get the chance, but it is fun to dream of gathering the news and reporting it. For this paper, you will have the chance to be a reporter. Each group will find a topic about the school or our neighborhood and report on it. Each group member will work on one part of the report, and then the whole group will put the parts together to make a complete paper. After the reports are finished, groups will read them to the class so we can have our own evening news! Remember to supply details for every story and to avoid making your report sound like a conversation.

Sample Assignment 12.   This assignment was generated for a class of twelfth graders:

> In the minds of most people, an expert is someone who knows all the answers in a given field. This is a common and somewhat misconceived view. But there is another way of looking at things. In this alternative view, a knowledgeable person, an expert, is not one who knows what the answers are, but one who knows what the questions are in a given field. On this assignment, each group will be responsible for explaining what the significant questions are in a given field, whether it be criminal law, local government, American history, film, computer technology, or whatever. Divide the work among group members such that everyone has a task and everyone writes part of the report. Give your papers a professional tone. Keep them free of spelling and punctuation mistakes. Be sure to explain the questions in detail, and discuss why they are relevant to all of us.

These sample assignments illustrate how collaborative assignments can be structured, although it is important to note that Sample Assignment 12 is not as strong as it could be because it fails to inform students what function the task serves. Generally, the only conceptual problem with collaborative assignments is finding tasks that lend themselves to group work. Monitoring collaborations is a bit more difficult because teachers have to guard against any effort in each work group to make one or two members responsible for the whole project. Although it is often a good idea to have one member act as a chief editor to delegate the work and to oversee combining the several parts into a coherent essay, each member must be productive. Perhaps the most effective way to monitor collaborative assignments is to pay careful attention to workshop activities. When students are idle or are not writing, teachers should ask them to show the draft they are working on. If they have little or no work to show, they may be shirking their responsibility.

Experience shows that students not only enjoy group projects enormously but also learn a great deal about the writing process from them. They gain a new appreciation of audience, for example, when their ideas, style, and tone have to be compatible with those of the rest of the group.

JOURNAL ENTRY

If you could give your students your ideal writing assignment, what would be its major characteristics?

RELATING WRITING TO THE REAL WORLD

Teachers need to recognize the rhetorical nature of written discourse—in part, through their assignments—before they can expect students to produce meaningful essays. In other words, meaningful assignments are likely to lead to meaningful writing. If students were performing a real writing task—one arising in the natural context outside school—their writing would be directed by the social conventions of the stimulus. Writing a love letter or making a diary entry, they would automatically take into account such factors as audience, purpose, intention, and tone. Most school-sponsored writing assignments, however, provide little in the way of context, so student responses often seem pointless, vague, and rambling. Developing a context for each writing assignment therefore is important. This does not involve simply describing a supposed audience or asking students to role play. Rather it involves setting tasks that allow students to do something with their writing other than simply turning it in for a grade.

A personal computer and the appropriate software now make it possible to produce, quickly and easily, high quality copy in either a newspaper or magazine format. Teachers with access to such equipment can organize a publishing program for the writing classes, where student writing is printed for everyone to read. Such programs seem to be particularly successful with elementary students, who are eager to enhance their writing with artwork (some of which can be done on the computer).

Students in junior and senior high schools can benefit greatly from contact with local businesses, either through field trips or classroom visits by business people, which introduces them to the demands of writing in the workplace. This introduction can be followed by a unit on business writing, where students establish their own company, with the work groups taking on the roles of its various divisions. Assignments can simulate the wide range of written discourse we find in business. In addition, assignments dealing with reports and proposals lend themselves nicely to oral presentations, so teachers can draw on the advantages inherent in a whole-language approach to activities.

Students of all ages can benefit from visits by working writers in the community. Some communities are fortunate to have published poets, essayists, or even novelists as residents, and many times these writers are pleased by invitations to visit schools. Most communities are served by newspapers and radio stations, and it is possible to have journalists, copywriters, or disc jockeys come to talk about their work. Radio disc jockeys are often especially popular because their music and on-air chatter make them local celebrities. Yet few students are aware of the fact that DJs are often reading a script when broadcasting. This discovery can make a lasting impact on their perception of writing.

EXPLORING KEY IDEAS

1. Planning good writing assignments involves knowing something about the students and the course you will teach. As a new teacher, where would you get this information?
2. A large number of teachers construct assignments with the primary aim of making them fun. What are some factors that may motivate teachers to concentrate on fun rather than learning? How will you deal with students who may be conditioned to expect all their classes and teachers to be entertaining?
3. Sample Assignment 5 is very popular, and many teachers conclude the activity by bringing bread, peanut butter, and jelly to class and having students attempt to make a sandwich using the directions that the assignment produced. What are some pros and cons of this activity?
4. What is the ever-present problem with collaborative assignments?
5. Many teachers assume that having students do something with their finished papers, such as send copies to school boards or legislators, necessarily makes the writing task meaningful. Too often, it does not. Why not?

Assessing Writing

OVERVIEW

Writing teachers probably devote more time to evaluating students than anyone else in education, yet as White (1986) noted in *Teaching and Assessing Writing*, they generally know little or nothing about assessment. This paradox is made even more problematic by the fact that most writing teachers are arrogant about their ignorance. The net result is that, with some important exceptions, such as the training provided by the National Writing Project, writing assessment in the United States may be characterized as chaotic and unprincipled.

Assessing student papers is one of the more important things teachers do because the decisions they make about how they give grades affect students' lives, sometimes significantly. For this reason alone, teachers need to know more about assessment. Reduced to its most basic principle, assessment is a comparison of one thing to another. In the case of student writing, the comparison is made on two levels: Teachers compare the writing of one student to another, and they compare the writing of each student so some pre-established standard of good writing. That standard may be one that the district has established and distributed to teachers; it may be one that the school has established among its teachers; or it may be one that a teacher has developed over the years through experience. The variability of the standard can be a source of trouble whenever there is a lack of consensus. That is, those who are most directly involved in assessment, including students, must agree on the suitability of the standard before meaningful assessment can take place.

Three of the most important topics in writing assessment are: *validity, reliability*, and *time. Validity* is related to matching what one is measuring to what one is teaching and to what the assignments ask students to do. For example, an instructor who devotes much of her class time to teaching grammatical terminology but who grades students on their skill at writing autobiography is involved in *invalid assessment*.

Reliability is related to consistency of evaluation. If an assessment procedure is reliable, then neither the administrator nor the time of administration will significantly affect the evaluation. *Time* often is a topic given too little attention, yet it is of central importance to teachers in public schools who are so heavily burdened that they commonly do not have time to grade frequent writing. A viable assessment procedure is one that does not take up a great deal of teachers' time.

Validity in writing assessment is a difficult issue to address because writing is such a complex behavior. Reliability, however, is strongly influenced by assessment methodology, which is in turn related to the time involved in evaluating student writing. Since the late 1970s, composition studies has generally adopted holistic scoring as a means of increasing reliability and decreasing the time required for evaluation. *Holistic scoring* is a procedure that allows teachers to reduce the amount of time they spend grading papers. Papers are read very rapidly by at least two people who aim at getting an overall impression of the quality of the writing. Reliability is ensured by *socializing* readers, that is, by cooperatively reaching a consensus regarding the characteristics of good writing, as defined in a pre-established rubric, or scoring guide. Analyzing writing samples that reflect the characteristics described in the rubric is part of the socialization process, and it ensures a high degree of reliability during assessment. This chapter presents holistic scoring as a method students can use to evaluate their own writing.

The second procedure, portfolio grading, is a variation of holistic scoring and is also highly reliable. Students periodically select the best papers they have written up to that point and submit them to a group of teachers for evaluation. The teachers then score the papers and calculate an average score for the entire portfolio.

WHAT IS ASSESSMENT?

Writing teachers have a much harder job than many of their colleagues when it comes to assessment. Not only does assessing writing take more time than assessing, say, math problems, but it is also more difficult. With a math problem, or even a social studies question, the answers on any test of student mastery are right or wrong. With writing, however, assessment must consider a complex array of variables, some of which are unrelated to specific mastery of a given writing lesson.

At its most basic level, assessment is a comparison. The comparison in many subjects is an objective standard of correctness. For example, students' answers to math problems on a test are compared to the objective standard that governs correct addition, multiplication, substraction, and division. Any deviation from the standard constitutes

error. With writing, the situation is significantly different because
assessment involves comparison on two levels: the standard set by other
students in the class and some pre-established standard of good writing.
This pre-established standard may be provided by the school district, in
which case it is often linked to districtwide or even statewide testing. It
may be provided by teachers—usually those in language arts—at a
given school, in which case the standard arises out of discussions and
finally a consensus regarding the features of good writing. The standard
may be one that individual teachers bring to their classrooms, formed
initially on the basis of experiences at a university during a degree and
then a credential program. The individual standard is the most problematic because it naturally varies from teacher to teacher, creating
uneven assessment of students engaged in similar activities.

The existence of a pre-established standard raises important questions that educators have to wrestle with daily: "What is the basis of the
standard?" "Is the standard appropriate for a given group of students?"
"Is the standard fair?" "What does a grade on a student's paper mean?"
These are hard questions for many reasons. Determining the basis of a
standard requires deep exploration of assumptions underlying comparisons among students and notions of excellence. Determining whether a
standard is appropriate involves analysis of student abilities in a given
school and consideration of how those abilities rank compared to students at similar grade level but from different circumstances. Questions
of fairness are likely to require jettisoning appealing ideas of equality
in favor of equitable treatment and opportunity. Contrary to popular
opinion, a low grade on a paper does not necessarily mean that the
assessment was unfair. Fairness in evaluation is related to consistent
application of the standard regardless of who any given student is—this
is equity. It is not related to equal outcomes.

It is not surprising, then, that scholars who study evaluation have
found widespread confusion among teachers regarding writing assessment. More troubling is that so many teachers know almost nothing
about writing assessment and that large numbers of them are arrogant
about their ignorance (White, 1986). They give little thought to what they
are measuring when they give students grades on their papers. Teachers
should be asking themselves: "Are we measuring the content of papers?"
"Are we measuring writing ability?" "Or are we measuring students'
performance on a given task at a particular time?" Some might argue
that they are measuring all of these factors and more, but this argument
is fraught with difficulties. The only content that most language arts
teachers deal with is literature, and writing instruction that focuses
exclusively on literature is so narrow as to lack meaning. Teachers who

have opted to focus on self-expressive writing are in even more dire straits because there is no content per se in self-expressive texts.

Many people, both in and out of education, assume that when teachers assess writing they are measuring writing ability, but careful consideration indicates that this assumption may be wrong, or at least simplistic. The patterns of students' writing growth shed light on the problem. Any given class has good, average, and poor writers. At the end of the term, all the students show growth; all have improved their language skills to some degree. Generally, however, the patterns remain the same: Those who were good writers at the beginning of the term may be excellent writers at the end, those who were average writers may be good writers, and those who were poor writers may be average writers. With respect to overall writing ability, it is unusual when students skip ability levels. Few students who start a term as poor writers end it as excellent writers, perhaps because growth in writing is such a slow, incremental process. Nevertheless, students of all ability levels may display performance that differs from assignment to assignment or from task to task. Students who have been writing *C* papers for weeks will get excited about an idea or a project, will work away at it for days, and will produce *B* work or better. Then, the next assignment finds them really struggling to put together something meaningful. By the same token, students who generally are very good writers occasionally will stumble, producing a paper that is barely passing. In both cases, it is hard to say that the grades on these uncommon papers truly reflect overall writing ability, but they do appear to reflect a degree of success on a particular task.

It may be that adding up all of a student's grades at the end of the term offers some indication of overall writing ability, but because assessment is a comparison, the question of the standard emerges again. "Will the good writer who shows little improvement receive the same grade as the poor writer who shows much improvement but who nevertheless still writes worse than the good writer?" "Will they receive different grades?" University writing teachers experience the reality of a comparative standard every fall, when tens of thousands of freshmen enter college having received nothing but *A*s on all their high-school essays. These students are crushed by the tens of thousands when they cannot earn anything higher than a *C* in freshman composition.

This analysis suggests that the terms *good, average*, and *poor writers* are constrained by context. They apply with a degree of accuracy only when the group that forms the basis of individual comparisons is fairly limited and well defined. But if this is the case, then even cumulative or averaged grades may not be true indications of writing

ability, at least not in any absolute sense. On this account, the grades
teachers put on papers are related to performance on a specific task at
a given time, not to the broader concept of ability. Indeed, many composition scholars now view successful writing as being the application of
quite specific rhetorical skills to equally specific rhetorical situations.
In other words, one does not simply learn how to write but rather learns
how to write very particular texts for particular audiences (Bizzell, 1987;
Faigley et al., 1985).

It is possible to measure writing ability, but any straightforward
effort to do so in a composition class is likely to have undesirable
pedagogical consequences. In most situations, what a teacher is evaluating is reflected in the way he or she teaches, because what one intends
to measure affects methodology (see Faigley et al., 1985; Greenberg,
Wiener, & Donovan, 1986). For example, teachers who want to evaluate
how successfully students use writing in a social context, how they
respond to specific writing situations, and how they revise are likely to
use a method that stresses making students feel good about themselves
as writers, providing realistic writing situations, and offering ample
opportunities for revision. They probably search for relevant, interesting
topics and make much use of workshops and conferences, where instruction is as individualized as possible. Grades, in this case, reflect a
complex array of abilities, such as cooperation with others during group
activities, not just writing ability.

Evaluation also can serve a pedagogical function, as when teachers
assign average grades to papers that are barely passing in order to build
poor writers' self-confidence and sense of accomplishment. Evaluation
in this case is not a measure of writing ability at all but is, if anything,
a pedagogical tool used to manipulate student behavior and attitudes.
If a teacher were concerned strictly with measuring writing ability,
however, there would be no need to consider the relevance of writing
assignments, and certainly, the use of grades to manipulate behavior
would not be an issue. The sole interest would be in making certain that
the assignments were valid tests of writing ability. Each assignment
would be structured so that the good writers would consistently receive
high grades on their responses and the poor writers would consistently
receive low grades. The issue would be how accurately the task and the
subsequent assessment measured students' abilities.

VALIDITY IN ASSESSMENT

The question of what teachers are measuring when they assess writing
is at the heart of assessment validity, which may be thought of as the
match between what is being taught and what is being evaluated. If a

lesson includes thesis statements, supporting evidence, and conclusions, and if the writing assignment calls for these features, then the assessment should consider how well students demonstrated mastery. In other words, writing assessment—like all other forms of assessment—should measure what was taught. Valid assessment will not measure anything that was not taught. Quite simply, teachers need to be certain that they are measuring what they are teaching (White, 1986).

Although this injunction appears commonsensical, observations of classroom practices indicate that it is rarely honored where writing is concerned. In the majority of language arts classes, the focus is on literature and grammar, with no direct instruction in writing at all. Teachers may assign some reading or may work on subject–verb agreement and then ask students to write an essay. The grade the teachers put on the essay does not reflect anything that students have learned because the task is unrelated to anything that was taught. Thus the first step toward validity in writing assessment is to teach writing. The second step is to grade what is taught. If revision is an important part of a teacher's instruction on every project, he or she needs some way to account for this skill when evaluating students' work. Some teachers therefore assign grades or scores to rough drafts, as well as to participation in work groups. However, this approach has at least two drawbacks. First, it reflects an attempt to grade process, even though composing processes appear to differ from person to person and from task to task. There really is no such thing as *the* composing process, and evaluation is valid only when teachers measure similar student behavior against a pre-established standard. Second, this approach defeats the purpose of formative evaluations by adding a summative component that too easily results in a shift in focus from, say, having a rough draft to having a good rough draft. Such a shift is significant and counterproductive because it reinforces the erroneous perception students have that the only difference between a first draft and a final draft is neatness.

A more effective means of evaluating something like revision skill therefore involves having students submit their rough drafts along with final drafts to allow for comparisons between the revisions and the finished product. By comparing the initial drafts and then matching them against the final draft, one can more clearly evaluate how successfully any given student is grasping the skill being taught. The grade on the final draft, the summative evaluation, reflects the quality of the finished paper, as well as revision skill, because realistically, the two are inseparable. In other words, one grade would indicate an overall assessment.

Assessment validity can be affected by the structure of assignments. Teachers have no principled way to evaluate responses when they give students poorly planned tasks that allow them to choose from a list of topics that call for different kinds of writing. If one student writes a narrative report and another an argument in response to the same assignment, which may ask for description, the criteria for what constitutes a successful response varies from essay to essay, seriously compromising assessment. Often students who attempt the more difficult task—the argument—receive a lower grade on the assignment than they would have received had they performed the easier task and written a narrative report. Under these circumstances, teachers have almost no way of knowing what they are measuring.

RELIABILITY IN ASSESSMENT

Reliability in assessment is related to the consistency of the comparison to the pre-established standard. In a paper that illustrated clearly the importance of reliability in writing assessment, Diederich, French, and Carlton (1961) distributed 300 student papers to 53 professors from six different disciplines. The professors were asked to read and grade the papers. About 90% of the papers received 7 different scores on a 9-point scale, indicating that the professors demonstrated no consistency at all with respect to assessment. Reliable assessment, however, will be consistent across evaluators and across time. It is generalizable. When dealing with a subject like math, it is easy to conceptualize the reasonableness of what this means: If a student gets a score of 85 on a math test from one teacher, he or she should get the same score if the test were graded by yet another teacher. Unfortunately, reliability just does not occur spontaneously with respect to writing but must be built into the assessment process through adherence to standardized procedures that reduce (if not eliminate) capriciousness and subjectivity. Standardized multiple-choice tests like the SAT are reliable, in part, because they have been piloted and normed against representative populations and because test administrators follow a specific protocol for administration and scoring.

There are several reasons why it is important that writing assessment be reliable. Students need to know that assessment is consistent and objective, not capricious and subjective. Just as important, reliable evaluations throughout schools avoid unacceptable (but recurrent) situations in which a student receives Ds on written tasks in one class and As in another. Unless teachers in a school work together to make their assessments reliable, some students indeed get high grades on papers in one class and low grades in another, even though their writing remains pretty much the same from teacher to teacher. The problem is that different teachers look for different things in a well-written assignment—hence, the inconsistency in evaluation. In such circumstances, students are forced to conclude, quite correctly, that writing assessment is largely subjective, which has the effect of motivating them to write to please the teacher while making them frustrated. Writing for an audience of one is a rhetorical exercise that does little to improve writing skills. The only way to make assessment more reliable is to reach agreement on what constitutes good writing and what does not. In other words, teachers who are responsible for writing instruction must reach a consensus on the standard that will form the basis of their assessments.

THE POSTMODERN POSITION ON ASSESSMENT

Although space constraints prohibit a detailed discussion of the postmodern position on assessment, it is important to provide some discussion of the main features. The analysis of validity and reliability in the previous sections is based on standard evaluation principles, and it is firmly rooted in new rhetoric. Postmodern rhetoric has a different view. Postmodernists reject notions of validity and reliability. As Hout (1996) noted: "Instead of generalizability, technical rigor, and large scale measures that minimize context and aim for standardization of writing quality, these new procedures emphasize the context of the texts being read, the position of the readers, and the local, practical standards teachers and other stakeholders establish for written communication" (p. 561).

The question of generalizability is important in the postmodern position (see Englehard, Gordon, & Gabrielson, 1992; Michael, 1995). One reason is that generalizability is based on the pre-established standard discussed earlier. The very nature of a standard entails absolute criteria for good writing, and traditional notions of teaching and learning maintain that it is the responsibility of teachers and students to strive to meet those criteria. The postmodern position, however, rejects absolute criteria and traditional notions of teaching and learning. Absolute criteria are considered to be antithetical to diversity, imposing not only a uniform level of achievement but also levels and types of performance that not all students can meet. In this case, the perspective is exactly the opposite of the new rhetoric perspective: When students cannot reach the pre-established standard, the problem does not lie in the students or the instruction they receive; it lies in the standard, which more often than not is deemed to be racist or sexist. Critics of this position have noted that it presumes that minorities and females cannot meet pre-established standards, and they have argued that this presumption is inherently prejudiced because it presumes inherent inferiority.

Rejecting generalizability has the immediate effect of eliminating concern for reliability. If evaluators believe that it does not matter whether their assessment of student writing is congruent with the assessment that evaluators at another school might make of those same pieces of writing, the imperative to provide reliable assessment disappears. In fact, the postmodern perspective celebrates the lack of consistency, claiming that it is impossible to assess writing objectively and that evaluation must recognize the inherent subjectivity of the process. Local criteria and an individual standard, rather than absolute criteria and a generalizable standard, govern the assessment. Several universities have embraced these notions. Smith (1993), for example, reported on the placement program implemented at the University of Pittsburgh that discarded traditional assessment methods. Student placement essays are evaluated by instructors who teach the composition courses in which students can be placed. They are not trained or socialized to ensure reliability but rather base their assessment on their knowledge of the class they teach. Smith reported that teachers were far more satisfied with this approach to placement than with the formal approach, largely because it eliminated the fairly elaborate training sessions, development of scoring guides, and general quantification of writing assessment required in the formal approach.

Perhaps the biggest problem with the postmodern position is that it makes it even more difficult to determine what an assessment means. If an assessment is dependent on context and the associated local criteria for success and if it lacks standards associated with general writing quality, then it is remarkably difficult to compare one response to another. All responses to a given assignment must be deemed equally acceptable and equally successful because any standard (or no standard) is a viable measure of success. Attempts to differentiate good writing from poor writing are rendered meaningless because what matters is not the writing but the evaluator's personal judgment and the act or performance that put words on the page. The effect is to return to the situation that Diederich et al. (1961) described, in which there is no consistency in the assessment of a given paper.

Those teachers and scholars with a new rhetoric orientation find this position unacceptable because they see it as inherently unfair to students. Any given assessment varies on the basis of those who happen to be evaluating the writing at any given time, leaving students exposed to the capriciousness and subjectivity of their evaluators. One group of evaluators applies their local standards to one assessment, whereas another group applies different standards. In the case of the University of Pittsburgh, students with identical writing skills are likely to experience completely different placement decisions.

JOURNAL ENTRY

Have you ever felt that a teacher graded your writing subjectively or capriciously? If so, what prompted those feelings? What lesson is there in your experience that you can apply to your teaching?

REDUCING THE PAPER LOAD

As important as validity and reliability are, there is a third problem in writing assessment that sometimes gets overlooked. It is the time it takes to evaluate student papers. The problem is especially acute at the junior and senior high-school levels, where teachers often have as many as three or four writing classes each term. Four classes with an assignment a week creates a crushing paper load. If teachers spend 15 minutes evaluating and commenting on each paper, they need 30 hours a week to assess them all. Faced with such a paper load, most instructors do not give an assignment each week. But reducing students' writing assignments is not really an acceptable way to reduce the paper load because students have to write frequently if they are going to improve.

The crux of the problem is the way teachers assess student writing. Most teachers, even those who have adopted a process approach to instruction, use a very traditional grading method. They read each finished paper, writing comments in the margins as they go along, concluding with a summary comment at the end of the essay then affixing a grade. This process is extremely time consuming, taking anywhere from 15 to 40 minutes per paper. In addition, research suggests that it is a largely ineffectual method, offering little that acts to improve students' writing performance.

Teacher Comments on Papers

Given the labor-intensive nature of writing comments, teachers have only two choices when deciding on a method. They can assign little writing but try to provide very effective written comments, or they can assign much writing but make few, if any, written comments. Most teachers opt for the former choice.

The rationale for this choice is that comments are an effective pedagogical tool. In theory, the teacher uses them to engage in a kind of discussion with writers, pointing to those things done well, those things done not so well, then offering suggestions and advice not only on how to fix the weak parts of the current paper but also on how to improve the next one. Students are expected to study the comments, learn from them, and transfer this learning to other assignments. When this theory is put into practice, however, several problems arise. Many teachers use abbreviations, such as *AWK* (for awkward), *AMB* (for ambiguous), and *MM* (for misplaced modifier), that students find cryptic. Even if a teacher takes the time to teach the various abbreviations and symbols to students, some question remains as to how effective they are pedagogically. Telling students they have misplaced a modifier does not really help them understand its proper placement. Furthermore, it does not do students much good to know what is wrong with a paper after the essay is completed and graded. Unless comments are made on a draft that students will revise, they have no chance to incorporate comments into their texts, and they have no chance to practice the immediate skills they are supposed to learn. Some educators have recommended marking rough drafts, but to do so increases a teacher's work load exponentially, especially in light of the fact that good papers commonly require three or more drafts.

Moreover, research indicates that students do not use written comments to improve their performance from one paper to the next (Gee, 1972; Hausner, 1976; Schroeder, 1973; Ziv, 1980). The only comments students pay attention to are personal ones that reflect an interested reader interacting with the text. Students are likely to remember comments like, "This is an interesting point; it reminds me of ...," but they are unlikely to remember comments about organization, rhetorical devices, or surface features.

Part of the problem is that when teachers make comments on final drafts, they almost always use them in an evaluative way to justify their grades, especially low ones. Students quickly learn how this works, so they tend to look at the grade and ignore the comments (see Sommers, 1982; Ziv, 1980). Regardless of research and theory, the pressures to apply comments must be acknowledged. Written comments on student essays are so thoroughly institutionalized that parents, administrators, fellow teachers, and certainly students expect them as a matter of course. To forgo them completely takes a bit of daring, even though everyone concerned may be better for it. The following suggestions may help make such comments more useful:

- The teacher should read papers twice rather than once. The first reading should be completed very quickly, almost skimming, without a pen or pencil in hand. The goal is to get a sense of the strengths and weaknesses of the papers, to grade them mentally, without making any marks.

- After finishing the first paper, the teacher should compare it with his or her internalized standard for an excellent response and then set it aside.
- When starting on the rest of the essays, the teacher should compare them not only to his or her internalized standard of an excellent response but also to one another.
- Upon finishing each paper, the teacher should put it with other papers of similar strength, setting up three stacks, one for excellent, one for adequate, and one for unsatisfactory.
- The teacher then should read the unmarked papers a second time, more slowly, making comments in the margins. If the teacher has conducted successful workshops, he or she already will have seen each paper at least once and will have established a dialogue concerning content and form. Comments should be continuations of each dialogue and should be the sort of things the teacher would tell the writers if they were there in a conference.
- Typical comments focus on changes students made or failed to make during revisions, what the teacher liked about the paper and why, and what impact the content had. They also (and quite effectively) may take the form of questions. In any event, it is extremely important that the teacher respond as a real, interested reader during such evaluations, not as a teacher. Remember, the grade is already fixed mentally, so there is no need to use the comments as a justification for the grade.
- Comments should be brief, and the teacher should avoid entirely the temptation to rewrite any sentences and to engage in any editing by circling spelling, usage, or punctuation errors; these problems should have been corrected during writing workshops.
- The teachers should remember that once a final draft is turned in, instruction is over for that assignment. Any weaknesses are better addressed on the first draft of the next task.
- Severe mechanical problems in final drafts indicate the need to monitor groups more closely.
- If the teacher provides a final comment at the end of the paper, it should not be next to the grade.
- As a reasonable goal, the teacher should try to limit commenting to about 5 minutes per paper.

JOURNAL ENTRY

Many teachers are reluctant to talk about how they evaluate student papers and how they arrive at grades. Reflect on how you might be able to stimulate more discussion when you are a teacher, discussion that may lead to more reliable assessments.

HOLISTIC SCORING

Until the 1960s, assessment of large numbers of students was performed using multiple-choice exams. Some teachers and researchers, however, were concerned that such exams were not very effective. Lack of reliability was deemed the largest problem with classroom assessment, and lack of validity was deemed the largest problem with large group assessment. In the latter case, people argued that the only way to measure writing was to ask students to write and that multiple-choice tests were invalid.

Largely in response to this criticism, Educational Testing Service (ETS), the group that sponsors the National Teachers Examination and the Advanced Placement tests, decided to explore the possibility of developing a valid and reliable way to evaluate writing. After several years of effort, ETS came up with the method known as *holistic scoring* (White, 1986). It quickly became popular as an effective means of testing large numbers of students, especially at the university level because it is valid, highly reliable, and does not take much time. More recently, individual teachers started using holistic scoring in their own classrooms as a means of reducing their paper load while increasing the reliability of assessment. This procedure requires training students to evaluate one another's writing, and it also requires teachers to give students more responsibility for their own success or failure on tasks. Although holistic scoring is used more frequently in junior and senior high schools, growing numbers of elementary school teachers are using it with their students.

The rewards of holistic assessment are significant for everyone involved. An entire batch of essays can be scored in a 50-minute class session, freeing evenings and weekends that otherwise would be devoted to marking papers. Because they are assessing their own writing, students gain an increased sense of control over their learning, especially if, as recommended, holistic scoring is used in conjunction with writing workshops. Also, the teacher–student relationship changes. Because the teacher is no longer assigning grades to papers, he or she can be accepted more readily as a resource person, or coach, who can help improve skills.

As the name suggests, holistic scoring involves looking at the whole essay, not just parts of it. The procedure is based on the notion that evaluating writing skill does not consist of measuring a set of subskills, such as knowledge of punctuation conventions, but rather of measuring what White (1986) called "a unit of expression" (p. 18). Clearly, some things are more important than others when it comes to a successful response. For example, quality is more important than quantity, and content and organization are more important than spelling and punctuation. The goal therefore is to make an overall assessment of the quality of the writing as a whole. Readers make this assessment more reliably when they read a paper very quickly. Skilled holistic readers take only about 1 or 2 minutes to go through a two-page paper. The more time readers take to get through a paper, the more inclined they are to begin mentally editing, focusing on the surface errors. A typical two-to-three-page paper should take student readers no more than 4 minutes to complete.

Scoring Rubrics

The earlier discussion of reliability noted that even good writers may receive different assessments from different people because each evaluator is likely to look for different qualities in a given paper. Unless evaluators agree in advance to look for the same qualities during an assessment—unless they reach consensus regarding the standard they will apply during assessment—there is little chance that their reliability will be high. Holistic scoring solves this problem through a process of *socialization*, during which evaluators agree to reach a consensus on a specific set of criteria, called a *rubric*. Sample rubrics appear later.

Rubrics for older students usually use a 6-point descending scale to gauge the quality of each response. A paper that scores a 6 is very good; one that scores a 2 is not very good at all. In addition, a rubric is divided into lower half and upper half to specify the general quality of a response. Upper half papers (6, 5, 4) are well written, whereas lower half papers (3, 2, 1) are not. No direct correspondence exists between numeric scores and letter grades. Translating scores into grades is a separate procedure and should not even be discussed as part of a round of holistic scoring.

IMPLEMENTING HOLISTIC SCORING
IN THE CLASSROOM

A workshop approach to writing instruction makes implementing holistic scoring easier because students already will have been working together in teams before their first scoring session. However, holistic scoring does not require a workshop approach to be successful.

Student evaluators have to agree on the characteristics of good writing before any scoring can begin, so the first task is to analyze some writing samples that show a range of skill, from good to bad. The goal is to help students develop a standard for good writing, which requires that students become more critical readers.[1] The first socialization is critical to the success of the entire procedure, and it requires about a dozen sample papers, which the teacher must evaluate carefully in advance and assign a score on the basis of a pre-established rubric that he or she has created for the assignment. The samples must all be on the same topic for valid assessment.[2]

The first step in socialization is to examine a *general rubric*. This rubric articulates the general standard of good writing that the teacher brings to every assessment. As noted earlier, this standard may be one that a given teacher bases on prior experiences, it may be one developed in conjunction with fellow teachers at a given school or it may be one provided by the school district. (The standard based on consensus is recommended whenever it is feasible.) In any event, the general rubric should be produced before classes begin. It serves as the basis for the *specific rubrics* that the class will develop for each writing assignment. The two sample rubrics that follow provide helpful examples. The first was developed for an elementary class, the second for a high school class focusing on argumentation.

General Rubric 1: Elementary

A Very Good Composition:
has a beginning that lets readers know clearly what the composition is about; gives readers much information, is interesting, and has fewer than three errors in capitalization and spelling.

---

[1]New teachers may have to borrow sample papers from more experienced colleagues.

[2]Photocopying enough samples for all students is expensive. Some teachers try to get around the problem by making transparencies of the samples for use on an overhead projector. Unfortunately, handwriting does not transfer very well, so some papers may require typing. In large classes, students at the back may not be able to see very well, which many will take as an excuse to disengage.

A Good Composition:
has a beginning that lets readers know what the composition is about; gives readers some information; has at least one interesting point; has fewer than five errors in capitalization and spelling.

A Composition That Needs More Work:
does not let readers know what the composition is about; does not give readers much information, has no interesting points; has more than five errors in capitalization and spelling.

General Rubric 2: Middle and Secondary

In general, thoughtful, critical responses to the assignment will be placed in the upper half; in addition, those that demonstrate global organizational and argumentative skills usually will be rewarded over those that merely demonstrate sentence-level competence.

Upper Half

6-point essays will:
have a clear aim, a strong introduction that clearly states the thesis to be defended, and a thoughtful conclusion; effectively recognize the complexities of the topic, thoughtfully addressing more than one of them; contain strong supporting details and a judicious sense of evidence; be logically developed and very well organized; use a tone appropriate to the aim of the response; show stylistic maturity through sentence variety and paragraph development; be virtually free of surface and usage errors.

5-point essays will:
have a clear aim and a strong introduction and conclusion; effectively recognize the complexities of the topic, addressing more than one of them, and contain supporting details and a good sense of evidence; be logically developed and well-organized; use a tone appropriate to the aim of the response; have adequate sentence variety and paragraph development; lack the verbal felicity or organizational strength of a 6-point essay; be largely free of surface and usage errors.

4-point essays will:
have a clear aim and a strong introduction and conclusion; recognize the complexities of the topic; contain supporting details and a sense of evidence; display competence in logical development and organization, although it may exhibit occasional organizational and argumentative

weaknesses; use a tone appropriate to the aim of the response and display basic competence in sentence variety, paragraph development, and usage.

Lower Half

3-point essays will:
acknowledge the complexities of the topic and attempt to address it, but the response will be weakened by one or more of the following: lack of a clear aim, thesis, or conclusion; lack of sufficient support or evidence; supporting details may be trivial, inappropriate, logically flawed; flaws in organization/development; inappropriate tone; stylistic flaws characterized by lack of sentence variety and/or paragraph development; frequent usage and/or surface errors.

2-point essays will:
address the topic, but will be weakened by one or more of the following: thesis may be too general or too specific; makes a vacuous or trivial argument; lack of support or evidence; lack of organization; inappropriate tone; serious stylistic flaws; serious usage and/or surface errors.

1-point essays will:
be seriously flawed in terms of argument, organization, style, or usage surface errors.

Before examining the sample papers, the class should study the general rubric and talk about what it means. The teacher then should hand out a specific rubric for the sample papers. This rubric, again written in advance by the teacher, describes the features of a range of possible responses, just as the general rubric does. However, the description is particular to this prompt and these responses.

The teacher's role is that of "chief reader." The chief reader uses his or her greater experience with writing to help students understand the rubric and see why one paper is better than another. This role is vital to the socialization process because it is common to have students disagree over the merits of a particular paper. Many will reward poorly written papers merely because they like the topic. Students need the chief reader to resolve disagreements and to help them understand that liking a topic is not a viable criterion for assessment. Also, the teacher must guide students to ensure that their assessments eventually agree with those articulated in the rubric. In other words, an important part of socialization is to get students to accept and then apply the teacher's standard for what constitutes good writing. This means that the teacher must allow enough time to discuss various features of the writing prompt, the characteristics of the samples, and the standard expressed in the rubric. Thus as chief reader the teacher models critical reading. Guidance in all cases must be persuasive rather than coercive. A rubric is invaluable in this regard because it objectifies evaluations: A paper is poorly written because it has lower half characteristics, not because readers do not like it (or vice versa).

The class should read three samples quickly, first ranking them informally as upper half and lower half and then applying scores.[3] Papers used in each socialization are read once. Papers in an actual scoring session, however, are read twice, by two different students, so that each paper receives two scores. If socialization was successful, these scores agree with a high level of reliability. The teacher then should ask students how they scored each sample response in the set. There will be a spread of scores, and on the first set of three papers the spread may be fairly wide. A paper that the teacher scored as an *anchor 5*,[4] for example, is likely to receive several scores of 6, several of 4, and some of 3 and 2. The teacher must guide students through these scores by asking those who were very wide of the target score to identify features in the response that correspond to characteristics in the rubric. When asked to make this connection, students begin to recognize that they misread the paper because it will not have the features they thought it had. Students who do not see this right away can be helped along, normally with comments and suggestions from the teacher as well as classmates. It is entirely appropriate for the teacher to tell individual students that their scoring is too harsh or too lenient and that they should adjust their scoring on the next set.

After the class has analyzed the first set of papers in this way, they go on to the second set, then the third, then the fourth, until they have scored each paper and discussed it with respect to the rubric. As they proceed through the sets, their reading becomes more consistent, more reliable, and the spread of scores decreases. This is a sign that socialization is succeeding.

This first socialization may take four class sessions and should use all 12 samples. With some classes, socializing may take even longer. It is important that students reach agreement, so effective teachers do not rush them. Subsequent socializations proceed more quickly, eventually taking about one class session. The time certainly is not wasted because

---

[3]It is a good idea to identify each sample paper without using names. Because the score is a number, many teachers follow an alpha format: paper GG, paper HH, paper ZZ, and so forth.

[4]Meaning that it is a representative 5-point response and should serve as a standard for other 5-point responses.

students are practicing critical-reading skills every time they evaluate samples. After completing this socialization, students are ready to score their own papers.

It is important to understand, however, that each time the class scores an assignment they must have a rubric designed specifically for that assignment. For older students, the class itself should generate these rubrics, with guidance from the teacher. The most effective approach is to spend some time talking with students about the assignment and then to ask them to offer suggestions for what a 6-point response to that assignment might look like. One student serves as secretary, taking notes that the teacher then types up after class with the understanding that he or she will devolve the 6-point response so as to provide descriptions for the other scores on the rubric. When the rubric is typed, the teacher should share it with the class and ask students whether they want to make any changes. If they do, the teacher then produces a revision for the next class. What's important in this procedure is that students need to feel that the rubric is theirs, that it reflects their views on what successful responses look like. The empowerment that comes from this procedure is highly beneficial to students and their progress as writers.

Split Scores

Perfect agreement on every paper scored by 25 to 30 people is very difficult to achieve. Some variation in the scores assigned to papers should be expected. For example, a given paper might receive a score of 3 from the first reader and a score of 4 from the second. This variation is acceptable because it does not exceed one point. A 3/4 score is viewed as a single score. A two-point difference, however, is not acceptable. In situations where the first reader gives a paper a 5, for example, and the second reader gives it a 3, the paper has what is called a *split score*. Papers with split scores go to the chief reader for another assessment. In other words, the teacher gives it a third reading. The chief reader is the final arbiter. The scores are not simply averaged; the teacher must carefully evaluate the paper and assign an appropriate score. Usually, this score agrees with one of the student scores, but not always.

SCORING STUDENT PAPERS

To reduce subjective factors during scoring, students' names should not appear on their papers. The teacher should assign each student a code number at the beginning of the term, recording the number in his or her record book next to each name. Teachers who use work groups should number them as well. If there are five students in Group 1, their code numbers would be 1–1, 1–2, 1–3, 1–4, and 1–5. Students use the code number rather than their names whenever they turn in a composition.

Teachers must help the class develop a new rubric for each writing assignment; every task is different and makes different demands on students. Students should have copies of the rubric before they begin writing their papers so that it functions as a concrete guide as they are working on drafts. With the exception of the general rubric and the rubric for the first socialization, students should have primary responsibility for generating each rubric; their participation gives them a greater sense of control over their achievement. Developing a rubric involves carefully examining the assignment and reaching a consensus regarding the characteristics of good, average, and weak responses. The best way to structure the activity is to have on hand at least three sample papers written in response to the assignment. Students can then analyze the papers and work through the rubric on the basis of their analysis of how other students responded to the assignment.

New teachers may find this approach difficult unless they have established a file of writing samples. Colleagues can serve as a valuable resource for sample papers, but this approach entails being willing to use their assignments. If it is not possible to obtain enough samples for both the initial socialization and the first round of assignments, teachers may want to analyze a professional model that approximates the type of task assigned. This approach has some drawbacks, however. Students are likely to have some difficulty relating the model, and therefore the rubric, to their own writing. In addition, they will have only one sample essay rather than several, which limits their understanding of the range of possible responses. The only other alternative is for the teacher to focus on the assignment and to use his or her experience with varieties of discourse to help students identify the characteristics they should strive for in their papers. In effect, the teacher helps them discover what characterizes an upper half response and what characterizes a lower half response.

Teaming With Another Teacher

Although students are perfectly capable of scoring one another's papers, they usually are not happy about it. Most complain about the responsibility, and the loudest complaints normally come from the better students. An effective way to help students feel more comfortable with holistic scoring is to team up with another teacher and to trade papers at the time of each scoring session. This approach requires some minimal cooperation. For example, the teachers must coordinate their writing assignments so that students are writing on the same topics at the same time. They also must coordinate their lessons to ensure that their units on writing instruction match, and they must coordinate due dates for papers and scoring sessions.

This sort of cooperation does not take much time, and it provides numerous benefits for teachers and students alike. When teachers work together and communicate their ideas and approaches, their teaching improves, as does the collegial spirit at the school. Students feel as though they have a real audience for their papers and are more motivated to succeed. As noted, exchanging papers with another class makes the scoring experience more positive.

Setting Anchor Scores

After collecting students' papers on a given assignment, the teacher has to resocialize the class. This requires a set of sample papers on the topic for students to evaluate. In this instance, however, the set need not be as large as the one used for the initial socialization because much of what constitutes good writing is already partially internalized. Three or four samples usually are sufficient. The aim is to provide samples that illustrate a range of responses, so the papers should reflect at least one very good response, an average one, and a weak one. Unless the teacher has sample papers from another class, he or she has to pull anchors from those the class is preparing to score.

Selecting samples from the papers students submit means that the teacher must read all the papers in advance of the scoring. Reading them holistically does not take very long; most teachers are able to read a set of 30 in about 1 hour. The procedure is identical to the one previously described in the section on reducing the paper load. The teacher should read the first paper and mentally evaluate it according to the rubric. The second paper should be compared to the first one. If the papers are of about the same quality, they go together in a pile, but if they differ, they go in separate piles. As the teacher completes each paper, he or she puts it in a stack of similar papers, so that when finished there are three stacks of papers grouped on the basis of similar quality. After this grouping, the teacher should pull a sample paper from each stack, read it holistically a second time and assign a score from the rubric. These papers are the scoring anchors that will be the basis for the socialization session prior to scoring all the other papers.[5]

---

[5] It is not fair to use the same students more than once for anchor papers, so teachers should note in their record book the names of whose papers were selected as sample papers.

Conducting the Reading

After analyzing the anchors and reaching a consensus on scores, the class is ready for the actual reading. Teachers who use work groups should separate the papers by group, giving Group 1 the papers of Group 2, and so forth. With each assignment, the teacher should alternate the arrangement to avoid any regularity of grouping. Reliability and validity are seriously compromised if readers are able to see one another's scores, so the teacher needs some self-adhesive patches—round labels available in any store that sells school supplies—to cover the first score. When the first reader finishes a paper, he or she must affix a patch over the score before passing the paper on for the second reading.

After all the papers have been scored, students remove the patches, check the scores, and then circulate the papers back to their owners. Students should have 1 to 2 minutes to look at their scores; then they should pass the papers back to the teacher. The teacher's task at this point is twofold. First, he or she must check for split scores. Those papers that have split scores must be given a third reading. Second, the teacher needs to read through all the papers another time to compare the scores the students gave with those he or she would give. This procedure acts as a support for students, most of whom doubt their ability to score accurately. They need to know that the teacher checks all scores to ensure that they are fair and accurate. In some cases the teacher may find that a paper has been evaluated incorrectly, which requires changing the score.

Converting Numeric Scores to Letter Grades

At some point, numeric scores must be converted to letter grades. Although some teachers do this early in the term, most delay conversion until the end of the term. The rationale is that they do not want students to be applying letter-grade criteria to papers during scoring sessions. This rationale is sensible, although teachers who apply it sometimes have problems with students who become anxious when they do not know what their grade is in writing.

There are no definite guidelines for converting numeric scores to letter grades because teachers differ in how they perceive grades. Some teachers, for example, may want a simple assignment: 6 = A, 5 = B, 4 or 3 = C, 2 = D, and 1 = F. This sort of distribution seems entirely appropriate for most grading situations, but it may make students unhappy, considering that grade inflation has boosted the average grade in most schools to a B or B+. Generally, it is a good idea to put the score distribution on the board for students because it gives everyone a chance to see how he or she did in comparison with everybody else. If no papers scored a 6, students are inclined to argue that *A* grades should begin with the highest score, even if it is a 3. The teacher should explain that it is not unusual for a class to have no *A*s on a given assignment and to resist grade inflation as much as possible. More often than not, establishing letter grades is a matter of compromise, with the teacher trying to reduce inflation and students trying to increase it.

After going through the process of compromise many times with many different groups of students, it seems that the following grade equivalencies arise again and again. It gives some idea of the direction the compromise is likely to take:

6 = A	4/5 = B	3 = C-
5/6 = A-	4 = C+	2 = D
5 = B+	4/3 = C	1 = F

JOURNAL ENTRY

The biggest obstacle to using holistic scoring in the classroom is student resistance. Consider ways you might reduce this resistance.

PORTFOLIO GRADING

Some teachers object to holistic scoring on several grounds. Many believe that putting grading in the hands of students aggravates the already bad state of grade inflation. There is no evidence to support this belief, however. Others believe that no matter how carefully one socializes students they will never be as accurate in their assessments as teachers, owing to the disparity in maturity and reading experience. Still others are convinced that it is a mistake to grade every composition students produce because students become inclined to focus on grades rather than process. Finally, some believe that student writing performance can be assessed accurately only by an outsider, not by the students' teacher or by the students themselves.

Many of these objections have some measure of truth, and portfolio assessment arose in response. Portfolio grading is based on holistic scoring procedures in that it involves a rubric, socialization of readers to the rubric, and rapid reading of compositions. It differs, however, in several respects. First, portfolio grading requires the participation of at least three faculty members. In a typical grading situation, three instructors evaluate student papers for one another, alternating with each scoring session. Second, to reduce the paper load, students' papers are not assessed as each one is completed, nor is every paper evaluated. Instead, students keep their work in individual files (portfolios) that are stored in the classroom. After several papers are finished, students select the best three or four, depending on the teacher's directions, for assessment.

In a hypothetical situation, a teacher would have students write a paper each week, for a total of 15 papers each semester. Five weeks into the term, the teacher would announce the first grading session and would ask students to select the best three of their first five papers. Additional grading sessions occur during Week 10 and at the end of the term. These three papers go into a folder along with each assignment and the rubrics the class worked out for each task. The participating teachers then meet with their students' folders. Together the teachers discuss the various rubrics and some sample papers until they reach a consensus on scoring standards. They then exchange folders and begin scoring, using the 6-point scale (or 3-point for elementary students) previously described. After each portfolio has been read twice, the scores on the individual papers are averaged into a single score for the entire portfolio. Thus if a student received 5s on one composition, a 5/4 on the second, and two 4s on the third, his average score would be 4.5. This score would then be converted to a letter grade.

Portfolio grading has some clear advantages. It forces students to consider readers other than their teacher and their peers as part of their audience. It may make the paper load slightly smaller than holistic scoring because there is no need to read papers to check student scoring. It also creates a sense of collegiality often missing among faculty members. On the other hand, it presents one obstacle that is frequently difficult to overcome: persuading other teachers with busy schedules to participate. What should be clear, however, is that either holistic scoring or portfolio grading is a significant improvement over traditional methods of assessment.

SAMPLE RUBRICS AND SAMPLE PAPERS

The following sample rubrics and papers are offered to illustrate further how rubrics are used to assess writing. The score—or in the case of the elementary samples, the evaluation—each paper received in holistic assessment is shown at the end of the response.

Assignment 1 (Grade 6)

Two years ago, the school board of Ocean View School District voted to ban gum chewing in all schools. At next month's meeting, the board members will evaluate the ban and decide whether or not to make it permanent. Write a composition either for or against gum chewing. Take a position and then support it with good reasons and examples. We will send the finished papers to the district office so the school board will know how students feel about the ban.

Rubric: Assignment 1

A Very Good Composition:
has a beginning that lets readers know clearly what the composition is about and what the writer's position is; gives several good reasons for that position; is interesting; has fewer than three errors in capitalization and spelling.

A Good Composition:
has a beginning that lets readers know what the composition is about and what the writer's position is; gives some good reasons for that position; has at least one interesting point; has fewer than five errors in capitalization and spelling.

A Composition That Needs More Work:
does not let readers know what the composition is about; does not state the writer's position clearly; does not give good reasons for why the writer takes that position; has no interesting points; and has more than five errors in capitalization and spelling.

Sample 1

The Right to Chew Gum

[1] The school board banned gum at school two years ago, probably because gum can be pretty messy if kids spit it on the ground or put it under desks. It banned gum because it believed that students cannot be responsible enough to handle gum chewing. I not only disagree with the ban but I disagree with the idea that we are not responsible.

[2] We know the board has the power to ban gum, but it is not so clear that it has the right. As long as students act responsible and do not spit their gum on the ground or pop it in class, gum chewing does not hurt anyone. It is a private act. We may be kids, but that does not mean that we do not have the right to eat what we want or say what we want or chew what we

want, as long as it does not bother others. The problem is that the board never gave us the chance to act responsible. If there was a problem with kids abusing the right to chew gum, the board should have explained the situation to us. It should have told us what would happen if we didn't stop abusing the right. But it didn't do that. Instead it just banned gum chewing without ever talking to us. That is not fair.

(A very good composition)

Sample 2

No gum On Campus!

[1] I agree with the school board's decision to ban gum chewing in Ocean View School District. Chewing gum is real messy. If you spit it on the ground it gets stuck to your feet and you cannot get it off your shoes. If you chew it in class it can be real loud so that you cannot hear what the teacher is saying. And maybe if you blow bubbles the other kids will not be able to hear either, especially if the bubble pops and makes a loud noise.

[2] If teachers step in the gum that you've spit on the ground they can get mad. That means that everybody gets into trouble because one person spit his gum on the ground. That is not right. Only the one who spit the gum should get into trouble. But if you do not know who spit it in the first place, then I guess it is right that everybody gets punished.

[3] We're here to learn things and I think that chewing gum in class can keep us from learning. We can get so involved with chewing that gum that we do not pay attention to what the teacher is saying. The next thing you know we end up dumb and we cannot find jobs when we grow up and we have to go on welfare.

[4] Chewing gum is just a bad idea. I support the ban.

(A good composition)

Sample 3

Chewing Gum

[1] I think the ban on chewing gum is stupid. I have friends in Sunnyside school district and they can chew gum. If they can chew gum we should be able to chew gum to. It does not hurt anything and it is relaxing. Also it keep us from talking in class. It is hard to talk and chew at the same time. So I think the school board should forget about the ban and let us chew gum like my friends in the sunnyside district.

(A composition that needs more work)

Assignment 2 (Grade 8)

The United States is a country of immigrants. Essentially we all have roots extending somewhere else. Over the last few years, more and more people have become interested in tracing their roots, turning into amateur genealogists. Using all the resources available to you, including interviews with family members, trace your family history as far back as you can and write a report of your investigation, telling readers what you discovered.

Rubric: Assignment 2

6—A six-point essay will be characterized by all of the following features: establishes a context for the essay by providing background and purpose; purpose will be easily identifiable, although not stated directly; addresses the complexities of human behavior; operates on a very high level of significance; is rich in detail; is well organized, easy to follow, easy to read; tone is entirely appropriate to the task and the audience; has variation in sentence and paragraph structure; is virtually free of spelling, punctuation, sentence/paragraph errors.

5—A five-point essay will be characterized by all of the following features: establishes a context for the essay by providing background and purpose; purpose will be identifiable, although not stated directly; addresses most of the complexities of human behavior; addresses significant points; has many details; is generally well organized, easy to follow, easy to read; tone is generally appropriate to the task and the audience; is generally free of spelling, punctuation, sentence/paragraph errors.

4—A four-point essay will be characterized by the following features: establishes a context for the essay by providing background and purpose, but the context will not be as detailed as the five-point response; purpose may not be easily identifiable; addresses some of the complexities of human behavior; addresses a few significant points; has some details; is organized, although may not be as easy to follow as the five-point response; tone may occasionally be inappropriate; may have occasional spelling, punctuation, or sentence/paragraph errors.

3—A three-point essay may be characterized as having some combination of the following features: attempts to establish a context for the essay by providing a background; attempts to provide an identifiable purpose; addresses few of the complexities of human behavior; attempts to address at least one significant point, but overall the composition tends to be trivial; is not very detailed; is not well organized; frequent errors in punctuation, spelling, and paragraph structure.

2—A two-point essay will significantly compound the problems of the three-point essay.

1—A one-point essay may be characterized by as having some combination of the following features: lacks background; the purpose may be unidentifiable or may be stated explicitly; lacks details; may be off topic; fails to address the complexities of human behavior; composition is trivial; is unorganized and hard to follow; uses inappropriate or inconsistent tone; serious surface errors in spelling, punctuation, or sentence/paragraph structure.

Sample 4

Realizing the American Dream

[1] I feel very unfortunate not to have known my great grandfather on my father's side of the family. He passed away in 1972, the year I was born.

[2] His name was Anton, but my mother says everyone called him Poppi. Poppi was born in 1880 in Norway, where he learned to be a tailor by apprenticing himself when he was only 13. At nineteen he was so well trained that he decided to open his own small shop, and during his first year of business he was successful enough to take on two apprentices. But at the end of that year he was ordered to fulfill his military service. Being against war and weapons, he preferred to leave his country rather than serve in the army. In the summer of 1900, he set sail for America.

[3] When he arrived on Ellis Island, he immediately arranged to travel to Minnesota, which at that time had several large Norwegian communities. Knowing almost no English, Poppi felt he would have an easier time surviving among people from a similar background, people who spoke his language. With the small sum of money he had brought with him, he opened another tailor shop. He owned the shop until 1940, making a modest living for himself and his wife and children. In 1940 he had to sell the shop because more and more people were buying ready-made clothes rather than having them tailored. Without a shop of his own, he had to find work where he could, so he and his family moved to St. Paul, where he worked in several department stores, altering the ready-made suits and pants customers bought off the rack.

[4] Poppi's only daughter married Paul Alphaus, who was my grandfather and who I always called Grandpa Alphi. He was born on a farm in Iowa. Even when he was a young boy he was determined not to become a farmer like his father, because there was no way to make a good living on the farm. So while many of the other farm boys quit school to go to work in the fields, Grandpa Alphi studied hard and finished high school. After he

finished, he enrolled in a small Lutheran college not far from his home. He got good grades and enjoyed the work, but he had to drop out at the end of his first semester because he ran out of money—his family couldn't help him, either.

[5] Grandpa Alphi was good with numbers, which may be a reason why he was offered a job as bookkeeper at a local insurance company. He worked hard in those early years. He took classes evenings and on weekends that were offered through the insurance company, and he studied banking and investments. Five years latter, after his studies were finished, he was given an award for his high grades. He worked at the insurance company for forty-six years, until the company went out of business. He then went to work at the local bank as a senior trust officer, a job he kept until 1986, when he finally retired at age 79. Living in a small town made job opportunities scarce, but Grandpa Alphi managed to succeed through determination.

[6] My grandfather on my mother's side was John Walter, who I knew as Pop Pop. He was born in 1915 in Pennsylvania. Pop Pop had to drop out of school after the ninth grade because of the Depression—his family needed him to work and to bring in extra money. Jobs were scarce, but he found work in a lumberyard, where he worked stacking lumber until the war started. Then he began working at a local arsenal making bullets. After a year, he went on to the shipyards in Philadelphia, where he worked as a welder.

[7] After the war, Pop Pop sold jewelry, while in his spare time he made lawn furniture out of scraps of metal, using the welding skill he had picked up during the war. He liked the furniture work so much that he borrowed money to open his own shop, where he made wrought iron railings, furniture, and interior rails. He never seemed to make much money, but somehow he managed to put his two daughters through college. After thirty years of welding, Pop Pop retired, only to die a year later of cancer. On his deathbed he told us not to feel sad, because he had lived a good life and had done just about everything a man could hope for.

(Holistic score = 5)

Sample 5

Mother's Love

[1] During World War II, with all its abandonment and loneliness, Harrison Richards met Mary Rogers. Harrison was from Port Orchard Washington, where, at age 18, he was drafted and sent to Southern California, where he was stationed. Mary was living in San Diego.

[2] They began seeing each other and before long Mary became pregnant at the age of 16. Harrison and Mary got married before the baby was born because the war was still going on and they wanted to be married in case Harrison had to leave for combat. Mary's parents accepted her pregnancy and the marriage because she was one of their favorite children. In the hot, dry month of July, 1942, Mary gave birth to a little baby girl she named Hilda LaVerne and she became a mother for the first time. Needless to say, at the age of 16 she was still a child herself and not responsible enough to handle a child. After the baby was born Harrison left for the war and was never heard from again. It had just been a wartime romance for him and he knew that it was too great a responsibility for him to handle. Mary didn't even acknowledge that she had a child, she didn't even want to give the child Harrison's last name.

[3] Mary would leave the baby with her brother and his wife to take while she went out on dates and late night parties. Mary's sister-in-law showed more love and attention to the baby than Mary did. In 1947 Mary decided to give the baby up for adoption, and her brother and sister-in-law decided to adopt the baby because they were unable to have children because she had Scarlet fever as child which caused her to get a hysterectomy. They changed the baby's name to Tonya LaVerne, and after that Mary never made any attempt to see her. Mary got remarried in 1955 to Bud Hevert who owned his own floor covering business. Mary owned her own beauty shop and was doing good for herself now that she had given up Hilda. When Bud and her would come to family get togethers she wouldn't even act like Hilda, who was now Tonya, was her real daughter. Even Mary's grandmother, Myrtle Lola Chrissy Moore, treated her like she wasn't part of the family.

[4] Mary met a construction worker and began to see him behind Bud's back. Bud became suspicious of her because she would work late hours to see this man and she was always acting tired. One night, in 1966, Bud followed her and waited in the parking lot to see what was going on. He saw the man enter the shop with a six pack so he decided to go in. He found them together in the back room and shot them both dead, then he turned the gun on himself. Tonya was 13 when she found out about being adopted and she has never acknowledged Mary as her mother. She is not ashamed of her and she does not hate her for giving her up because she got a mother who would show her the love she needed. Tonya married Wayne my father in 1966 and they had a daughter that they named Trisha in 1972. Tonya gives her daughter the love and attention that a natural mother should give a child but that she received from an adopted mother.

(Holistic score = 3)

Sample 6

Brothers

[1] The year was 1865 and it was the beginning of the Civil War. Samuel Lloyd was 17 years old. He had never fought in a war before. Now here he was assigned to General Rosser's troop and he was expected to fight and to kill. He had been called in for duty from his West Virginia home and had expected to be in battle within days. However, he and the other troops found themselves marching South for weeks only to see the abandoned burned down plantations and homes of Southern Virginia farmers. They continued this monotony until they reached the border. He found there the action that he had anticipated in the previous weeks.

[2] The North fought a long and hard battle. The casualties number almost 600 for the South. As they set out the next morning to head North and take their prisoners to a camp, Sammy Lloyd was called to the back of the line to help a dying prisoner. While he was approaching the man, he could hear him coughing with all his might in his body. Sammy reached over to roll the man on his back to ease the coughing. As he did so he saw that it was the face of his only brother staring up at him. Sam Lloyd never forgave himself for having been a part of the killing of his own flesh and blood. The war that he so anxiously awaited had brought him nothing but hardship and sorrow and it left him cold and bitter.

(Holistic score = 2)

Assignment 3 (Grade 12)

In the minds of most people, an expert is someone who knows all the answers in a given field. This is a common and somewhat misconceived view. But there is another way of looking at things. In this alternative view, an expert is not one who knows what the answers are, but one who knows what the questions are in a given field. Your task for this assignment is to find out what the questions are in a given field, whether it be math, chemistry, history, or business. Begin by interviewing one of your teachers, asking him or her about the significant questions in the field. Then use the library to get additional information. Your paper should be about 5 pages. It should not only identify the questions but explain why they are significant, how they are being investigated, and why they are relevant to readers.

Rubric: Assignment 3

6—A six-point essay will be characterized by all of the following features: It will be well organized: (a) it will clearly introduce the topic and provide an interesting and detailed background for the essay; (b) it will then move to the body of the paper, where it will identify the significant questions, explain in depth why they are significant, how the questions affect the field, how the questions are being investigated, and why the questions are relevant to readers; in each case the author will provide abundant details and examples to illustrate his or her points; (c) it will have a conclusion or summation that offers a more explicit statement of relevance; it will be factual and highly informative, providing readers with new information; it will be coherent; each of the several parts will flow together smoothly; the tone will be objective and appropriate to the task; stylistically, the essay will demonstrate variety in sentence structure and paragraph development; the essay will be virtually free of surface errors.

5—A five-point essay will be characterized by all of the following features: It will be well organized: (a) it will introduce the topic and provide an interesting background for the essay; (b) it will then move to the body of the paper, where it will identify the significant questions, explain why they are significant, how the questions affect the field, how the questions are being investigated, and why the questions are relevant to readers; in each case, the author will offer details and examples to illustrate his or her points; (c) it will have a conclusion or summation that offers a more explicit statement of relevance; it will be factual and informative, providing readers with new information; it will be coherent, although the various parts will not flow together as smoothly as in the six-point essay; the tone will be objective and appropriate to the task; stylistically, the essay will demonstrate variety in sentence structure and paragraph development; the essay will be largely free of surface errors.

4—A four-point essay will be characterized by all of the following features: It will be organized: (a) it will introduce the topic and provide a background for the essay; (b) it will then move to the body of the paper, where it will identify the significant questions, explain why they are significant, how the questions affect the field, how the questions are being investigated, and why the questions are relevant to readers; the author will offer some details and examples to illustrate his or her points, but they may not always be effective or appropriate; (c) it will have a conclusion or summation that offers a more explicit statement of relevance; it will be factual; there may be occasional transitional flaws that prevent the various parts from flowing together as smoothly as they should; the tone will be objective; stylistically, the essay will demonstrate some variety in sentence structure and paragraph development; the essay may have occasional surface errors.

3—A three-point essay may be characterized as having one or more of the following features: It will not be well organized, as characterized by one or more of the following: (a) it will introduce the topic but will not provide an adequate background for the essay; (b) it will move to the body of the paper, where it will identify the significant questions, but it will fail to explain in much detail why they are significant, how the questions affect the field, how the questions are being investigated, and why the questions are relevant to readers; the author may attempt to offer some examples to illustrate his or her points, but they will generally be ineffective; (c) it will have a conclusion or summation that attempts to offer a more explicit statement of relevance, but the conclusion may be confused or may be merely a repetition of what has already been said; it will be factual but uninformative, telling readers things they already know; it will have significant transitional flaws that prevent the various parts from flowing together smoothly; the tone will be inconsistently objective or inappropriate to the task; stylistically, the essay will lack variety in sentence structure and paragraph development; the essay may have frequent surface errors.

2—A two-point essay may be characterized by as having one or more of the following features: Organization will be seriously flawed in that the writer fails to offer adequate background information; there will be insufficient details in the body of the paper, and the summation may not be relevant to the topic; the tone may be inconsistent; the frequency of mechanical errors increases.

1—A one-point essay may be characterized by as having one or more of the following features: Will be unorganized, lacking background and context, details of fact, and a summation; the tone will be subjective and inappropriate; the essay will have serious mechanical errors.

Sample 7

Math

[1] When most of us think of mathematics, we think of practical applications, such as using math to balance a checkbook. Such applications of math are used everyday by many different types of people. For example, economists use differential calculus to determine the maximum and minimum points on supply and demand curves. Civil engineers use principles of trigonometry to calculate the tensions on certain beams on truss bridges. Even school teachers use algebra to set bell curves for exams.

[2] But the field of mathematics is actually much more complex. Another aspect of math is theory, which deals with explanations of why mathematical equations and theorems, such as the quadratic equation, work. This side of math is also called pure mathematics. If this pure math cannot be applied, it is virtually useless. Therefore, a very significant question in the field is brought forth: How can pure math be related to applied math?

[3] This important question has had a great effect on the field of math. The field has been split into two parts: pure math and applied math. Researchers in pure math deal with theoretical principles and come up with abstract theorems. Although pure math by itself is not practically used, research is very important because it broadens the field of math. A broader field in turn gives applied mathematicians more to work with. Greater importance is being given to applied mathematicians, because they make math useful, by applying it to practical matters. They include researchers in many fields, some of which are in the natural sciences, engineering, and business. They in turn broaden many other fields, such as chemistry, economics, and electrical engineering.

[4] Many different approaches have been tried to find a sure method to apply pure math to answer all the questions in a given field. In one technique, trial and error is used to try to apply mathematical principles to a certain case. If a mathematical principle works, it is attempted with many other similar situations. If this approach can be repeated over and over in every case, a formula or equation is derived, which can be applied in practical situations. Unfortunately, this technique does not always work, because the same repetitive steps can rarely be used for all cases. Also, numerous complexities frequently come up, which in turn bring up more questions to be answered.

[5] In another technique, abstract mathematical principles are converted into physical models. These models link the pure math to certain applications. A good example of this method is the differential analyzer. Most problems in physics and engineering involve differential equations. The problem was that in theory the solutions of this type of equation are rarely expressed in term of a finite number and therefore cannot be practically used. But in 1928, an engineer named Vannevan Bush, along with his staff at MIT discovered that when differential equations are applied to physical situations, a finite answer is not necessary if a graphic solution is obtainable. Using this fact, they designed and constructed the first differential analyzer. Today these analyzers are used throughout industry.

[6] In conclusion, how we can relate pure math to applied math is a very significant question, not only in the field of mathematics itself, but also in many other fields. A universal answer to this important question would make many aspects of mathematics more useful. For normal people like you and me, the answer would greatly speed up technology. Many more practical applications would lead to many new inventions and break throughs that would have a great impact on the way we live.

(Holistic score = 5 / 6)

Sample 8

The World of Economics

[1] Most people do not notice that the movies shown during the summer are either comedies, adventures, or teen related, while those played in the winter are dramas and adult comedies. We might wonder why this is. During the summer months, what type of audience can a film bring it? Young people. Also for us, the summer means good times and lots of adventure. Most of us want to keep those good times rolling and do not wish to take on a serious film. This interesting observation has to do with economics, because economics has to do with each and every one of us.

[2] The people who create and produce films we watch need to answer three questions before they can get the film rolling. In fact these are the same questions that every nation, economist, businessman, and individual needs to be able to answer, because without them products would not be created and an economy would not exist. We need to know what to produce, how much to produce, and whom to produce it for.

[3] The question what to produce is significant because if we do not know what to produce then we will not have certain goods or services. An economy cannot exist without production, and the more products available the stronger the economy and the cheaper the product. The cheaper the product the greater the demand for the product. The more demand means more product sold, which creates a healthier economy. Therefore if we can answer what to produce, more of our wants will be satisfied, the goods and services will be cheaper, and the economy will be growing. This makes us happier and our nation stronger.

[4] However before the good or service can be produced, it must be known for whom you are producing it for. We need to know if there is a market for the product. If there is not a market for the product, there is no reason to produce it. Music groups are a good example. Music groups provide a service however if there is not a demand for their type of music they will not be able to sell albums. If they do not produce a product that is desired, it does not help economy. In fact groups in demand could increase the cost of their material, because they now hold a monopoly on the music that is in demand. This means higher prices for you and me. This question is investigated through market research. These individuals study the market system and predict what is and what will be in demand. This helps companies create future products, which help satisfy our wants and desires.

[5] Although what and for whom to produce it for is not known, how much to supply or produce is still unanswered. The less product that is produce the cheaper it is to produce it. For example, it is cheaper to buy the materials to wall paper one room then it is for a whole apartment complex.

More materials, supplies, and hired help need to be bought and it takes more time. However, items with little demand are not heavily produced and cost more. For example, there is little demand for dialysis machines, so few are produced. There is a monopoly on these machines because they are needed. So manufacturers can charge as much as they see fit because, although it is small, there is always a demand for it. Therefore, how much product is produce affects the price that you and I have to pay. However, we decide how much demand there is for the product by deciding whether to purchase it or not.

[6] As it can be determined, these questions are always being asked and answered. They affect everyone because the products are produce for us and bought by us. They are investigated through market systems and market research. These questions affect the field of economics, because they are economics. Without these questions, there would be no products and therefore no economy. Economics is the study of how goods and services get produced and how they are distributed. Consequently the study of what, for whom, and how much to produce, is economics. The attempt to answer them gives us the field of economics.

(Holistic score = 3)

Sample 9

Questions in french

[1] At one time, people concentrated on learning as much as possible about their native language. This was sufficient until society became more complex and knowing more than one language was almost essential. As one strolls the isles of a local grocery store, one notices products with names derived from the french language. Some examples are Lean Cuisine, Au Gratin and Le Jardin, all three of this parents have french words in their title. The television companies even broadcast a Perma Soft commercial spoken in french. These are just two subtle examples used to show the need to have a knowledge of the french language is increasing. This has caused many people to seriously consider or go forth with the learning of french. One can not simply learn a language overnight. It requires determination along with an effective method. This has raised a very significant question in learning the french language. Despite research, the question still remains of what is the most effective method to adopt in learning the french language.

[2] One of the methods of teaching concentrates on grammar translation. This method involves translating from french to english as well as from english to french. Students translate sentences, paragraphs, and even complete sentences. The translations are checked for accuracy in grammar

usage, proper word placement in sentences, accent marks, and consistency of the choice of words. This method has advantages but is not free of disadvantages. Since there is little oral work, the students are not familiar with correct pronunciation, the ability to perform well on dictation and communicate with other french speakers. Researchers have found this is an effective method in learning how to read and write the language but feel more oral activities. They also have found through grammar translation, students appear to be able to retain their knowledge of french over a long period of time.

[3] A second method of teaching french involves audiolinguism. This method is based on listening to cassettes of french conversation and students will learn by repetition. There is some written work involved since students are asked to write what is heard on the cassette. The information heard ranges from daily conversation to sentences with specific exceptions in french. Researchers have found this method to be less practical since one is confined to listening to the french spoken and many are bored with this. Since many people learn through repetition, it is quite effective.

[4] The final method is communative competence. Their is a great amount of concentration on distinguish this "method" the ability to understand french in day today situation and the culture. The majority of this would include oral work. Students learn greetings, answering and asking questions, interests and information concerning the french culture. There is more emphasis on the ability to be able to say a sentence correctly than the ability to write one. Researchers have found students in this type of class were able to communicate but their writing and grammar skills were not quite strong. They felt a student had a liberal education in french but more precision was needed to help the student have a better grasp of the language.

[5] Deciding on which method to adopt in teaching french is an unanswerable task. Choosing one method would satisfy all french students. Researchers have found a certain amount of certains performed will in each method of teaching. Experts in the field of foreign language study feel they are not at liberty to pick a single method because, as mentioned earlier, who is to say which is the best method. Research on the french language continues. There have been many cons found since many feel the purpose of learning a foreign language is the ability to communicate. Researchers have stated there should always be a purpose behind taking the foreign language. The question remains unanswered concerning the most effective method to adopt in teaching a foreign language.

(Holistic score = 1)

EXPLORING KEY IDEAS

1. Which do you think is a larger problem in the assessment of writing as it currently exists in our schools, validity or reliability? Why?
2. Even teachers who know that their comments on student papers do not serve any effective pedagogical function find it hard to resist writing comments when grading. What are some reasons they find it so difficult?
3. When students are using holistic scoring, why is it important to develop a rubric before they start writing an assignment?
4. Consider the sample rubric on pages (273–274). What implicit message does it convey with respect to global features, such as audience and support, and local features such as punctuation and spelling?
5. Why is it so important that the teacher select good anchor papers?
6. Why is it important that students feel that the teacher closely monitors their holistic scoring?
7. Portfolio assessment offers several advantages over holistic scoring? What are the two most significant?
8. If finished papers do not have any written comments on them, how do students get feedback on their work?

Appendix *A*

Writing Myths

All writers are concerned with form to one degree or another. At the elementary and secondary levels, the focus of writing instruction often is on simply producing complete sentences, correct spelling, and correct punctuation. More complex matters related to organization, content, and purpose are ignored or treated inadequately. A focus on form generally involves a reliance on rules to explain to students what writing is about. These rules can come to regulate every aspect of writing, such as spelling, the number of paragraphs that make an essay, sentence length, and so on. In some classes, the consequences for violating these rules are dire. A misplaced comma or a misspelled word has been enough to earn more than a few students an *F* on a given assignment.

Accuracy and correctness in form are important. Also, classroom experiences can be trying, as when a student asks for the 20th time why commas and periods go inside quotation marks rather than outside. It is just easier to tell them, "Because that's the rule!" Nevertheless, we need to keep in mind that a large part of what people do with writing is governed by conventions—conventions of spelling, genre, and punctuation. Rules too commonly are understood as laws, which they are not. Conventions are quite arbitrary and therefore changeable. At any point, it would be possible to hold a punctuation conference of teachers, writers, and publishers to adopt some alternative to what writers currently use.

Several rules are not matters of convention but rather are outright myths. They seem to get passed on from teacher to student year after year. This appendix is intended to summarize and discuss a few of the more egregious writing myths that nearly everyone has received as absolute truth.

SENTENCE OPENERS

Every year, thousands of students are told that they never should begin a sentence with a coordinating conjunction, such as *and, but*, and *for*. They also are told that they never should begin a sentence with the subordinating conjunctions *because* and *since*. The origin of this prohibition probably lies in the fact that many students transfer some speech patterns to writing. Most conversations have a strong narrative element, which means that they consist of strings of actions and events linked chronologically. The most common way to connect these events is through the coordinating conjunction *and*. When students apply conversational patterns to their writing, *and* appears with great frequency. Yet most sentences in written English begin with the subject, not with a coordinator, and teachers may unconsciously be attempting to reduce conversational patterns through the injunction against starting sentences with the conjunction. Although well-intentioned, this injunction is incorrect.

With respect to subordination, information supplied by the context of a conversation allows us to use sentences in speech that are shorter than those we characteristically use in writing. Moreover, we often express utterances that are not sentences at all, in the strict sense, but are simply parts of sentences, which in composition we usually term as *fragments*. If, for example, a man were to tell his roommate that he is going to the market in the afternoon, and the roommate were to ask why, most likely the man would respond with, "Because we're out of milk." This response is not a sentence; it is a subordinate clause. It has a subject and a predicate, making it a clause, but the subordinating conjunction *because* makes it a modifier, in this case, supplying information related to the reason for going to the market. Because modifiers must modify something, they are dependent, and by definition, dependent clauses are not sentences. If the speaker had not taken advantage of context in this exchange, the response to the roommate's question would have been "I am going to the store because we're out of milk." Here the dependent clause is attached to its independent clause, "I am going to the store," but having already declared the intention to go to the store, the speaker could limit his response to the subordinate clause.

This rather long explanation is designed merely to suggest how prohibitions against certain sentence openers may have originated. The goal may have been to reduce the number of fragments that potentially could be produced when students transfer a very common pattern in speech, like "Because we're out of milk," to writing. Yet the answer to sentence fragments lies in students understanding the nature of sentences, not in arbitrary prohibitions that have no basis in fact. There simply are no rules, conventions, or laws that decree sentences cannot begin with conjunctions.

Actually, sentences in English can begin just about any way one chooses, which is apparent to anyone who looks closely at published writing. Authors will open sentences with *and* or *for* or *because* quite regularly. In an unpublished study (Williams, 1976) of sentence openers that I conducted some years ago on 100 well-known authors of fiction and nonfiction, using 500 word excerpted passages, 9% of the sentences began with a coordinating conjunction.

SENTENCE CLOSERS

Teachers also tell students that they never should end a sentence with a preposition—another myth. There is evidence that this myth has circulated for many years; Winston Churchill is commonly reported to have mockingly responded to the injunction against prepositions by saying, "This is the sort of English up with which I will not put." In certain types of constructions, such as questions, English grammar allows for movement of prepositions. The following two sentences, for example, mean the same thing and are both grammatical:

1. In what did you put the flowers?
2. What did you put the flowers in?

One might argue that Sentence 1 is more formal than Sentence 2, but one cannot argue that it is more correct. Issues of formality have nothing at all to do with correctness; they are related to appropriateness, much like questions of dress. Sentence 1 probably sounds a bit awkward to most readers, and it would sound awkward and probably incorrect to elementary and high-school students.

The most common situation that might leave a preposition at the end of a sentence occurs when using a relative clause (actually, Sentences 1 and 2 involve relative clauses). Relative clauses begin as sentences, and then they are joined to an independent clause. Consider Sentences 3 and 4:

3. Fritz waited for the boat.
4. Macarena arrived on the boat.

These sentences can be combined to provide Sentences 5 or 6:

5. Fritz waited for the boat on which Macarena arrived.
6. Fritz waited for the boat which Macarena arrived on.

The details of relativization can be a bit complex, but essentially, the process involves taking a duplicate noun phrase—in this case *the boat*—and replacing it with a relative pronoun. In Sentence 4, *the boat* becomes *which*. Notice, however, that the preposition *on* remains. When relativization involves noun phrases at the end of constructions, as in Sentences 3 and 4, English grammar provides the option of shifting the whole prepositional phrase (*on which*) to the front of the relative clause or shifting the relative pronoun. The second option produces Sentence 6, which is perfectly grammatical and correct, even though it ends with a preposition.

For inexplicable reasons, people with an overconcern for matters of structure actually spend time thinking up truly ungrammatical constructions that occur when a sentence ends with a preposition. Consider the following examples, which are from a popular handbook on writing:

7.   * It was really funny, the way which Fred ate in.
8.   * We gave money for fame and fame for love up.

These sentences are variations of:

7a.   It was really funny, the way in which Fred ate.
8a.   We gave up money for fame and fame for love.

The problems here are interesting. The writer of Sentences 7 and 8 actually violated English grammar to produce examples of ungrammatical sentences ending with prepositions. Sentence 7a is understood to begin as two sentences:

7b.   The way was really funny.
7c.   Fred ate in a way.

When these are combined through relativization, the result is:

7d.   The way in which Fred ate was really funny.

In addition, Sentence 7a has undergone a process known as *topicalization*, which increases the focus of the sentence on the funniness of Fred's eating. The process involves taking the predicate *was really funny*, putting *It* in place as a pseudo subject, and fronting the new construction, *It was really funny*:

7e.   It was really funny/the way in which Fred ate.

This construction, however, is fundamentally different from the result of combining Sentences 3 and 4 because the noun phrase *the way* was not at the end of both. It was at the beginning of 7b and at the end of 7c. Consequently, the preposition cannot be moved—movement simply is not an option here. Thus Sentence 7 is ungrammatical because the writer made it so, not because it ends with a preposition.

In Sentence 8 the problematic *up* is not even a preposition. It is called a *particle* and is part of the verb *gave*. Although English grammar does allow particles to move, they can do so only under certain conditions, as in the following sentences:

9.   Fred looked up the number.

9a.   Fred looked the number up.

That is, particles can move *only* to the right of the noun that immediately follows the verb plus particle phrase.

Students do have problems with prepositions, especially nonnative speakers. Producing ungrammatical constructions by putting prepositions at the end of sentences, however, is not one of these problems. Because so many English sentences can and do end with a preposition, passing on the myth that they cannot confuses students.

TO BE OR NOT TO BE:
WEAK VERBS–STRONG VERBS

This myth maintains that writers should avoid using forms of *to be*. Very often forms of *to be* are classified as "weak verbs," and all other verb forms are classified as "strong verbs." The idea that some words are better than others lies at the heart of the weak verb–strong verb myth. A kernel of truth exists here, but it is a truth that must be qualified. Words themselves have no value. They only assume value when they are put together with identifiable intentions in specifiable contexts, thereby achieving specifiable effects. The origin of this myth lies, in part, in the tendency of many young writers to focus on two aspects of their individual realities: the existence of things and the classification of things. The short essay that follows, written by a sixth grader and presented unedited except for name changes, illustrates this focus in a typical manner. The assignment asked students to describe an important experience in their lives:

> The Olympics at my school *were* on June 6, 7, 1986. There *was* a lot of different events and I was in a 400 meter relay with three other people. We *were* from South America. we had very fast runners. They *were* Erica, Peter, Jack, and myself and my name is Jason. Peter *was* first to run 100 meters then Erica then Jack, and I *was* anchor. I came in 1st place. It changed the way people felt about me in a positive way. Now I have races against more people.

The italicized type highlights the various uses of *to be*; we see how this verb form establishes existential relations ("The Olympics at my school were on June 6, 7, 1986") and classifications ("We were from South America"). The difficulty the student faces in focusing on existence and class is that he captures none of the excitement that he assuredly felt when he won his race. His tone is that of a police report or an insurance policy (typical narrative reporting). It is inappropriate for this particular assignment. In this case, the various forms of *to be* simply reflect a much larger problem, one related to the purpose of the writing task. The writer does not appear to have a solid grasp of what exactly a description of a memorable event is supposed to do.

A more likely source of the injunction against forms of *to be* is the tradition of the belles-lettres essay, which is a literary genre that stands in stark contrast to the utilitarian prose of reports, proposals, and journal articles. From this perspective, the injunction is intended to make student writing more literary. Such a goal would be appropriate if the belles-lettres genre were not moribund or if the existing need for competent writers of utilitarian prose were not so great. The reality is that most of the writing that people produce is related to business and government, and that it relies heavily on forms of *to be* out of sheer necessity. When teachers make artificial distinctions between verb forms based on humanistic preferences, they run the risk of hindering students who need to master a variety of prose forms.

THE POOR PASSIVE

Passive constructions are interesting for several reasons. They allow us, for example, to reverse the most common order of subject–object positions in sentences, as in:

10.   Betty kicked the ball.
10a. The ball was kicked by Betty.

Sentence 10 is a simple active sentence, where *Betty* is also the subject, *kicked* is the verb, and *the ball* is the object or the recipient of the action conveyed by the verb. *Betty* is also the topic of the sentence. In Sentence 10a, however, the situation is different. The terms subject, verb, and object still apply, but now there are additional words and *Betty* is no longer the topic of the sentence—the ball is. Also, there is some question as to whether the meaning of an active sentence changes if one switches it to the passive. In most cases the meaning does not appear to change, but in others a strange ambiguity arises:

11.   Everyone at the party spoke a foreign language.
11a. A foreign language was spoken by everyone at the party.

Most students are told that they never should use passive constructions, that all sentences should be active, yet as this sentence demonstrates, passives are very useful constructions. They allow for a distancing among writer, object, and agent that is essentially mandatory in some forms of writing and that is tactful and polite in others. They also allow for greater sentence variety. In certain types of writing, lab reports, reports of data collection, and so forth, the passive is required by convention, and to fail to use it is to violate the writing conventions of the disciplines that produce lab reports.

The real problem with student writers is that they frequently use a passive construction when it is not appropriate or necessary. They hide subjects or delete them entirely, in part because they are insecure about their work and the passive allows them to equivocate. The role of teachers with respect to passive constructions, therefore, should not be to issue a universal ban against them but rather to help students understand when passive constructions are useful and necessary.

MISCONCEPTIONS ABOUT SENTENCE LENGTH

Another prevalent myth involves sentence length. Teachers generally tell students that short sentences are better than long ones—that is the myth. They then go on to tell students to make their sentences as short as possible. The basis for the myth, as well as the command, is shrouded in impenetrable mystery, but it may be connected to an effort on the part of teachers to help students avoid writing run-on sentences.

Research on writing maturity indicates that children's sentences increase in length and complexity as they grow older. Fourth graders in Hunt's (1965) study, for example, wrote very long sentences, averaging about 70 words each, because they compounded clauses, generally using the conjunction *and*. The following passage illustrates this sort of compounding. It comes from a sixth grader who was asked to write a response to a recent ban on gum chewing at his school:

> I think children at this school should be able to chew gum and I think it should be for fourth and up because those grades are the more mature grades and they would not spit it on the floor. If you were chewing gum you would not be able to talk but you must throw away your wrappers, and spit out your gum in the trash before recess, lunch, and Physical Education. This morning Rita Brown was chewing gum, the teacher caught her and she didn't get in trouble. You could only chew it, not throw it, or play with it and if it started getting out of hand you could abolish the priviledge.

The sentences in this passage are not especially long, but they tend to be run-on; that is, the student has joined independent clauses with conjunctions, without a comma at each joining. It is easy to see why one might be tempted to tell the student, "Write short sentences!" The student understands where to put a period, if not a comma, so dotting the essay with periods will take care of some of the run-on sentences. However, breaking each of these long sentences into shorter ones simply would trade one problem for another. If the change were made on the basis of independent clauses, the result would be choppy, at best, as we see in the altered version of the Rita Brown sentence:

> This morning Rita Brown was chewing gum. The teacher caught her. She didn't get in trouble.

The effect is a Dick-and-Jane style that becomes virtually unreadable after a paragraph or two.

Christensen (1967) observed that really good writers, professionals who make a living at writing, do not write short sentences. They write long ones, short ones, and some in between. Students, he noted, usually have little trouble with the last two categories, but they have serious difficulty with long sentences because the tendency is to engage in compounding with *and* and subordinating with *because* until the sentence approaches gibberish. An important task of the writing teacher, in his view, is to help students master long sentences that truly reflect maturity in writing. The key, according to Christensen, lies in short independent clauses that have modifying constructions attached to them, usually following the clause. Sentence 12 illustrates this principle:

12. The misconceptions have existed for decades, being passed from teachers to students, year after year.

The independent clause in Sentence 12 is *The misconceptions have existed for decades*, and it is followed by two modifying constructions: *being passed from teachers to students* and *year after year*.

Several studies have found a relation between overall writing quality in student essays and sentences that fit the pattern of short independent clauses followed by modifiers. These findings suggest that when working with students at the sentence level, teachers should not ask for shorter sentences, but for longer ones with short independent clauses.

CONCLUSION

The attitudes teachers bring to the classroom and the things they tell students have long-lasting effects on their lives. Students seem particularly susceptible to attitudes and assumptions about writing and writing ability. Teachers' attitudes and assumptions become students' attitudes and assumptions. Given the importance of writing, not only to students' education but also to their work and place in society, teachers do them a terrible disservice if they perpetuate the misconceptions that prevent a clear understanding of what writing is about. One of the more difficult problems a teacher can face is the student who has come to believe that he or she cannot write and, moreover, cannot learn to write. Too often this false assumption is accompanied by a set of rules related to sentence structure that can lead to so much attention to form that ideas never have a chance to be developed. Nothing of worth gets written, and the student reinforces his or her own sense of defeat.

As stated at the outset, this appendix discusses only some of the myths that surround writing. The purpose here was not to be comprehensive but to provide a starting point for discussion and learning, to stimulate readers to examine critically their own understanding of what writing is about. It is often said that teachers teach just the way they themselves were taught, and this observation may explain, in part, why the myths in this appendix have been handed down from generation to generation. In trying to dispel them, this appendix dares readers to become risk takers, to challenge their preconceptions about writing.

Appendix *B*

Sample Essays

The following essays are offered for the purpose of practice evaluations. They were written in class by a group of high-school seniors in Southern California who had studied argumentative strategies in English class. They had 45 minutes to complete the task. For several weeks before the assignment, the community and the campus had been talking about establishing a smoking area for students who smoke. The proposal was controversial because it is illegal in California for anyone under 18 to buy, possess, or use tobacco. Thus the school would be condoning an illegal activity were it to establish the smoking area.

The writing assignment was as follows:

> The school principal is proposing to establish a smoking area on campus for students who smoke. In an argumentative essay, take a stand either for or against this proposal. Completed essays will be forwarded to the principal for his consideration. Be certain to state your position clearly after providing appropriate background information. Provide good reasons or support for your position, using convincing details. Finally, include a conclusion that states the significance of the topic for the whole campus.

Essay 1

On Campus Smoking

[1] The fact that more students than ever before are smoking on campus has caused a lot of discussion among students and teachers. Our school newspaper, The Scroll, even ran a series of articles about it. On the one hand, smoking is illegal for anyone under 18, so students who smoke, and teachers who let them, are breaking the law. On the other hand, by the time a person reaches high school he/she is old enough to make some decisions on his own, so restricting smoking may be a limitation on his/her rights.

[2] Now the district is toying with the idea of setting up a special area for smokers. The aim is to clear out the restrooms, which would reduce the

305

fire hazard that comes from students lighting up around wastepaper bins that are often overflowing, and to put an end to the silly game of "hide and seek" played out between students and teachers. The students hide to have their cigarettes, and the teachers try to find them.

[3] There's no doubt that the idea seems initially to make sense. Students could be open about their habit. They wouldn't have to sneak around behind the gym or in the restrooms to have a smoke. Nonsmokers would really appreciate being able to walk into the restrooms without choking on the smoke-filled air. Smokers wouldn't have to dodge cars as they rush across the street to Paris Liqour to grab a quick one between classes, which means they would have fewer tardies. They could simply step over to the smoking area, have their cigarette, then go on about their business. Everyone would be happier: students, teachers, and administrators.

[4] What all these good arguments ignore, however, is that existing California law prohibits minors from buying, possessing, or smoking cigarettes. That law isn't likely to change in the near future, considering the clear health problems tobacco causes. Until the law does change, the school district is really in no position to even propose a smoking area, unless administrators want to put themselves in the awkward position of aiding and encouraging criminal behavior among students. That's a bad position to be in, and it comes from their considering a bad idea.

Essay 2

[1] Our school newspaper recently reported that the school district is thinking about setting aside a special area for smokers. I think this is good idea because so many students at W.H.S. smoke. They smoke out in the parking lot or in the restrooms. They smoke out behind the gym or across the street at the liqour store. There are probably more smokers at this school than there are nonsmokers.

[2] The simple truth is that if a teenager wants to smoke there's no way to stop him/her. I know that a lot of parents don't want their kids to smoke, but the kids do it anyway. They are always willing to take a chance of getting caught whenever they want to smoke, because they are as addicted to their cigarettes as a junky is to heroine. Talking to them isn't going to help, neither is having teachers chase them out of the restrooms. All that does is make them resent their teachers more than they already do and make them dispise school more than they already do.

[3] In some ways it's like so many other things that adults do but don't want teenagers to do. Sex is a good example. Grown ups are all the time telling teenagers they shouldn't have sex, but we do anyway because it feels good and we figure we're old enough to make our own decision about it. And there

sure aren't many adults who would give up sex. Sex isn't bad for us if we're in the Pill, so it's our decision regarding what we want to do with our bodies. Alcohol is another example. Adults are always telling us not to drink, that it's bad for us, but those same adults will have a drink before dinner, wine with their meal, and then a nightcap before going to bed.

[4] Smoking is a little more complex because it is bad for our health. But its our lungs and our health problems. In fact, the smoking area would let us smoke away from nonsmokers, so that our cigarettes don't pollute the air for them. All in all, it's a good idea. We are old enough to decide what to do with our bodies. We're going to do it anyway because we're addicted. And it would be good for nonsmokers.

Essay 3

I Don't Think There Should Be a Smoking Area

[1] It seems that everyday we hear another report on the news about how bad smoking is for smokers and nonsmokers around them. Now the principal's office is thinking about putting in a smoking area at Westminster High School. In my opinion, this would be a mistake, and in this essay I'll point out some of the reasons why.

[2] First, the school would in effect be encouraging students to smoke if it set aside this special area. Given the fact that smoking is illegal as well as the fact that it causes lung cancer, heart disease, and emfazima, smokers should be given help to kick their habit. They shouldn't be told by their school that it's o.k. to ruin their health and comit a crime.

[3] Second, we know that cigarette smoke is not only bad for smokers—it's bad for people. who don't smoke but who just happen to be standing around. If there was a spot on campus for smokers, what would their nonsmoking friends do? The smokers would probably smoke more freely and more often, which means that they would spend all their free time in the "smoking zone." Their nonsmoking friends sure wouldn't want to be around all that smoke, so they would stay away. The result would be that the smokers and the nonsmokers would rarely talk to each other. Friendships might end, and that wouldn't be good for anyone. As it is now, smokers have to sneek a quick smoke between classes or at lunch, so their nonsmoking friends have time to be with them.

[4] Finally, a lot of students probably wouldn't use the smoking zone because they would just go back to smoking where they usually do. A lot of students smoke at certain places where they can meet their friends before and after school. Most of them have been doing this for a long time. Why would they change now?

[5] In this essay I have expressed my opinion on a smoking area on campus. As you can see, there are many different reasons why there shouldn't be a smoking spot. It's just a bad idea.

Essay 4

Smoking in the Schools

[1] I think people have a right to smoke, as long as it doesn't bother others, and I would not mind if the schools set up a special place for smokers if the smoke did not effect the other people in the school. If a place for smokers was provided then smokers might stop smoking around people who don't smoke. This is important because many people are allergic to smoke and some of them could become sick.

[2] The place set aside for smokers should in some way keep the smoke away from other areas so that it will not bother other people. We see this all the time in restaurants. In fact, it is now a law that restaurants must have a nonsmoking area for people who don't smoke. If someone comes in with a cigarette, they have to sit in the smokers area. If the smoke still bothers someone in the restaurant, the smoker has to put out the cigarette or leave the restaurant. I work at Denny's on weekends and we have this happen all the time. Sometimes the smoker gets mad and refuses to put out the cigarette, but then the manager comes and forces him to either put it out or to leave.

[3] This is a good idea because smoke causes so many diseases and it smells so bad. When I have to work the smoking section I come home with cigarette smoke on my clothes and in my hair. It doesn't do any good to wear a nice perfume because the smoke kills the fragrance so that all anyone can smell is cigarettes. Well the same thing happens at school in the restrooms because of all the girls in there sneaking a smoke. I come out stinking.

[4] As I say, people have the right to smoke, but only if it doesn't bother anyone else. If the place on campus is set up for smokers and the smoke bothers the nonsmokers, then the smoking area should be removed and smoking should be stopped in the school altogether.

Essay 5

[1] Smokers seem to be everywhere on this campus. A person can't even go to the toilet without having to wade through clouds of smoke puffed into the air by all the guys hanging out in the restrooms sneaking a cigarette. A designated smoking area might put an end to this problem, but in my opinion it would create more trouble than it's worth.

[2] Let's face it, smoking is a dirty habit that's not only bad for the person smoking but that's bad for the health of any innocent bystanders. In addition, it's illegal for minors to smoke. They aren't even supposed to have cigarettes. So what is the school going to do, help students break the law? That's stupid.

[3] Also, think of what a mess a smoking area would be. In my experience smokers are basically inconsiderate slobs. Rather than use an ashtray, most of them will just drop a butt on the floor. They also don't care where they put their ashes. They'll drop them anywhere. Concentrate a bunch of smokers in one small area, and you'll not only have ashes and butts to contend with, you'll have burned out matches and empty cartons everywhere. If you think convenient trash containers will help, you don't know many smokers. The result will be that our school will look trashy, which would bring the whole schools reputation down.

[4] In all respects, of course, the area would be condouning the illegal possession and use of cigarettes by minors. Those who aren't of age are prohibited by law from buying cigarettes. So why should they be allowed to smoke them on campus? What would the parents of these children think if they didn't allow their son or daughter to smoke, only to find out later that the school districts not only allow them to smoke on campus, but even set up a reserved area for them? I don't think the parent would find this at all amusing.

[5] And finally, there's the second hand smoke. Not only is smoke bad for the smoker but tests show that the second hand smoke is twice as bad for a person to breathe than what is going directly into the lungs of the smoker. If you concentrate all the smokers on this campus in one spot, you're going to generate a whole lot of smoke, and there's no way you're going to prevent it from affecting others. This means that the district would be endangering the lives and well being of innocent bystanders. Those who don't smoke would be getting a bad deal, and the school would be opening itself up to potential law suites.

[6] Given all these reasons, I feel that to allow smoking on campus isn't right and shouldn't even be considered.

Essay 6

Smoking on Campus

[1] The peer pressure applied on students in high school is very hard to cope with. Some people can ignore it, but most cannot. Those who are unfortunate get pulled into doing drugs, promiscuos sex, smoking, and other illegal acts. Probably the worst pressure would be to begin smoking,

because unlike drugs it is more or less socially acceptable, and unlike promiscuos sex it is harmful. Cigarette smoking is proven to cause cancer and heart disease. The problem is that teens either don't know this or they don't believe it, so they experiment. This is where the problem starts, because once they try it they get addicted. I therefore feel that giving students a place to smoke is wrong because it will only encourage more students to smoke because of the peer pressure. It may also encourage teens to loiter, and it may turn into a "hang out" where kids can sell and take drugs.

[2] Teens are already under a lot of peer pressure and giving them a place to smoke is almost like saying, "smoking is what everybody does." Every time they get bored they'll go out to smoke a cigarette. This will probably be thier biggest reason for being tardy to class and for ditching or cutting class. It already is, of course, with teens hanging out in the restrooms and behind the gym. But it could be worse. Also, there is no guarante that this will stop students from smoking where they're not allowed.

[3] Instead of adding to the problem, the school should be trying to do something about it. It should be trying to get teens off cigarettes. It should work on a way of controlling students urge to smoke, ending the addiction. Maybe then some of these students would concentrate more on learning rather than on sneaking another smoke.

Essay 7

Essay

[1] I think it would be all right if we had a smoking area on campus. I think then the kids wouldn't go the liquor store and smoke there. It would be a good idea to get the smokers out in the open so the teachers could talk to them about quiting the habbit. This idea is to the bennafit of the people that smok, so they would support this idea.

[2] On the other hand, I think that the smokers only smok to get atention. And having a smok area at school will only make it almost right for the High school kids to smoke Also they would incorage the people that don't smok to smok too. Then you would just have more of a problum with smoking at Westminster High school. I also think it's a fier hazzard and we shouldnt have that at our school We have enof to worrie about without this idea.

[3] It is my opinion that there should be a smoking area on campus. If they want to muss up their lives by smoking it all right with me. I think it would be graet to teach the smokers the hard way just because they want to fit in. That way I think people suold be alowed to smok wereever they want

or they suold stop selling cijrettes all together and take care of this problum once and for all!!

Essay 8

[1] Upon entering high school students are faced with several important decisions. Among these decisions is whether or not to smoke. There is much pressure put upon the adolescences by their peers to "light up" with most parents having the oppisite veiws. Caught in the middle of this heated battle are the schools. A recent proposition made by the schools is to set aside an area for smoking on the schoolgrounds. Does this mean the school is condoning smoking? Yes, to a very large degree it does. If the students are given this area to use for smoking more students will begin "lighting up." There is no useful reason for such an area, and much to the dismay of many parents this proposition may someday come into affect.

[2] With the awareness of the cancer-causing affects of the cigarettes the schools should be condemning their use. On each package reads a warning label to warn off that person from using the harmful product, yet millions of teenagers and adults alike, are still smoking. Doctors warn of serious results from smoking, such as lung cancer, deadening of the cilia that line the throat, and several others as well. Yet still we keep smoking. If areas are set aside in our schools we are leading our children into an addiction from which some may never return. The cons far outweight the pros in this situation, especially those from a medical stand point.

[3] The future of these smoking teenagers is a factor as well. Studies have shown that smoking takes as much as five years off the life of a smoker, and that of those who begun smoking in their teens fewer were able to quit. Some of these students may die of cancer before attaining their goals, and take away the contributions they might have put forth.

Essay 9

Smoking Area

[1] I think setting aside an area on campus for students who smoke on their break is the most absurd idea I have ever heard. Smoking is bad enough already as it is and to even encourage it is something school administrators shouldn't be involved in. Most of the teenagers who smoke are too young. A person cannot purchase cigarettes legally until they are eighteen years of age, even though most liquor stores sell them to children well under the legal age.

[2] By establishing this area on campus, smoking would be encouraged more among teenagers because it would be accepted. In no way would this

eliminate smoke; high schoolers have thirty-five minutes of lunch to go off campus and smoke to their heart's content. Being an occasional smoker myself, I know that is plenty of time to have a few cigarettes. When there is an urge, even though seldom, I get tempted to spend class in a bathroom stall puffing on a cigarette, so somethimes I do. I never get caught, and if I did it wouldn't be a big deal like possession of drugs such as marijuana, alcohol, cocain, etc.

[3] Smoking is a major cause of many diseases, we all know. So why should teachers, administrators, and the campus police augment the growth and popularity of smoking by providing a "special" place for teens to practice their habit? Many people die each year of cigarette-related deaths. Smoking causes cancer, emphysema, high blood pressure and underweight babies at birth. These deadly diseases wouldn't show up in teenagers immdiately, but in ten or twenty years from now, many more people would be dying because smoking was accepted so much in the one place where drugs and alcohol weren't. And that's saying to students that smoking is okay.

References

Abbott, V., Black, J., & Smith, E. (1985). The representation of scripts in memory. *Journal of Memory and Language, 24,* 179–199.

Ackerman, J. (1993). The promise of writing to learn. *Written Communication, 10,* 334–370.

Addison, R., & Homme, L. (1965). The reinforcement of event (RE) menu. *National Society for Programmed Instruction Journal, 5,* 89.

Albano, T. (1992). The effect of interest on reading comprehension and written discourse. *Dissertation Abstracts International, 53,* 111A.

Allen, J. (1993). Discerning communities: Uniting theory and practice in the social epistemic composition. *Dissertation Abstracts International, 53,* 2718A.

Amastae, J. (1981). The writing needs of Hispanic students. In B. Cronnell (Ed.), *The writing needs of linguistically different students.* Washington, DC: SWRL Educational Research and Development.

Amastae, J. (1984). The Pan-American Project. In J. Ornstein-Galicia (Ed.), *Form and function in Chicano English.* Rowley, MA: Newbury House.

Anastasi, A. (1980). Culture-free testing. In G. Lindzey (Ed.), *A history of psychology in autobiography* (Vol. 7). San Francisco: Freeman.

Andres, S. (1993). *Images bridging home and academic cultures.* (ERIC Document Reproduction Service No. ED 359 536).

Artz, F. (1980). *The mind of the middle ages.* Chicago: University of Chicago Press.

Austin, J. (1962). *How to do things with words.* Cambridge, MA: Harvard University Press.

Bain, A. (1866). *English composition and rhetoric.* New York: Appleton-Century-Crofts.

Bamberg, B. (1983). What makes a text coherent? *College Composition and Communication, 34,* 417–429.

Bateman, D., & Zidonis, F. (1964). *The effect of a knowledge of generative grammar upon the growth of language complexity.* (ED 001241). Columbus: Ohio State Research Foundation..

Bateman, D., & Zidonis, F. (1966). *The effect of a study of transformational grammar on the writing of ninth and tenth graders.* Champaign, IL: National Council of Teachers of English.

Bates, E. (1976). *Language and context.* New York: Academic Press.

Bates, E. (1979). *The emergence of symbols: Cognition and communication in infancy.* New York: Academic Press.

Bates, E., Camaioni, C., & Volterra, V. (1975). *Communicazione nel primo anno di vita* [Communication in the first year of life]. Rome: Mulino.

Baugh, J. (1983). *Black street speech: Its history, structure, and survival.* Austin: University of Texas Press.

Baugh, J. (1984). *Language in use: Readings in sociolinguistics.* Englewood Cliffs, NJ: Prentice-Hall.

Beach, R., & Liebman-Kleine, J. (1986). The writing/reading relationship: Becoming one's own best reader. In B. Petersen (Ed.), *Convergences: Transactions in reading and writing.* Urbana, IL: National Council of Teachers of English.

Beck, F. (1964). *Greek education, 450–359 B.C.* London: Methuen.

Beesley, M. (1986). The effects of word processing on elementary students' written compositions: Processes, products, and attitudes. *Dissertation Abstracts International, 47,* 11A.

Belanoff, P. (1991). The myths of assessment. *Journal of Basic Writing, 10*, 54–67.

Berlin, J. (1990). Writing instruction in school and college English, 1890–1985. In J. Murphy (Ed.), *A short history of writing instruction from ancient Greece to twentieth-century America*. New York: Hermagoras.

Berlin, J. (1992a). Freirean pedagogy in the U.S.: A response. *Journal of Advanced Composition, 12*, 414–421.

Berlin, J. (1992b). Poststructuralism, cultural studies, and the composition classroom: Postmodern theory in practice. *Rhetoric Review, 11*, 16–33.

Berliner, D. (1996). Nowadays, even the illiterates read and write. *Research in the Teaching of English*, 30, 344–351.

Berthoff, A. (1981). *The making of meaning: Metaphors, models, and maxims for writing teachers*. Montclair, NJ: Boynton/Cook.

Berthoff, A. (1983). A comment on inquiry and composing. *College English, 45*, 605–606.

Berthoff, A. (1990). Killer dichotomies: Reading in/reading out. In K. Ronald & H. Roskelly (Eds.), *Farther along: Transforming dichotomies in rhetoric and composition*. Montclair, NJ: Boynton/Cook.

Bever, T. (1970). The cognitive basis of linguistic structures. In J. Hayes (Ed.), *Cognition and the development of language*. New York: Wiley.

Bilingual Education Act. (1968). *United States Statutes at Large, 81*, 817.

Bissex, B. (1980). Patterns of development in writing: A case study. *Theory into Practice, 19*, 197–201.

Bizzell, P. (1987). What can we know, what must we do, what may we hope: Writing assessment. *College English, 49*, 575–584.

Bizzell, P. (1992). *Academic discourse and critical consciousness*. Pittsburgh, PA: University of Pittsburgh Press.

Bleich, D. (1995). Collaboration and the pedagogy of disclosure. *College English, 57*, 43–61.

Bloom, B. (1956). *Taxonomy of educational objectives: The classification of educational goals*. New York: David McKay.

Bloom, L. (1970). *Language development: Form and function in emerging grammars*. Cambridge, MA: MIT Press.

Bloom, L. (1973). *One word at a time: The use of single-word utterances before syntax*. The Hague, The Netherlands: Mouton.

Bloomfield, L. (1933). *Language*. New York: Holt, Rinehart & Winston.

Bluck, R. (Ed.) (1947). *Plato's seventh and eighth letters*. Cambridge, England: Cambridge University Press.

Boas, F. (1911). *Handbook of American Indian languages*. Washington, DC: Smithsonian Institution.

Boethius. (1978). *De topicis differentiis* [Topics]. (E. Stump, Ed. & Trans.). Ithaca, NY: Cornell University Press.

Bonner, S. (1977). *Education in ancient Rome: From the elder Cato to the younger Pliny*. Berkeley: University of California Press.

Braddock, R., Lloyd-Jones, R., & Schoer, L. (1963). *Research in written composition*. Champaign, IL: National Council of Teachers of English.

Britton, J., Burgess, T., Martin, N., McLeod, A., & Rosen, H. (1975). *The development of writing abilities* (pp. 11–18). London: Macmillan Education Ltd.

Broca, P. (1861). Remarques sur le siège de la faculté du langage articulé, suivies d'une observation d'amphemie (perte de la parole) [Remarks on the seat of the faculty of language articulation, following an observation of the loss of speech]. *Bulletin de la Société Anatomique* (Paris), *36*, 330–357.

Brown, P. (1987). Late antiquity. In P. Ariès & G. Duby (Eds.), *A history of private life: Vol. 1. From pagan Rome to Byzantium*. Cambridge, MA: Harvard University Press.

Bruck, M., Lambert, W., & Tucker, G. (1974). Bilingual schooling through the elementary grades: The St. Lambert project at grade seven. *Language Learning, 24*, 183–204.

Bruffee, K. (1993). *Collaborative learning.* Baltimore: Johns Hopkins Press.

Bruner, J., & Olson, D. (1979). Symbols and texts as the tools of intellect. In J. Bruner (Ed.) *The psychology of the 20th Century: Vol. 7. Piaget's developmental and cognitive psychology within an extended context.* Zurich, Switzerland: Kindler.

Calkins, L. (1983). *Lessons from a child.* Exeter, NH: Heinemann.

Callaghan, T. (1978). The effects of sentence-combining exercises on the syntactic maturity, quality of writing, reading ability, and attitudes of ninth grade students. *Dissertation Abstracts International, 39*, 637-A.

Carlson, N. R. (1994). *Physiology of behavior* (5th ed.). Boston: Allyn & Bacon.

Cattel, R. (1971). The structure of intelligence in relation to the nature–nurture controversy. In R. Cancro (Ed.), *Intelligence.* New York: Grune & Stratton.

Chall, J. (1996). American reading achievement: Should we worry? *Research in the Teaching of English, 30*, 303–310.

Charney, D. (1996). Empiricism is not a four-letter word. *College Composition and Communication, 47*, 567–593.

Chauvin, P. (1990). *A chronicle of the last pagans.* (B. Archer, Trans.). Cambridge, MA: Harvard University Press.

Chomsky, N. (1957). *Syntactic structures.* The Hague, The Netherlands: Mouton.

Chomsky, N. (1965). *Aspects of the theory of syntax.* Cambridge, MA: MIT Press.

Chomsky, N. (1972). *Language and mind.* New York: Harcourt Brace Jovanovich.

Chomsky, N. (1975). *Reflections on language.* New York: Pantheon.

Chomsky, N. (1979). *Language and responsibility.* New York: Pantheon.

Chomsky, N. (1980). *Rules and representations.* New York: Columbia University Press.

Chomsky, N. (1981). *Lectures on government and binding.* Dordrecht, The Netherlands: Foris.

Chomsky, N. (1986). *Knowledge of language.* New York: Praeger.

Chomsky, N. (1988). *Generative grammar: Its basis, development, and prospects.* A special issue of *Studies in English Linguistics and Literature.* Kyoto, Japan: Kyoto University of Foreign Studies.

Chomsky, N. (1992). *A minimalist program for linguistic theory.* Cambridge, MA: MIT Press.

Christensen, F. (1967). *Notes toward a new rhetoric: Six essays for teachers.* New York: Harper & Row.

Christiansen, T., & Livermore, G. (1970). A comparison of Anglo-American and Spanish-American children on the WISC. *Journal of Social Psychology, 81*, 914.

Cicero. (1970). De oratore [On oratory]. In J. Watson (Ed. & Trans.), *Cicero on oratory and orators.* Carbondale: Southern Illinois University Press.

Clark, A. (1993). *Associative engines: Connectionism, concepts, and representational change.* Cambridge, MA: MIT Press.

Clark, E. (1980). Here's the top: Nonlinguistic strategies in the acquisition of orientational terms. *Child Development, 51*, 329–338.

Clark, G. (1994). Rescuing the discourse community. *College Composition and Communication, 45*, 61–74.

Clark, H., & Clark, E. (1977). *Psychology and language.* New York: Harcourt Brace Jovanovich.

Colby, B., & Cole, M. (1976). Culture, memory and narrative. In R. Horton & R. Finnigan (Eds.), *Modes of thought.* New York: Academic Press.

Combs, W. (1977). Sentence-combining practice: Do gains in judgments of writing quality persist? *Journal of Educational Research, 70*, 318–321.

Conley, T. (1990). *Rhetoric in the European tradition*. New York: Longman.

Conrad, R. (1972). Speech and reading. In J. Ravanaugh & I. Mattingly (Eds.), *Language by ear and eye*. Cambridge, MA: MIT Press.

Cooper, M. (1986). The ecology of writing. *College English, 48*, 364–375.

Corrigan, R. (1978). Language development as related to stage 6 object permanence development. *Journal of Child Language, 5*, 173–189.

Coulson, A. (1996). Schooling and literacy over time: The rising cost of stagnation and decline. *Research in the Teaching of English, 30*, 311–327.

Courts, P. (1991). *Literacy and empowerment: The meaning makers*. New York: Bergin & Garvey.

Crawford, J., & Haaland, C. (1972). Predecisional information seeking and subsequent conformity in the social influence process. *Journal of Personality and Social Psychology, 23*, 112–119.

Crowhurst, M., & Piche, G. (1979). Audience and mode of discourse effects on syntactic complexity in writing at two grade levels. *Research in the Teaching of English, 13*, 101–109.

Cummins, J. (1976). The influence of bilingualism on cognitive growth: A synthesis of research findings and explanatory hypothesis. *Working Papers on Bilingualism, 9*, 143.

Cummins, J. (1988). The cross-lingual dimensions of language proficiency: Implications for bilingual education and the optional age issue. *TESOL Quarterly, 2*, 175–187.

Daiker, D., Kerek, A., & Morenberg, M. (1978). Sentence-combining and syntactic maturity in freshman English. *College Composition and Communication, 29*, 36–41.

Davis, S. (1990). Natural restoration. *Whole Earth Reiew, 66*, 102–114.

Day, P., & Ulatowska, H. (1979). Perceptual, cognitive, and linguistic development after early hemispherectomy: Two case studies. *Brain and Language, 7*, 17–33.

Delpit, L. (1988). The silenced dialouge: Power and pedagogy in educating other people's children. *Harvard Educational Review, 58*, 280–298.

Dennis, M., & Kohn, B. (1975). Comprehension of syntax in infantile hemiplegics after cerebral hemidecortication: Left hemisphere superiority. *Brain and Language, 2*, 475–486.

Dennis, M., & Whitaker, H. (1976). Language acquisition following hemidecortication: Linguistic superiority of the left over the right hemisphere of right-handed people. *Brain and Language, 3*, 404–433.

Derrida, J. (1976). *Of grammatology*. (G. Spivak, Trans.). Baltimore: Johns Hopkins University Press.

De Ste. Croix, G. (1981). *The class struggle in the ancient world*. Ithaca, NY: Cornell University Press.

Diaz, D. (1986). The writing process and the ESL writer: Reinforcement from second language research. *Writing Instructor, 5*, 167–175.

Diederich, P., French, J., & Carlton, S. (1961). *Factors in judgments of writing quality*. Princeton, NJ: Educational Testing Service. (ERIC Document Reproduction Service No. ED 002 172).

Dillard, J. (1973). *Black English: Its history and usage in the United States*. New York: Vintage Books.

Dillon, G. (1981). *Constructing texts: Elements of a theory of composition and style*. Bloomington: Indiana University Press.

Docker, J. (1994). *Postmodernism and popular culture: A cultural history*. Cambridge, England: Cambridge University Press.

Dodds, E. (1951). *The Greeks and the irrational*. Berkeley: University of California Press.

Donaldson, M. (1978). *Children's minds*. London: Fontana.

Dulay, H., Burt, M., & Krashen, S. (1982). *Language two*. New York: Oxford University Press.

Duncan, S., & De Avila, E. (1979). Bilingualism and cognition: Some recent findings. *National Association of Bilingual Education Journal, 4,* 15–50.

Dyson, A. (1982). The emergence of visible language: The interrelationship between drawing and early writing. *Visible Language, 16,* 360–381.

Dyson, A. (1983). The role of oral language in early writing processes. *Research in the Teaching of English, 17,* 130.

Eco, U., Ivanov, V., & Rector, M. (1984). Frames of comic freedom. In T. Sebeok (Ed.), *Carnival!* Amsterdam: Mouton.

Edelsky, C. (1986). *Writing in a bilingual program: Había una vez* [Once upon a time]. Norwood, NJ: Ablex.

Edfelt, A. (1960). *Silent speech and silent reading.* Chicago: University of Chicago Press.

Elbow, P. (1973). *Writing without teachers.* New York: Oxford University Press.

Elbow, P. (1981). *Writing with power.* New York: Oxford University Press.

Elbow, P. (1991). Some thoughts on expressive discourse: A review essay. *Journal of Advanced Composition, 11,* 83–93.

Elbow, P., Berlin, J., & Bazerman, C. (1991). The second stage in writing across the curriculum. *College English, 53,* 209–212.

Elley, W., Barham, I., Lamb, H., & Wyllie, M. (1976). The role of grammar in a secondary school English curriculum. *New Zealand Journal of Educational Studies, 10,* 26–42.

Emig, J. (1971). *The composing processes of twelfth graders.* Urbana, IL: National Council of Teachers of English.

Englehard, G., Gordon, B., & Gabrielson, S. (1992). The influences of mode of discourse, experiential demand, and gender on the quality of student writing. *Research in the Teaching of English, 26,* 315–336.

Enos, R. (1993). *Greek rhetoric before Aristotle.* Prospect Heights, IL: Waveland Press.

Enos, R. (1995). *Roman rhetoric: Revolution and the Greek influence.* Prospect Heights, IL: Waveland Press.

Epstein, H. (1978). Growth spurts during brain development: Implications for educational policy and practice. In J. Chall & A. Mirsky (Eds.), *Education and the brain* (Vol. 2). Chicago: University of Chicago Press.

Erickson, F. (1984). Rhetoric, anecdote, and rhapsody: Coherence strategies in a conversation among black American adolescents. In D. Tannen (Ed.), *Coherence in spoken and written discourse.* Norwood, NJ: Ablex.

Eunapiaus. (1968). *Lives of the philosophers.* (W. Wright, Trans.). London: Heinemann.

Faigley, L. (1993). *Fragments of rationality: Postmodernity and the subject of composition.* Pittsburgh, PA: University of Pittsburgh Press.

Faigley, L., Cherry, R., Joliffe, D, & Skinner, A. (1985). *Assessing writers' knowledge and processes of composing.* Norwood, NJ: Ablex.

Farr, M., & Daniels, H. (1986). *Language diversity and writing instruction.* Urbana, IL: National Council of Teachers of English.

Farr, M., & Janda, M. (1985). Basic writing students: Investigating oral and written language. *Research in the Teaching of English, 19,* 62–83.

Farr Whitemann, M. (Ed.). (1981). *Variation in writing: Functional and linguistic-cultural differences.* Hillsdale, NJ: Lawrence Erlbaum Associates.

Fasold, R. (1972). *Tense marking in Black English: A linguistic and social analysis.* Washington, DC: Center for Applied Linguistics.

Ferreiro, E., & Teberosky, A. (1982). *Literacy before schooling.* London: Heinemann.

Finnegan, R. (1970). *Oral literature in Africa.* London: Oxford University Press.

Fitts, K., & France, A. (Eds.). (1995). *Left margins: Cultural studies and composition pedagogy*. Albany, NY: SUNY Press.

Flavell, J., Botkin, P., Fry, C., Wright, J., & Jarvis, P. (1968). *The development of role-taking and communication skills in children*. New York: Wiley.

Flesch, R. (1955). *Why Johnny can't read—and what you can do about it*. New York: Harper.

Flower, L., & Hayes, J. (1981). The pregnant pause: An inquiry into the nature of planning. *Research in the Teaching of English, 15,* 229–243.

Fodor, J. (1983). *The modularity of mind*. Cambridge, MA: MIT Press.

Fodor, J., Bever, T., & Garrett, M. (1974). *The psychology of language*. New York: McGraw-Hill.

Fodor, J., & Garrett, M. (1966). Some reflections on competence and performance. In J. Lyons & R. Wales (Eds.), *Psycholinguistics papers: Proceedings of the 1966 Edinburgh Conference*. Edinburgh: Edinburgh University Press.

Foster, S. (1985, March). The development of discourse topic skills by infants and young children. *Topics in Language Disorders,* 31–45.

Freire, P., & Macedo, D. (1987). *Literacy: Reading the word and the world*. South Hadley, MA: Bergin & Garvey.

Fries, C. (1962). *Linguistics and reading*. New York: Holt, Rinehart and Winston.

Furth, H. (1966). *Thinking without language: Psychological implications of deafness*. New York: The Free Press.

Gale, I. (1968). An experimental study of two fifth-grade language-arts programs: An analysis of the writing of children taught linguistic grammar compared to those taught traditional grammar. *Dissertation Abstracts, 28,* 4156A.

Garcia, E. (1983). *Early childhood bilingualism*. Albuquerque: University of New Mexico Press.

Gardner, R. (1980). On the validity of affective variables in second language acquisition: Conceptual, contextual, and statistical considerations. *Language Learning, 30,* 255–270.

Gardner, R. (1983). Learning another language: A true social psychological experiment. *Journal of Language and Social Psychology, 2,* 219–239.

Garibaldi, A. (1979). *Teamwork and feedback: Broadening the base of collaborative writing*. (ERIC Document Reproduction Service No. ED 174 994).

Gee, T. (1972). Students' responses to teachers' comments. *Research in the Teaching of English, 6,* 212–221.

Genishi, C. (1981). Code switching in Chicano six-year-olds. In R. Duran (Ed.), *Latino language and communicative behavior.* Norwood, NJ: Ablex.

Gibson, E., & Levin, H. (1975). *The psychology of reading*. Cambridge, MA: MIT Press.

Gilbert, J. (1987). Patterns and possibilities for basic writers. *Journal of Basic Writing, 6,* 37–52.

Giroux, H. (1987). Literacy and the pedagogy of political empowerment. In P. Freire & D. Macedo (Eds.), *Literacy: Reading the word and the world*. South Hadley, MA: Bergin & Garvey.

Glass, A., Holyoak, K., & Santa, J. (1979). *Cognition*. Reading, MA: Addison-Wesley.

Glucksberg, S., & Danks, J. (1969). Grammatical structure and recall: A function of the space in immediate memory or recall delay? *Perception and Psychophysics, 6,* 113–117.

Goodlad, J. (1984). *A place called school: Prospects for the future*. New York: McGraw-Hill.

Goodman, K. (1967). Reading: A psycholinguistic guessing game. *Journal of the Reading Specialist, 6,* 126–135.

Goodman, K. (1973). *Miscue analysis*. Urbana, IL: ERIC Clearinghouse on Reading and Communication Skills.

Goody, J. (Ed.). (1968). *Literacy in traditional societies*. Cambridge, England: Cambridge University Press.

Goody, J. (1972). Literacy and the nonliterate. In R. Disch (Ed.), *The future of literacy*. Englewood Cliffs, NJ: Prentice-Hall.

Goody, J. (1977). *The domestication of the savage mind*. Cambridge, England: Cambridge University Press.

Goody, J. (1987). *The interface between the oral and the written*. Cambridge, England: Cambridge University Press.

Goody, J., & Watt, I. (1968). The consequences of literacy. In J. Goody (Ed.), *Literacy in traditional societies*. Cambridge, England: Cambridge University Press.

Graff, H. (1987). *The legacies of literacy: Continuities and contradictions in western culture and society*. Bloomington: Indiana University Press.

Grant, M. (1992). *A social history of Greece and Rome*. New York: Macmillan.

Graves, D. (1975). Examination of the writing processes of seven year old children. *Research in the Teaching of English, 9*, 227–241.

Graves, D. (1979). Let children show us how to help them write. *Visible Language, 13*. 16–28.

Graves, D. (1981). The growth and development of first grade writers. In D. Graves (Ed.), *A case study observing the development of primary children's composing, spelling, and motor behaviors during the writing process: Final Report*. Durham: University of New Hampshire Press.

Green, E. (1973). An experimental study of sentence combining to improve written syntactic fluency in fifth-grade children. *Dissertation Abstracts International, 33*, 4057A.

Green, S. (1992). Mining texts in reading to write. *Journal of Advanced Composition, 12*, 151–170.

Greenberg, K., Wiener, H., & Donovan, T. (Eds.). (1986). *Writing assessment: Issues and strategies*. New York: Longman.

Greenfield, P. (1972). Oral or written language: The consequences for cognitive development in Africa, the United States and England. *Language and Speech, 15*, 169–177.

Greenfield, P., & Bruner, J. (1966). Culture and cognitive growth. *International Journal of Psychology, 1*, 23–59.

Griswold del Castillo, R. (1984). *La familia: Chicano families in the urban Southwest 1848 to the present*. Notre Dame, IN: Notre Dame University Press.

Gumperz, J. (1982). *Discourse strategies*. Cambridge, England: Cambridge University Press.

Gunderson, B., & Johnson, D. (1980). Promoting positive attitudes toward learning a foreign language by using cooperative learning groups. *Foreign Language Annals, 13*, 39–46.

Gundlach, R. (1981). On the nature and development of children's writing. In C. Frederiksen, M. Whiteman, & J. Dominic (Eds.), *Writing: The nature, development, and teaching of written communication*. Hillsdale, NJ: Lawrence Erlbaum Associates.

Gundlach, R. (1982). Children as writers: The beginnings of learning to write. In M. Nystrand (Ed.), *What writers know: The language, process, and structure of written discourse*. New York: Academic Press.

Gundlach, R. (1983). *How children learn to write: Perspectives on children's writing for educators and parents*. Washington, DC: National Institute of Education.

Guthrie, W. (1971). *The Sophists*. Cambridge, England: Cambridge University Press.

Hakuta, K. (1984). Bilingual education in the public eye: A case study of New Haven, Connecticut. *NABE Journal, 9*, 53–76.

Hakuta, K. (1986). *Mirror of language*. New York: Basic Books.

Hakuta, K., & Diaz, R. (1984). The relationship between bilingualism and cognitive ability: A critical discussion and some new longitudinal data. In K. Nelson (Ed.), *Children's language* (Vol. 5). Hillsdale, NJ: Lawrence Erlbaum Associates.

Hall, M. (1972). *The language experience approach for the culturally disadvantaged.* Newark, DE: International Reading Association.

Halliday, M. (1979). One child's protolanguage. In M. Bullowa (Ed.), *Before speech.* Cambridge, England: Cambridge University Press.

Halloran, M. (1993). Conversation versus declamation as models of written discourse. In T. Enos (Ed.), *Learning from the histories of rhetoric: Essays in honor of Winifred Bryan Horner.* Carbondale: Southern Illinois University Press.

Hardyck, C., & Petrinovich, L. (1967). Subvocal speech and comprehension level as a function of the difficulty level of reading material. *Journal of Verbal Learning and Verbal Behavior, 9,* 647–652.

Harris, J. (1989). The idea of community in the study of writing. *College Composition and Communication, 40,* 11–22.

Harris, R. (1993). *The linguistics wars.* New York: Oxford University Press.

Harrold, V. (1995). An investigation of faculty attitudes and oral communication programs for African American speakers of Black English at selected two-year private and public institutions of higher education in Michigan. *Dissertation Abstracts International, 56,* 1676.

Harste, J., Burke, C., & Woodward, V. (1983). *Children's language and world: Initial encounters with print.* (Final Report No. NIE-G-79-0132.) Bloomington, IN: Language Education Departments.

Harter, S. (1981). A model of intrinsic mastery motivation in children: Individual differences and developmental change. In A. Collins (Ed.), *Minnesota Symposium on Child Psychology* (Vol. 14). Hillsdale, NJ: Lawrence Erlbaum Associates.

Haswell, R., & Wyche-Smith, S. (1994). Adventuring into writing assessment. *College Composition and Communication, 45,* 220–236.

Hatch, E. (1978). *Second language acquisition: A book of readings.* Rowley, MA: Newbury House.

Haugen, E. (1966). *Language conflict and language planning: The case of modern Norwegian.* Cambridge, MA: Harvard University Press.

Hausner, R. (1976). Interaction of selected student personality factors and teachers' comments in a sequentially developed composition curriculum. *Dissertation Abstracts International, 36,* 5768A.

Havelock, E. (1982). *The literate revolution in Greece and its cultural consequences.* Princeton, NJ: Princeton University Press.

Hawisher, G. (1987). The effects of word processing on the revision strategies of college freshmen. *Research in the Teaching of English, 21,* 145–159.

Hawkins, T. (1980). The relationship between revision and the social dimension of peer tutoring. *College English, 40,* 64–68.

Hayes, B. (1992). *On what to teach the undergraduates: Some changing orthodoxies in phonological theory.* Paper presented at the International Conference on Linguistics, Seoul, Korea.

Heath, S. (1981). *Language in the USA.* Cambridge, England: Cambridge University Press.

Heath, S. (1983). *Ways with words.* Cambridge, England: Cambridge University Press.

Herrnstein, R., & Murray, C. (1994). *The bell curve: Intelligence and class structure in American life.* New York: Free Press.

Hillocks, G. (1986). *Research on written composition: New directions for teaching.* Urbana, IL: National Conference on Research in English.

Hirsch, E. (1977). *The philosophy of composition*. Chicago: University of Chicago Press.

Hoenigswald, H. (1978). The annus mirabilis 1876 and posterity. *Transactions of the Philosophical Society, 14*, 191–203.

Hoffer, B. (1975). Spanish interference in the English written in south Texas high schools. In E. Dubois & B. Hofrer (Eds.), *Papers in southwest English: Research techniques and prospects*. San Antonio, TX: Trinity University Press.

Howie, S. (1979). A study: The effects of sentence combining practice on the writing ability and reading level of ninth grade students. *Dissertation Abstracts International, 40*, 1980A.

Hudson, R. (1980). *Sociolinguistics*. Cambridge, England: Cambridge University Press.

Huff, R., & Kline, C. (1987). *The contemporary writing curriculum: Rehearsing, composing, and valuing*. New York: Teachers College Press.

Hughes, M. (1975). *Egocentrism in preschool children*. Unpublished doctoral dissertation, Edinburgh University, Scotland.

Hunt, J. (1975). Reflections on a decade of early education. *Journal of Abnormal Child Psychology, 3*, 275–336.

Hunt, K. (1964). *Differences in grammatical structures written at three grade levels*. (Cooperative Research Project No. 1998). Tallahassee: Florida State University.

Hunt, K. (1965). *Grammatical structures written at three grade levels*. (NCTE Research Report No. 3). Champaign, IL: National Council of Teachers of English.

Huot, B. (1996). Toward a new theory of writing assessment. *College Composition and Communication, 47*, 549–566.

Hymes, D. (1971). Competence and performance in linguistic theory. In R. Huxley & E. Ingram (Eds.), *Language acquisition: Models and methods*. New York: Academic Press.

Jarratt, S. (1991). *Rereading the Sophists: Classical rhetoric refigured*. Carbondale: Southern Illinois University Press.

Jarvis, L., Danks, J., & Merriman, W. (1995). The effect of bilingualism on cognitive ability: A test of the level of bilingual hypothesis. *Applied Psycholinguistics, 16*, 293–308.

Jencks, C. (1972). *Inequality: A reassessment of the effect of family and schooling in America*. New York: Basic Books.

Jensen, A. (1969). How much can we boost IQ and scholastic achievement? *Harvard Educational Review, 39*, 11–23.

Johnson, D. (1980). Group processes: Influences of student-vs-student interaction on school outcomes. In J. McMillan (Ed.), *The social psychology of school learning*. New York: Holt, Rinehart and Winston.

Johnson, D. (1993). The relationship of reading, attitudes, and learning strategies to writing in college freshmen. *Dissertation Abstracts International, 53*, 3815A.

Johnson, D., & Ahlgren, A. (1976). Relationship between students' attitudes about cooperation and competition and attitudes toward schooling. *Journal of Educational Psychology, 68*, 92–102.

Johnson, D., Johnson, R., & Maruyama, G. (1983). Interdependence and interpersonal attraction among heterogeneous and homogeneous individuals: A theoretical formulation and a meta-analysis of the research. *Review of Educational Research, 53*, 554.

Johnson, T., & Louis, D. (1985). *Literacy through literature*. Melbourne, Australia: Methuen.

Johnson, D., Maruyama, G., Johnson, R., Nelson, D., & Skon, L. (1981). The effects of cooperative, competitive, and individualistic goal structures or achievement: A meta-analysis. *Psychology Bulletin, 89*, 47–62.

Johnson-Laird, P. (1983). *Mental models*. Cambridge, MA: Harvard University Press.

Jones, S., & Tetroe, J. (1983). Composing in a second language. In A. Matsuhashi (Ed.), *Writing in real time*. Norwood, NJ: Ablex.

Kantor, K. (1985). Questions, explorations, and discoveries. *English Journal, 7,* 90–92.

Karmiloff-Smith, A. (1992). *Beyond modularity: A developmental perspective on cognitive sciecne.* Cambridge, MA: MIT Press.

Kay, P., & Sankoff, G. (1974). A language-universals approach to pidgins and creoles. In D. DeCamp & I. Hancock (Eds.), *Pidgins and creoles: Current trends and prospects.* Washington, DC: Georgetown University Press.

Kelso, J. (1995). *Dynamic patterns: The self-organization of brain and behavior.* Cambridge, MA: MIT Press.

Kennedy, G. (1980). *Classical rhetoric and its Christian and secular tradition from ancient to modern times.* Chapel Hill: University of North Carolina Press.

Kennedy, G. (1991). *Aristotle on rhetoric: A theory of civic discourse.* New York: Oxford University Press.

Kent, T. (1991). On the very idea of a discourse community. *College Composition and Communication, 42,* 425–445.

Kerek, A., Daiker, D., & Morenberg, M. (1980). Sentence combining and college composition. *Perceptual and Motor Skills, 51,* 1059–1157.

Killian, L. (1971). WlSC, Illinois test of psycholinguistic abilities and Bender Visual-Motor Gestalt test performance of Spanish-American kindergarten and first grade school children. *Journal of Consulting and Clinical Psychology, 37,* 383.

Kinneavy, J. (1971). *A theory of discourse.* Englewood Cliffs, NJ: Prentice-Hall. (Reprinted 1980. New York: Norton)

Kinneavy, J. (1979). Sentence combining in a comprehensive language framework. In D. Daiker, A. Kerek, & M. Morenberg (Eds.), *Sentence combining and the teaching of writing.* Conway, AR: University of Akron and University of Central Arkansas.

Kinneavy, J. (1982). Restoring the humanities: The return of rhetoric from exile. In J. Murphy (Ed.), *The rhetorical tradition and modern writing.* New York: Modern Language Associates.

Kintsch, W., & van Dijk, T. (1978). Toward a model of text comprehension and production. *Psychological Review, 85,* 363–394.

Kirscht, J., Levine, R., & Reiff, J. (1994). Evolving paradigms: WAC and the rhetoric of inquiry. *College Composition and Communication, 45,* 369–380.

Kohn, B. (1980). Right-hemisphere speech representation and comprehension of syntax after left cerebral injury. *Brain and Language, 9,* 350–361.

Krashen, S. (1980). The input hypothesis. In J. Alatis (Ed.), *Current issues in bilingual education.* Washington, DC: Georgetown University Press.

Krashen, S. (1981a). *The role of input (reading) and instruction in developing writing ability.* (Working paper). Los Angeles: University of Southern California.

Krashen, S. (1981b). *Second language acquisition and second language learning.* Oxford, England: Pergamon.

Krashen, S. (1982). *Principles and practice in second language acquisition.* Oxford, England: Pergamon.

Krashen, S. (1985). *Writing research, theory, and applications.* New York: Pergamon.

Labov, W. (1964). Phonological indices to social stratification. In J. Gumperz & D. Hymes (Eds.), *The ethnography of communication.* Washington, DC: American Anthropological Association.

Labov, W. (1966). *The social stratification of English in New York City.* Washington, DC: Georgetown University Press.

Labov, W. (1969). Contraction, deletion, and inherent variability of the English copula. *Language, 45,* 715–762.

Labov, W. (1970). *The study of nonstandard English.* Urbana, IL: National Council of Teachers of English.

Labov, W. (1971). The notion of system in creole studies. In D. Hymes (Ed.), *Pidginization and creolization of language*. Cambridge, England: Cambridge University Press.

Labov, W. (1972a). *Language in the inner city: Studies in the Black English vernacular*. Philadelphia: University of Pennsylvania Press.

Labov, W. (1972b). *Sociolinguistic patterns*. Philadelphia: University of Pennsylvania Press.

Labov, W. (1980). The social origins of sound change. In W. Labov (Ed.), *Locating language in time and space*. New York: Academic Press.

Labov, W. (1994). *Principles of linguistic change: Internal factors*. London: Blackwell.

Lakoff, G. (1987). *Women, fire, and dangerous things*. Chicago: University of Chicago Press.

Langacker, R. (1987). *Foundations of cognitive grammar: Vol. 1. Theoretical prerequisites*. Stanford, CA: Stanford University Press.

Langacker, R. (1990). *Concept, image, and symbol: The cognitive basis of grammar*. New York: de Gruyter.

Laughlin, P., & McGlynn, R. (1967). Cooperative versus competitive concept attainment as a function of sex and stimulus display. *Journal of Personality and Social Psychology, 7*, 398–402.

Lee, J. (1987). Prewriting assignments across the curriculum. In C. Olson (Ed.), *Practical ideas for teaching writing as a process*. Sacramento, CA: State Department of Education.

Lehmann, W. (1983). *Language: An introduction*. New York: Random House.

Leiber, J. (1975). *Noam Chomsky: A philosophic overview*. New York: St. Martin's Press.

Lenneberg, E. (1967). *Biological foundations of language*. New York: Wiley.

Lévi-Strauss, C. (1966). *The savage mind*. Chicago: University of Chicago Press.

Lévy-Bruhl, L. (1926). *How natives think*. (L. Clare, Trans.). New York: Knopf.

Lévy-Bruhl, L. (1975). *The notebooks on primitive mentality* (P. Riviere, Trans.). New York: Harper & Row.

Lindemann, E. (1993a). Freshman composition: No place for literature. *College English, 55*, 311–316.

Lindemann, E. (1993b). *A rhetoric for writing teachers* (3rd ed.) New York: Oxford University Press.

Loban, W. (1976). *Language development: Kindergarten through grade twelve*. (NCTE Research Report No. 18). Urbana, IL: National Council of Teachers of English.

Love, G., & Payne, M. (Eds.). (1969). *Contemporary essays on style*. Glenview, IL: Scott, Foresman.

Luges, A. (1994). A descriptive study of writing in a secondary ESL classroom. *Dissertation Abstracts International, 56*, 482.

Lunsford, A., Moglen, H., & Slevin, J. (1990). *The right to literacy*. New York: Modern Language Association.

Luria, A. (1976). *Cognitive development: Its cultural and social foundations*. (M. Lopez-Morrillas & L. Solotaroff, Trans.). Cambridge, MA: Harvard University Press.

Lyons, J. (1970). *Noam Chomsky*. New York: Penguin.

Lyons, J. (1977). *Semantics* (Vol. 1). Cambridge, England: Cambridge University Press.

Lyons, J. (1977). *Semantics* (Vol. 2). Cambridge, England: Cambridge University Press.

Macaulay, R. (1973). Double standards. *American Anthropologist, 75*, 1324–1337.

Mack, N., & Zebroski, J. (1992). Remedial critical consciousness? *Pre/Text, 13*, 82–101.

Macnamara, J. (1972). Cognitive basis of language learning in infants. *Psychological Review, 79*, 1–13.

Macrorie, K. (1968). *Writing to be read* (3rd ed.). Upper Montclair, NJ: Boynton/Cook.

Macrorie, K. (1970a). *Telling writing* (4th ed.). Upper Montclair, NJ: Boynton/Cook.

Malt, B. (1985). The role of discourse structure in understanding anaphora. *Journal of Memory and Language, 24*, 271–289.

Mano, S. (1986). Television: A surprising acquisition source for literacy. *Writing Instructor, 5*, 104–111.

Mansfield, M. (1993). Real world writing and the English curriculum. *College Composition and Communication, 44*, 69–83.

Marcuse, H. (1941). *Reason and revolution: Hegel and the rise of social theory*. Boston: Beacon Press.

Marcuse, H. (1955). *Eros and civilization: A philosophical inquiry into Freud*. Boston: Beacon Press.

Marcuse, H. (1964). *One-dimensional man: Studies in the ideology of advanced industrial society*. Boston: Beacon Press.

Marcuse, H. (1965). Repressive tolerance. In R. Wolff, B. Moore, & H. Marcuse (Eds.), *A critique of pure tolerance*. Boston: Beacon Press.

Mathews, M. (1966). *Teaching to read, historically considered*. Chicago: University of Chicago Press.

Matsuhashi, A. (1981). Pausing and planning: The tempo of written discourse production. *Research in the Teaching of English, 15*, 113–134.

McClure, E. (1981). Formal and functional aspects of the code-switched discourse of bilingual children. In R. Duran (Ed.), *Latino language and communicative behavior: Advances in discourse processes* (Vol. 6). Norwood. NJ: Ablex.

McCrum, R., Cran, W., & MacNeil, R. (1986). *The story of English*. New York: Viking.

McGuigan, F. (1966). *Thinking: Studies of covert language processes*. New York: Appleton.

McGuigan, F. (1978). *Cognitive psychophysiology: Principles of covert behavior*. Englewood Cliffs, NJ: Prentice-Hall.

McKowski, N. (1993). A postmodern critique of the modern projects of Fredric Jameson and Patricia Bizzell. *Journal of Advanced Composition, 13*, 329–344.

Mellon, J. (1969). *Transformational sentence-combining: A method for enhancing the development of syntactic fluency in English composition*. (NCTE Research Report No. 10). Champaign, IL: National Council of Teachers of English.

Mencken, H. (1936). *The American language: An inquiry into the development of English in the United States*. New York: Knopf.

Michael, J. (1995). Valuing differences: Portnoy's first year. *Assessing Writing, 2*, 67–90.

Michaels, B. (1982). *Black rainbow*. New York: Congdon & Weed.

Miller, C. (1993). Rhetoric and community: The problem of the one and the many. In T. Enos & S. Bron (Eds.), *Defining the new rhetorics*. Newbury Park, CA: Sage.

Miller, G. (1962). Some psychological studies of grammar. *American Psychologist, 17*, 748–762.

Miller, G., & McKean, K. (1964). A chronometric study of some relations between sentences. *Quarterly Journal of Experimental Psychology, 16*, 297–308.

Miller, J., Chapman, R., Branston, M., & Reichle, J. (1980). Language comprehension in sensorimotor stages V and VI. *Journal of Speech and Hearing Research, 23*, 284–311.

Miller, S. (1982). Classical practice and contemporary basics. In S. Murphy (Ed.), *The rhetorical tradition and modern writing*. Davis, CA: Hermaguras Press.

Moffett, J. (1968). *Teaching the universe of discourse*. Boston: Houghton Mifflin.

Moffett, J. (1985). Liberating inner speech. *College Composition and Communication, 36*, 304–308.

Murphy, J. (1974). *Rhetoric in the middle ages: A history of rhetorical theory from St. Augustine to the Renaissance*. Berkeley: University of California Press.

Murray, D. (1982). *Learning by teaching*. Upper Montclair, NJ: Boynton/Cook.

The National Assessment of Educational Progress. (1994). *NAEP reading: A first look: Findings from the National Assessment of Educational progress.* Paul Williams. Washington, DC: N.S. Department of Education.

Nelson, K. (1973). Structure and strategy in learning to talk. *Monographs of the Society for Research in Child Development, 38(1–2, Serial No. 149).*

Norris, C. (1993). *The truth about postmodernism.* London: Blackwell.

North, S. (1987). *The making of knowledge in composition: Portrait of an emerging field.* Upper Montclair, NJ: Boynton/Cook.

O'Hare, F. (1972). *Sentence combining: Improving student writing without formal grammar instruction.* (NCTE Committee on Research Report Series, No. 15). Urbana, IL: National Council of Teachers of English.

Ober, J. (1989). *Mass and elite in democratic Athens.* Princeton, NJ: Princeton University Press.

Ohmann, R. (1969). Prolegomena to the analysis of prose style. In G. Love & M. Payne (Eds.), *Contemporary essays on style.* Glenview, IL: Scott, Foresman.

Olson, D. (1977). From utterance to text: The bias of language in speech and writing. *Harvard Educational Review, 47,* 257–281.

Olson, D. (1987). Development of the metalanguage of literacy. *Interchange, 18,* 136–146.

Ong, W. (1978). Literacy and orality in our time. *ADE Bulletin, 58,* 1–7.

Ong, W. (1982). *Orality and literacy: The terminologizing of the word.* London: Methuen.

Ostwald, M. (1986). *From popular sovereignty to the sovereignty of law.* Berkeley: University of California Press.

Owens, D. (1994). *Resisting writings (and the boundaries of composition).* Dallas, TX: Southern Methodist University Press.

Paratore, J., Homza, A., Krol-Sinclair, B., Lewis-Barrow, T., Melzei, G., Stergis, R., & Haynes, H. (1995). Shifting boundaries in home and school responsibilities: The construction of home-based literacy portfolios by immigrant parents and their children. *Research in the Teaching of English, 29,* 367–389.

Parker, R. (1979). From Sputnik to Dartmouth: Trends in the teaching of composition. *English Journal, 68(6),* 32–37.

Patterson, O. (1991). *Freedom.* New York: Basic Books.

Peal, E., & Lambert, W. E. (1962). The relation of bilingualism to intelligence. *Psychological Monographs, 76* (27, Whole #546).

Peck, M. (1982). *An investigation of tenth-grade students' writing.* Washington, DC: United Press of America.

Pedersen, E. (1978). Improving syntactic and semantic fluency in writing of language arts students through extended practice in sentence-combining. *Dissertation Abstracts International, 38,* 5892-A.

Penalosa, F. (1980). *Chicano sociolinguistics: A brief introduction.* Rowley, MA: Newbury House.

Penfield, J., & Ornstein-Garcia, J. (1985). *Chicano English: An ethnic contact dialect.* Amsterdam: John Benjamins.

Perron, J. (1977). *The impact of mode on written syntactic complexity.* Athens: University of Georgia Studies in Language Education Series.

Peterson, L. (1985). Repetition and metaphor in the early stages of composing. *College Composition and Communication, 36,* 429–449.

Petrosky, A. (1990). Ritual poverty and literacy in the Mississippi delta: Dilemmas, paradoxes, and conundrums. In A. Lunsford, H. Moglen, & J. Slevin (Eds.), *The right to literacy.* New York: Modern Language Association.

Piaget, J. (1953). *The origins of intelligence in the child.* London: Routledge & Kegan Paul.

Piaget, J. (1955). *The child's construction of reality.* London: Routledge & Kegan Paul.

Piaget, J. (1962). *Plays, dreams, and imitation in childhood*. New York: Norton.

Piaget, J. (1974). *The language and thought of the child*. New York: New American Library.

Piaget, J., & Inhelder, B. (1969). *The psychology of the child*. New York: Basic Books.

Pinker, S. (1994). *The language instinct: How the mind creates language*. New York: Morrow.

Plato. (1937). Apology. In B. Jowett (Ed. & Trans.), *The dialogues of Plato* (Vol. 1). New York: Random House.

Plato. (1961). Letter VII. In E. Hamilton & H. Cairns (Eds. & Trans.), *The collected dialogues of Plato, including the letters*. Princeton, NJ: Princeton University Press.

Poe, E. A. (1962). To Helen. In K. Campbell (Ed.), *The poems of Edgar Allen Poe*. New York: Russell & Russell.

Putnam, H. (1975). The meaning of meaning. In H. Putnam (Ed.), *Philosophical papers: Vol. 2. Mind, language, and reality*. Cambridge, England: Cambridge University Press.

Quine, W. (1960). *Word and object*. Cambridge, MA: MIT Press.

Raimes, A. (1985). What unskilled ESL students do as they write: A classroom study of composing. *TESOL Quarterly, 19*, 229–258.

Raimes, A. (1986). Teaching ESL writing: Fitting what we do to what we know. *Writing Instructor, 5*, 153–166.

Raschke, C. (1996). *Fire and roses: Postmodernity and the thought of the body*. Albany, NY: SUNY Press.

Restak, R. (1979). *The brain: The last frontier*. New York: Warner Books.

Rice, M., & Kemper, S. (1984). *Child language and cognition*. Baltimore: University Park Press.

Robinson, J. (1990). *Conversations on the written word: Essays on language and literacy*. Upper Montclair, NJ: Boynton/Cook.

Rohman, D., & Wlecke, A. (1964). *Prewriting: The construction and application of models to concept formation in writing*. East Lansing: Michigan State University Press.

Rosch, E. (1973). Natural categories. *Cognitive Psychology, 4, 328–350*.

Rose, M. (1984). *Writer's block: The cognitive dimension*. Carbondale: Southern Illinois University Press.

Rose, M. (1988). Narrowing the mind and page: Remedial writers and cognitive reductionism. *College Composition and Communication, 39*, 267–302.

Rumelhart, D., & McClelland, J. (1986). *Parallel distributed processing: Explorations in the microstructure of cognition* (Vol. 1). Cambridge, MA: MIT Press.

Rumelhart, D., & McClellan, J. (1986). *Parallel distributed processing: Explorations in the microstructure of cognition* (Vol. 2). Cambridge, MA: MIT Press.

Russell, D. (1987). Writing across the curriculum and the communications movement: Some lessons from the past. *College Composition and Communication, 38*, 184–194.

St. Augustine. (1962). *The confessions of St. Augustine*. (R. Warner, Trans.). New York: New American Library.

St. Augustine. (1958). *On Christian doctrine*. (D. Robertson, Trans.). Indianapolis, IN: Bobbs-Merrill.

Sanchez, N. (1987, June). Bilingual training can be a barrier to academic achievement for students. *Chronicle of Higher Education*.

Sanchez, R. (1983). *Chicano discourse: Socio-historic perspectives*. Rowley, MA: Newbury House.

Sanford, A., & Garrod, S. (1981). *Understanding written language*. New York: Wiley.

Scardamalia, M., & Bereiter, C. (1983). The development of evaluative, diagnostic, and remedial capabilities in children's composing. In M. Martlew (Ed.), *The psychology of written language: A developmental approach*. London: Wiley.

Scargill, M., & Penner, P. (Eds.). (1966). *Looking at language: Essays in introductory linguistics*. Glenview, IL: Scott, Foresman.

Schank, R., & Abelson, R. (1977). *Scripts, plans, goals and understanding*. Hillsdale, NJ: Lawrence Erlbaum Associates.

Schlesinger, I. (1971). The production of utterances and language acquisition. In D. Slobin (Ed.), *The ontogenesis of grammar*. New York: Academic Press.

Schroeder, T. (1973). The effects of positive and corrective written teacher feedback on selected writing behaviors of fourth-grade children. *Dissertation Abstracts International, 34*, 2935-A.

Scinto, L. (1986). *Written language and psychological development*. San Diego: Harcourt Brace Jovanovich.

Scollon, R., & Scollon, S. (1979). *The literate two-year-old: The fictionalization of self*. Austin, TX: Southeast Regional Laboratory.

Scribner, S., & Cole, M. (1981). *The psychology of literacy*. Cambridge, MA: Harvard University Press.

Searle, J. (1969). *Speech acts: An essay in the philosophy of language*. New York: Cambridge University Press.

Searle, J. (1992). *The rediscovery of the mind*. Cambridge, MA: MIT Press.

Searle, J. (1995). *The construction of social reality*. New York: Free Press.

Seidman, S. (Ed.). (1994). *The postmodern turn: New perspectives on social theory*. Cambridge, England: Cambridge University Press.

Self, C. (1986). Reading as a writing strategy: Two case studies. In B. Petersen (Ed.), *Convergences. Transactions in reading and writing*. Urbana, IL: National Council of Teachers of English.

Shankweiler, D., & Crain, S. (1986). Language mechanisms and reading disorder: A modular approach. *Cognition, 10*, 139–168.

Shaughnessy, M. (1977). *Errors and expectations: A guide for the teacher of basic writing*. New York: Oxford University Press.

Shayer, D. (1972). *The teaching of English in schools, 1900–1970*. London: Routledge & Kegan Paul.

Shin, F. (1994). Korean parents' perceptions and attitudes of bilingual education. *Dissertation Abstracts International, 56*, 850.

Skinner, B. F. (1957). *Verbal behavior*. New York: Appleton-Century-Crofts.

Slobin, D. (1973). Cognitive prerequisites for the development of grammar. In C. Ferguson & D. Slobin (Eds.), *Studies of child language development*. New York: Holt, Rinehart & Winston.

Slobin, D. (1977). Language change in childhood and history. In J. Macnamara (Ed.), *Language, learning and thought*. New York: Academic Press.

Slobin, D. (1982). Universal and particular in the acquisition of language. In L. Gleitman & E. Wanner (Eds.), *Language acquisition: State of the art*. New York: Cambridge University Press.

Slobin, D., & Welsh, C. (1973). Elicited imitation as a research tool in developmental psycholinguistics. In C. Ferguson & D. Slobin (Eds.), *Studies of child language development*. New York: Holt, Rinehart & Winston.

Smith, F. (1972). *Understanding reading*. New York: Holt, Rinehart and Winston.

Smith, F. (1983). *Essays into literacy*. London: Heinemann.

Smith, W. (1993). Assessing the reliability and adequacy of using holistic scoring of essays as a college composition placement program techique. In M. Williams & B. Huot (Eds.), *Validating holistic scoring for writing assessment*. Cresskill, NJ: Hampton.

Sokolov, A. (1972). *Inner speech and thought* (G. Onischenko, Trans.). New York: Plenum.

Sommers, N. (1982). Responding to student writing. *College Composition and Communication, 33*, 148–156.

Spear, K. (1993). *Peer response groups in action: Writing together in secondary schools.* Portsmouth, NH: Boynton/Cook.

Staats, A., & Butterfield, W. (1965). Treatment of nonreading in a culturally deprived juvenile delinquent: An application of reinforcement principles. *Child Development, 4,* 925–942.

Steinbeck, J. (1937). *Of mice and men.* New York: Collier & Son.

Sullivan, M. (1978). The effects of sentence-combining exercises on syntactic maturity, quality of writing, reading ability, and attitudes of students in grade eleven. *Dissertation Abstracts International*, 39, 1197-A.

Sullivan, M. (1979). Parallel sentence-combining studies in grades nine and eleven. In D. Daiker, A. Kerek, & M. Morenberg (Eds.), *Sentence combining and the teaching of writing.* Conway, AR: University of Akron and University of Central Arkansas.

Tannen, D. (1982). Oral and literate strategies in spoken and written narratives. *Language, 58,* 1–21.

Tannen, D. (1990). *You just don't understand: Women and men in conversation.* New York: Morrow.

Tarvers, J. (1988). *Teaching writing: Theories and practices.* Glenview, IL: Scott, Foresman.

Tate, G. (1993). A place for literature in freshman composition. *College English, 55,* 317–321.

Trevarthen, C. (1974). Communication and cooperation in early infancy: A description of primary intersubjectivity. In M. Bullowa (Ed.), *Before speech: The beginnings of human communication.* Cambridge, England: Cambridge University Press.

Trimbur, J. (1987). Beyond cognition: The voices of inner speech. *Rhetoric Review, 5,* 211–221.

Trudgill, P. (1974). *Sociolinguistics: An introduction.* New York: Penguin.

Tufte, V. (1971). *Grammar as style.* New York: Holt, Rinehart & Winston.

Turner, C. (1973). *Stylistics.* London: Penguin.

Ullmann, J. (1963). *Semantics: An introduction to the study of meaning.* Oxford: Basil Blackwell & Mott.

Vaillant, J. (1977). *Adaptation to life.* Boston: Little, Brown.

Vernant, J. (1982). *The origins of Greek thought.* Ithaca, NY: Cornell University Press.

Vygotsky, L. (1962). *Thought and language.* Cambridge, MA: MIT Press.

Vygotsky, L. (1978). *Mind in society.* (M. Cole, V. John-Steiner, S. Scribner, & E. Souberman, Eds.). Cambridge, MA: Harvard University Press.

Wadsworth, O. (1971). *Over in the meadow.* New York: Scholastic.

Wald, B. (1985). Motivation for language choice behavior of elementary Mexican-American children. In E. Garcia & R Padilla (Eds.), *Advances in bilingual education research.* Tucson: University of Arizona Press.

Walters, K. (1990). Language, logic, and literacy. In A. Lunsford, H. Moglen, & J. Sledd (Eds.), *The right to literacy.* New York: Modern Language Associates.

Walvoord, B. (1996a). The future of writing across the curriculum. *College English, 58,* 58–79.

Walvoord, B. (1996b). *WAC in the long run: A study of faculty in three writing-across-the-curriculum programs.* Urbana, IL: National Council of Teachers of English.

Warren, R., & Warren, R. (1970). Auditory illusions and confusions. *Scientific American, 223,* 30–36.

Waterfall, C. (1978). An experimental study of sentence combining as a means of increasing syntactic maturity and writing quality in the compositions of college students enrolled in remedial English classes. *Dissertation Abstracts International, 38*, 7131A.

Watson, R. (1985). Toward a theory of definition. *Journal of Child Language, 12*, 181–197.

Weber, H. (1968). The study of oral reading errors: A survey of the literature. *Reading Research Quarterly, 4*, 96–119.

Welch, K. (1990). Writing instruction in ancient Athens after 450 BC. In J. Murphy (Ed.), *A short history of writing instruction from ancient Greece to twentieth-century America.* Davis, CA: Hermagoras Press.

Wernicke, C. (1874). *Der aphasische symptomenkomplex* [Aphasia]. Breslau, Poland: Cohen & Weigert.

White, E. (1986). *Teaching and assessing writing.* San Francisco: Jossey-Bass.

White, L. (1977). Error analysis and error correction in adult learners of English as a second language. *Working Papers in Bilingualism, 13*, 42–58.

White, R. (1965). The effect of structural linguistics on improving English composition compared to that of prescriptive grammar or the absence of grammar instruction. *Dissertation Abstracts, 25*, 5032.

Whitehead, C. (1966). The effect of grammar diagramming on student writing skills. *Dissertation Abstracts, 26*, 3710.

Whorf, B. L. (1956). *Language, thought and reality: Selected writings of Benjamin Lee Whorf* (J. B. Carroll, Ed.). Cambridge, MA: MIT Press.

Williams, J. (1976). *Sentence openers.* Unpublished study.

Williams, J. (1983). Covert language behavior during writing. *Research in the Teaching of English, 17*, 301–312.

Williams, J. (1985). Coherence and cognitive style. *Written Communication, 2*, 473–491.

Williams, J. (1987). Covert linguistic behavior during writing tasks: Psychophysiological differences between above-average and below-average writers. *Written Communication, 4*, 310–328.

Williams, J. (1992). Politicizing literacy. *College English, 54*, 833–842.

Williams, J. (1993). Rule-governed approaches to language and composition. *Written Communication, 10*, 542–568.

Williams, J., & Snipper, G. (1990). *Literacy and bilingualism.* New York: Longman.

Winterowd, W. (Ed.). (1975). *Contemporary rhetoric: A conceptual background with readings.* New York: Harcourt Brace Jovanovich.

Winterowd, W. & Blum, J. (1994). *A teacher's introduction to composition in the rhetorical tradition.* Urbana, IL: National Council of Teachers of English.

Witte, S. (1980). Toward a model for research in written composition. *Research in the Teaching of English, 14*, 73–81.

Witte, S. (1985). Revising composing theory and research design. In S. Freedman (Ed.), *The aquisition of writer language: Response and revision.* Norwood, NJ: Ablex.

Witte, S., & Cherry, R. (1986). Writing processes and written products in composition research. In C. Cooper & S. Greenbaum (Eds.), *Studying writing: Linguistic approaches.* Beverly Hills: Sage.

Witte, S., & Faigley, L. (1981). Coherence, cohesion, and writing quality. *College Composition and Communication, 32*, 189–204.

Witte, S., Nakadate, N., & Cherry, R. (Eds.). (1992). *A rhetoric of doing: Essays on written discourse in honor of James L. Kinneavy.* Carbondale, IL: Southern Illinois University Press.

Wittrock, M. (1977). The generative processes of memory. In M. Wittrock (Ed.), *The human brain.* Englewood Cliffs, NJ: Prentice-Hall.

Wolfram, W. (1969). *A sociolinguistic description of Detroit Negro speech*. Washington, DC: Center for Applied Linguistics.

Wolfram, W., Christian, A., & Adger, L. (in press). *Dialects in schools and communities*. Mahwah, NJ: Lawrence Erlbaum Associates.

Young, I. (1990). The ideal of community and the politics of difference. In L. Nicholson (Ed.), *Feminism/postmodernism*. New York: Routledge.

Zamel, U. (1983). The composing processes of advanced ESL students: Six case studies. *TESOL Quarterly, 17,* 165–187.

Zebroski, J. (1990). The English department and social class: Resisting writing. In A. Lunsford, H. Moglen, & J. Slevin (Eds.), *The right to literacy*. New York: Modern Language Association.

Ziv, N. (1981). *The effect of teacher comments on the writing of four college freshmen*. (ERIC Document Reproduction Service No. ED 203 317).

Zoellner, R. (1968). Talkwrite: A behavioral pedagogy for composition. *College English, 30,* 267–320.

Author Index

331

Subject Index

A

Aristotle, rhetoric and, 2–3, 14–17, 24
  and ethos, 16
  and logos, 16–17
  and pathos, 16–17
Assessment, writing
  comparison standards, 258–262, 264 266
  and grammar, 148–150
  holistic scoring, 270
    anchor scores, 278
    assignment reading, 279
    classroom experience of, 272–276
    letter grade conversion, 279–280
    scoring rubrics, 271–277, 281–294
    socialization in, 259, 271, 274–276, 278
    split scores, 276, 279
    and student codes, 276–277
    student–teacher teams for, 277–278
  invalid, 258
  portfolio grading, 259, 280–281
  postmodern, 265–267
  reliability in, 258–259, 264–265, 271
  and style, 168–170
  time factor in, 258–259, 267
  validity in, 258–259, 262–264
  written comments, 267–270
Assignments, writing, *see also* Classroom workshop
  argumentation in, 243, 249–252
  collaborative, 254–255

  features of, 245
  meaningful, 72–73, 240, 256–257
  narrations, 242–243, 249–251
    and expressive discourse, 251
  narrative reports, 249–250
  rhetorical complexity in, 242–243
  samples of, 246–248, 252–254, 307–314
  sequence development for, 242–244, 250–252
  teacher planning of, 244

B

Belles-lettres movement, 1–2, 27, 45
Bilingual education, *see* English as a Second Language (ESL)
Bilingual Education Act (1948), 178, 181
Bilingual Inventory of Natural Language (BINL), 178
Black English Vernacular (BEV)
  cultural factors of, 199 201
  Ebonics, 194–196
  and grammar, 197–201
  origins of, 192–194
  and pidgin, 192–193
  and standard English, 34, 191
  and style, 164–165
  and writing, 201–206
    cognitive deficiency, 205–206
  oral language interference, 202–206
Bottom-up process (reading), 99, 104, 111, *see also* Phonics

C

Case grammar, 120
Categorical level (grammar), 120

337